# Collaboration

# IBM Center for
# The Business of Government

## THE IBM CENTER FOR THE BUSINESS OF GOVERNMENT BOOK SERIES

### Series Editors: Mark A. Abramson and Paul R. Lawrence

The IBM Center Series on The Business of Government explores new approaches to improving the effectiveness of government at the federal, state, and local levels. The Series is aimed at providing cutting-edge knowledge to government leaders, academics, and students about the management of government in the 21st century.

Publications in the series include:

# Collaboration: Using Networks and Partnerships

EDITED BY

JOHN M. KAMENSKY
IBM BUSINESS CONSULTING SERVICES
and
THOMAS J. BURLIN
IBM BUSINESS CONSULTING SERVICES

ROWMAN & LITTLEFIELD PUBLISHERS, INC.
*Lanham • Boulder • New York • Toronto • Oxford*

ROWMAN & LITTLEFIELD PUBLISHERS, INC.

Published in the United States of America
by Rowman & Littlefield Publishers, Inc.
A wholly owned subsidiary of The Rowman & Littlefield Publishing Group, Inc.
4501 Forbes Boulevard, Suite 200, Lanham, Maryland 20706
www.rowmanlittlefield.com

PO Box 317
Oxford
OX2 9RU, UK

British Library Cataloguing in Publication Information Available

**Library of Congress Cataloging-in-Publication Data Available**

0-7425-3513-4 (alk. paper) — 0-7425-3514-2 (pbk.: alk. paper)

Printed in the United States of America

♾™ The paper used in this publication meets the minimum requirements of American National Standard for Information Sciences—Permanence of Paper for Printed Library Materials, ANSI/NISO Z39.48-1992.

# TABLE OF CONTENTS

# PART I

## Understanding Networks and Partnerships

**CHAPTER ONE**

# Networks and Partnerships:
# Collaborating to Achieve Results
# No One Can Achieve Alone

John M. Kamensky
Associate Partner
IBM Business Consulting Services

Thomas J. Burlin
Vice President, IBM Global Services
IBM Business Consulting Services

Mark A. Abramson
Executive Director
IBM Center for The Business of Government

# Collaboration Is More Pervasive
# Than Most Think

"[I]n the information age," notes journalist Brian Friel, "successful organizations behave more like computer networks than assembly lines and look more like Chinese Checker boards than hierarchies."[1] This is not the result of simply following the latest management fad. As government faces more complex problems, and citizens expect more, the way government delivers services and results is changing rapidly.[2] The traditional model of government agencies administering hundreds of programs by themselves is giving way to one-stop services and cross-agency results. This transition implies collaboration—within agencies; between agencies; between levels of government; and between the public, private, and nonprofit sectors.

The desire for individuals to collaborate is old, reaching back to the efforts of the ancient Greek city-states to band together to defend themselves against a common enemy. But applying collaboration in diverse policy arenas such as law enforcement, social services, transportation, homeland security, and the environment is relatively new. Also, the evolution of technology is now allowing new approaches that just a decade ago were seen as belonging to the realm of science fiction. The first part of this book describes what networks and partnerships are. The second part presents case examples of how collaborative approaches have actually worked in the public sector, when they should be used, and what it takes to manage and coordinate them.

In chapter two, Robert Klitgaard and Gregory Treverton note that two drivers of the increased use of public sector networks and partnerships are the communication revolution brought about by technology, which makes collaboration easier, and the shift in societal power to the "market state," which "respects neither the borders nor the icons of the traditional state." Other factors include the changing nature of work from labor-based production to the integration of knowledge-based work, which again does not respect hierarchical boundaries. In addition, the changing nature of government means that problems cannot easily be divided into pieces and addressed in isolation from each other. In addition, the role of government is shifting from the traditional model where it directly operated programs to one where it now takes on a developmental or steering role. In a more pragmatic approach, notes Elaine Kamarck in chapter four, "as bureaucratic government has failed in one policy area after another, policy makers have looked to implement policy through networks instead."

As networks and partnerships take on many new shapes, explains public management expert Russell Linden, organizations are shifting their focus on change from "within" to "between."[3] In fact, because of the many different forms this shift is taking, we often fail to recognize them. But we are now seeing examples of this change in our daily lives:

- ⸱ When Department of Homeland Security Secretary Tom Ridge raises the national terrorist threat level to "orange," a collaborative network reacts: Within hours, the local subway system flashes an advisory to passengers to be on the lookout for suspicious behavior. Creating a network among thousands of law enforcement agencies and public transit systems allows quick response times in conveying information and enlisting everyone in anti-terror efforts.

- Swiping your debit card through a card reader at the grocery store to pay your bill is commonplace today. But the nationwide system, which works in virtually all 83,000 grocery stores in America today, started a decade ago as a collaborative venture sponsored by the federal food stamp program in its efforts to reduce the administrative costs of delivering benefits and reducing fraud. This collaboration included banks, state governments, the National Association of Clearinghouse Administrators, as well as the grocery stores themselves.

- In mid-April 2000, a census taker knocking at doors in Chicago was accompanied by a neighbor who encouraged residents to take the time to complete the survey. Chicago was home to several of the 140,000 partner networks created by the Census Bureau to encourage the highest possible response rate to the decennial census.

These are only a few examples of new ways in which government can effectively use networks and partnerships as vehicles for increased collaboration between the public and private sectors, as well as between levels of government itself. Collaboration through the use of networks and partnerships to get results citizens care about is a growing trend that appears to have staying power. But as it grows, it is challenging government leaders and managers in new ways because it requires them and their employees to behave far differently than they have in the past. One part of this shift is a change from the historical bureaucratic model focused on agencies and individual programs run by separate agencies to a model that places increased emphasis on services and results. The new model implies organizing around customers and outcomes, not agencies and programs. The General Accounting Office (GAO) notes in a January 2003 report on the status of management in the federal government that "… national goals are achieved through the use of a variety of tools and, increasingly, through the participation of many organizations that are beyond the direct control of the federal government." In other words, government is now turning more and more to networks and partnerships to achieve many national objectives.

The value of collaboration as a new approach or tool for government managers is receiving increasing appreciation and notice throughout the federal government. GAO notes, "Promoting effective partnerships with third parties in the formulation and design of complex national initiatives will prove increasingly vital to achieving key outcomes...."[4] The Office of Personnel Management's list of core competencies for the federal senior executive of the future now includes not only the ability to work in a team environment, but also the ability to develop "alliances with external groups (e.g., other agencies or firms, state and local governments, Congress, and clientele groups)," and the ability to engage in cross-functional activities, as well as find common ground with a widening range of stakeholders.[5] In chapter three, Robert Agranoff notes, "How to manage in a network is an important 21st century issue because of networks' prevalence in the managerial enterprise."

---

## Dark Networks

H. Brinton Milward notes that "most of the literature on networks and collaboration is quite positive" and that these approaches are appropriate ways of tackling public management problems and coordinating political, social, and economic action. But he also notes that the pioneers in the use of networks include disruptive radical activists, drug dealers, arms traffickers, and terrorists.[6] For example:

- Journalist Matthew Brzezinski describes the decentralized model for the illicit drug smuggling trade as a "surprisingly sophisticated industry, market-driven just like any consumer-products business"—except that it must operate in the shadow of the law. Since transportation is a key element, consolidation and vertical integration—mainstays of multinational corporations—are impossible. As a result, the drug trade has developed sophisticated networks.[7]

- As Brian Friel describes Osama bin Laden: "He decentralized decision-making authority and created a flat management structure to quickly respond to changes in his operating environment. He overcame turf battles by creating an overarching sense of mission and doctrine. He used the Internet, the globalization of news, and the revolution in telecommunications to advance his organization's goals worldwide. He developed a complex organizational network in which information gets only to the right people at the right time. In his network, connections between individuals and groups are activated at key times to get work done and severed when they are no longer necessary."[8]

Observers note that the best offense against "dark networks" is counter-networks. A case in point: While the new Department of Homeland Security is composed of traditional agencies, to be successful they must work together in non-traditional ways, largely via networks and partnerships that reach beyond their organizational boundaries.

While the reliance on networks and partnerships is increasing, many unresolved challenges in how to effectively use these two new tools still remain. For example, as networks and partnerships grow, how do you fund them? As agency lines blur, who gets the credit? When things go wrong, whom do you hold accountable? As networks go beyond the traditional approaches of cooperation and coordination between hierarchical agencies, how are they held accountable in the context of traditional "rule of law" paradigms? GAO's Robert Goldenkoff expands on this list of unresolved management and accountability challenges:

- Should the Office of Management and Budget develop decision guidance for when it is appropriate for agencies to partner outside the federal government?
- Which incentives/tools work best with different partners? Choices can affect who is willing to partner.
- How do First Amendment issues apply to partnerships with religious organizations?
- How can federal agencies ensure adequate performance and accountability in a collaborative arrangement where the federal government may not be the dominant partner?
- Will partnerships create more government-dependent entities and interest groups?
- Is it a valid premise that nonprofits can deliver services better than federal agencies can with their own staffs?[9]

Even though key policy and operational challenges are unresolved, the use of networks and partnerships continues to grow in response to pressing public demands for governmental action and the availability of new technologies that make collaboration easy. Public managers are no longer waiting for answers to these potentially nettlesome but crucial policy questions; they are moving forward. They have little choice in a fast-moving world.

# What Do We Mean by Using Networks and Partnerships for Collaboration?

Since government executives are increasingly using collaborative arrangements despite the many open policy questions, it is important to determine which approaches work better under which circumstances. This book seeks to bring together some of the best practices from the front lines. To establish a common understanding among public managers, the first step is to define what is meant by using networks and partnerships for collaboration, the theme of Part I of this book.

## What Is Collaboration?

Russ Linden writes, "Collaboration is about co-labor, about joint effort and ownership. The end result is not mine or yours, it is ours." Collaboration occurs when people from different organizations produce something together through joint effort, resources, and decision making, and share ownership of the final product or service. The focus is often on producing or implementing something.

Collaboration, however, can mean using one tool or a mix of tools on a continuum that ranges from the traditional approaches of coordination and cooperation to the creation of new networks, some of which may contain formal partnership agreements. The use of traditional coordination and cooperation generally involves independent entities that continue to pursue their own missions and programs independent of other actors, but with an informed understanding about what the others are doing. For example, the long-standing federal "single point of contact" network between state governments and the federal government is a forum where a representative from the Office of Management and Budget meets face-to-face with the 50 state counterparts several times a year. They share information and concerns, and they may agree to certain standard approaches to selected issues. But, generally, that is as far as it goes. The Congressional Research Service in 2002 described a wide array of coordination and cooperation groups across the government and observed, "Interagency coordinative mechanisms at the federal level have become more prominent and prevalent recently."[10]

In other cooperative ventures, government managers may use task forces, councils, or committees to address a specific issue, such as the Department of the Interior's interagency task force to preserve the health of coral reefs, the government-wide Chief Information Officers Council, and the joint council of the Departments of Defense and Veterans Affairs to implement the sharing of medical facilities and improve medical services for the nation's veterans. In these efforts, government managers represent the interests of their home agencies while working jointly on common interests.

At the other end of this continuum is the use of networks and partnerships. While both networks and partnerships reach across organizational boundaries (and oftentimes across levels of government as well as sectors), partnerships tend to be more formal joint ventures with binding obligations for action. In contrast, networks tend to consist of more informal relationships with voluntary obligations to act. In chapter six, William Snyder and Xavier de Souza Briggs describe communities of practice, which have proven to be an effective type of voluntary network. Networks such as communities of practice are organized around common shared goals; more formal partnerships tend to be organized around common outputs and results.

## Potential variations of federal government collaboration

1. Within a department (agency to agency)

2. Across departments (department to department)

3. Intergovernmental I (federal/state)

4. Intergovernmental II (federal/local)

5. Intergovernmental III (federal/state/local)

6. Intersectoral I (public/private)

7. Intersectoral II (public/nonprofit)

8. Intersectoral III (public/nonprofit/private)

9. International I (federal/international organization)

10. International II (federal/single nation)

11. International III (federal/multiple nations)

## Using Networks

According to Mandell and Steelman, networks are "a spectrum of structures that involve two or more actors and many include participants from public, private, and nonprofit sectors with varying degrees of interdependence to accomplish goals that otherwise could not be accomplished independently."[11] In chapter seven, William Waugh, Jr., notes that "... networks are more common in policy arenas in which issues are complex or ambiguous." They can be permanent or temporary in nature. Robert Atkinson, in a 2003 report on the evolution of network government, observes that the traditional management concepts of hierarchy and control are "built on three assumptions: predictable processes, a stable environment, and a fixed output. But these conditions no longer describe the environment" in which government finds itself today. As a consequence of this change, networks are becoming an increasingly important management approach or tool. Atkinson concludes, "In the networked world, much of government will shift from managing programs to guiding and funding networks."[12]

In chapter four, Kamarck observes that the term *network* has come to have three separate meanings. First, it is used to describe the constellation of public, private, and semi-public organizations that influence a policy world. Second, it is used to describe emerging relationships between organizations that work together to solve important governance problems, such as drug crimes or poverty. And third, the term is used to describe government's power to contract and fund a network of non-governmental organizations to jointly deliver public services.

Friel also notes that there are different types of network structures. They can include:

- Customer or product-based networks, such as local-level Head Start programs.
- Matrix or project-based structures, such as the 2000 census field operations.
- Cellular structures, which are autonomous and self-organizing, such as CIA overseas spy operations.
- Hub-spoke networks, such as the Department of Labor's state and local job training Private Investment Councils.
- Chain networks, where information or goods must pass from one intermediary to another, such as drug smuggling.
- All-channel networks, where all participants are connected to and can communicate with all others, such as an e-mail system.

Networks, because of their more informal nature, tend to be time-consuming to develop and fragile to maintain. The decision on whether to use this approach depends on an initial assessment of whether the right dynamics exist and whether they reflect the characteristics of a successful network. Key dynamics include such factors as leadership styles, success measures, the use of technology, and the approaches to accountability. Also, successful networks share five characteristics: shared vision and trust, independent members, voluntary links, multiple leaders, and clearly defined roles. Conducting a hard-headed assessment upfront as to the probability of a network approach succeeding will save many headaches later.

Despite the difficulties in creating them, networks offer many advantages that cannot be easily created by other vehicles. Network-based structures:

- Provide a boundary-spanning mechanism.
- Are "soft structures" held together by formal/informal agreements, which allow great flexibility.
- Increase capacity of participating organizations to combine capabilities.
- Spur innovation and adaptation to local conditions.
- Promote social capital, thereby reducing transaction costs.

In chapter three, Agranoff notes that participating in networks changes the nature of how public managers operate. In a network, a government manager serves as a convener and becomes a participant, not a leader. In some cases, the network may play a mediation role. Resources are more dispersed and cannot be controlled centrally. And, program implementation occurs through the partners involved pooling knowledge and technologies—not through government owning or operating programs through traditional government agencies.

However, Agranoff also observes that government agencies are not simply bystanders in a network. Government organizations still possess the legitimacy to deal with public problems and policy solutions, retain authority to set rules and norms, contribute resources, and retain and share knowledge. As a result, important networks cannot be sustained without the participation of government managers assigned to such roles by their traditional organizations.

Using networks does have disadvantages. While government by network is non-bureaucratic and flexible, and provides the ability to innovate, Kamarck, in chapter four, notes that there is a 100 percent probability that some actor in some part of the network will mess up. Government has traditionally been risk-averse. However, she concludes, rather than avoiding risk, government needs to better learn how to manage risk. Also, Snyder and Briggs, in chapter six, note that network-based organizational structures decrease a central authority's power to control activities, but that this is compensated with increased control by the network over the end outcomes that may be desired by the central authority (which presumably sanctions the network).

## Using Partnerships

Partnerships tend to be a more formal approach to collaboration. GAO's Goldenkoff says that *partnering* refers to "government agencies engaging third-party or non-governmental actors to deliver or administer a public service." The tools of engagement include the use of contracts, grants, and memoranda of agreement.[13] A two-year study of high-performing partnerships by the National Academy of Public Administration, released in April 2003, offers two defining characteristics: "First, it must have a structure for the individual [member] organizations to share authority, resources, and accountability for achieving a mutually decided goal.... Second, it must produce significant results."[14]

In chapter two, Klitgaard and Treverton define public-private partnerships as "working together in the provision of service, financing, and development of infrastructure, and the administration of government.... a cooperative venture between the public and private sectors, built on the expertise of each partner, that best meets clearly defined public needs through the appropriate allocation of resources, risks, and rewards.... The essence is the sharing of risks."

Much like networks, different types of partnerships can be created depending on the particular circumstances, and they too can happen in different places. For example, is the nature of the activity inherently governmental or inherently commercial? And, is the incentive for the partnership driven by financial considerations, or is it driven by voluntary, mission-based considerations? Depending on what this mix turns out to be, the framework and approaches may differ.

Because partnerships tend to be more defined than networks, they may face more difficulties in adapting to a chaotic environment. However, they have some distinct advantages. First, partnerships tend to be more resilient when there is a transition in leadership among its members. Since networks are based largely on interpersonal relationships rooted in trust among members, they are more vulnerable to falling apart when there is substantial turnover of membership or sponsorship. Second, because partnerships involve more of a formal set of relationships, it is easier to leverage the resources of others. And, third, because partnerships often involve frontline service delivery agents, the pipeline is shortened between service providers and recipients—and partnerships also improve decision making by taking advantage of the street-level knowledge of partners.

# Where and When Should You Collaborate?

While collaboration is a powerful approach to getting results, it cannot work in all circumstances. Experience shows that there are certain preconditions that need to be present for networks and partnerships to be successful. Successful collaborative ventures are premised on the existence of trust, a mutual obligation to succeed, and the ability to build consensus. Creating trust is not a one-way street. As former Governor John Kitzhaber of Oregon once remarked, "Trust means both sides having something at risk." Likewise, all parties have to be committed to a common outcome, and when there is not agreement on how to achieve that outcome, the ability to work together to find agreement is essential.

In chapter two, Klitgaard and Treverton provide a handy checklist for assessing the costs and benefits of using partnerships. They say that the decision to use a partnership approach must be evaluated from three perspectives: the value to the participating organization, the value to the collective members of the partnership, and the value to society as a whole. Professor Marsha Guffey, who studies public sector networks, identifies four operational prerequisites as well: (1) the political climate has to be right, (2) there must be a champion dedicated to providing the necessary leadership, (3) the leader must be able to engender trust among the participants, and (4) the network members have to be able to forge a shared vision of what they want to collectively achieve.[15]

Once the decision is made to collaborate, the next question is whether one should create a network or partnership and how it should be designed. In chapter three, Agranoff describes four types of networks that can be created:

- *Informational networks*—partners agree to exchange information, but nothing more.
- *Developmental/capacity-building networks*—partners agree to not only share information, but also jointly learn so individual members' capacities to implement solutions in their home agencies is improved.
- *Outreach/information-exchange networks*—partners exchange information and technologies, pool client contacts, and design their programs so their customers see a more seamless network, but the network partners still operate within their own agencies.
- *Action/collaborative networks*—partners formally adopt collaborative courses of action in which they depend upon each other for their joint success.

Guffey maintains that who sets up a network, and what kinds of conditions are placed on its creation, can affect its design, dynamics, and ultimate success. For example, she found that if legislation mandates one agency to be in charge and play a major role, the result is a mediated coordination group, with a vertical system of coordination. The group cannot extend itself to become an action/collaborative network, as described by Agranoff, because the success of collaborative networks generally depends on unmediated, voluntary participation in which participants are co-equal. However, Guffey found that legislatively mandated collaboration, where the lead agency's role is merely to facilitate interaction of members, can be successful. However, such legislative initiatives historically have not provided funding or granted any authority to implement agreed-upon measures.

When the right conditions exist for creation of a network or partnership, and the design issues are directly addressed, networks and partnerships can make a significant difference. The presence of good leadership is also crucial. Part II of this book is devoted to four chapters describing various collaborative ventures, ranging from the creation of virtual teams and communities of practice to formal partnerships.

## Collaboration through the Use of Virtual Teams

In chapter five, Samuel DeMarie describes the value of using virtual teams within an agency. "Virtual teams," he writes, "are groups of geographically and/or organizationally dispersed collaborators that are brought together to address a specific task." These teams rarely, if ever, meet face-to-face. Most are temporary, created to address a specific task.

DeMarie's case study focused on the Department of Energy's Radioactive Waste Management Project at Yucca Mountain, Nevada, which operates largely through about 1,000 ongoing virtual teams composed of several Energy offices, two prime contractors, and about 40 significant subcontractors spread across six states. The teams include scientists, engineers, managers, administrative staff, and media specialists. Technology plays a key role. All members of the organization were given laptops with a common server platform so they could readily communicate. Teleconferencing and video-conferencing were important communication tools as well.

The study found that creating virtual teams (without any face-to-face meetings) did not allow for the informal communication needed to develop interpersonal levels of trust. DeMarie concluded that all new teams should be launched with a "significant face-to-face interaction." The study also found that it takes training to learn how to work collaboratively in a virtual team environment. DeMarie determined that having a common body of knowledge and team norms greatly improves team communication on a virtual team. In addition, he concluded that having a strong cadre of technical support to keep the technology working was essential.

## Collaboration through the Use of Communities of Practice

In chapter six, Snyder and Briggs describe a new tool for public managers called "communities of practice." This particular type of network features peer-to-peer collaborative activities that build members' skills. Used successfully by many large companies in the private sector, communities of practice are "social learning systems" where practitioners informally "connect to solve problems, share ideas, set standards, build tools, and develop relationships with peers and stakeholders." As informal networks, these communities complement an organization's formal units by reaching across organizational boundaries. Because they are inherently boundary-crossing entities, they are particularly suited to large organizations and federal systems.

Snyder and Briggs not only describe the concept of communities of practice and when and how to build them, they also provide a series of four case studies of communities of practice in action. Have you ever hit a rumble strip on a highway? They are designed to reduce the number of run-off-road accidents. While well-known in the safety engineering community, it was not until the Federal Highway Administration created a community of practice among safety engineers across the country that state governments began to actively install them on their highways. Members of the Rumble Strips Community created broad support for this initiative by linking engineers with policy makers in each of the 50 states.

Other examples of federally sponsored communities of practice that Snyder and Briggs describe include three pilot federal, state, local, and nonprofit networks created in the late 1990s. One focused on "results for kids," such as school readiness and health insurance; another focused on "safe cities," with an emphasis on reducing gun violence; and a third focused on worker skills for 21st century jobs. Each of these started as conventional technical assistance programs, but evolved into peer-to-peer models that linked all the participants together. In each case, these were more than networks for fixing local problems; they were communities of practice where practitioners with mutual interests and a collective drive to solve problems spanned all organizational boundaries. In each of these pilot cases, the communities were ultimately disbanded because the federal community coordinator was withdrawn. But the lessons of each of these communities of practice show the potential power they can bring to problem solving and the importance of having a dedicated coordinator to ensure the endurance of a community.

Snyder and Briggs describe key roles in creating a community of practice: a dedicated coordinator, a steering committee, a sponsor, etc. They also lay out an approach for growing communities of practice from several dozen participants to thousands, if federal policy makers choose to leverage this approach more broadly.

## Collaboration through the Use of Agency-Sponsored Networks and Partnerships

In chapter seven, Waugh describes how the Federal Emergency Management Agency (FEMA) turned to the use of networks and partnerships to achieve a goal it could not achieve by itself.

Historically, a major FEMA responsibility was to respond to natural disasters. Although FEMA improved its disaster response capabilities during the 1990s, an increasing number of natural disasters occurred in this period, including hurricanes and floods. Congress and stakeholders, such as the major insurance companies, became increasingly concerned about the rising costs of responding to these disasters. In response, FEMA included an increased emphasis on the prevention of disasters in its 1995 strategic plan. FEMA began this initiative by dedicating a relatively small investment, equivalent to about 15 percent of its disaster spending, to this new preventive approach. The agency quickly found, however, that it would have very little direct control over the solution and that it would be a big job, with diverse state/local dynamics and huge political problems. As a result, it turned to the use of existing networks that had common interests. One of its first major initiatives in the prevention effort was to mitigate, or lessen, the effects of a disaster by strengthening buildings in areas prone to natural disasters. This involved using existing networks in the building and the insurance industry, as well as state and local regulators involved in setting building codes and other key stakeholders. The FEMA goal was to "create a culture for mitigation that in turn creates a commercial market demand for safe construction."

Based on his analysis of the FEMA experience in using existing networks and creating new partnership arrangements, Waugh concludes:

> ... national goals can be pursued through indirect means but that there may be less control when agencies work through networks. Agencies must be prepared to deal with non-hierarchical relationships, invest time and energy in relationship building, separate regulatory and partnership-building functions, be open to participation by organizations and individuals who are not typically included in governmental or even public/private programs, and operate with more transparency than might be expected in traditional programs. However, building trust and interpersonal relationships may be more important than formal agreements and contracts.

Waugh also found that, when compared to other policy tools (such as government-supported insurance, buyouts, regulation, and land use planning), networks and partnerships were effective approaches for achieving the goal of disaster mitigation. However, he found there were some necessary preconditions for successful application. First, interdependence among stakeholders had to exist, with shared goals and a strong interest in solving problems. Second, the relationships among network members had to be built on respect and trust and less on positional authority. Third, working in a network meant that the lead federal agency had limited authority and must pursue its goals through persuasion, bargaining, and coalition building. Being too directive can destroy the network. And, finally, the key to success is ultimately building local capacity at the grass roots. Individual leaders on the front line are crucial and must be engaged from the beginning.

In chapter eight, John Scanlon describes how another federal agency, the Bureau of Primary Health in the United States Department of Health and Human Services, created networks and partnerships that could achieve an ambitious "national goal" well beyond the reach of the agency's traditional programs: to provide 100 percent of the uninsured in every community access to quality health care while eliminating health-status disparities among population groups.

Scanlon describes how a group of managers in the Bureau of Primary Health moved beyond their individual program and agency goals to pursue a national goal by using a "bottom-up approach." Because of their professional commitment to improving public health, they created a self-organized group with a common vision and an impossible goal. Over a three-year period, they created a self-sustaining movement with multiple networks and partnerships. By collaborating with leaders in government (at national, state, and local levels) and in the private and nonprofit sector, the Bureau pursued an ambitious common vision with measurable objectives to achieve a national goal.

The core leadership group at the Bureau consisted of a small handful of senior career federal employees. For most of these employees, the initiative was not a full-time responsibility. They did, however, function as a group of peers who saw the world from the perspective of a grand vision they were collectively committed to carrying out: They articulated an impossible national goal and crafted a plan to achieve it. They leveraged events and activities that were going to happen anyway to link to their grand vision. They leveraged key personnel in other institutional networks to make it happen. And they used a campaign-style approach along with a series of performance metrics to create the momentum and sense of urgency to act.

While this initiative represented entrepreneurship within a government organization, many challenges can be pursued in the context of an organization's broader mission statement. When senior political leaders craft a compelling vision, career leaders many layers down in the organization often find creative ways to translate this vision into action in ways unimaginable by the senior leadership, increasingly by using collaborative approaches.

## How Do You Successfully Collaborate by Using Networks and Partnerships?

One of the biggest challenges in using collaborative approaches in the public sector is that most public managers are not trained in how to lead through the use of networks or partnerships. In chapter three, Agranoff notes, "How to manage in a network is an important 21st century issue because of networks' prevalence in the managerial enterprise." He reviewed the experiences of over a dozen networks in the Midwest and observed, "The public organization actor often serves as a convener, but once the process begins those persons are among the many participants." He identified a range of roles that government actors perform, as well as what managers do and what kinds of personal characteristics they bring to their jobs to be successful.

The roles included activities such as creating the governance framework for the network; leveraging resources, such as technology and expertise; being a strategic investor; finding collaborators and brokering linkages; being a champion and breaking down barriers; tracking, monitoring, and collecting data; providing an electronic communications system; and handling public relations.

Similarly, in his story of the Bureau of Primary Health Care's campaign to increase access to health care, Scanlon identified a series of activities that contributed to its success. Both he and Agranoff distilled their observations of successful public sector network managers. While Scanlon focused on lessons in creating a network, Agranoff presents 10 lessons in managing a network once it is in place.

---

**Lessons Learned About Networks**

**Stage One: How to create a network around a compelling goal (from Scanlon, chapter eight)**

- Collaborate and network
- Reveal hidden assets
- Operate in campaign mode
- Search for national goals
- Find the leadership below the surface
- Accept the natural resistance
- Distinguish the ready and the not ready
- Make and secure commitments
- Tell leadership stories
- Practice the discipline of leadership

**Stage Two: How to manage in a non-hierarchical, self-organizing network (from Agranoff, chapter three)**

- Be a representative of both your agency and the network
- Take a share of the administrative burden
- Operate by agenda orchestration
- Recognize shared expertise-based authority
- Stay within the decision bounds of your network
- Accommodate and adjust while maintaining purpose
- Be as creative as possible
- Be patient and use interpersonal skills
- Recruit constantly
- Emphasize incentives

---

## Next Steps

In chapter six, Snyder and Briggs see a clear role for the federal government in the use of collaboration through the use of communities of practice, especially in social policy arenas. They write, "the federal government is in a unique position to cultivate an influential system of communities of practice that embrace a variety of problem or issue domains that span the nation." Snyder and Briggs envision a clear role for the federal government in launching and sustaining innovation and learning networks in a wide range of policy arenas. After analyzing the four case studies in chapter six, Snyder and Briggs conclude that the federal government can stimulate the creation of communities of practice by:

- Providing agency sponsorship, which can provide strategic focus, seed funding, and institutional legitimacy;
- Designating community coordinators to develop a learning agenda, build the community, and lead outcome-oriented initiatives; and
- Encouraging agency champions and support staff to bridge formal unit barriers, coach community initiatives, and liaise with sponsors and stakeholders.

# Conclusion

As the government moves forward in the decades ahead to meet challenges in such diverse arenas as the environment, homeland security, education, jobs and training, health care, and poverty, the use of collaboration through networks and partnerships is an approach that allows greater leverage to achieve national goals than the more traditional "stovepipe" approach to individual federal programs that still predominates.

Based on the studies presented in this book, a critical success element seems to be having the right kind of people involved in the creation of these networks and partnerships. As noted earlier, collaboration requires a different set of skills than those used in "traditional government," which depends more heavily on institutional arrangements, legislation, and the budget process. Developing this new set of skills will be a major challenge for government leaders whose future policy success will increasingly depend on their ability to collaborate with others by creating networks and partnerships.

# Endnotes

1. Brian Friel, "Hierarchies and Networks," *Government Executive*, April 2002, pp. 31–39.

2. Mark A. Abramson and Ann M. Kieffaber, *New Ways of Doing Business* (Lanham, Md.: Rowman & Littlefield Publishers, 2003).

3. Russell M. Linden, *Working Across Boundaries: Making Collaboration Work in Government and Non-Government Organizations* (San Francisco: Jossey-Bass, 2002).

4. General Accounting Office, "Major Management Challenges and Program Risks: A Governmentwide Perspective," GAO-03-95, January 2003, p. 5.

5. Office of Personnel Management, Senior Executive Service, Executive Core Qualification #5, Coalitions/Communications http://www.opm.gov/ses/ecq5.html.

6. H. Brinton Milward and Joerg Raab, "Dark Networks as Problems," *PA Times*, November 2002, p. 5.

7. Matthew Brzenzinski, "Re-engineering the Drug Business," *New York Times Magazine*, June 23, 2002.

8. Friel.

9. Robert Goldenkoff, "Opportunities and Challenges of Public/Private Partnerships," *The Public Manager*, Fall 2001.

10. Fredrick M. Kaiser, "Federal Interagency Coordinative Mechanisms: Varied Types and Numerous Devices," Congressional Research Service, RL031357, (July 22, 2002).

11. Myrna Mandell and Toddi Steelman, "Understanding What Can Be Accomplished through Different Interorganizational Relationships: The Importance of Typologies, Context and Management Strategies," a paper delivered at the national conference of the American Society of Public Administration, March 2001, p. 3.

12. Robert Atkinson, *Network Government for the Digital Age* (Washington, D.C.: Progressive Policy Institute, 2003), pp. 15, 21.

13. Goldenkoff.

14. National Academy of Public Administration, *Powering the Future: High-Performance Partnerships* (Washington, D.C.: NAPA, April 2003), p. 5.

15. Marsha Guffey, "Collaborative Networks: The Initial Design Strongly Influences the Outcomes," *The Public Manager*, Summer 2003.

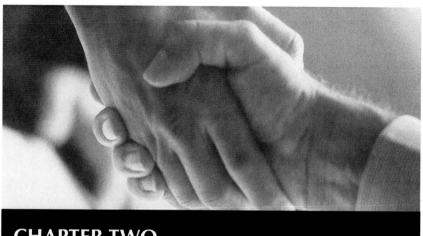

**CHAPTER TWO**

# Assessing Partnerships:
# New Forms of Collaboration

Robert Klitgaard
Dean and Ford Distinguished Professor of
International Development and Security
RAND Graduate School

Gregory F. Treverton
Associate Dean and Senior Policy Analyst
RAND Graduate School

*This report was originally published in March 2003.*

# Introduction

We are entering an era of "hybrid governance," where the lines between the public, nonprofit, and private sectors are quickly eroding. A remarkable transition is under way in the institutions of government, the market, and civil society, especially in the United States but also around the world.

The transition is:

- *From* layer-cake governance, where different tasks are taken on separately by different sectors (public, private, nonprofit)
- *To* marble-cake governance, with new forms of partnerships across sectors at all levels.

This transition raises a host of practical issues—what forms these public-private partnerships might take, when various kinds of partnerships are worthwhile (for each partner and for society), and how partnerships should be stimulated or constrained. This chapter outlines frameworks for better understanding these issues, uses these frameworks to assess partnerships, and suggests promising approaches for practitioners and researchers alike.

## Partnerships: The Rage

"Partnerships" are the rage in the government, business, and nonprofit worlds alike. A recent RAND study found government respondents almost overwhelmed, especially after September 11, by the need to reach out to new partners, in government and out, at home and abroad.[1] In the blizzard of commentary, it is easy to be confused about the value and risks of partnership, all the more so because those partnerships come in many sizes and shapes.

Businesspeople talk of a "partnership craze," as described in the 2001 annual report of the World Economic Forum.[2] The CEO of Hewlett-Packard, Carleton Fiorina, told the Forum that companies are functioning more like living organisms in an ecosystem of other organisms. Corporations can no longer be self-sufficient. They must be constructed around partnerships.

David Komansky, former CEO of Merrill Lynch, noted how rapid this change has been. "For over a hundred years, Merrill Lynch never did a thing that wasn't strictly Merrill Lynch. In the past three to five years, [we] have developed more joint ventures and partnerships than you could count."

In international circles, too, the word "partnership" is popular.[3] In the past, but more so recently, it has been applied to both relations between rich and poor countries, and between donors and recipients.[4] More to our point, public-private-citizen partnerships are increasingly in vogue. The World Bank's James Wolfensohn has been among the most enthusiastic: "I cannot stress enough the importance of partnerships. The task ahead is too formidable for any single institution or set of institutions to tackle. Every one of us has a role to play. Halving poverty by 2015 is possible, but only if we concert our efforts in a new way."[5]

## Partnerships Arise in Many Policy Areas

In this chapter, we consider areas of public policy, including international, that are addressed by government, business, and civil society trying to achieve together more than any one of them could achieve on its own. Partnerships are emerging in many areas of public life, and they pose challenging questions for potential partners as well as for policy makers. For example:

- *Better schools* are being forged through partnerships of communities and education providers, including public schools but also the private sector. Results-oriented education demands excellent evaluation, including better measures of quality, the design of incentive systems, and the design and management of public-sector/citizen/private-sector interactions. But how might we assess the many kinds of partnerships that have been formed between businesses, the schools, and parents' groups?

- *Health care* will become fairer and more efficient by becoming more client driven, more sensitive to competition, and more accountable for results. Again, it becomes crucial to forge and manage effective partnerships among the public, private, and nonprofit sectors, and the consumers of health care. But how might we assess the various kinds of institutional hybrids and overlaps that have arisen in our health care systems?

- From roads to water supply, from electrification to environmental projects, *infrastructure* increasingly involves partnerships of the public and private sectors in their design, finance, and management. Communities also play a key role in deciding what is done and how, and in monitoring progress. How should such partnerships be assessed?

- *International security* involves increasing sophistication in the ways of the private sector and in the management of military-business relationships such as privatization and outsourcing. "Operations other than war" involve the military in new kinds of relationships with civil society, government, international organizations, and business. Moreover, defense policy requires greater understanding of public-private collaboration to deal with terrorism, organized crime, and the vulnerability of the information infrastructure. What kinds of partnerships between businesses, communities, and government seem most promising for what kinds of security risks? What are the dangers and costs of such partnerships?

## What's Driving the Rise of Partnerships

The rise of hybrid governance can be traced to several sources. One pre-dominant driver is technology, including the communications revolution, which enables partnerships within and across borders.[6] While much has been written about the role of technology as a driver of change, another factor is equally critical—societal power is increasingly passing from government to the private sector, leading to a "market state."[7] For example, from 1983 through 1988, the ratio of "official" to private flows of capital to the poorer countries averaged just under 2:1. By 1991, the two were about equal. By 2000, the ratio had reversed dramatically, and was about 1:7 private over offi-cial.[8] For another context, each of the 10 largest companies in the world has annual total receipts larger than the GNP of 150 of the 185 members of the United Nations, including countries such as Portugal, Israel, and Malaysia.

The market respects neither the borders nor the icons of the traditional state. It does not care about a worker's national origin, gender, sexual pref-erence, or veteran status. If the person can do the job, he or she is rewarded, and if not, not. "Made in America" is not a label of interest to the market. Nor are national cultural symbols of interest, except as marketing devices: Ask any American who has traveled and seen sweatshirts bearing English words that make no sense, or ventured to ask a foreigner wearing a Harvard T-shirt which class she was in, only to get a blank stare in return.

The circumstances of the market state are transforming the role of government—and the roles of business and civil society as well. The gov-ernment of a traditional territorial state was a doer; students of public administration and public policy learned that government's choice was "make, buy, or regulate." For tomorrow's public managers, the triad will be "cajole, induce, or facilitate" (or "carrots, sticks, or sermons"[9]). Of course, all three may be involved simultaneously.

To these emerging partnerships, government will provide its power to convene, its infrastructure, its legitimacy, and its information or intelligence. But it will often rely on business and civil society to provide public goods and services. The shift in mind-set this will require of government can hardly be overstated. It will not come easily to governments that they must work with, and indeed sometimes for, CARE and Amnesty International, not to mention Shell and Loral.

These shifting roles will also challenge businesses and nonprofits. Both have been used to acting within a framework established by governments. Increasingly, they will be asked to take greater responsibility for shaping and implementing that framework. "Private" actors will be more and more responsible for "public" purposes, often in new and different partnerships with governments at various levels.[10] That responsibility, and the careful thought about partnerships it should entail, will run through issues ranging from welfare and school reform, to humanitarian relief operations, to the protection of America's critical infrastructures.

## Partnerships: No Panacea

As public-private partnerships are increasing in popularity, their benefits may be oversold. One evening at a dinner party, George Bernard Shaw was seated across from Isadora Duncan, the celebrated and beautiful dancer. She flirted with him outrageously. Finally, she said for all to hear, "Oh, my dear Bernard, wouldn't it be simply wonderful if you and I should have a child? Just imagine—a child with your brain and my body."

To which Shaw replied: "But what if it should be the other way around?"

The "Shaw-and-the-dancer problem" abounds in partnerships of other kinds. Yes, partnerships have potential benefits, but things may not turn out as planned. How can leaders of government agencies, international organizations, businesses, and NGOs understand partnerships more systematically as they decide whether to partner, with whom, how much, and how?

# What Are "Partnerships"?

These questions are all the harder to address because partnerships come in so many sizes and shapes. Their range is broad. The Canadian Council for Public-Private Partnerships defines a partnership as "a cooperative venture between the public and private sectors, built on the expertise of each partner, that best meets clearly defined public needs through the appropriate allocation of resources, risks, and rewards."[11]

## Degrees of Partnership

Defined this way, partnerships stretch from partial collaboration on one end to virtual integration on the other. In *Privatization and Public-Private Partnerships,* E. S. Savas characterizes the degree of partnership (see Table 2.1). His subject is the provision of municipal services, yet even in this relatively narrow field, kinds of arrangements vary widely. At the extremes, there is little partnership to speak of. If the government "makes" and provides the service—as in traditional public schools or police departments, for instance—any partnership will be relatively incidental, taking the form of parent-teacher associations or community groups that meet with police.

**Table 2.1: A Continuum of Partnerships in Municipal Services**

| Type of Partnership (or Not) | Education | Police Protection | Streets and Highways | Parks and Recreation | Hospitals | Housing | Refuse Collection | Transportation |
|---|---|---|---|---|---|---|---|---|
| Government service provision | Conventional public school system | Traditional police department | Municipal highway department | Municipal parks department | County hospital | Public housing authority | Municipal sanitation department | Public transit authority runs a bus service |
| Government vending | Local public school accepts out-of-district pupil and is paid by parents | Sponsor pays city for crowd control by police at concert | Circus pays town to clean streets after parade | Sponsor pays town to clean park after company picnic | | | Stores pay town to collect their solid waste | Company hires city bus and driver for a special event |
| Inter-governmental agreements | Pupils go to school in the next town; sending town pays receiving town | Town buys patrol services from county sheriff | County pays town to clean county roads located in town | City joins special recreation district in the region | City arranges for residents to be treated at regional hospital | Town contracts with county housing authority | City joins regional solid-waste authority | City is part of a regional transportation district |
| Contracts | City hires private firm to conduct vocational training program | City hires private guard service for government buildings | City hires private contractor to clean and plow city streets | City hires private firm to prune trees and mow grass | County hospital hires firm for cafeteria service | Housing authority hires contractor for repairs and painting | City hires and pays contractor to collect garbage | School board hires bus company for pupil transport |
| Franchises | | | | Firm is authorized to operate city-owned golf course and charge fees | | | City franchises private firm to collect garbage and charge residents | Government gives company exclusive right to operate bus service |

**Table 2.1: A Continuum of Partnerships in Municipal Services (continued)**

| Type of Partnership (or Not) | Education | Police Protection | Streets and Highways | Parks and Recreation | Hospitals | Housing | Refuse Collection | Transportation |
|---|---|---|---|---|---|---|---|---|
| Grants | Private colleges get government grant for every enrolled student | | | | Government grant to expand non-profit hospital | Grant to private firm to build and operate low-income housing | City charges user fee but subsidizes elderly and low-income households | Government subsidizes bus purchases for private bus firm |
| Vouchers | Tuition voucher for elementary school, GI Bill for college | | | | Medicaid card permits holder to get medical care anywhere | Voucher enables low-income tenant to rent any acceptable, affordable unit | | Transportation vouchers for elderly and handicapped to use for taxis, etc. |
| Free market | Private schools | Banks hire private guards | Local merchant association hires street cleaners | Commercial tennis courts and golf driving range | Proprietary (for-profit) hospitals | Ordinary private housing | Household hires private firm to provide service | Free market for jitneys, private cars for hire |
| Voluntary Service | Parochial schools | Block association forms citizens' crime-watch unit | Homeowners' association hires firm to clean local streets | Private tennis club and fitness center | Community-based non-profit hospital | Housing cooperative | Homeowners' association hires firm to provide service | Carpools organized by groups of suburban neighbors |
| Self-service | Home schooling | Install locks and alarm system, buy gun | Merchant sweeps sidewalk in front of his shop | Swimming pool at home | Self medication, chicken soup, other traditional cures | Do-it-yourself home construction | Household brings refuse to town disposal site | Driving one's own car, cycling, walking |

Source: E. S. Savas, *Privatization and Public-Private Partnerships. New York and London: Chatham House Publishers, Seven Bridges Press, 2000.*

At the other extreme, if citizens provide the service themselves (home schooling, for instance) or buy it on the free market (private schools), the "partnership" is limited and standoffish. The local school authority is likely to *regulate* in the form of setting some minimum standards.

In the last column of Table 2.1, note that urban transportation services simultaneously include every degree of public-private partnership. There is pure government provision, when a public transit authority runs a bus service. There is the free market or pure business provision model, when rental car companies compete on the open market. There is pure citizen self-provision of transportation services, when people drive their own cars or bicycles. And there are many hybrids in between.

## How Partnerships May Evolve

Partnerships evolve as partners move from limited and wary collaboration to realizing that they have more common interests and joint possibilities. In his study of partnerships between for-profits and nonprofits, James Austin identifies three phases in partnerships and labels them "philanthropic," "transactional," and "integrative."[12]

The first phase is arm's-length and limited. Companies give nonprofits money, but otherwise there is hardly any interaction between the two. The for-profits get the benefits of having been good citizens, benefits that are at this stage as much directed inward toward the company's staff as outward toward its potential customers.

With time and better understanding of one another—an understanding that, in Austin's observations, usually begins with some chance encounter involving the senior executives of the corporation—the partners may discover other values in each other. At the second stage, the most obvious of the additional values for the for-profits is the "branding" value of visible association with a highly regarded nonprofit. The nonprofits receive more and more predictable funding from the companies. Depending on the institutions involved, the values may include leadership training (in either direction within the partnership), publicity for the nonprofit, jobs for its trainees, and so on.

Austin finds that few partnerships reach the integrative stage. When they do, the alliance becomes strategic, and the boundaries between "us" and "them" begin to blur. The partnership comes to resemble an integrated joint venture that is critical to the strategies of both partners. Exchanges multiply in everything from money to people to ideas. At this point, the partnership is able to effectively respond to the changing environment. When, for instance, one high-flying corporate partner suffered its first-ever bad year, that downturn did not undercut the logic of the partnership; the reasons that had made it a good strategic idea remained valid.

# Evaluating Partnerships: Three Perspectives

How can we begin to assess all these varieties of partnership? What does experience so far seem to indicate? What insight might we derive from analogies elsewhere—and from theory?

For most public sector managers contemplating partnerships, the first questions are self-interested. What's in it for me and my organization? How will this proposed partnership help my government agency do what it is supposed to do? The government agency has a mission and a way of doing things—and it has to see what the partnership would accomplish in the agency's own terms.

The questions are good ones, and they are the first ones to ask. They are not, however, the only ones. It is worthwhile to distinguish three perspectives on partnerships. They are perspectives that people in different roles—government manager, outside evaluator, government policy maker—will emphasize, or that different managers will adopt at different times.

The first focuses on the interests of a specific partner. It asks the first question, "How good is this kind and degree of partnership for us?" This perspective tries to understand the benefits and risks of the particular partnership that is being contemplated compared with alternatives.

Perspective 2 seeks to understand the overall results of a particular partnership and the allocation of tasks within it. Beyond the specific partners, how has society more broadly been affected, again compared with alternatives? Different questions of accountability emerge from this perspective.

Perspective 3 concerns the environment in which partnerships of various kinds emerge or don't emerge, function well or function badly. The analogy with industrial policy may make this perspective clearer. For industrial policy, a perspective 2 question would be, what sort of industry should a government subsidize? For partnerships, by analogy, the question would be, what kind of partnership benefits society, given the alternatives? The perspective 3 question in industrial policy is, how can the government create

**Table 2.2: Perspectives on Partnerships**

| Perspective | Focus | Concern |
|---|---|---|
| 1 | Each partner | Each partner's interests |
| 2 | Each partnership | Broader effects on society for this particular partnership |
| 3 | All partnerships (over time) | Broader effects on society over partnerships and over time |

an environment where industries will best develop over time? For partnerships, the question from perspective 3 is, how can government—and the public, nonprofit, and private sectors working together—create an environment in which the right partnerships develop over time?

## Perspective 1: Understanding "What's in It for Me?"

Put somewhat more precisely, the "what's in it for me and my institution?" question becomes: "What are the advantages and risks to us and our mission from various kinds of partnerships, structured how, managed how?"

The advantages may be of many kinds. A recent publication of the World Bank's Business Partnership and Outreach Group lists eight possible benefits for business, among them "to enhance or rebuild brand image/corporate reputation" and "to address public accountability issues or market failures." Among the seven possible benefits for "communities/our clients" are efficiency, effectiveness, equity, and sustainability.[13]

Some of the hoped-for benefits are often not enunciated publicly, including prestige, political insulation, and co-optation. These motives have been dominant in many recent business-NGO partnerships. They may also be crucial to the huge increase in partnerships at organizations such as the World Bank, which may be designed in part "to enhance or rebuild brand image/corporate reputation."

What nonprofits bring to the partnership can range across:[14]

- **Cost.** In the case of nonprofits, the most visible cost advantage is usually access to volunteer labor, though they may have innovative process or service delivery mechanisms as well.
- **Quality.** There may be reason to believe that a nonprofit will deliver a higher quality service, usually because its ethos is thought to be more caring than the government's or a private company's. For the nonprofit organization, providing the service may be a mission, not simply a way to make a profit. And it may have stronger connections to the target population. In his study of nursing homes and handicapped facilities, for instance, Burton Weisbrod found some evidence of quality advantages in nonprofits, at least those that were church related.[15] They ranked higher than for-profits in surveys of customer satisfaction.
- **Access.** For similar reasons, a not-for-profit may be thought to be a more likely way to access a hard-to-reach target population. It may have earned the trust of that population through its commitment and image as "one of us" and from its previous work and connections.
- **"Identity."** The not-for-profit may have some advantage that derives from its commitment and identity, one that is related to but not fully captured by its perceived advantages in quality or cost, or both.

---

## Questions to Ask When Considering Partnerships

- How efficient are partnerships?

- What are the costs of the partnership?

- What do partners from various sectors bring to the table?

---

There are risks as well, as any manager who has tried to coordinate things among government agencies, or even different parts of a local office, knows all too well. The "hassle factor" can be even more difficult across the public-private divide, and it is often overlooked in many discussions of partnerships, especially by advocates. For example, a British public-private alliance called InterAct "believes that the shift to a focus on collaborative processes is key to democratic renewal, social inclusion, sustainable development, and a vibrant civil society." InterAct recognizes the importance of evaluating partnerships. But its interesting working paper "Evaluating Participatory, Deliberative, and Co-operative Ways of Working" lists many potential benefits but not the direct and indirect costs.[16]

And yet, when one looks at examples, one hears worried voices among those being asked to enter partnerships. The mundane transaction costs of interacting, coordinating, and partnering can loom large in practice. For example, these costs have been highlighted in internal World Bank studies that interviewed managers involved in partnerships. These studies evoke the adage, "No one likes to be coordinated."

There also can be opportunity costs—that is, things left undone because partnerships consume the time and attention of senior managers. For example, the World Bank recently discovered to its alarm that it is a member of 87 global and regional partnerships. Worried about the risk of having too many partnerships, the Bank's management asked how such partnerships could be evaluated. How should the Bank decide in advance which partnerships to join and how to participate?

In response to this question, a "discussion note" laid out these criteria for judging partnerships:

> [I]n order to ensure that the Bank fulfills its mission, it needs to be able to be selective in its role and only participate in initiatives with the greatest possible development impact, the best leverage of resources, and the strongest synergies with other partners. A clear direction for the Bank, then, is to make sure that its work at the global level contributes to poverty reduction, and builds on its core expertise—developing and helping to implement country-based programs.[17]

Other costs are important but difficult to measure—and sometimes difficult even to talk about. NGOs, for example, have been fearful of partnerships diluting their mission, silencing their voices, and bureaucratizing their cultures.[18] Similar worries have been expressed about government institutions being undermined by outsourcing, public-private partnerships, even by regulation. Consider the phenomenon of "regulatory capture," where regulatory agencies are deviated from their public purposes through their interactions with those being regulated.[19]

## How Efficient Are Partnerships?

The wide range of possible forms of partnership gives rises to questions about what form will be best for a would-be partner. Suppose an antipoverty agency accepts the idea that potential partners can provide advantages that will complement what it does, making what it does even more effective. Does this mean that the partnership needs to be set up as some kind of formal administrative integration? Or could the partnership be a kind of understanding, where both take advantage of each other in a good way but don't try to merge?

"A Checklist for Assessing Costs and Benefits of Partnerships" can help an agency think through where and how to partner. It also raises questions that are useful from perspectives 2 and 3 as well—understanding the effects on society of particular partnerships and of partnerships more generally.

On the plus side for the would-be partner are complementary capabilities provided by another sector. For instance, in protecting our nation's information infrastructure, the technical know-how and resources of the private sector, the distinctive capabilities and authority of the Department of Defense, and the knowledge and authority of the Justice Department all may complement each other. In successful policing, community awareness complements police action. In fostering rural development, services such as water, agricultural extension, roads, health, education, and credit complement one another. The presence of each enhances the value of the others.

Even if a would-be partner sees complementary capabilities, is a partnership of some sort required? Perhaps the goods and services can come together without any sort of administrative partnership among the service providers. Sometimes, people's choices and the market itself can be the integrating mechanism. In developed rural areas, once the government has provided roads, the other services may be left to the market, with individual farmers deciding how much of each to buy. As one expert asserted, "The major requirement is that such services be *simultaneously* available, and it is frequently possible for that to be achieved without administrative integration."[20]

But markets may malfunction in ways that partnerships can ameliorate.
- What one citizen does may affect another's productivity—for example, through practices that affect erosion, the use of water, and the control

of pests. When the incentives individual citizens face do not reflect these spillovers, or externalities, the classic economic solution uses prices and taxes to adjust those incentives. If this is not possible for some reason, a partnership among the service providers may improve the results. For example, a program might "integrate" the purchase of cows with mandatory vaccination and dipping services. Another program might require welfare recipients to undergo training, psychological assessment, and drug testing in order to be eligible for job placement—using a partnership of service providers and enforcers.

- Citizens may save time and travel costs by obtaining services from a single supplier—or at least from suppliers in one location. This is a major argument for combining services in a single agent, clinic, or project.

- Years ago, poverty experts routinely cited the tradition-boundedness and ignorance of the poor as obstacles. This is no longer in fashion. Today one tends to hear that poor people know best what they need and what works for them. Actually, both positions may have validity. The poor may indeed "rationally" respond to the prevailing incentive structure, but this structure may itself contain encrusted constraints, and unreliable or biased sources of information and knowledge. Another plus for partnerships may be gains in efficiency.

- Private firms that merge often justify the action by saying that each firm can profit from the strengths of the other. In the merger between two pharmaceutical companies, Merck with Sharp and Dohme, it was said that Merck had a strong research organization, whereas Sharp and Dohme had an effective sales force. By integrating, resources that are in effect underutilized in one firm are shifted to a more productive combined use. Economists, however, have been skeptical of this logic. Empirical research seems to show that instead of the weaker unit profiting from the stronger one, the process often works the other way around—the Shaw-and-the-dancer problem.

- A common rationale for pursuing partnerships in poor areas is the supposed paucity of trained managers. Combining institutions under a single chief may exploit what are called economies of scale, in this case in management. Economies of scale may also be realized by integrating common organizational functions such as research and development, finance, legal services, political functions, marketing, and information gathering. Integration may reduce redundancy. If agencies separately replicate part or all of a common task, then after integration what was done many times need be done only once. If the Department of Water and Power has established a citizens' council to obtain the views of local residents, it may seem nearly cost-free for the electricity provider or the transportation authority to utilize the same mechanism.[21]

# A Checklist for Assessing Costs and Benefits of Partnerships

1. Complementarity among the services provided
   a. Which goods and services exhibit complementarity? To what extent, at what levels of output? Focus attention on outputs whose synergies are most marked.
   b. Why can't consumers themselves integrate the goods and services optimally?
      - Externalities among consumers
      - Transaction costs
      - Consumer ignorance
   c. How would the partnership for the supply of the goods and services overcome these problems? Might other measures be preferable (such as providing information, adjusting prices, education)?
2. Economies of combined inputs for producing services
   a. Reallocating resources across institutions
      - Does having a partnership allow resources to be reallocated among the partners?
      - If so, with what resulting efficiencies? Consider the "comparative advantages" of the different partners in various functions (such as planning, marketing, delivery, evaluation, political connections).
      - Could the desired reallocation take place without a partnership?
      - Consider the risks of misallocation ("the Shaw-and-the-dancer problem").
   b. Economies of scale from integrating inputs
      - How large would the economies of scale be, for what functions (such as planning, research, capital equipment and other overhead, top management, delivery costs)?
      - What economies exist in the provision of collective goods (such as information, political organization, public relations)?
   c. Externalities
      - To what extent do partners and their activities affect each other via externalities? Consider especially the external effects of lumpy investments in capital, space, and time, such as infrastructure.
      - How well might the institution partners adjust to externalities without partnering (such as information exchange, changing prices, and so forth)?

3. The creation of a monopoly
   a. What benefits might arise from the monopoly powers that could result from the partnership? Consider increased bargaining leverage in relation to local citizens and clients, the provincial and national governments, and donors of foreign aid.
   b. What negative consequences might ensue? Consider the ease of co-optation by elites, corruption, politicization, and excessive expansion, as well as resistance by people in the individual partner institutions themselves.
4. Overcoming transaction costs via partnering
   a. Do the independent institutions now engage in transactions with each other, analogous to the purchase of inputs and the sale of outputs? If not, this argument for partnering may not apply.
   b. How would partnering lower these transaction costs and to what extent?
5. Allowing financial diversification via partnering (portfolio effects)
   a. To what extent would such financial benefits follow from partnering?
   b. Could the same benefits be obtained more efficiently through financial markets, investments, and so forth?
6. Direct financial costs of creating partnerships (such as the costs of starting an integrated organization, new personnel costs, changes in staffing patterns, training, information and publicity, and so forth)
7. Indirect and managerial costs of partnerships
   a. How large are learning costs (for changes in budgeting, personnel, political linkages, standard operating procedures, evaluation and information systems, and so forth)? Consider the costs for clients as well as employees.
   b. How serious will bureaucratic resistance be? Consider the legitimacy and power of the integrated authority, the similarity of missions among the partner organizations, and possible conflicts of politics and culture.
   c. Are the managerial tools available for inducing agencies to partner effectively? Consider incentives, authority, information, control over workloads, and career paths.
   d. How large are the returns to institutional specialization? To what extent is specialization sacrificed in the attempt to partner? Consider the technical aspects of the production function, but also the role of routines, measurable outcomes, morale, and so forth.

• Just as one person's consumption of something produces spillover effects, so, too, one institution's lumpy decisions in space and time may spill over to the operations of another. The analysis of such spillover effects is a classic topic in development planning, but how to include them in designing an integrated project is controversial in theory and difficult in fact.

When spillovers exist, it may be possible to share information and change incentives so that independent institutions will make the right choices. Joint planning may be called for—indeed, this is a fundamental argument for planning—but the administrative integration of various institutions is not necessarily implied. A key question is whether mutual adjustment by each individual institution is rapid and relatively cost-less. If so, then there is little need for integration. Mutual adjustment will be easier if information is widely available, and if rewards depend on results.

In some cases, though, it may be better for separate institutions—public, private, and nonprofit—to present a united front. As opposed to a set of independent actors that can be pitted against one another or fragmented in negotiations, the integrated unit can in theory bargain for better outcomes in negotiations with local citizens, the regional or national government, or international agencies.

The downside is that this sort of integrated partnership creates a kind of monopoly, and so it also entails costs and risks. One is that the monopoly will be captured or co-opted by a local elite or by one specific set of consumers.

It is argued that partnerships create a single interest, a combined set of objectives, which in turn reduces the "frictions" and costs that arise from different organizational interests and objectives. The temptation to hide information, for example, is reduced, given that "we're partners now." In partnerships, it is hoped that information will be shared and incentives aligned in the common purpose.

In practice, one would ask several questions. Do the potential partners already have to interact with each other, and do they experience large frictions in doing so? If so, how might partnering reduce these costs?

Finally, in the private sector, sometimes firms merge to take advantage of portfolio effects—combining assets or activities whose risks and returns are not perfectly correlated. Risk sharing is a common rationale for co-operatives, credit unions, and other sorts of partnering arrangements. It may be less relevant to public-private partnerships, but it is still worth asking, "How might a partnership help pool risks of various kinds to all partners' benefit?" The Canadian Council emphasizes partnerships not just as a way to import private sector techniques into public policy but also as a way to share risks, perhaps allowing the government to undertake initiatives that would not be possible otherwise.

## What Are the Costs of the Partnership?

The theoretical benefits of partnerships can make theorists swoon. Practical people may also be attracted. They may be swayed by the apparent costs of a *lack* of partnership—the misunderstandings, the failures to coordinate, the duplications—and tend to ignore the costs of sustaining a partnership and the benefits of staying separate.

It is fair to say that the costs of partnership often turn out to be higher than anticipated. Some of these costs can be measured directly in currency, but others involve reduced effectiveness because of drains on managers or staffs. Creating a new partnership, organization, committee, staff, or council costs time and money. So do training a multipurpose worker, sharing data and reports and impressions, and designing and implementing joint incentive and evaluation systems.

Creating a partnership and then learning how to make it work can entail indirect costs not only for employees but for clients and citizens as well. That is the case because institutions differ in budgets, organizational styles and traditions, connections to local and national clients and powers, personnel systems (pay scales, prescribed duties, career lines), and standard operating procedures.

In addition to dead-weight or start-up costs, organizational conflict often ensues. Those working inside a particular institution may perceive a partnership as an invasion of their turf. These costs will be greater the weaker the legitimacy and power of the partnership, the less that partnership helps each participating organization by its own standards, and the more different these separate standards turn out to be. The resistance and conflict are not just among organizations but also among personalities. Careers are built on the fight over who gets to control budgets and workloads. New partnerships can threaten that control.

Once again, the question to ask is whether appropriate incentives are available to induce integration. Without financial incentives in the short run and career incentives down the line, managers may be unable to motivate agencies and personnel to be partners. Once again, information and incentives are crucial to success.

Note, too, that there may be a trade-off between integrating activities in a partnership and the specialized excellence of each partner institution. Consider this advice from an old business-school textbook:

> The effective solution to any integration problem is the one that costs the least and that does not seriously undermine the effectiveness of the *specialized subunits*.... More than one well-intentioned company president has managed to "get his people to start pulling together," but in the process, made them less effective at their respective specialized tasks.[22]

Specialization has its own returns—familiarity, expertise, and savvy. Often routines are more readily established, outcomes more easily measured, and uncertainties reduced. Partnership may involve integrated activities that are not just more but different. Managing an integrated organization often requires qualitatively different skills and systems. Rarely will two organizations partner and find that their management systems align seamlessly.

The merits of various methods of partnering depend on a host of specific considerations, case by case. The framework in "A Checklist for Assessing Costs and Benefits of Partnerships" (see pages 34–35) is designed to help policy makers think more systematically and creatively about the alternatives—and to question whether administrative integration is the best method for partnering.[23]

## What Do Partners from Various Sectors Bring to the Table?

A different approach to "what's in it for me?" looks at the kinds of goods and services that various sectors provide best. One begins by analyzing carefully what a contemplated project is intended to accomplish. What goods and services in the broadest sense are to be produced?

Economists classify goods along two dimensions. The first is whether consumption of the good by one person reduces what is available to another, and the second is whether any individual can easily be excluded from consuming the good. The answers to those questions then produce four different kinds of goods.

For *private goods,* like groceries or automobiles, the answers to both questions are yes. If I buy a car, you can't buy it too. But both of us can easily be denied the chance to buy it if, for instance, our friend who owns it refuses to sell. At the other end, for *public goods,* the answers to both questions are no. Once these goods, like national defense or clean air, are provided, your access to them does not diminish mine, nor can you be easily excluded from enjoying the benefit. The general presumption is that private goods can be left to the private market, but public goods cannot. The nature of the latter gives rise to the familiar problem of free-riding: Because no one can be excluded from "consuming" national defense, all of us want it but would like to have the rest of our fellow Americans pay for it. As a result, voluntary contributions will produce too little defense, and the presumption is that the government must act.

For two other goods, the answers are mixed. For a *toll good*—like toll roads or water systems or other public utilities—once it is built, within some limits of crowding or scarcity, your consumption does not diminish my ability to benefit, but either of us can readily be excluded. In such cases, some combination of the private market and government supervision or regulation seems appropriate.

Finally, if one person's consumption does subtract from another's, but no one can easily be excluded, the good might be called a *common-pool good*. Open pastures or irrigation systems are examples. For them, the toll good mix of market and government may not work, because the incentive to free-ride will be large, and monitoring how much you and I consume will be difficult. These goods may require some cooperative or participatory mechanism to accomplish the monitoring.

E. S. Savas illustrates this classification scheme in Figure 2.1.[24] It locates a variety of goods in a kind of a continuum between the four corners of private good (or individual good), common-pool good, toll good, and public good (or collective good).

In Table 2.3, Robert Picciotto employs this same classification scheme and then adds two other dimensions based on the work of Albert O. Hirschman—exit and voice.[25] *Exit* refers to how easy it is for one person to opt in or out of consuming a particular good, while *voice* refers to how much say a person will have in decisions about producing the good. When a good or service is provided under conditions of low exit and low voice, Picciotto calls it a *government good*. When both exit and voice are high, he calls the good a *civil good*. In the corner characterized by low voice but high exit, he places *both private goods* and *toll goods*—you or I can readily opt in or out but individually don't have much say about producing it. *Common-pool goods* and *public goods,* by contrast, are low exit but high voice.

## Figure 2.1: Classifying Goods

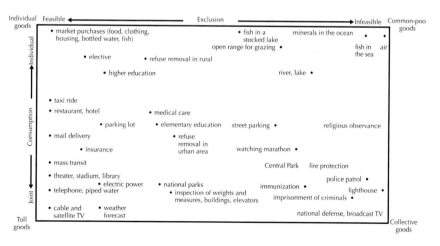

*Source: E. S. Savas, Privatization and Public-Private Partnerships.*

**Table 2.3: A Classification of Goods**

|  | **Low Voice** | **High Voice** |
|---|---|---|
| **Low Exit** | Government good | Common-pool good; public good |
| **High Exit** | Private good; toll good | Civil good |

Based on Robert Picciotto, Putting Institutional Economics to Work: From Participation to Governance.

Picciotto goes on to identify loyalty with hierarchy—that is, loyalty to due process over time. He then asks which goods can be left to the market and which require hierarchy in their provision. He argues that common-pool goods rank low in both market and hierarchy: Markets for them will not work, because people cannot readily be excluded from consuming them, but hierarchy will be frustrated by the difficulty of monitoring. By contrast, toll goods rank high on both. Public and government goods rank low on market but high on hierarchy, while private and civil goods have reverse rankings.

In Figure 2.2, Picciotto builds on these typologies to derive the distinctive advantages of each of the three sectors: government (or hierarchy), business, and civil society. Like Savas, he points out that some kinds of goods seem particularly suited to one or another of these institutions. For example, government goods, like the enforcement of contracts, are well suited to the government, private goods to the market, and common-pool resources to NGOs or other participatory or cooperative mechanisms.

Importantly, Picciotto's framework also identifies intermediate goods where partnerships may be particularly important. He argues that by their nature toll goods should involve both state and market. He describes "civil goods" and argues they would best be provided by a combination of the state and NGOs or participatory organizations (see Figure 2.2). Civil goods lie between market and participation in several respects. They will involve voluntary organizations or NGOs of all sorts, where both exit and voice are high. They will be non-hierarchical. Those NGOs or civil organizations will act to both exhort the state and restrain it, and to call attention to the excesses of pure private markets.

Picciotto's framework helps us understand partnerships in another way. A particular problem or project may require some combination of a public good, a civil good, a private good, and a common-pool resource. Without that combination, it will fail. That understanding has implications not just for how partnerships are built but for what kinds of partners make sense. This takes us to perspective 2, the broader effects on society of a particular partnership.

**Figure 2.2: A Typology of Goods and Institutions**

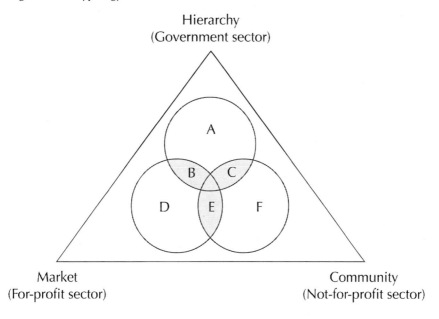

Hierarchy
(Government sector)

A

B C

D E F

Market
(For-profit sector)

Community
(Not-for-profit sector)

|   | Type of Good | Type of Institution | Examples |
|---|---|---|---|
| A | Government | State agencies | Justice, police |
| B | Toll | Public or regulated private corporations | Public utilities |
| C | Public | Hybrid organizations | Policy, rural roads |
| D | Market | Private corporations, farmers, and entrepreneurs | Industry, farming, many services |
| E | Civil | Non-governmental organizations, private voluntary organizations | Public advocacy, professional standards, civic action |
| F | Common pool | Local organizations, cooperatives | Natural resource management |

*Based on Robert Picciotto, Putting Institutional Economics to Work: From Participation to Governance. World Bank Discussion Paper 304. Washington, D.C: The World Bank, 1995.*

## Perspective 2: Assessing Partnerships as a Whole

This perspective focuses on the overall results of a partnership and on the allocation of tasks within it. What are the effects on society as a whole from the partnership as a whole, as compared with alternatives? Under what conditions, and for what problems, would it be socially useful for government, business, and NGOs to partner?

Practitioners have developed useful checklists to guide the analysis of benefits and costs in a partnership. An example is the outline for a benefit cost analysis of "cross-sector collaboration" distributed by The Prince of Wales Business Leaders Forum. It describes some of the social benefits (and also the partner-specific benefits) that may result from a partnership.[26] (See Tables 2.4 and 2.5.)

### Table 2.4: Advantages of "Cross-Sector Partnerships"

| | |
|---|---|
| **Greater Efficiency** | • Pooling resources and optimizing "division of labor"<br>• Decreasing costs associated with conflict resolution and societal disagreement on policies and priorities<br>• Creating economies of scale<br>• Promoting technological cooperation<br>• Facilitating the sharing of information<br>• Overcoming institutional rigidities and bottlenecks |
| **Improved Effectiveness** | • Leveraging greater amounts and a wider variety of skills and resources than can be achieved by acting alone<br>• Accommodating broader perspectives and more creative approaches to problem solving<br>• Shifting away from "command and control" to more informed joint goal setting<br>• Obtaining the "buy in" of recipients and local "ownership" of proposed solutions, thereby ensuring greater sustainability of outcomes<br>• Offering more flexible and tailored solutions<br>• Speeding the development and implementation of solutions<br>• Acting as a catalyst for policy innovation |
| **Increased Equity** | • Improving the level and quality of consultation with other stakeholders in society<br>• Facilitating broader participation in goal setting and problem solving<br>• Building the trust needed to work toward shared responsibilities and mutual benefit<br>• Building community-level institutional structures, networks, and capacities to enable local control and ownership |

**Table 2.5: Potential Positive Outcomes from Partnerships**

| Outputs of Societal Partnership | • Development of human capital<br>• Improved operational efficiency<br>• Organizational innovation<br>• Increased access to information<br>• More effective products and services<br>• Enhanced reputation and credibility<br>• Creation of a stable society |
| --- | --- |
| Outputs— Private Sector | • Increased shareholder and societal value<br>• Greater competitiveness and long-term success<br>• Enhanced reputation—among employees and other stakeholders |
| Outputs— Public Sector | • National governance and competitiveness<br>• Less bureaucracy—in reality and perception<br>• Cost reductions |
| Outputs— Civil Society Sector | • Social cohesion<br>• Human development<br>• Empowerment<br>• Access to resources<br>• Reputation enhancement |

Source: Measures for Success: Assessing the Impact of Partnershi ps.London: The International Business Leaders Forum, August 2000. http://www.pwblf.org/csr/csr webassist.nsf/content/ f1d2a3b4c5.html

Even these lists are incomplete, as their designers emphasized. For example, at the practical level of possible benefits, one might also look for reduced vandalism, better maintenance, leverage for additional funding, and impact on the policy process. Even there, though, the document admits that "there remains insufficient hard evidence on these benefits for them to be widely acknowledged."

Partnerships may have other effects that are difficult to measure but in any particular case can be among the most valued. For example, a partnership can build trust, enable negotiation, reduce violence, undergird a social contract, inhibit government discretion, and enable freer flows of information. InterAct's "Evaluating Participatory, Deliberative, and Co-operative Ways of Working" lists as possible benefits increases in information and understanding, trust among stakeholders, ownership, "capacity" among stakeholders, openness and transparency, "representativeness of participation," and "level of understanding about the process and the specific project"— as well as "changes in values, priorities, aims and objectives" and new relationships between organizations (formal and informal).

Some possible social costs are also hard to measure, but they are potentially crucial. For example, partnerships between government and business may enable corruption and cronyism. Jose Edgardo Campos and Hilton Root studied various policy partnerships in East Asia, especially "deliberation councils" involving people from industry, the government, academia, and, in some cases, the press, consumer groups, and labor.[27] Campos and Root extolled the benefits of these partnerships as the key to the East Asian economic miracle. But after the East Asian economic crisis of 1997, some critics cited these same partnerships as catalysts of crony capitalism and corruption, which rendered these countries more vulnerable. Our conclusion: Experience indicates that partnerships may have important benefits and costs that go beyond the level of service provided and the financial costs.

## What Do Various Partners Bring?

One may also appraise partnerships by how well they function in providing an ensemble of goods and services. Robert Picciotto's work again suggests a valuable approach. One begins with an issue or problem and asks, "To address this issue, what kinds of goods and services need to be provided?" Then one asks, "Which of the potential partners can provide each good and service the best?"

The issue or problem may be as grandiose as "homeland security" or "provision of relief services," or as narrow as "nursing home services." To address it, many different kinds of goods and services may be required. These in turn might be provided by a government agency, an international institution, a private business, or an NGO, or perhaps by all of them working together in a partnership. Each combination of these different goods and services "produces" an outcome. One evaluates the different partnerships by asking how much homeland security or nursing home services is produced by what combinations of public, private, and nonprofit inputs.

For example, consider a program to improve the seeds available to farmers in the African country of Malawi. Upon analysis, it became clear that various kinds of goods and services would be essential. Eventually, a partnership was formed. Some parts of the overall solution were provided by government—for example, funding research and development and setting agricultural pricing policies. Some of the necessary goods and services were provided by the private sector—for example, the distribution of the new seed varieties. And still others were provided by community organizations—for example, mobilizing farmers to enable group credit.

As another example, consider welfare-to-work programs. Social experiments in the United States are pitting government agencies against both community groups and private employment firms to see which "does the best job" of placing welfare recipients. Picciotto's framework focuses on the comparative advantages of the three kinds of institutions. Might government employment agencies, private employment firms, and community organizations each have distinctive advantages in providing different relevant services? For example, community groups might do best in bringing in certain kinds of participants and giving them confidence in the process of job seeking, while for-profits might have an advantage in teaching marketable skills and work habits to another clientele. And then the partnership question would arise. How might it be possible to blend the distinctive features of businesses, government, and nonprofits in this endeavor—for example, trying to draw on the efficiency of private providers and the commitment or superior access of nonprofit institutions?[28] Might it be possible that for some sorts of welfare recipients, community groups would work best; for others, private firms; and for still others, government agencies?

Along with benefits, one must assess costs. What are the various kinds of costs that accrue to each combination of public, private, and nonprofit inputs? The costs would be financial, as when the government provides so many soldiers, the private sector so much medicine, and the NGO so many volunteer physicians. But the costs could also be transactional—including the management and administrative costs of combining, coordinating, creating a hybrid, or otherwise entering into a partnership.

The ideal partnership will be arrived at by a careful assessment of both benefits and costs. As perspective 1 made clear, experience with public-private partnerships shows that the products and the costs come in many forms, and these may be valued differently by different partners. For example, quite apart from the amount of homeland security produced, or the amount of nursing home services provided, there may be benefits in image building, trust building, communication efficiencies, and so forth. And quite apart from the dollar costs, there may be costs in terms of mission dilution, loss of specialization, greater propensities for corruption, and loss of diversity.

## Who Should "Own" a Partnership's Project?

One critical issue bridges perspectives 1 and 2. That is, who should "own"—figuratively or literally—a project that emerges from a partnership? There is promise in applying contract theory to partnerships between government, business, and civil society. Contract theory begins with the premise that all the future contingencies that may arise cannot be specified beforehand, and so no fully specified contract can be written among potential partners. This means that the partnership will not be able to live up to its full promise, because whenever the contract is not specific, each individual institution will look first to its own interests rather than the partnership's interests.

Contract theory responds by focusing on the allocation of residual rights (those that cannot be specified in the partnership "contract").[29] A public official or agency might, for instance, want to contract with a private firm or an NGO to provide some service that is a public good, like education or environmental cleanup. The contracting process is, however, incomplete—that is, many critical contingencies of the project, like the size of the investments the two will make or the quality of the resulting services, cannot be written into binding contracts in advance. That is so because there are too many contingencies to be identified, and often too many uncertainties to enable probability estimates even for the contingencies that can be named.

Suppose the public manager of a school system contemplates a project, an investment, to improve the quality of a local school, perhaps as measured by better test scores. She imagines partnering in some way with an NGO that is active in the locality and cares deeply about education; suppose, indeed, that the NGO values the public good that the test scores project produces more highly than the school system. The NGO, however, cannot undertake the project on its own, perhaps for legal reasons or because it lacks the appropriate technology. If the two cannot make a binding contract beforehand on either the size of their relative investments or the resulting quality, then—following the logic of incomplete contracts—they will choose the size of their investment according to what would happen if, after having made it, they disagreed with one another and the partnership fell apart.

In this case, the school system values the higher test scores, but the NGO values them more. Once the investments were made, if the partnership fell apart, the school system would continue the project because it values it. The NGO, however, values the project more, and it would receive that value without contributing anything. Thus, it could not be induced to contribute anything; knowing that, the school system will not make the investment. Both it and the NGO will thus be worse off.

Suppose, by contrast, that the NGO "owned" the project. If the partnership broke down, the project would not continue because the NGO could not do so on its own. If the two then bargained over the value of the project, they might agree that the value for each was roughly half the total value to both. That would be a positive value for the school system, and the project would go forward. Moreover, since the NGO as owner could not finish the project on its own, it would be willing to contribute to the school system to complete the project.

The logic is complicated, but the critical practical insight is this: In a situation of incomplete contracts, the party that values the public good produced by some partnership more highly than the other should retain residual ownership rights, *regardless of who made the original investment*. This logic suggests why it is increasingly common for public agencies to fund service facilities that then become privately owned. It also suggests, more metaphorically, the value of arranging partnerships to convey a sense of "ownership" to the partner that values the public good more highly— even if that ownership is not formal legal title.

What if the project produces both private and public goods? For instance, costs could be cut in running the school, producing a private good between the partners, but at the price of reducing quality as measured by test scores, which is the public good. In that case, who owns the project should depend on the balance between private and public goods. If the public good is important enough, the NGO should be the owner even if it is not the investor.

One way for the school system manager to think about the test scores project is illustrated in Table 2.6.

In the Appendix, we apply the framework to several examples, and in two of them the question of ownership arises front and center. NGOs and other humanitarian organizations value the public good produced by international relief operations more highly than do the nations and militaries with whom they partner. Those NGOs, by the logic of the framework, ought to "own" the operations, but they don't. In a second example, protecting the nation's critical infrastructures for information, finance, and power, the first thing a government manager notices is that while the public good of infrastructure protection is important, it is dwarfed by the stakes of the infrastructure owners, which are predominantly private. That suggests that the for-profits probably will have to be the main "owners" of any protection system, and that the government will have difficulty getting into the game. Indeed, that has been the case.

**Table 2.6: Deciding on "Ownership" in Partnership**

|  | Who invests in project? | Who values public good more? | Who should "own" the residual rights? |
|---|---|---|---|
| **Basic case** | Only Partner A | Partner B | Partner B |
| **Both partners invest** | Both partners | Partner B | Partner B |
| **Private and public goods** | Either one partner or both | Partner B | Depends on how important the public good |

## Perspective 3: Understanding the Conditions That Help Partnerships Work Best

Perspective 3 considers the conditions under which partnerships of various kinds emerge or don't emerge, function well or function badly.

At RAND and elsewhere, researchers are exploring this question. We are investigating how the existence, efficiency, and sustainability of partnerships are affected by:

- Better measures of quality of service and quality of life
- Better estimates of institutional performance[30]
- How well incentives are aligned with performance, within and across institutions
- The cost of information flows, which in turn affects learning and feedback

In general, one finds more and better partnerships when measures of quality of service are plentiful and accurate; when estimates of institutional performance are relatively easy; when incentives are plentiful and aligned with performance; and when information flows are inexpensive.

In this work, once again we find it crucial to recognize the nether side of partnerships, how from society's perspective they may unwittingly abet market power, cronyism, and corruption. We must examine not just the enabling conditions for partnerships but also what might be "disabling conditions." Pranab Bardhan has pointed out the troubling persistence of dysfunctional institutions. He criticizes a benign view that tends to "understate the tenacity of vested interests, the enormity of the collective action problems in bringing about institutional change, and the differential capacity of different social groups in mobilization and coordination."[31]

We are struggling with another broad and important category of conditions, those having to do with the social and cultural setting of the partnership. Many contextual factors can affect the benefits and costs of partnerships, indeed their likelihood to emerge at all. How to grasp the many possible interactions between aspects of partnerships and aspects of the social and cultural setting remains a daunting challenge, in theory and in practice.[32]

This line of inquiry runs into two taboos in discussions of partnerships. The first is simple *incompetence*. One of the partners may not only have less capacity technically or managerially but actually be incompetent. In international development, technical assistance is sometimes woeful, as are so-called experts; this much we are allowed to say. But so-called local partners are often so poorly paid and so badly trained that partnering with them creates special challenges and perils. This much is taboo to say, at home or abroad.

Second is the problem of *dysfunctional institutions*. Calls for partnership and local ownership ring hollow if one of the "owners" is systematically corrupt. This issue arises most forcefully in developing countries, where the places most in need of partnerships are those with the gravest problems of incompetence and dysfunctional institutions. To put it another way, advocating local ownership now in countries such as Indonesia, Peru, and Nigeria is hard to square with simultaneous criticism of how local politicians exercised ownership in the past. Similarly, a renewed emphasis in donor circles on capacity building and on fighting corruption combines awkwardly with calls for local ownership, causing rhetorical and practical tensions in development donor organizations, both national ones and the World Bank.

We have discovered that research on these questions may be helpful in creating the conditions for healthy partnerships to emerge. For example, serious evaluations of partnerships may actually enable them to succeed under conditions of low capacity and dubious probity. Evaluations abet accountability. Objective, independent information about performance enables credible commitments to be made, on both sides of the partnership. But any evaluation must face up to the levels of technical competence that can be expected in practice on all sides of the partnership, and must both recognize and counteract the temptations for corruption, self-congratulation, and conceptual hectoring that plague evaluations. Evaluation can be part of the problem (when vitiated by incompetence or nullified by corruption), but it also can be part of the solution to both taboo topics.

Assessing partnerships through perspective 3 should focus on such aspects as the availability of good information about quality of service and about performance, the incentives within and across organizations, and (admittedly poorly theorized) the social and cultural context. It also should frankly assess the capacities of the partners and the likelihood of abuse of power and corruption. Finally, it should recognize the possibly strategic role of evaluation in difficult settings: Evaluations can, in fact, be enablers of productive partnerships and antidotes to abusive ones.

# The Process of Assessing Partnerships

There is no magic algorithm that can tote up all the considerations in a specific case and tell a manager whether a particular partnership is worthwhile. We do not have anything approaching a full model of the benefits and costs of partnerships. Theorists would imagine identifying all the factors that affect the various benefits and costs of partnership, including external forces and dynamics. They would then imagine pulling together valid and reliable data on all the benefits and costs and other factors, including those that are laden with values and deeply affected by perceptions. With enough cases, a researcher might then be able to say which partnerships work (in what senses) when, and therefore provide rich guidance to the designers of and participants in partnerships.

But we are a long way from this ideal. Not only are we just beginning to understand the benefits and costs and the various perspectives for identifying them, we have little experience with public-private partnerships. History is not a good guide, either. A look at the history of public transport or municipal water supply over the last century displays the changing boundaries of public and private—changes that have been driven, then as now, by fashion as well as culture or technology.[33]

And yet, we need as never before to assess partnerships. They are an emerging feature of the way we deal with public problems. Like it or not, we are entering the era of hybrid governance. More and more issues raise the desirability not just of changing the boundaries of who does what— privatizing or, as the United States has done recently with airport security, re-nationalizing—but of considering something more: real partnerships.

And so our task is to make assessments together in the face of incomplete theory and sparse experience. Under such circumstances, we believe that the task of improving partnerships may be better pursued through a process rather than through any pretense of a mathematical calculation.

We recommend that potential partners work through checklists like "A Checklist for Assessing Costs and Benefits of Partnerships" and Tables 2.4 and 2.5. Probe together each dimension. The result may be the shared conclusion that a particular advantage or risk is paramount, and then the partners can actively focus on it. Or all participants may discover that there are angles to the problem that they had overlooked—and by talking them through together, they are able to manage them more effectively.

This process of understanding should itself be a kind of partnership. "In today's world," a colleague of ours who's been a CEO of a private company and a nonprofit recently wrote, "the role of the CEO is no longer to huddle behind the crystal ball and oracle out strategic directions, but rather one of coaching (and being the accountability boss) of a team of unit managers around him. He gets his team to work through the analysis together. The role model there of course is Jack Welch: He spends a lot of time in his book explaining the tools he used to make GE tick."

The same is true for partnerships. It isn't the job of the leader to do the analysis alone and tell others the results. Nor should this be left to a technical analyst working alone. Rather, we should seek a kind of participatory diagnosis, where the agency's managers work through the checklists, perhaps facilitated by the leader and with inputs from a technical evaluator. For each bullet, there is a discussion. What does this category trigger in your imaginations? How big might this category of benefits be, and what does it depend on? Which of these headings seems most important to our agency's mission? Which of the synergies or complementarities across partners seems most crucial? Which most fragile? And so forth.

In this context, research may have a valuable role to play. Can we identify and then study together examples of successful partnerships (and perhaps also failed ones, but let's begin with whatever successes we can find)? Working with practitioners will be crucial here in defining what "success" might mean and carrying out the case studies.

We also might aspire to identify excellent examples of understanding the benefits and costs of partnerships—from the perspective of a single partner, from the perspective of the entire partnership, and from the perspective of how various conditions enable or discourage effective partnerships of many kinds.

Finally, once we have done such research, how might we together learn from the results and see what further insights they generate in practitioners and analysts alike?

These questions may suggest new ways to assess and improve the "business" of government.

# Appendix:
# Analysis of Three Examples
# of Partnerships

Consider several examples that we believe illustrate the usefulness of the framework in analyzing partnerships.

## Integrating Family Planning Services

What are the pros and cons of a partnership of many public, private, and community services? Working through the specifics of the goods and services and the possible costs and benefits of partnership might enhance the chances of success.

For example, perspective 1 questions about economies of scale in managerial talent would be helpful in assessing integrated family planning. Whatever the theoretical attractions, partnering health clinics with family planning centers and community organizations is a managerial challenge. A classic evaluation by David Korten concluded:

> Integration in itself is not likely to improve the acceptance of family planning and indeed may result in serious deterioration in program performance.... It should be clear that integration is not a panacea for poor program performance.... Indeed I would suggest as a tentative hypothesis that on the whole, integrated programs require stronger management to maintain the same level of performance as a comparable vertical program.[34]

## Managing Complex Humanitarian Emergencies[35]

Using perspectives 1 and 2 to assess humanitarian emergencies sharpens the focus on what good is being produced and thus who should "own" the operations. With the end of the Cold War, international relief missions have moved from one-shot responses to natural disasters to complex, and often lengthy, operations to assist the victims of conflict. From northern Iraq to Turkey, Somalia, Haiti, Rwanda, Zaire, Bosnia and Kosovo, it has come to be recognized that hungry people hardly ever result from an absolute shortage of food; rather, famine is usually the byproduct of conflict, and so relief becomes an issue between combatants. The missions range from simply delivering food, albeit in perilous circumstances, to trying to rebuild states that have lost control of their territories, to trying to end civil wars.

The operations have involved partnerships as varied as the missions. On the relief side, the major partners have been the large humanitarian organizations—CARE, Oxfam, Save the Children, and others. The founding ethos of these organizations was that of the volunteer fire brigade— volunteers rushing to alleviate this or that famine in a particular country, then returning to their ordinary lives. The organizations tended to have skimpy infrastructure and not much capacity for learning lessons. It has caused some pain to their sense of mission to realize that humanitarian emergencies, somewhere, are a permanent condition, and that their organizations need to become more permanent, more professional, and more specialized.

The military forces involved have also covered a wide range—from next to none in Rwanda, to U.N. peacekeepers in Somalia, to heavy-armored forces of the North Atlantic Treaty Organization (NATO) operating with a U.N. mandate in Bosnia. The adjustment in perspective these complex operations have required of participating militaries has been at least as wrenching as that imposed on the humanitarian organizations. The original military model was that of U.N. Cold War peacekeeping, when lightly armed forces were interposed as reassurance between combatants who could not make peace but were presumed to be beyond making war. If that presumption was shattered, the peacekeepers withdrew; they were neither equipped nor prepared to stand and fight.

Now the peacekeepers often have to be prepared to be peacemakers or enforcers, not only protecting themselves and relief operations when doing so is likely to appear to one set of combatants as taking sides, but also sometimes separating or pacifying combatants. The "partnership" between the militaries and the humanitarian NGOs has been uneasy at best. To the militaries, the NGOs have often looked like rag-tag amateurs. For their part, the NGOs know they need protection, but many cherish their image as neutral humanitarians. They are wary of too close an association with governments, fearing that they will lose their independence and animating spirit.

The first observation the framework suggests is that "ownership" in the existing partnerships is badly mismatched in terms of how much the partners value the good produced.

That good is, for the international community, almost entirely a public one, some combination of lessened suffering and enhanced order. For the militaries, and especially the United States, there is also some private good, in the form of enhanced influence. But what is striking is that the public good often is valued much more highly by the NGOs than by the participating nations and militaries. Vital interests have not been at stake for the nations; Bosnia and Kosovo were perhaps exceptions, at least for the Europeans, and much larger operations resulted. Participating has been discretionary, and opting out is always possible.

The NGOs ought therefore to own the operations, but they don't. The military partners do. That has been the result of the overriding need for protection, as well as the fact of clear chains of command on the military side. By contrast, the civilian side is at best cobbled together, often from a welter of different and sometimes competing organizations. The U.N. High Commissioner for Relief is a symbolic focal point, but not one that is in a position to exercise real operational control, surely not with regard to the participating militaries.

The more venturesome NGOs have begun to draw the unpleasant implications of the misbegotten partnerships. They have accepted that the United Nations or the United States or NATO cannot be counted on to provide security for these complex operations. That protection will be a sometime thing. That fact suggests, first, that the NGOs and their community need much better capacity to analyze the circumstances of any given emergency to understand just how much and what kind of danger they run. Second, some NGOs have gone so far as to imagine drawing the private sector into their partnership if government protection cannot be assured. They would, in effect, "privatize" the security function. By one calculation, the 1990s operation in eastern Zaire could have privatized security for about $50 million, out of a total relief budget of about a billion dollars.

Finally, the NGOs have begun to realize that they may have to refuse to intervene. To do so would be to directly contravene their mission. But if the operation is very risky, national partners are not available for protection, and privatizing security is impossible or unacceptable, then saying no may become necessary.

## Protecting the National Information Infrastructure[36]

For this issue, too, the framework provides insights about the nature of the goods and who should "own" projects, as well as the forms the partnerships might take. These are factors to think through together more carefully, not a kind of accounting sheet or a specific recommendation.

September 11, 2001, drove home the vulnerability of the United States to terrorist attack. Even before the attack, concern about the nation's infrastructures—telecommunications, finance, electric power, air traffic control—had spawned a presidential commission and set of new government institutions. All the infrastructures are vulnerable to threats ranging from bad weather and careless clerks, to joy-riding hackers and petty criminals, to determined terrorists. Information networks are central to all of them.

Yesterday's solution was a tight but limited partnership between the federal government and its controlled monopoly, AT&T. In those years, government communications, particularly military communications, were much more segregated from civilian communications than they are now. To the extent that elements of the civilian information infrastructure were deemed dangerously vulnerable, the solution was easily at hand: Subsidize AT&T to bury the cables deeper, to build redundancy, or to otherwise harden the system.

Now, no such government solution is at hand. AT&T is long since dissolved, and the infrastructures themselves are simultaneously global, or at least international (in the case of power), and mostly in private hands, not public. Moreover, information technology leaders, especially at home but also abroad, have spent their careers getting the government off their backs. So the last thing they seek is a government role even if they might privately accept that intense competition does drive them to spend too little safeguarding the infrastructures. Given the pace of technology, any government regulations would be almost bound to be dead on arrival, or worse.

For its part, the government instinctively views the problem as one of either law enforcement or national security, neither one an irrelevant perspective but both destined to frighten off the private infrastructure managers, both in making policy at home and negotiating abroad. As the government seeks to reach out to the for-profit sector, it sees a set of people, none of whom have security clearances and all of whom are driven by competitive advantage, not in the first instance national security.

Starting to parse the issue using the framework, then, the first thing a government manager notices is that while the public good of infrastructure protection is important, it is dwarfed by the private stakes of the infrastructure owners. That suggests that the for-profits probably will have to be the main "owners" of any protection system, and that the government will have difficulty getting into the game. Indeed, that has been the case. Before September 11, the government created a set of rather traditional government institutions—the Critical Infrastructure Assurance Organization at Commerce and the National Infrastructure Protection Center at the Federal Bureau of Investigation. Its "partnerships" with the private sector, ISACs, or Information Sharing and Analyses Centers, have thus far mostly been public relations ventures. In areas like banking or energy, where effective trade associations already existed, the government has anointed them as ISACs.

What the government might offer a partnership is money, intelligence or information, and, ultimately, the prospect of treating the public good as such and regulating or setting standards. The last—the use of hierarchy—is precisely, though, what the for-profits fear most. One possible institutional model is the existing National Institute of Science and Technology, which grew out, in part, of the last generation's infrastructure wake-up call, the 1977 New York City blackout. Perhaps more suggestive still are the Centers for Disease Control. They are very nonpolitical and very professional, out of Washington, and dominated by the private sector. Public health professionals need them, and can be confident that information provided to the centers will not be released.

The frameworks suggest to us the utility of using NGO or other participatory mechanisms in several ways. When the Melissa virus struck the web in 1999, its perpetrators were identified within a matter of days. What was striking, though, was that none of the government's fledgling machinery for protecting infrastructure was a significant part of the hunt. Rather, a loose network of private hackers shared tips and pursued leads. They did so, so far as one can tell, not from any sense of public duty or animosity toward the perpetrators, but rather for the simple challenge of solving the puzzle. Still, that might be thought of, in Picciotto's terms, as a public good.

Perhaps there is also a role for more organized participation, a kind of civil good, as a check on both the pursuit of profit by the infrastructure owners and the heavy-handedness of government involvement. The existing trade associations are probably too self-interested to play that role. But the evolution of the Silicon Valley's TechNet from a trade association to a policy group with interest in what Washington did, or might do, is suggestive of one kind of new NGO in the infrastructure area.

# Endnotes

1. See Gregory F. Treverton and Tora Bikson, New Challenges for International Leadership: Positioning the United States for the 21st Century, RAND Issues Paper, forthcoming.

2. Michael R. McAdoo, "Tying the Knot: The Partnership Craze," in Sustaining Growth and Bridging the Divides: A Framework for Our Global Future. Annual Meeting 2001 Report. Davos, Switzerland: World Economic Forum, 2001: 40.

3. An internal document from the World Bank defines partnership as "a collaborative relationship between entities to work toward shared objectives through a mutually agreed division of labor," including specific programs and "ongoing, often open-ended relationships." "Partnership Oversight and Selectivity: A Discussion Note," March 2000, p. 2.

4. For a review of recent usage, see Simon Maxwell and Tim Conway, "Perspectives on Partnership," OED Working Paper Series No. 6. Washington, D.C.: The World Bank, 2000; and John Eriksson, The Drive to Partnership: Aid Coordination and the World Bank. Washington, D.C.: The World Bank, 2001.

5. http://www.worldbank.org/partners/

6. Philip S. Antón, Richard Silberglitt, and James Schneider, The Global Technology Revolution: Bio/Nano/Materials Trends and Their Synergies with Information Technology by 2015. Santa Monica: RAND, 2001.

7. Philip Bobbitt, The Shield of Achilles: War, Peace, and the Course of History. New York: Knopf, 2002.

8. The World Bank, Global Development Finance 2001: Building Coalitions for Effective Development Finance. Washington, D.C.: The World Bank, 2001, chapter 2.

9. Carrots, Sticks, and Sermons: Policy Instruments and Their Evaluation, ed. Marie-Louise Bemelmans-Videc, Ray C. Rist, and Evert Vedung. Somerset, N.J.: Transaction Publishers, 1998.

10. For example, see Burton Weisbrod, "The Future of the Nonprofit Sector: Its Entwining with Private Enterprise and Government," Journal of Policy Analysis and Management. 16, 4 (1997): 541-555; Nonprofits and Government: Collaboration and Conflict, ed. Elizabeth T. Boris and C. Eugene Steuerle. Washington, D.C.: The Urban Institute Press, 1999; and Public-Private Policy Partnerships, ed. Pauline Vaillancourt Rosenau. Cambridge: MIT Press, 2000.

11. http://www.pppcouncil.ca/aboutppp.htm.

12. See James E. Austin, The Collaboration Challenge: How Nonprofits and Businesses Succeed through Strategic Alliances. San Francisco: Jossey-Bass Publishers, 2000, especially chapter 2.

13. Business Partnership and Outreach Group, "Partnering with Business: Questions and Answers." Briefing Note No. 2. Washington, D.C.: The World Bank, Nov. 2000. http://www.worldbank.org/business/files/note2.pdf It is, of course, a long way from a typology of benefits to their careful measurement in a specific case, and we know of no exemplar.

14. See Public-Private Policy Partnerships, op. cit., especially chapter 13.

15. Burton Weisbrod, op cit.

16. Brighton, England: InterAct, June 2001.

17. "Addressing Global Dimensions in Development, A Discussion Note," The World Bank, March 20, 2000: 9. The document later notes (p. 10): "Key aspects of the Bank's comparative advantage are global reach and a broad developmental mandate, ability to mobilize and manage resources, and operational competence at the country level."

Again, it is easier to list these aspects than to monitor and evaluate them across a range of potential partnerships.

18. For example, NGOs, States and Donors: Too Close for Comfort? ed. David Hulme and Michael Edwards. London: Macmillan, 1997.

19. Jean-Jacques Laffont and Jean Tirole, "The Politics of Government Decision-Making: A Theory of Regulatory Capture." Quarterly Journal of Economics, 106, 4 (Nov. 1991): 1089-1127.

20. Arthur T. Mosher, Thinking about Rural Development. New York: Agricultural Development Council, 1976.

21. Samuel Paul, Holding the State to Account. Bangalore: Public Affairs Centre, 2002.

22. John P. Kotter, Leonard Schlesinger, and Vijay Sathe, Organization: Text, Cases, and Readings in the Management of Organizational Design and Change. Homewood, Ill. Irwin, 1979: 133, emphasis in original.

23. "A Checklist for Assessing Costs and Benefits of Partnership" also suggests pointers for our other two perspectives on partnerships. For instance, from perspective 3, governments can take steps to enhance information flows and make incentives more flexible. If so, partnerships will be easier to organize and more efficient in their operations. By providing an information-rich environment and appropriate incentives, independent agencies and the citizens they serve are able to do their own "integrating" efficiently. Partnerships, which are often thought of only in terms of organization charts and training and law, may be usefully refocused in terms of information and incentives.

24. E. S. Savas, Privatization and Public-Private Partnerships New York and London: Chatham House Publishers, Seven Bridges Press, 2000, pp. 46-47.

25. Robert Picciotto, Putting Institutional Economics to Work: From Participation to Governance, World Bank Discussion Paper 304. Washington, D.C.: The World Bank, 1995.

26. "Measures for Success: Assessing the Impact of Partnerships." London: The International Business Leaders Forum, August 2000. http://www.pwblf.org/csr/csrwebassist.nsf/content/f1d2a3b4c5.html

27. The Key to the Asian Miracle: Making Shared Growth Credible. Washington, D.C.: Brookings, 1996.

28. See, for instance, Paul C. Light, Making Nonprofits Work: A Report on the Tides of Nonprofit Management Reform. Washington, D.C.: The Brookings Institution, 2000.

29. Oliver Hart, Andrei Shleifer, and Robert W. Vishny, "The Proper Scope of Government: Theory and an Application to Prisons," Quarterly Journal of Economics, 112:4 (Nov. 1997): 1126-1161. Timothy Besley and Maitreesh Ghatak, "Public-Private Partnerships for the Provision of Public Goods: Theory and an Application to NGOs." The Development Economics Discussion Paper Series, No. 17, London School of Economics, August 1999. http://econ.lse.ac.uk/staff/tbesley/papers/ngo.pdf.

30. This builds upon better measures of quality, but is separable from them. An example: Suppose we have a fuller set of measures of educational quality. To judge a school's performance, in the sense of value added, we would have to adjust for changes in the quality of the intake and for other features of the environment that affect the quality of education but are not under the school's control.

31. Pranab K. Bardhan, "Understanding Underdevelopment: Challenges for Institutional Economics from the Point of View of Poor Countries," Journal of Institutional and Theoretical Economics 156, 1 (March 2000): 224.

32. Robert Klitgaard, "Including Culture in Evaluation Research," New Directions for Evaluation, No. 67, Fall 1995; and Robert Klitgaard, "Applying Cultural Theories to Prac-

tical Problems," in *Culture Matters*, ed. Richard J. Ellis and Michael Thompson. Boulder: Westview, 199 .

33. Charles D. Jacobson and Joel A. Tarr, "No Single Path: Ownership and Financing of Infrastructure in the 19th and 20th Centuries," in *Infrastructure Delivery: Private Initiative and the Public Good*, ed. Ashoka Moody. EDI Development Studies. Washington, D.C.: The World Bank, 199 .

34. David C. Korten, "Integrated Approaches to Family Planning Services Delivery." Development Discussion Paper 24. Cambridge: Harvard Institute for International Development, 19 5: 24.

35. See Michael Bryans, Bruce J. Jones and Janice Gross Stein, *Mean Times: Humanitarian Action in Complex Political Emergencies—Stark Choices, Cruel Dilemmas*, University of Toronto, January 1999, available at www.toronto.ca/cis/conflict.html or www.care.ca Daniel Byman and others, *Strengthening the Partnership: Improving Military Coordination with Relief Agencies and Allies in Humanitarian Operations*. RAND, MR-11 5-AF 2000 , pp. 59- 9, 101-19 and Marc Lindenberg and Coralie Bryant, *Going Global: Transforming Relief and Development NGOs*. Bloomfield, Conn.: Kumarian Press, 2001.

3 . See "National Plan for Information Systems Protection," January 2000, and Report of the President of the United States on the Status of Federal Critical Infrastructure Protection Activities, January 2001, both available on the CIAO website, www.ciao.ncr.gov. See also the FBI's National Infrastructure Protection Center, whose website is www.infragard.net. For examples of public-private partnerships to build the information infrastructure, see http://www.ncppp.org/casestudies/ ConnectingMinnesota.htm.

# CHAPTER THREE

## Leveraging Networks:
## A Guide for Public Managers
## Working across Organizations

Robert Agranoff
Professor Emeritus
School of Public and Environmental Affairs
Indiana University–Bloomington

*This report was originally published in March 2003.*

# Networks and Network Management

## Scope of the Study

Do public managers operate differently in interorganizational networks than they do in their home organizations? Is management in networks different from that of hierarchical organizations? Some may answer no, because both entail a type of boundary spanning and "dealing with people" that is common to traditional management functions. Others respond definitely yes, because of the absence of all the trappings of standard management—for example, hierarchy, authority, and direction. One state official said, "We manage by consensus in the Partnership for Rural Nebraska," one of the networks studied in this chapter. "In my department I supervise and direct, based on the legal authority vested in my position ... in the network I am an equal partner."

This chapter investigates public managers as they participate in collaborative undertakings with other governments and the nongovernmental sector. These experiential lessons about "network management" are derived from the responses of managers in federal government, state government, local government, and universities, as well as nongovernmental organization (NGO) officials, as they work together to approach issues that cross the boundaries of their organizations. The 12 focal networks studied operate in Midwest states. "Networks Studied," at the end of this section provides a thumbnail sketch of each one.

How to manage in a network is an important 21st-century issue because of networks' prevalence in the managerial enterprise. No single agency or organization at any level of government or the private sector has a monopoly on the mandate, resources, or information to deal with the most vexing of public problems. Moreover, a century of knowledge building in management—public and private—has focused on hierarchy and its derivatives, for example, POSDCORB (Planning, Organizing, Staffing, Directing, COordinating, Reporting, and Budgeting). Such targeted focus on running the single organization was appropriate during a time when the concept of management—as a guidance function—within organizations was developed. The importance of organization management is likely to continue. But research also demonstrates a parallel importance of managers working across organizational boundaries. One study of collaborative management in economic development found that about 20 percent of public managers' time is spent in collaborative activity outside of the home government organization.[1] In a number of public policy arenas—for example, environmental protection—an increasing portion of this time is spent in formal networks.[2] As a result, both a knowledge base[3] and a practical literature[4] in network management are beginning to emerge.

## About Networks

The study focuses on networks of public organizations, involving formal and informal structures, composed of representatives from governmental and nongovernmental agencies working interdependently to exchange information and/or jointly formulate and implement policies and programs that are usually designed for action through their respective organizations. However, not all networks are alike. Some come together primarily to provide information and some do more by also mutually developing capabilities, whereas others additionally provide new programming opportunities for their component organizations, and still others make joint decisions and take action.

Networks bring the nonprofit and for-profit sectors together with government in a number of policy arenas, including economic development, health care, criminal justice, human services, information systems, rural development, environmental protection, biotechnology, transportation, and education. Their activities are purposeful efforts to access knowledge and technology and to guide, steer, control, or manage. And the public and private actors involved do not act separately but in conjunction, operating as a network. Since the networks under study involve government, interest is in patterns that emerge from the governing activities of the actors, for example, codiscovery, coregulation, costeering, coproduction, cooperative management, and public-private partnerships.

## Study Focus

In this chapter, we do not analyze the structure and operation of the Midwest networks but try to answer important generic managerial questions that emanate from their experiences. As a result, the chapter does not go beyond a categorization-by-decision structure. The chapter emphasizes general management processes. In particular, managers were asked how various tasks and roles in the promotion and operation of these networks are different from their other public role, that of working within bureaucratic organizations (see "Appendix: Research Method"). Among the many issues discussed, the following questions guide this chapter:

1. How do public managers promote networks? That is, are there important organizing, convening, and operational issues that are essential for maintenance of these bodies?
2. What processes of management are different and tend to replace traditional approaches when working in networks?
3. How do managers working together across organizational lines replace authority with mutual understanding or trust levels so that they can work together and respect one another?

4. How do network managers broker decisions and results? In other words, what processes do they engage in to reach agreement and ultimately decisions?
5. Since information exchange is a key element of networking, how are technical information, knowledge, and expertise mobilized?
6. What operational information and advice can the network managers studied offer other public managers about the techniques and approaches they have experienced?

Answers to these questions will not only help other public managers as they operate in networks, but add to the network management knowledge base.

## Importance of Networks

Why do public managers find themselves working in networks today? One force is the changing nature of work from labor-based production and services to the integration of knowledge-based symbolic-analytic work, which places greater value on human capital. Knowledge is specialized and must be integrated collaboratively to solve many problems, a core issue in change management. As a result, government agencies, once thought to be the monopolistic holders of key information and expertise relating to public issues, now possess only part of the information needed to solve problems.

A second force is the changing nature of government. The 20th century was a time of growth of welfare states and, consequently, government agencies and programs at national and state levels. The government took on more and more problems and created many new policy areas. As public efforts grew, however, it became apparent that the government could not garner the resources, investments, expertise, or commitments needed to solve all public problems. New structures involving several organizations became one of a number of collaborative efforts to try to approach some of society's "wicked problems" or challenges that could not be handled by dividing them into simple pieces, in isolation from one another.[5]

A related factor is the idea that government should not only operate programs but also should take on more of a developmental or steering role, promoting, regulating, and encouraging various types of nongovernmental activity and operations. This engagement philosophy has, in many fields, unfolded in the 1980s and 1990s, and it has led to greater variety in government-nongovernment organizational interaction.

A number of research streams have also confirmed the prominence of networks. The urban-politics work of Clarence Stone on regime theory is seminal. In his study of urban power, he concludes that in a fragmented world where power, resources, knowledge, and the other means to solve problems reside with so many individuals and organizations, "the issue is how to bring about enough cooperation among disparate community elements to get things done—and to do so in the absence of an over-arching command structure or a unifying system of thought." He labeled this process as "governance," which is the ability to combine the necessary elements toward a result, that is, the capacity to assemble and use needed resources for a policy initiative.[6]

Intergovernmental researchers have also recognized the importance of networks, often operating in complex and overlapping fashions[7] and, in many ways, changing the traditional role of governments and their links with nongovernmental organizations and with the various tools and strategies that lead to different public-private configurations.[8] A study by Radin and associates reveals how federal-state-private councils in rural development have led to many program changes and demonstration approaches.[9] In the same vein, economic development research at the state and local levels has demonstrated how networked officials enhance their economies by stimulating private sector action, engaging in partnerships with such organizations as chambers of commerce and industry groups, and jointly formulating developmental policies in human resource development, technology advancement, and global marketing.[10] Finally, research in environmental policy also demonstrates that emergent solutions to such problems as nonpoint source pollution (for example, agricultural chemicals) and watershed and forest management can be approached by formally and informally convening government agencies, conservation advocacy groups, industry representatives, land developers, and the scientific community into joint bodies.[11]

## The Public Agency and the Network

Operating in networks is changing the nature of government organizations, at least with regard to shared policies and programs. Of primary importance is that representatives of public agencies become partners with other organization representatives in examining problems, establishing strategies, and formulating policy responses. The public organization actor often serves as a convener, but once the process begins those persons are among the many participants.

Second, the public agency representative does not have nearly the monopoly or the corner on technical expertise that previous public administrators possessed. Many stakeholders—such as scientists, organizational researchers, interest groups, and advocacy groups—bring needed knowledge and information to the table.

Third, resources are more dispersed. In the past, a government agency possessed the major allocation or appropriation needed to launch a program, and money (and indirectly control) was dispensed through a chain of agencies, public and non-public. Resources are now more dispersed throughout the network, as government increasingly tries to use its role in governance to leverage investments and broker program actions through other government agencies and a host of nongovernmental organizations.

Fourth, program implementation occurs through many of the same organizations that were involved in pooling knowledge and technologies, enhancing capacities, or in formulating strategies and policies. As government has taken on more of a guidance role, and has encouraged nongovernmental investments, the carrying out function is no longer exclusively through the familiar intergovernmental chain of public organizations or by contract or mutual agreement. The process involves a variety of grantees, contractees, and, most important, collaborating partners.

Some analysts have concluded that this renders the government agency unimportant and a bystander to a series of private actions. Networks do change the role of government in democratic systems. Government agencies are not, however, marginal players in the multiple organization process. They remain core actors, because they continue to possess a legitimacy to approach public problems and policy solutions, retain important legal authority to set rules and norms, contribute financial resources to programs, and retain some of the information and scientific knowledge needed to approach problems. This research reveals that government agencies are almost always among the key partners in networks.

## Network Prospects

The future holds even greater promise for these collaborative structures, and, therefore, a body of knowledge about how to manage them is important for public management. The demand for knowledge will increase as an important resource, as will the demand for new capital that resides in human resources or knowledge workers. Knowledge capital will continue to need some form of collective that will bring it together. Knowledge is nonhierarchical in that it is required for a situation where professional performance needs to be applied, regardless of organizational position, social status, or possession of wealth. As a result, portable knowledge application plus rapid access to information can and has led to the disintegration of large-scale organizations into more flexible structures, such as the networks studied here. In the future, several different types of organizations are expected to interlock along these lines. These trends will also accelerate the need for greater study of the new forms of organizing and operating. As Peter Drucker concludes, "Despite all the present talk of 'knowledge management,' no one yet really knows how to do it."[12] Finally, these structures will increasingly be used to deal with social problems. David Korten concludes that knowledge and reformation have provided powerful new collective intelligence that can be used to master social and institutional discovery and innovation through problem solving.[13] A portion of this body of knowledge entails a newer form of management knowledge that can be applied in both public and private institutions.

## Types of Networks

Not all networks are alike, as other researchers have also discovered.[14] Of the networks examined for this study (see "Types of Networks Studied"), three limit their interorganizational actions to exchange of information. The Darby Partnership (Darby), the Lower Platte River Corridor Alliance

---

### Types of Networks Studied

1. *Informational Networks:* Partners come together exclusively to exchange agency policies and programs, technologies and potential solutions. Any actions that might be taken are entirely up to the agencies on a voluntary basis.

   Darby, LPRCA, IEDC

2. *Developmental Networks:* Partner information and technical exchange are combined with education and member service that increases member capacity to implement solutions within home agencies or organizations.

   PRN, IRDC, IGIC, IEN

3. *Outreach Networks:* Partners come together to exchange information and technologies, sequence programming, exchange resource opportunities, pool client contacts, and enhance access opportunities that lead to new programming avenues. Implementation of designed programs is within an array of public and private agencies themselves.

   SCEIG, USDA/RD

4. *Action Networks:* Partners come together to make interagency adjustments, formally adopt collaborative courses of action, and/or deliver services along with exchanges of information and technologies.

   EDARC, DMMPO, ICN

(LPRCA), both environmental or natural resource networks, and the Indiana Economic Development Council (IEDC) are included in this category. *Informational networks* tend to involve large numbers of stakeholders, many of whom have quite opposite views, who come together to exchange information, examine the depths of a given problem, and explore "possible actions" that stakeholders might take. Such actions are not mandated but are almost always voluntary and exclusively taken within the partner agencies. As such, informational networks tend to be broad convening bodies or "sounding boards," but never decision bodies. In many ways they are like councils of organizations that most volunteers are familiar with, such as a health and welfare council. Nevertheless, with the exception of not deciding, they experience the exchange and information/knowledge management patterns as other networks.

Three of the networks studied, in stark contrast, take the kind of joint action that is commonly associated with a number of other collaborative organizations, for example, partnerships and joint ventures. The Indiana Electronic Data Access Review Committee (EDARC), the Des Moines Metropolitan Planning Organization (DMMPO), and the Iowa Communications Network (ICN) all have developed interactive working procedures to collectively adopt programs and to implement them through component organizations. To be sure, these *action networks* also are heavily engaged in information exchange, capacity development, and discovering new programming opportunities, but they are distinguished by their ability to engage in collective action. In many ways their decision component makes them the most different and means that they have the most difficulty achieving aims, because they make collective win/lose decisions among governments and organizations, and they share implementation with their partner organizations.

Standing between these two types of networks are two others, one that exchanges information and increases partner capabilities to take own-source actions, and one that not only increases capacity but develops new program venues that are implemented through partner agencies. The former category, *developmental networks,* includes the Partnership for Rural Nebraska (PRN), the Indiana Rural Development Council (IRDC), the Iowa Geographic Information Council (IGIC), and the Iowa Enterprise Network (IEN). Each relies heavily on partners implementing those strategies and capabilities developed within the network itself, and as such, the network goes beyond the mere exchange of information.

The latter category, *outreach networks,* includes the Ohio Small Communities Environmental Infrastructure Group (SCEIG) and the Nebraska U.S. Department of Agriculture Rural Development (USDA/RD) program. These networks not only exchange information, technologies, and opportunities, but they carve out programming strategies for clients (for example, funding packages, usable technologies) that are carried out elsewhere, usually by the partner organizations. In other words, potential action frameworks for clients are developed, but action is not formally adopted by the network, it is merely suggested. Managerially, both of these types of networks are like consortia or confederations where information and potential action is collectively arrived at but not taken by the bodies themselves. In terms of operational decisions, both of these types experience most of the managerial challenges of all types of networks, except that they stop short of those binding decisions that imply joint action.

## Management Differences

When administrators from different agencies come together to solve problems or to inform one another, most operate differently than in their home agencies. One informational network leader said, "Inside, I manage a program, and I have a line role. When in a partnership I dispense and exchange information." Another said, "I am a typical 'fed,' with administrative structure, rules, programs ... whereas in this [network] group the activity is exchange, equal input." Another state official stated, "At the network there are no bosses, many players." A federal official stated, "We do loans, fund and operate programs within the agency. At the network, we build capacity." Another state official said, "We do programs and contracts here. In the network I am not the answer." All of these responses suggest that another type of management is going on in these networks.

What kind of management is it? First and foremost, agency representatives come to the table as delegates from their agency and form a "pooled" authority system that is based more on expertise than on position. In most of the networks studied, despite differential informal authority, official authority is more or less one delegate, one *opportunity* to influence the recommended/ agreed course of action. One federal official said, "I am the orchestra leader in [agency], in the Council I am a partner." Authority generally flows in the following manner. Agency designation to the network usually brings a measure of delegated authority, that is, ability to speak on behalf of and to commit agency resources. That seat at the table offers the venue to offer home agency information and technical expertise to the joint experience. Potential resources—funding opportunities, access to programs, new technologies, educational opportunities—are entered into the transactional mix. These inputs are thrust into the discussions, which are joint learning experiences based on exchange. Then, if the network takes a form of action—for example, outreach and decision networks—the accommodations are made. In this sense, authority is based on expertise and the ability to reach agreement as a collective. These agreements carry more "moral" weight because they have the backing of many experts and managers even though traditional program authority normally remains in the participating organizations. One state official concluded that "while [the network] provides the input, and we work as a team, and try to reach agreement, ... this agency is the final decision maker."

## Decision Making

Decision making is different in networks, where reaching ultimate overall agreement based on joint learning from many organizational representatives is paramount. In the networks where actual joint decisions are made, discussion, discovery, adjustment, and consensus are clearly the rule. When authority is delegated and divided and based on expertise, there are few alternatives. Because most network participants usually come together with some shared beliefs, this is easier than it would appear on the surface. Where strident differences are present—for example, between landowners and environmentalists in natural resource networks—the process does not work as well. The transportation network resorts to voting whereas natural resource networks like the Lower Platte River Corridor Alliance (see "Lower Platte River Corridor Alliance: An Informational Network") have no choice but to remain informational. In general, networks do decide on programs of mutual benefit or of technical and informational value, and some make policy recommendations. These decisions are mostly ones that all can agree upon. One network leader said, "Our decisions come naturally as a product of our discussions and interventions. We only vote once a year when we adopt our work plan."

## Planning

Planning in all of the different types of networks is vision and problem driven. "The work plan is a catalyst for what we do." The partners come together and articulate what they want to work on, and the collective body by agreement or a token vote adopts it. For example, one of the rural development networks, PRN, has a steering committee of second-level executives and an education committee composed of program specialists. The former group agrees on the networks' work program whereas the latter plans an annual Rural Institute. The executive committee composed of the ratifiers of the overall agreement approves the programming decisions made by program and second-level staff. In each process it is a matter of finding and tapping available expertise and delegated authority. Planning then becomes organizing what the network has decided to do. One net-

## The Lower Platte River Corridor Alliance (LPRCA): An Informational Network

The Lower Platte River Corridor Alliance is a consortium of three natural resource districts and seven state agencies in Nebraska, joined together in an effort to address natural resource management issues in the Lower Platte River Corridor area. With the passage of an interlocal agreement, the Lower Platte River Corridor Alliance was established in 1996. Members contribute to an administrative fund totaling $65,000 annually to support a coordinator's position for the Alliance, and agree to provide technical and other assistance within their authority to the coordinator. Quarterly meetings are convened to share progress reports on programs and projects of all involved.

The Alliance seeks to assist counties and communities spanning 100 river miles to become fully informed about the natural-resources impact of their decisions, and to promote consistent decision making across jurisdictions so as to promote natural-resources conservation in the river corridor area. The Alliance provides a forum for concerned, interested citizens and local elected officials to bring their different perspectives to the table and seek common solutions. The goals of the alliance are: to foster increased understanding of the Platte River's resources; to support local efforts to achieve comprehensive and coordinated land use to protect the long-term vitality of the river; and to promote cooperation among local, state, and federal organizations, private and public, to meet the needs of the many and varied interests in the river corridor. The Alliance furnishes easy access to relevant information on key issues and proposed projects, opportunities for dialogue and discussion for individuals wishing to influence the decision-making process, and a forum for consensus. Community participation is an integral part of this process. Opportunities for public involvement include river tours, a water quality golf tournament, stakeholder summit meetings, and regional planning workshops and charettes.

*Source: www.lowerplatte.org*

work coordinator related, "In my other work, in this organization, we administrators lay out what we need to do to make programs work. In the [network] a committee plans everything."

## Implementation

Programming, or what might be called network implementation, follows planning, and in all types of networks it is normally through participating agencies. Most of the networks studied have either a minuscule staff presence, usually one coordinator, or program support comes out of the home agency of whoever is chair or president. Meeting arrangements, the listserv, and a website are the norm for this activity. The real programs that flow from the decisions of a network, which need to be carried out, happen back in the agencies themselves. For example, both the rural development and natural resource networks, which are not decision makers, rely on substate, state, and federal agencies to do the actual remediation or development work needed to deal with their challenges and agreed courses of action. In the same fashion, the Iowa Communications Network, an action network, is the data transmission and narrowcast agency for dozens of federal, state, and local government agencies that are responsible for their own programming. With this type of programming, one state official reported, "I have less control over what is done by the members because they are agencies and I can't tell them what to do."

## Staffing

Staffing follows programming. With the exception of the action networks, where there is a larger staff presence, once what to do is decided, one must go back to the table and see who is willing to take on the various tasks beyond core maintenance activities. "We rely on each partner to identify and offer expertise." In a network with pooled resources and expertise, this is not merely a matter of asking for "volunteers." Indeed, the process rarely works that way. More often in the course of the discussion of an issue, participating agencies make the group aware of staff within their organization who might contribute time and/or expertise. Several of the networks rely on the federal-state Extension Service located at land grant universities in this way, whereas others point out the expertise of planners, engineers, information specialists, finance experts, and many others. Then it is a question of "convincing the person to contribute some of their [agency] time or resources to the overall cause."

## Organizing

Finally, organizing flows from all the other management activities. In a network, the form of organization more closely resembles a voluntary organization than a bureaucracy. Officers are "elected" on a rotating basis. Normally, that means tapping one who has been immediately active and has the technical and political respect of the other network activists. Often it is someone who can also command one's agency or university resources. Other officers may or may not be utilized, and their presence is more or less a formality beyond forming an executive committee to decide between meetings.

The real organization within most networks is through its voluntary committees, where the basic and detailed work gets done. For example, the Iowa Geographic Information Council operates with the following committees: Executive, Remote Sensing, Newsletter, Conference, Strategic Planning, and Clearinghouse. The MPO transportation network organizes with two committees: Policy and Technical. The Indiana Rural Development Council organizes with these committees: Executive, Community Visitation, Housing, Environmental Infrastructure, Leadership Development, and Agricultural Development. The particular structure for each network is a product of a self-organizing process where partners bring issues to the table and the group decides to focus on specific issues. Then specialization and expertise is pooled into committees. It is an incremental process. Initially, discussants report that the process resembles "herding cats." One state official asserted that eventually "our activities fall into categories, more or less, and we agree to a structure of some kind, at some time, about when we decide on our work plan."

Working in a network is thus quite different for most managers, who are normally more heavily engaged in their own structures and operations. The only exception to this would be a notable number of agency "boundary spanners," or staff who represent their department/agency nearly full time as a liaison person to other organizations and who are network participants. Their inside and outside work is in many ways similar as they reach across and represent their program as full-time partner or network participant. Only about 10 percent of the informants fell into this category. But even the boundary spanner who does different work is within a hierarchy with standard management processes as he/she communicates with the home organization. In the network, all managers face a nonhierarchical self-organizing situation where "jointly agreed focus and purpose prevails."

**Networks Studied**

| Name of Network | Description and Purpose | Type | Enabling Authority | Primary Agencies |
|---|---|---|---|---|
| 1. *accessIndiana* Enhanced Data Access Review Committee (EDARC) | Portal to Indiana State government information; EDARC regulates *accessIndiana*, (www.state.in.us) supported by a contractor for web development; sets policies for *accessIndiana*, reviews, modifies, and approves audit agency agreements; encourages public and private use; and establishes fees for enhanced access to public records. | Action | State Government | Indiana State Library; Indiana Departments of Administration, Bureau of Motor Vehicles, Secretary of State, Indiana Commission on Public Records, Indiana Commission for Higher Education; Chair, Indiana Intelnet Commission; Division of Information Technology; Office of Attorney General; State Budget Agency; and six citizen/NGO/media representatives |
| 2. Des Moines Area Metropolitan Planning Organization (DMMPO) | Responsible for transportation planning for metropolitan area under §450 of Title 23 of U.S. Code (TEA-21) through its Transportation Policy and Technical Committees. | Action | Intergovernmental Agreement | Thirteen cities, three county government members, and two associate cities. Advisory participants include Iowa Department of Transportation, U.S. Federal Highway Administration, U.S. Federal Transit Authority, Des Moines Metropolitan Transportation Authority, and Des Moines International Airport. |
| 3. Indiana Economic Development Council (IEDC) | Created by the Indiana General Assembly to serve as a research and ideas consultant for statewide public-private economic development strategic planning. | Informational | Not-for-profit 501c(3) | Seventy-two-member board of directors from state government, universities, private sector, business and labor interest groups, and NGOs. Chaired by the governor. Lt. Governor is chief executive officer of the Council (Note: in Indiana the Lt. Governor is head of the Department of Commerce and is Commissioner of Agriculture). |

**Networks Studied (continued)**

| Name of Network | Description and Purpose | Type | Enabling Authority | Primary Agencies |
|---|---|---|---|---|
| 4. Indiana Rural Development Council (IRDC) | Provides a forum to address rural issues, seeks community input to identify problems, establishes partnerships to find solutions, enables partners to take action, and educates the public on rural issues. | Developmental | Intergovernmental Agreement/Not-for-profit 501c(3) | U.S. Department of Housing and Urban Development, U.S. Small Business Administration, U.S. Department of Agriculture/ Rural Development Service, Indiana Commissioner of Agriculture, Indiana Department of Health/ Rural Health, Indiana Department of Commerce, four local government elected officials, eight state legislative and U.S. Congress staff appointees, and four for-profit appointees. |
| 5. Iowa Communications Network (ICN) | A statewide, state-administered, fiber-optics network that enables authorized users such as hospitals, state and federal government, public defense armories, libraries, schools, and higher education to communicate via high-quality, full-motion video; data; high-speed Internet communications; and telephones. | Action | State Government | Iowa Telecommunications and Technology Commission, Iowa Public Television, Iowa National Guard, Iowa Department of Corrections, Iowa universities and colleges, Iowa Department of Transportation, U.S. Veterans Administration, U.S. Social Security Administration, public schools, public libraries, and others. |
| 6. Iowa Enterprise Network (IEN) | Supports home-based and micro enterprises; provides mutual assistance and information through conferences, workshops, and web links. | Developmental | Not-for-profit 501c(3) | U.S. Small Business Administration, Iowa Department of Economic Development, Iowa Rural Development Council, Iowa Area Development Council, Small Business Development Center–Des Moines, U.S. Department of Agriculture/Rural Development, Iowa Department of Cultural Affairs, and micro business owners. |

## Networks Studied (continued)

| Name of Network | Description and Purpose | Type | Enabling Authority | Primary Agencies |
|---|---|---|---|---|
| 7. Iowa Geographic Information Council (IGIC) | Clearinghouse for coordinated geographic information systems (GIS), data sharing, exploring standards, and facilitating cooperation among Iowans who use GIS. | Developmental | State Government | Representatives on 25-member board include university/private colleges, state government, planning organizations, county governments, local governments, federal government, private businesses, and community colleges. |
| 8. Lower Platte River Corridor Alliance (LPRCA) | Fosters the development and implementation of locally drawn strategies, actions, and practices to protect and restore the river's sources; fosters increased understanding of the river's resources; supports local efforts to achieve comprehensive and coordinated land use; promotes cooperation among local, state, and federal organizations, private and public, to meet the needs of the many and varied interests of the corridor. | Informational | Intergovernmental Agreement | Lower Platte South, Lower Platte North, and Papio–Missouri Natural Resources Districts; Nebraska Departments of: Natural Resources, Health and Human Services, Environmental Quality; Nebraska State Military Department; and University of Nebraska Conservation and Survey Division. Ex-officio links with U.S. Environmental Protection Agency, U.S. Geological Survey, U.S. Army Corps of Engineers, and U.S. National Park Service. |
| 9. Partnership for Rural Nebraska (PRN) | Cooperative commitment to address rural opportunities and challenges identified by rural Nebraskans; to work together to meet those challenges and provide resources and expertise to enhance development opportunities. | Developmental | Intergovernmental Agreement | State of Nebraska—Departments of Agriculture, Economic Development, Environmental Quality, Health and Human Services Systems, and the Rural Development Commission; federal government—USDA/RD and Natural Resources Conservation Services; the University of Nebraska; Nebraska Development Network. |

## Networks Studied (continued)

| Name of Network | Description and Purpose | Type | Enabling Authority | Primary Agencies |
|---|---|---|---|---|
| 10. Small Communities Environmental Infrastructure Group (SCEIG) | Coordinated efforts to assist small governments in Ohio in their development, improvement, and maintenance of their water and wastewater systems. | Outreach | Non-formal group | State of Ohio Water Development Authority, Ohio Environmental Protection Agency, Ohio Department of Natural Resources, U.S. federal-state Extension Service/Ohio State University, U.S. Department of Agriculture/Rural Development, U.S. Department of Commerce, Economic Development Administration, private lending representatives, university rural centers, nongovernmental organizations, and regional development districts. |
| 11. The Darby Partnership (Darby) | Facilitated by the Nature Conservancy of Ohio, this partnership of federal, state, and local agencies, environmental groups, and watershed citizens share information and resources to address stresses to the streams and serve as a "think tank" for conservation efforts in the watershed. | Informational | Non-formal group | U.S. Department of Agriculture, Natural Resources Conservation Service, Ohio Department of Natural Resources, Ohio Environmental Protection Agency, U.S. Geological Survey, six county Soil and Water Conservation Districts, City of Columbus, Columbus and Franklin County Metro Parks, Mid-Ohio Regional Planning Commission, The Nature Conservancy, The Darby Creek Association, and several NGOs. |
| 12. United States Department of Agriculture/Rural Development Nebraska Outreach Programs (USDA/RD) | Uses outreach to leverage funds of other programs to augment its funding as well as assisting rural cooperatives, value-adding businesses, small municipal water systems, public facilities, and housing for small communities. | Outreach | Federal Government | USDA/RD, Partnership for Rural Nebraska, Nebraska Department of Economic Development, Nebraska Rural Development Commission, Nebraska Development Network, University of Nebraska–Extension, Development Districts, Nebraska colleges, and county and city governments. |

# A Guide to Network Participation
# and Operation

## Promoting Networks

Networks do not just happen, but many other experiences suggest that they must be developed. Those composed of public managers will need to be advanced by some of the managers. This is because few networks have a pre-existing mandate to operate. With the exception of the Des Moines Area Metropolitan Planning Organization (MPO) and the Iowa Communications Network, the other networks are based on voluntary action, a non-profit charter, or voluntary intergovernmental agreements. Their operation and continuation therefore depends on self-generated actions. They have to be "held together." This requires a heavy dose of developmental activity on the part of some partners who are champions and promoters as well as partners.

All networks depend on one or a small number of champions. A state program head of a federal agency in one of the rural development networks stated that every network must "have a catalytic leader who has a passion for it." Another state official said, "We need an overall champion, and each subcommittee project needs a mini champion!" Even though authority is more equal in networks, and is based primarily on expertise, someone needs to come forward and help orchestrate a vision, follow through on the work plan, contact key partners, orchestrate meetings, and so on. Ordinarily this is someone who holds an administrative position in one key agency, can command modest professional staff resources if needed, has control over potential donated in-house clerical and communication resources, and has the technical or professional respect of the other members. A network champion can be but is not always the convener or chairperson. Often it is the director of one of the participating agencies who, through staff time, holds the modest network records, operates the listserv, and maintains the website. In other cases it is a "volunteer" who has the capacity to do the work within the organization, for example, a federal or state agency/program or unit of a college or university. In a few cases, the role of champion has rotated with the chair, who is expected to be temporary champion. The risk is that "with an inactive chair we go a year or so with very little activity." As in the case of voluntary organization committee work, behind most long-term networks lies the energy work of a network champion.

Networks need promoters around their champions. One network promoter referred to himself and others like him as "vision keepers." "These are the people at the middle or working level of federal and state agencies where the links up and down have to be made." As persons who work with programs on a daily basis, they have the technical knowledge to share with others. They do more than be present and present. They provide a technical and organizing energy that champions need to keep the process going. They become involved in developing joint information events and activities, and engage extensively in information sharing, are at meetings to access information and emerging technologies, and communicate the networks' concerns with their home agencies. In this sense these vision keepers promote the information and access to expertise/information within their agencies and help carry the work of the network. Each network needs a reasonable number (three to six) of these persons representing a range of different agencies, who in a collaborative are as essential as the champion. Indeed, it would be very hard to be a successful champion, or even think of a viable network, without the complementary work of the vision keepers.

## Broad Participation

The vision keepers must work with the champion to broaden participation. In nonprofit-organization parlance, this means identify the stakeholders and bring them in. Networks, too, must find those organizational representatives who have the needed resources—information, expertise, authority, money—to advance the overall cause. One network champion said, "We try to mobilize all the people in a similar capacity: funders, regulators, educators, and technology experts." Many networks have categories of council or board members to signify broad involvement: federal government, state government, local government, nonprofit, for-profit, and university/college. This type of activity involves reaching out and inviting new resource persons to an "ever-widening circle." Once people come to the table, it is important to see that everyone's issues are put on the table. It keeps and holds partners, meeting after meeting, year after year.

## Communication

The network is also promoted by a steady flow of communication. Electronic communication—e-mail, websites, and, to a lesser extent, video conferencing—constitute the channels of non-face-to-face communication. Meeting notices, announcements of relevant events and programs, and newly available technologies are all transmitted this way. "They save a lot of telephone tag, and contact with one can be contact with all." All the networks have websites, which provide an instant introduction and a contact point for potential participants. Before the availability of the World Wide

# The Partnership for Rural Nebraska (PRN): A Developmental Network

## What Is the Partnership for Rural Nebraska?
The PRN is really a name applied to a vision:
- A vision of local, state, and federal groups working together to stretch resources, thereby benefiting more Nebraskans: The whole of the PRN is greater than the sum of its parts.
- A vision of educating each other on available resource and rural development needs, using educational opportunities such as the annual Rural Institute, agency orientations, and seminars: PRN organizations learn from each other.
- A vision of communicating to Nebraskans and others regarding rural development activities, opportunities, and challenges through the newsletter, *Rural News Bits*. The PRN shares a common voice.
- A vision that is admired outside Nebraska. The PRN is seen as a model for the rest of the country.

## As a Result of the Partnership, We Have:
The *Nebraska Rural Institute*. Held every year in September, the Rural Institute has become the preeminent conference of its kind in Nebraska. Focused entirely on rural development issues, the Institute brings together providers, practitioners, researchers, and community activists to network, share, discuss, and learn about rural issues, opportunities, challenges, and solutions. Over 750 people have participated in the Institute since 1998, including people from South Africa and Australia.

The *PRN Education Committee*. The Education Committee is the education arm of the PRN. The Education Committee is responsible for the planning and implementation of the Nebraska Rural Institute, cross-training the staff of PRN organizations on each organization's programs, and conducting one- and two-day seminars on topics of interest to rural development practitioners.

*Rural News Bits*. Over 6,000 persons working on rural development in Nebraska receive this monthly newsletter. Contributing organizations share ideas, educational and financial opportunities, announcements, and general news. In a survey conducted last year, 76 percent of the survey respondents indicated they used the information from *Rural News Bits* to assist their community, business, or self. Only 15 percent of the respondents indicated that they receive the same type of information that is available in *Rural News Bits* from other sources.

*Nebraska Rural Poll*. The annual Rural Poll, conducted through the University of Nebraska–Lincoln's Center for Applied Rural Innovation, is the most extensive, comprehensive research of its kind anywhere in the world. Real information on the trends happening in rural Nebraska and the attitudes of the people who live there is gathered and analyzed, providing an invaluable snapshot of rural

Nebraska that can be considered and used in policy development. Rural Poll results have been cited in the *Wall Street Journal, New York Times,* and *USA Today.*

*Nebraska Cooperative Development Center.* This is a network of people with access to local state and national resources, dedicated to keeping people in rural areas by helping them work together to increase their income, and dedicated to helping in the creation of agricultural opportunities by working cooperatively. The NCDC is staffed and funded by three of the PRN agencies.

*Shared Staff.* Because of the improved communications and recognition of common needs, some of the partner agencies have been able to share staff. While one agency may not have been able to afford a new staff person to meet a pressing need, by working cooperatively with another PRN agency, they are able to fund a position that meets the demands of two or more organizations. Shared staff includes two staff positions with the Cooperative Development Center and two shared positions with the Education Committee and *Rural News Bits.* In addition, agency staff works together on a variety of projects that aren't jointly funded. This extends and expands capability without stressing limited resources.

*Communication.* Perhaps most important of all is the heightened level of communication and its value to the partner organizations. The enhanced communication and the relationships that have been built allow the partner organizations to eliminate "turf" issues, collaborate to provide the needed service to rural Nebraska, and focus on the final result: that of providing the highest level of assistance to the greatest number of projects and communities, and stretching tax dollars to the maximum.

*Source: http://cari.unl.edu/prn1*

Web, it could take weeks to find out about and contact someone in a network. E-mails link individuals so that the work of the network can be transmitted, and, between meetings, e-mail is the transmission belt of technological and/or program information.

Electronic means, however, are not substitutes for face-to-face communication, particularly at network meetings. Here the network business and one-to-one interagency business is transmitted, once again avoiding "telephone tag." Most meetings observed informally "convened" 10 or 15 minutes before the formal meeting and "continued" for up to 45 minutes after the meeting. At the annual Rural Institute of one developmental network that the author attended, The Partnership for Rural Nebraska (PRN), hundreds of informal contacts were made over the two and a half days (see "Partnership for Rural Nebraska: A Developmental Network"). These contacts are important since PRN does not take direct action beyond its capacity-building activities. Communication promotes networks by offering participants vital information, new capabilities and opportunities, and contact venues. They are central to conducting transorganizational affairs in all types of networks.

## Agency Head Role

Network promotion, as other research has revealed, also relies on the tacit support of most partners' agency head. It proves to be hard for anyone in the hierarchy to devote scarce agency resources—time, personnel, information—if the person at the top has not bought into the idea of agency presence in a network. "Our council is struggling right now because it was the idea of a Republican governor two governors ago. The previous and current Democrats see less of a need for such a body." As a result, appointed department heads in this situation were reported as offering only token support. On the other hand, another network coordinator stated, "The only way we have survived political resistance from local people is that the state and [special] district chief executive officers are steadfast in their support of this joint undertaking." In this case the executives are not directly involved, but they have committed dollars to support a coordinator and have made their staff available to become involved in network activity. Top-level support is essential promotional activity.

In effect, network promotion beyond a modest amount of publicity through electronic venues and an occasional brochure and newsletter is primarily operational activity. Acts or deeds in development and maintenance amount to the major elements of promotion. A sort of natural contacting of like-minded agency managers, specialists, and knowledge holders over commonly held aims or interests moves champions and vision keepers to engage in an inclusive involvement that brings in others, and those who benefit personally/professionally/organizationally will participate, and sometimes become potential vision keepers. Media advertisements, news releases, newspaper and magazine articles, and other aspects of mass publicity can create some visibility but are rare forms for network building. Networks' real promotion is by organizing and operating.

## Brokering Decisions and Results

One clear factor about networks is that because they are self-organizing and nonhierarchical, they approach their form of decision process carefully, whether it be to adopt an agenda or to take some form of action. Why the trepidation over decisions? Several reasons are apparent. First, these bodies are rarely program bodies, but they exist to *exchange* information and become aware of potential adjustments that the network actors can make in their own organizations.[15] Second, most members come to the table on a *voluntary* basis (a few report they were assigned network duty), and the nature of their participation suggests some form of shared participation in decisions. Third, network actors come together from very *different organizational cultures,* and the risk of clashing styles is great if not managed. Fourth, in most networks, decision comes as a result of *shared learning* experiences in which the product is the creative solution that emanates from the discussion.[16] Fifth, decisions that create winners and losers, most zero-sum situations, discourage involvement and *contribution.* These concerns make clear why so few of the networks make many hard and fast core policy/program decisions. It is also clear that consensus is the mode of agreement. It almost always prevails over parliamentary voting.

It is important to understand that many networks are not the joint decision bodies they are assumed to be. In all but the action networks, the process of decision is limited to such organizing issues as adopting the annual work plan, approving the agenda for the annual meeting or program for the conference, forming workgroups or committees, reviewing the website, or electing officers. With the exception of Des Moines MPO, where plans and funding priorities are adopted, and ICN and EDARC of *accessIndiana,* where agency use rates are approved and communications operations are regulated, the networks operate without the kind of formal work schedules or major project designs that single organizations are familiar with. Often studies are conducted, as with the two natural resource networks, after which the partners "hear the results," ask questions, and then are free to bring the studies back to their agencies for implementation. Also, with the exception of the transportation and natural resource networks, little that is on the table is really controversial. Decisions are not core issues for most networks.

## Decision Process

How are decisions that are made brokered in most of the networks? Clearly by achieving consensus through joint exploration and discussion until agreement is at hand. Then another issue is brought to the table. A state official described the process this way: "Proposals are made by participating agencies; the staff there researches the proposal and does a market feasibility study; the report is distributed electronically before the meeting; at the meeting, discussion is held and questions are asked; if there are too many questions we table the issue until more research can be undertaken; in between, meetings, phone calls, and one-to-one discussions ensue; the issue is brought back to the table; and if there are a lot of head nods in the yes direction, we consider it to be approved." A process like this, with lots of brokering, is followed in most of the networks, although normally "staff" research tends to be the partners themselves who go back to their own programs and work with their agency colleagues, later bringing the agency-derived results to the network.

One partner described the network decision process as similar to "a rural community meeting." "You get the people out, connect them, let them identify the issues, and let them come up with a solution over time." Another said that beyond setting priorities on work, and staff doing some studies, "we let consensus rise to the top." Another said, "We have Robert's Rules in our by-laws, but only use them after we have reached agreement." Another network chair said that "parliamentary procedure rules won't work—as a last resort when we are near consensus we may resort to informal Robert's Rules to move things along."

Therefore, agreement must be brokered in some way. The prevailing mode is to use the discussion to identify the barriers posed by the people at the table and, if possible, acknowledge them by making accommodations. As mentioned, most of the administrators at the table have the delegated authority to make such adjustments. In other cases an ominous silence by a key partner may signal disagreement but unwillingness to hold up the emerging consensus. Voiced disagreement, on the other hand, often leads to tabling and protracted discussions and e-mails among administrators between network meetings.

In some information networks, consensus is often hard to reach. The parties—for example, landowners and environmentalists—may simply agree that they disagree. Action is individual. The Des Moines MPO must by law make two types of decisions that are virtually impossible to reach by consensus, project funding priorities and the metropolitan transportation plan. For the former, they have adopted elaborate decision rules that all have bought into by prior agreement, deflecting major conflict over choosing projects, whereas with regard to the plan, a weighted (by population) voting scheme has been employed, but these devices have not always built consensus.

## Network Power

The decision-brokering role also operates within the context of network power. Beyond the façade of consensus and collaborative management, stronger partners may be able to take advantage of weaker partners. In each of the networks studied, some organization representatives sit in positions where their knowledge, financial resources, organization position, or legal authority accrues power within the collective.[17] While such power can be used to impede consensus, it is more often used to forge general agreements. For example, in the rural development networks—both outreach and developmental—the USDA/RD, university Extension, and state economic development departments tend to be powerful and committed actors. Their partner members do a great deal of the persuasion and, ultimately, adjustment work required to foster the common mission by getting others to make the adjustments needed for essential consensus. On the other hand, the absence of the support of any of the "big three" can slow progress in these networks.[18]

## Negotiated Support

Brokering within networks is, as one partner suggested, "very much like project management within our agency, where you try to make adjustments to build agreement to move forward." Working together and discussing reasonable accommodations and proposals needs to carry the support of a wide range of organizations. Like project management, it is a negotiated support.

## Developing Trust

It is clear that networks are held together by purpose and social capital, plus mutual respect or trust. Generally held beliefs in the purpose—geographic information system (GIS), rural development, micro and home-based business, economic development—of the network contribute to attracting and holding people in the collective.[19] Social capital, or the built-up reservoir of good will that flows from different organizations working together for mutual productive gain, no doubt is the "glue" that holds people together or the "motivator" that moves the process along.[20] But in terms of what helps to steer networks, it is clearly trust, the obligation to be concerned with others' interests, that allows for the network to do its work, select its leaders, keep its members, and, most important, to broker those decisions it must make.

To some degree, many network partners bring pre-existing trust-based relationships with them into the network. "Some of us have been working together for up to 30 years," said one natural resource administrator. The author was repeatedly reminded that many of the state and federal officials work with one another in multiple settings: interagency funding awards committees, task forces, councils, and consortia. In this way, familiarity breeds subsequent understanding through prior or other ongoing work.

The process of mutual learning through exploration leads to additional trust. "As we educate one another we take advantage of diverse backgrounds."

When participants hear technical presentations by colleagues, or hear about others' programs, they develop more than a passing level of understanding about them. One learns not only about the other agency and its programs, but is able to make deeper judgments regarding the competence of the agency, along with that agency's potential contribution to the network's mission. As participation in the network increases over time, individuals demonstrate key technical and managerial abilities, which in turn build the collective confidence of the group. Indeed, the more knowledge that is extended, the greater the opportunity to build trust in others' abilities.

Discussants in virtually all networks agreed that procedurally the consensus-building process builds trust. "We give up some autonomy for a new paradigm shift, collaboration. This leads to mutual understanding and a passion about partnering." As deliberations ensue, the details and positions are put on the table, and adjustments are made, people feel more comfortable about one another. One federal official stated that a great group dynamic means, "Don't let your power get in the way." Each instance of consensus cements this obligation-based trust.

Another operating rule in most networks is that trust is maintained by non-encroachment on any participating agency's domain. One state official put it bluntly, "Let each agency put their details and concerns on the table; respect each agency's needs and interests. They come first!" Most network actors will tell you it is better to keep agency agendas from being hidden, but when agendas do come forward, it may be impossible to force an agency to change. Mild persuasion and minor adjustment may follow, but intransigence on the part of an agency, particularly a powerful one, usually means that a network must pull away from a controversial issue.

## Action Builds Trust

The individual information-sharing dimension of network activity cements relationships in a very subtle way. In the Ohio Small Communities Environmental Infrastructure Group, a key portion of every meeting is the time allotted for agencies to share their own outreach experiences and agendas. This unfolds *before* they tackle joint outreach activities (see "Small Communities Environmental Infrastructure Group: An Outreach Network"). This way partners know what the others are undertaking; agendas get put on the table. In most of the networks, meeting time is usually devoted to an around-the-table report on the issues of relevance in each agency or program. These "show-and-tell" sessions are important for all members to fulfill their liaison role for their organizations, whether they are official boundary spanners or not. In the process of opening up one's agency to others, the kind of trust that emanates from openness is advanced.

## Small Communities Environmental Infrastructure Group: An Outreach Network

### What is SCEIG?

The Small Communities Environment Infrastructure Group is an association of federal and state agencies, local governments and groups, service organizations, and educational institutions designed to help small communities in meeting their environmental infrastructure needs.

The SCEIG was formed in 1990, by state, federal, local, educational, and service agencies that provide regulatory, technical, financial, and educational assistance for environmental infrastructure projects. These agencies saw a need to coordinate efforts to assist small governments with the difficult task of developing, improving, and maintaining their water and wastewater systems. This group of experts has quarterly meetings to discuss the needs of small communities and what responses or remedies are appropriate and feasible.

The goal of the group is to assist small communities in identifying the most appropriate resources to help the communities resolve problems associated with environmental infrastructure. To this end, the group has established three committees to address the most pressing needs of small communities: Finance Committee, Curriculum Committee, and Technology Committee.

A committee on financing was formed to coordinate the financial resources administered by state and federal agencies to address environmental infrastructure needs of small communities. The Finance Committee meets bimonthly to address the needs of specific communities if a member agency feels that a project cannot be funded without a coordinated effort.

The Curriculum Committee offers workshops in what local officials need to know about water and wastewater systems; the training session includes: review of system alternatives, visits to nearby facilities, understanding management requirements, analysis of community needs, and resources available to assist in designing, funding, and operating water supply systems and wastewater treatment facilities.

The committee for technology transfer works together to identify and develop new or under-utilized technologies to meet the specific needs of small communities. The Technology Committee prepares manuals, offers workshops, and has developed a resource library to help engineering consultants and regulators find the right systems for small communities.

In addition, the SCEIG has published various documents and compiled a list of Internet resources for the use of small communities in considering the installation, repair, or expansion of environmental infrastructure.

*Source: http://www.cpmra.muohio.edu/sceig/sceig.htm*

The sense of trust can also be built through progressive accomplishment. "Start with something small and build from there" was a sentiment echoed by a number of discussants. Another suggested that starting with low-risk efforts helps. As each network carves out the possible, achievement produces "results" and proves to the group that they can work together. Committee work is critical here. When small groups of networkers work together at a smaller table on focused projects, it leads to a higher level of intimacy, and if all goes well and the work gets done, it breeds deeper understanding. Failure to do committee work, or failure to deliver a promised information component, a data set, or some other work necessary for network operation, contributes to loss of trust. Since networks rely on the "volunteer contribution" of mostly full-time administrators, each is expected to do his/her share and come forth with any commitments made to the group.

Extended timeframe conferences or meetings are important social platforms upon which trust is extended. The Iowa GIS network has a biannual conference at a university where prepared papers and panel presentations are offered. The Iowa Enterprise Network holds periodic conferences where self-help projects are demonstrated, along with useful presentations on maintaining small businesses. The Partnership for Rural Nebraska's annual community economic development Rural Institute is planned by its component partners; it provides substantive panel presentations and mobile workshops. The Indiana Rural Development Council holds a one-day annual conference, and in 2002 hosted the two-day National Rural Development Council Partnership workshops. These meetings bring the key actors together in planning the sessions, and the sessions, formally and informally, provide the type of social and intellectual bonding that reinforces preexisting trust.

Many network participants thus build on the relationship-based trust from numerous prior contacts. The act of working in the network as a team on a "common cause" as information bearers for their agencies usually leads to greater mutual respect. In the outreach and action networks, there is the opportunity to build trust by "delivering" on implementation.

## Problematic Trust

Trust is not guaranteed. The transportation Des Moines MPO has some difficulty getting representatives to think metropolitan rather than for their own jurisdiction's interests. Their policy body, composed of elected officials and local managers, finds this particularly difficult. They also suffer from turnover of local elected official members. The organization's technical committee finds this to be less of a problem, as it is composed of appointed

administrators who have worked together over time. The informational natural resource networks—Lower Platte and Darby—also find developing
mutual respect among conflicting interests difficult. In these cases, trust is
harder to develop, though there appears to exist among administrators, and
with the others, a level of working familiarity, if not trust. In these cases,
where the conflict potential is greater, the issues addressed mean that it is
more difficult to develop trust. The other networks, however, rely heavily on
their interactive processes to orchestrate mutual obligation.

## Enlisting Technical Expertise

Information is at the heart of network operations. Since only a small
number take direct mutual action, there would not be much left to do without a solid information base. Both program and technical information, from
different organizations running in the opposite directions of agency autonomy and integrative solution, take the form of a double helix, which constitutes the "transactional DNA" of these interorganizational exchange
relationships. Most of the network management practices already identified—such as roundtable information sharing, annual/biannual conferences, agency presentations at full network and committee meetings, web
postings, and e-mail transmissions—compose the set of ordinary vehicles of
finding and transmitting information. This constant flow of expertise is a part
of the ongoing operations of networks. As one nonprofit administrator
related, "A lot of expertise resides in the people who are in the network."
Dedicated expertise vehicles also play a prominent role in many of
the networks studied. The Des Moines MPO has a technical advisory
committee that both looks at feasibility of contemplated projects and
finds and brings state-of-the-art planning and transportation technology to
the MPO. The committee's technical conclusions and advice prove to be
essential for making the kind of joint-action decisions the MPO is required
to make (see "Des Moines Area Metropolitan Planning Organization: An
Action Network").
The Small Cities Environmental Infrastructure Group in Ohio has a
Technology Transfer Committee, composed mostly of consulting engineers,
who bring advice and information to small cities as an alternative technical
source to paid consultants. The committee maintains a technology library,
and also serves to educate the other group members. The Iowa GIS group
(IGIC) has several technical committees, for example, the Global Positioning Committee. Network actors sometimes call on network staff or agency
staff to provide expertise. IGIC has a state GIS coordinator who works for
Iowa State Extension, spending part of his time in GIS training and development at the county government level. *accessIndiana's* EDARC relies

## Des Moines Area Metropolitan Planning Organization (MPO): An Action Network

The Des Moines Area MPO is responsible for transportation planning within a geographic area called the Planning Area. The MPO approved the Planning Area on May 21, 1992. It is nearly double the area that was used for previous transportation plans in the Des Moines area. It is the same area used to develop the MPO's *HY 2020 Transportation Development Report,* published and adopted by the MPO in October 1994. It is the same area used to develop this plan, *The Horizon Year 2025 Long-Range Transportation Plan* (Plan). The Planning Area includes portions of Dallas, Madison, Polk, and Warren Counties. The Planning Area is intended to include the area that is expected to be developed or urbanized by the year 2025.

MPO membership is open to any county or city government located in the Planning Area having at least 2,400 population and that adopts the MPO's 28E Agreement (agreement entered into under Chapter 28E, Code of Iowa, establishing the MPO and its responsibilities). Currently, MPO membership includes the following cities and counties: Altoona, Ankeny, Carlisle, Clive, Dallas County, Des Moines, Grimes, Johnston, Norwalk, Pleasant Hill, Polk County, Urbandale, Warren County, Waukee, West Des Moines, and Windsor Heights. The city of Polk City is an associate MPO member. Associate membership allows a nonvoting representative to actively participate in the transportation planning process. Associate membership is available to governments within the MPO that do not meet the population threshold for full membership.

Representation on the MPO (the Transportation Policy Committee) is based on population, with each member government given at least one vote. The MPO gives additional representatives to larger member governments based on reaching determined population thresholds. The Iowa Department of Transportation (DOT), the Des Moines Metropolitan Transit Authority (MTA), the Des Moines International Airport (Airport), the Federal Highway Administration (FHWA), and the Federal Transit Administration (FTA) serve as nonvoting, advisory representatives to the MPO.

The MPO receives technical guidance and recommendations from the MPO's Transportation Technical Committee (Tech Committee). The Tech Committee representation differs from the MPO in that the MTA and Airport are voting members of this committee. The MPO Tech Committee's representatives, primarily senior staff from the MPO's member governments and agencies, are appointed by their respective councils or boards.

Additionally, the MPO has established and supports other committees on various transportation-related issues relevant to the MPO's responsibilities. The MPO also requests citizens to serve on these committees, as appropriate. As part of an adopted public participation process, the MPO strongly encourages input by and communication from citizens.

*Source: Des Moines Area Metropolitan Planning Organization, Horizon Year 2025: Long-Range Transportation Plan (Urbandale, IA: DMMPO, 1999).*

almost completely on contract-based technical and marketing staff. The Indiana Economic Development Council, a strategic planning group composed of high-level public and private sector executives and elected officials, relies almost completely on project staff, or the staff of the Indiana Department of Commerce, to conduct its research and provide needed information.

Finally, many of the networks dedicate up to half of their meetings to technical presentations. These presentations are reported to be invaluable in keeping and holding partner members, who become more comfortable if they attend a two- to four-hour meeting in which more than housekeeping business items are discussed. These presentations are made by network participant experts, university researchers and professors, or external vendors.

## Finding Expertise

Internal and external expertise is a mainstream source of technical knowledge. Most participants will ask staff scientists or specialists, along with university-based researchers, to share their technology knowledge with the body. For example, in the environmental and natural resource networks, engineering knowledge that deals with flooding and floodplain concerns, water supply, water quality, agricultural use, and recreation and wildlife management are all at the forefront of participating agency needs. Researchers and vendors have knowledge that may not be within the network. A good example of external knowledge in environmental management would be in various facets of precision agriculture. As a result, external experts are called in, usually with some "coaching." As one federal official observed, "The university research people usually need to be reminded that the audience is most interested in the practical applications, and how feasible and cost-effective it is. The vendors need to be reminded that they are not here to sell us a product, but to make us aware of a technology so we can explain it to the communities we work with." Individual agency partners then can access these external presenters if they choose to do so.

## Informal Expertise Development

The Iowa Communication Network accesses information differently through its informal networking processes. It is a different kind of action network, its physical network being the nearly 4,000 miles of fiber-optic cable that has been laid, and it is a statutory agency governed by a state commission. At the first level, expertise is exchanged through a set of advisory committees and councils: Education, Regional Telecommunications, Telemedicine (also statutory), Administrative Telecommunications, Telecommunications, Telejustice, and Library Network. At another level there are the interactions of the policy and operational people, such as the director of education for Iowa Public Television, the Iowa Department of Public Health chief information officer, the Iowa Department of Transportation information officer, the operations director for the Public Safety Department, the associate dean/telecommunications director of the University of Iowa School of Medicine/Hospitals, and ICN management staff and division heads. Technical expertise, however, is transmitted informally as ICN operating staff (some of whom are contract employees) interact with the information executives previously mentioned and their immediate staff. As needs are exchanged and programs adjusted, valuable telecom expertise is accessed and exchanged. Technical knowledge is enhanced by transactional contacts between service provider and client through this informal networking.

The other networks come together formally to access expertise and to share information. Holding many partners in the fold in most networks requires that technical knowledge be transmitted; they will not attend repeatedly unless there is something to gain beyond the usual collaboration slogans of who is doing what and can we work together. As one federal official related, "We try to find out who is riding the appropriate technology horse and get it out in a viable form."

# Ten Lessons on How to Manage in Networks

The network managers were asked, at the end of each discussion, for observations and suggestions to other public managers about how to manage in networks as opposed to managing within single administrative organizations. It provided them an opportunity to reflect on the network experience in a broad way and, most important, to contrast the two types of management, in hierarchies versus networks. Very few managers were reluctant to speak, reflect, and provide advice.

## 1. Be a representative of your agency and the network.

To be an effective network participant, one must balance the dualism of agency and collective concerns. As a formal or informal boundary spanner, one must first of all know your own agency, its programs, administrators, technologies, funding bases, regulations, and so on. "Others in the network will turn to you with questions and expect answers." This requires a con-

## The Ten Lessons

1. Be a representative of your agency and the network.
2. Take a share of the administrative burden.
3. Operate by agenda orchestration.
4. Recognize shared expertise-based authority.
5. Stay within the decision bounds of your network.
6. Accommodate and adjust while maintaining purpose.
7. Be as creative as possible.
8. Be patient and use interpersonal skills.
9. Recruit constantly.
10. Emphasize incentives.

stant flow of communication within the home agency. In this sense the boundary spanning activity extends to intraorganizational as well as interorganizational domains. "Do the lateral networking within your agency," said one state liaison officer. If expertise is called for that you cannot supply, bring the right person from the organization to the meeting. "It is your responsibility (as agency representative) to see that the right need for technical information from your agency is satisfied."

"Continuous involvement, no matter what the trade-offs might be, is also essential." "Always be there! No one will protect your interests but you." Several persons relayed that they don't want to miss the information that is exchanged around the table. One federal manager concluded that network involvement is a necessary evil. "It takes great time commitments, I would call it 'drudge' work; you have to make yourself network when there is so much on your desk, and go to night meetings; it is hard to keep the momentum going, so we all have to do our part."

At the same time, one must be concerned for the overall mission or purpose of the network. "We're not here just for departmental 'show-and-tell,' but to investigate and solve problems that touch all of us." Those at the table are, as mentioned, expected to contribute information or expertise or resources. And when the problem being faced is nettlesome, solutions require that most all administrators help focus on the issue at hand and contribute. That is a major reason why the network is demanding of managers' time. One must think in terms of the whole enterprise as well as represent one's agency.

## 2. Take a share of the administrative burden.

Most of the active and long-standing networks either have a small co-ordinating staff, or the maintenance work is conducted by a staff person as a small part of his or her regular duties. Only half of the agencies have any kind of full-time staff. The other half relies on a small portion of one person's duties, which were devoted to network maintenance/continuity. As a result, many individuals in the network may have to take on all or some of the necessary support chores. The point is to "have someone to do the staff work."

A great deal of the administrative load is carried by old-fashioned volunteering or stepping up. This is usually the case with regard to committee or taskforce chairpersons. When a network member agrees to become a chair there is a tacit understanding that this person will arrange meetings, keep records of proceedings, oversee necessary investigations, contact outside experts, and report at network plenary meetings. The network itself also makes designations of persons responsible for gathering information or making contacts. This designee is expected to absorb any necessary research assistance and e-mail or clerical resources within the home agency, and to personally perform the leadership aspects. The task leadership function is not expected to be delegated to an assistant or deputy, unless that person is or is about to become a working member of the network. In a network, many managers are expected to become workers in terms of critical committee or assignment work.

An active president/chair or coordinator is also essential. "Our good years have been those with a committed, active chairperson; the bad years when [the network] was low on the chair's agenda, or something came along to overwhelm or distract him." An active chair plus a champion is a real administrative advantage, as the champion can fill in the gaps with a less active chair and urge active chairs to greater heights.

## 3. Operate by agenda orchestration.

Networks that just let the discussion roll and hope for the best do not do as well as those who "manage the interaction time." The advice of the discussants, in their words, goes something like this: "Learn the players," "get people to work across their silos," "keep the formal and the informal going," "don't step on agency toes," "keep politics out of the core issue," and "always steer toward the vision."

This is why the work plan and a focused agenda are important in virtually all of the networks. An annual work plan focuses on mission-driven goals that can be accomplished within a timeframe. The plan is not only a statement of the quality and the quantity of the work, but an important message that the network is not a social gathering of like-minded managers, but a serious collaborative body that has concrete reasons for existence and can accomplish tangible results. The agenda is a signal to partner managers that meetings are devoted to objectives for which their participation is required. One network champion flatly asserted, "Without a work plan and real issues on the agenda, we would slowly lose program directors, or they would begin to send staff members, and then expendable employees. Then it [the network] is over!"

In other words, the interaction must not only be led but oriented to purpose, guided to some tangible level of accomplishment, while respecting partner interests and positions. In networks, one would call this the essential part of the guidance function.

## 4. Recognize shared expertise-based authority.

One discussant reminds herself "that every time I enter the world of the network I change hats from *the* boss to *one* member." Another state agency head concluded that every clergyperson—rabbi, minister, priest—could learn from his network experience. "They should all be required to not be the person in charge for at least a year before they take the pulpit. They would learn to work with people at different levels, formally and informally. This means that as one works though the network, different aspirations, goals, and missions must come together." Another administrator said, "You can't operate in this collective if you think you have all the answers. We come together to find answers. That makes us more equal. We all have expertise in different ways." Another administrator concluded, "It is not a matter of no one being in charge, but that everyone is in charge ... and that is how you have to operate." One middle manager related how important implicit authority among his peers in the network is, particularly in subcommittees: "We just do without our agency head's support. At the top level they have to be protective of their turf. It is easier for us to take certain actions." Finally, one full-time network coordinator underscored not only the presence of collective authority, but the low authority profile that networks often have to take in this regard: "We are most useful when no one is scared of us."

## 5. Stay within the decision bounds of your network.

If your network is designed to inform others or to build capacity so individual agencies can make better decisions, don't tread on agency decision prerogatives, or you will not be a network for long. The three information networks studied report they are constantly watched so that they do not cross that line to decision/action/implementation. Several discussants in one of these networks observed that the network was particularly threatened in 1999 when one of its core partners unilaterally came out in support of a national wildlife refuge proposal for the watershed. "The wildlife refuge issue almost blew us apart. People thought [the network] was in favor of it, and we lost a lot of public and agency support. Some people dropped out for two years and, now that the issue is dead, they are just coming back."

Developmental networks can decide on programs that help partner agencies, but they must stop short of deciding on courses of action that their agencies might take. "We demonstrate lots of different business development strategies and hope the conference participant will go home and use them!" Outreach networks stop short of hard decisions, but provide opportunities to access agency programs and no more. "We can't do programming as a network. Only the programs themselves are authorized by law to provide funding or some type of services!" On the other hand, action networks must fulfill their charge by delivering services, funding programs, making legal plans, and so on. It is thus important to know that all types of networks decide on work plans, agendas, officers, committees, and information programs, but not all make the kind of operational decisions that are familiar to agencies and organizations.

## 6. Accommodate and adjust while maintaining purpose.

The earlier discussion of the brokering role suggests the importance of moving beyond the recognition of individual concerns toward new ideas and forms of collaborative agreement. This requires recognition of the "long lead time that is needed for adjustment and reaching consensus." This comes, according to a state department head, "after an open and frank discussion on the big issues." "This means to be ready for give-and-take while reminding all of our vision," said another manager. Another program manager echoed this sentiment, "Talk it out, back off a bit from the agenda to get agreement, but stay within your bounds. Remember what you are there for." The individual member of the network is there to use agency knowledge/ expertise/resources to help explore problems and develop creative solutions while being concerned for the interests of the home agency. This is not an easy undertaking. One state official suggested that "informed discussion helps, but there is still a lot of work to get everybody on board." Many informants described the process as, in effect, protracted.

## 7. Be as creative as possible.

Because networks rely so heavily on shared information, a lot gets put on the table. Then the participants must go further and turn the pooled information into a new, group-based direction that is based in joint-learning experiences. One state program head reminded other managers to "think outside the box, because the whole must be something different than the sum of its parts." Another federal government state program director said that as a group, network actors must "get outside of their normal comfort zone." One thing that helps this process along is to focus on who ultimately is being served and what results will help them. "We try to focus on clients," said one state administrator. Another state official said, "If we forget about why we are here and who we are serving, we will slide into the same ruts. If we keep our focus on the purpose, we can extend our ability to experiment and utilize innovative technology." Finally, a former Extension worker concluded that the network he was involved in almost died because it "failed to take into account how all of the interests, all of the ideas, and all of the institutions could lead to solutions that all persons with a stake could live with."

## 8. Be patient and use interpersonal skills.

A university professor who was present at the founding of two networks said that he learned to "be incredibly patient; if you push you lose. You must adopt the style of 'wait for the teachable moment.'" Others similarly referred to the "long learning curve" required, as well as the strategy of "slow introduction, and wait for support later," as well as the need for "good listening skills because everybody's view is valued to some extent." Many discussants suggested that the same type of team-building skills that are necessary within agencies are valued, except that there is an extra burden on getting every person's involvement and agreement. It is a slower team process, because there is no ultimate authority, and the team management process evolves at the same time the content does. Finally, the ability to communicate openly is identified as an essential skill: "You have to talk it through and see that someone is responsible for institutional memory." In a sense, managers appear to bring similar skill sets to networks as they do for single organizations. In the absence of legal authority, however, they are applied with greater degrees of difficulty.

## 9. Recruit constantly.

As the scope of knowledge increases, and problems become more complex and interactive, the quest for information broadens. For networks this means a continuing effort at expanding the involvement base. "Touch as many bases as you can, get as many sectors as are important involved, and welcome them," said one federal administrator. Another state official said, "Get the top decision makers, the managers who do the work, and the technical people involved … but don't let the 'techies' get control." If there are key stakeholders who are potential opponents or impediments to solutions, "engage them early … don't wait for them to attack you from outside the tent." Involving some opponents means meeting them on their ground, as the natural resource network managers concluded. "We started having evening meetings in the communities, and new positions and opposition came out in numbers. Now we know how hard it is going to be, and how hard it is to keep them participating." In these situations, networks have no choice if they wish to inform and educate. Networks are inclusive. Exclusivity or limited involvement leads to information and support gaps, as well as lost potential in interagency adjustment as well as potential resources.

## 10. Emphasize incentives.

Most informants agreed that the two greatest incentives to participate are the opportunity to work toward solutions that are important to them and their agencies, and the possibilities of information/ knowledge expansion. Thus "keeping the information flowing," said one state program head, is "what I expect to give and to get." Another said, "The rewards are intrinsic but great. I learn how to keep rural Nebraska communities, and I help communities by my involvement." Another federal rural development administrator said, "Outreach is part of our agency's mission. All of our different rural bodies help us do this. The same people who are at the meetings are the ones we contact in the field. The meetings help keep the process going." It is also important to let people in the broad program arena that a network operates in know about your existence. "Let people know who you are." At some point awareness may lead to critical participation. Information or the potential to receive it, plus shared purpose, can at some point be the incentive that brings in other agencies or organizations to the network.

# Appendix:
# Research Method

Finding networks that can become objects of study is not as easy as looking at a government organization directory and choosing agencies whose missions equal one's scope of a study. Locating them involves following leads from federal, state, and local government managers, and listening carefully when networks are mentioned in the course of other research, or remembering those that surfaced during the hunt for "real life" teaching examples. The initial search for this project led to about three dozen possibilities. Their website home pages were visited to see if they really qualify as networks. That reduced the number to around 20. E-mail contacts were made with a potential principal contact and an abstract of the study included. That was followed by phone calls to answer questions and to request permission to enter into the "space" of the network, and to seek assistance for names of potential informants. If the answer was in the affirmative and if the body was a true network, documentation from the network's website and through mailings was gathered. After the initial document examination, the networks to be studied were selected.

The study itself encompasses a grounded theory/field study that includes observation and limited participation, guided discussions with principal network actors, and document analysis. The latter included extensive review of each network's annual reports, strategic plans, action plans, major studies, legislation and executive orders, meeting minutes, conference programs, and other published sources. For each network the discussions were conducted on-site in Ohio, Indiana, Iowa, and Nebraska. Site visits were scheduled in several cases to coincide with observation at regular network meetings and, in two cases, attendance at an annual conference. Rather than interviews, guided discussions were employed, where discussants were asked to respond to a standardized set of questions, but in a conversational form. All discussants received an e-mail copy of the study abstract in advance.

One hundred discussions were held with network staff coordinators and/or chairpersons/presidents, along with federal and state agency managers and program heads, and in most cases network activists from substate and local governments, nongovernmental organizations and university researchers and program specialists. Because the study focuses on management issues, priority was placed on public managers, particularly those who work both in large bureaucratic organizations and in networks. A mixture of agency heads or state directors, program managers, program specialists, and agency liaison persons or "boundary spanners" was included. This inevitably led to a weighted or purposive sample that included larger numbers of federal and state officials who were managers, along with network chairs and coordinators. The topic under study seemed to justify this approach, because the focus is not on the structure and operations of the networks themselves, but on how managers from agencies might manage differently in networks. As a result, some very important network contributors no doubt were missed. Their slighting was totally a function of topic.

The use of mixed methods allowed for a richer and deeper understanding of a murky arena, part of that 20 percent of public managers' time that is spent crossing organizational lines to do their jobs. Discussants had a chance to reflect on the presubmitted study abstract and to answer in their own words. Face-to-face allowed the researcher to read more stimuli, i.e., nonverbal expressions, and to get instant clarification of any point made. Also, additional but valuable information not on the discussion guide was usually added, including political and administrative tactics that would never be offered in a questionnaire response. Often the information was sufficiently sensitive to "drop the pen." The discussions were also the time to find out who really "carried" the network by their knowledge and efforts, and if unequal power is a relevant factor within the network, it was likely to come out during some discussions.

Meanwhile, the scientific documentation and information produced by the networks allowed for a clearer understanding about how research and technology are interlinked with interagency possibilities and, ultimately, action. Indeed, it allowed for an understanding of how information is as essential as interaction. Finally, the observation opportunities, while uneven, helped not only to understand relationships between the formal and informal, but also to see how networkers both give and receive valuable information and knowledge. It also provided a level of personal contact with many actors beyond the scheduled discussion in a considerably more informal and personal way. Together, the three types of data gathering allow for a more holistic picture of these semi-amorphous networks.

# Endnotes

1. Robert Agranoff and Michael McGuire, *Collaborative Public Management: New Strategies for Local Governments* (Washington, D.C.: Georgetown University Press, 2003).

2. Julia M. Wondolleck and Steven L. Jaffee, *Making Collaboration Work: Lessons from Innovation in Natural Resource Management* (Washington, D.C.: Island Press, 2000); Thomas W. Church and Robert T. Nakamura, *Cleaning Up The Mess: Implementation Strategies in Superfund* (Washington, D.C.: Brookings Institution, 1993); Denise Scheberle, *Federalism and Environmental Policy: Trust and the Politics of Implementation* (Washington, D.C.: Georgetown University Press, 1997).

3. Robert Agranoff and Michael McGuire, op. cit.; Walter J. M. Kickert, Erik-Hans Klijn, and Joop F. M. Koppenjan (eds.), *Managing Complex Networks* (London: SAGE, 1997); Eugene Bardach, *Getting Agencies to Work Together: The Practice and Theory of Managerial Craftsmanship* (Washington, D.C.: Brookings Institution, 1998); Michael McGuire, "Managing Networks: Propositions on What Managers Do and Why They Do It," *Public Administration Review* 62(September/October 2002), pp. 599-609.

4. Jessica Lipnack and Jeffery Stamps, *The Age of the Network* (New York: John Wiley, 1994); James E. Austin, *The Collaboration Challenge* (San Francisco: Jossey-Bass, 2000); David D. Chrislip and Carl E. Larson, *Collaborative Leadership* (San Francisco: Jossey-Bass, 1994).

5. Lawrence O'Toole, "Treating Networks Seriously: Practical and Research-based Agendas in Public Administration," *Public Administration Review* 57(January/February 1997), p. 46.

6. Clarence Stone, *Regime Politics* (Lawrence, Kan.: University Press of Kansas, 1989).

7. Robert Agranoff and Michael McGuire, "Multi-Network Management: Collaboration and the Hollow State in Local Economic Policy," *Journal of Public Administration Research and Theory* 8(January 1998), pp. 67-91.

8. Michael McGuire, "Collaborative Policy Making and Administration: The Operational Demands of Local Economic Development," *Economic Development Quarterly* 14(2000), pp. 276-291.

9. Beryl Radin, Robert Agranoff, Ann Bowman, G. Gregory Buntz, Steven Ott, Barbara Romzek, and Robert Wilson, *New Governance for Rural America: Creating Intergovernmental Partnerships* (Lawrence, Kan.: University Press of Kansas, 1996).

10. Susan Clarke and Gary Gaile, *The Work of Cities* (Minneapolis: University of Minnesota Press, 1998); Peter Eisinger, *The Rise of the Entrepreneurial State* (Madison: University of Wisconsin Press, 1988); R. Scott Fosler, "State Economic Policy: The Emerging Paradigm," *Economic Development Quarterly* 6(2)(1992), pp. 3-13.

11. D. John, *Civic Environmentalism* (Washington, D.C.: Congressional Quarterly Press, 1993).

12. Peter Drucker, "The Next Society," *Economist* (November 3, 2001), AQ3, p. 16.

13. David Korten, *Getting to the 21st Century: Voluntary Action and the Global Agenda* (West Hartford, Conn.: Kumarian Press, 1999).

14. Catherine Alter and Gerald Hage, *Organizations Working Together* (Beverly Hills, Calif. SAGE, 1993).

15. Ibid.

16. Robert Agranoff and Michael McGuire, "Big Questions in Public Network Management Research," *Journal of Public Administration Research and Theory* 11(3)(2001), pp. 295-326.

17. Ibid.

18. Radin et al.

19. Myrna Mandell, "Community Collaborations: Working Through Network Structures," *Policy Studies Review* 16(January 1999), pp. 42-64.

20. Jane E. Fountain, "Social Capital: Its Relationship to Innovation in Science and Technology," *Science and Public Policy* 25(1998), pp. 103-115.

**CHAPTER FOUR**

# Applying 21st-Century Government to the Challenge of Homeland Security

Elaine C. Kamarck
John F. Kennedy School of Government
Harvard University

*This report was originally published in June 2002, revised November 2003.*

# Introduction

For some time now Americans have been dissatisfied with their government. This dissatisfaction has lasted for nearly 40 years. It has lasted in spite of economic ups and downs, in spite of changes in administrations, and through war and peace.[1] It has affected Democrats as well as Republicans, liberals as well as conservatives.[2] Unhappiness with government has even spread to first-world countries where benevolent welfare states used to be very popular.[3] Alongside declining trust in government is dissatisfaction with a particular kind of government—bureaucratic government. Government organizations have long looked obsolete to some and downright counterproductive to others. Expensive, inflexible, and unfriendly, bureaucracy has become the enemy despite the public purposes to which it has been dedicated. Citizens who used to argue about the ends of government now also find themselves more or less universally dissatisfied with the means of government.

In the immediate aftermath of the attacks on New York and Washington of September 11, 2001, Americans expressed increased levels of trust in their government not seen since the 1960s. However, a few months later, a more nuanced poll, one that separated the government's role in preventing terror from the government's role in the economy and in social policy, showed that the surge in trust in government was all about the war on terrorism and had not spread to the government in general.[4]

Against this backdrop it is not surprising that government the world over has been shrinking.[5] No one seems to be a fan of government anymore, especially not of "big" government. Politicians throughout the world—even those who still call themselves Marxists—are following in the footsteps of former President Bill Clinton and Prime Minister Tony Blair in trying to forge a new "third way."[6] And the largest remaining Communist country in the world, China, recently signaled that it too would be withdrawing from state ownership of industries.[7]

If free-market, first-world countries, developing countries, and avowedly Communist countries are all moving away from big government, what comes next? These trends seem to herald the end of government. And, in a sense, it is ending. Until the attacks on the World Trade Center and the Pentagon, it was hard to imagine that any politician would propose the creation of a new bureaucracy or the rapid expansion of government control over the economy. And even in the aftermath of that attack, discussion of new government organizations is strictly limited to the realm of security. In my experience in government in the Clinton administration, policy options that involved new bureaucratic offices were routinely rejected (if not hooted down) in internal policy meetings of Democrats. The first Democratic administration in 12 years created exactly one new government agency, the Corporation for National Service, and made sure it was a public corporation.

Not only were bureaucratic policy proposals continually rejected, but speechwriters were called upon to extol the virtues of new proposals by emphasizing that they were "market oriented" and did not involve the creation of any new bureaucracies.

But to the dismay of many, the international trends toward smaller government and the revolt against bureaucracy do not mean the end of government; rather, the end of government as we know it. For much of the 20th century, the governmental response to a problem was to create a bureaucracy. This was certainly the case in the four mid-century decades, the 1930s through the 1960s, when the Great Depression, followed by World War II, the Cold War, and the civil rights movement, caused the creation of most of what we know as government today. As the 20th century ended, politicians in modern democracies did not lose their enthusiasm for solving public problems, but they became aware that they had to solve them in ways that did not create bureaucracy. And, so, we have seen the beginning of a remarkable era of experimentation in government, driven by a sense that the bureaucracies of the 20th century were simply not up to the job of 21st-century government.

This chapter describes the emerging implementation strategies of government for the 21st century. The first section outlines three models of government available to policy makers who believe that the bureaucratic model cannot solely solve the problems at hand. The last section applies these new models to the problem of homeland security in an attempt to show how they allow us to deal with a complex problem in a comprehensive and appropriate way.

# 21st-Century Government: Three Models

The modern government of the 20th century was built problem by problem, agency by agency. But as government matured, it became clear that some of the most difficult problems defied jurisdictional boundaries and were resistant to bureaucratic routines. Whether the problem was crime, homelessness, drug addiction, or terrorism, the bureaucratic structures of 20th-century government seemed increasingly inadequate.[8]

The limits of bureaucratic government resulted in innovations that moved beyond the formal structures of government and included other, nongovernmental actors. As a result, in recent years scholars have noted that "governance" is replacing "government" as the modus operandi of democratic societies.[9] Governance is a broader term, encompassing not just the state but also all sorts of organizations (public, private, semipublic, and even religious) that somehow contribute to the pursuit of the public interest. The evolution of the bureaucratic state has led some to conclude that "... governance without government is becoming the dominant pattern of management for advanced industrial democracies."[10]

But even governance theory presupposes the existence of the state. What will the postbureaucratic state of the 21st century look like and how will 21st-century government contribute to governance? Will these new arrangements work in all areas of policy, or will they work in some better than in others? Will they serve democratic ideals better than the bureaucratic state of the 20th century? These are topics we are just beginning to understand. But first we need to understand the outlines of this new state—the alternative, if you will, to government as we know it.

Three key assumptions underlie the movement toward new modes of implementing public policy. First is the assumption that the problems of monopoly, lack of innovation, insufficient responsiveness, and inefficiency that plague both the private sector and the public sector can be overcome or at least mitigated in the public sector (as they are in the private sector) by the injection of greater competition. Second is the assumption that, at the operational level, few major differences exist between management in the public sector and management in the private sector. And third is the assumption that the public interest can be articulated and measured and that this will create a "market proxy" for the public sector—thus allowing the public sector a new, and stronger, form of accountability.

The search for new modes of government to replace the bureaucratic state yields three new governmental forms: reinvented government, government by network, and government by market.

## Reinvented Government

The term "reinventing government" was first coined by David Osborne and Ted Gaebler in their best-selling book by the same name, *Reinventing Government*.[11] It is the basis of many of the government reform movements currently in vogue around the world. Stripped to its essence, reinvented government is entrepreneurial. Another way to look at it is that reinvented government is bureaucratic government without all the things that have made bureaucratic government so irritating to the citizens of Information Age economies. Reinvented government is government that is run as much like a private sector business as is possible. The literature and practice of reinvented government are replete with praise for competition, flexibility, employee empowerment, and customer service. These governments have often shed the civil service and centralized procurement. They have adopted performance goals, they use bonuses to reward their workers, and they place a premium on service to the citizen and on productivity.

Reinvented government, however, is still government. But it is government shorn of many public sector trappings, especially the rigid budget, personnel, and procurement rules that impose restrictions on government managers that are unusual, if not unheard of, in the private sector. The underlying assumption behind reinvented government is that there are few significant differences between the public and the private sectors when it comes to management. And a second, but equally important, assumption is that the goals of public sector organizations can be clearly articulated and measured.[12]

This second assumption is vital to the success of reinvented government because it allows government organizations freedom from the central control agencies that so dominate public sector life. These agencies were invented to identify and track the spending of every single bit of government money. But the accountability associated with 20th-century bureaucracy came with a price. In practice, civil service personnel agencies often made it impossible for line managers to hire the best people and fire the worst people; centralized procurement agencies often made it impossible for line managers to buy what they needed at good prices; and central budget agencies often made it impossible to move funds from one category to another in order to get the job done.

Finally, reinvented government seeks to use information technology to improve productivity and service in much the same way that the private sector increased its productivity and service delivery through information technology. Information technology is the secret to the success of third-way politics because it allows governments to maintain service without increasing the size of the bureaucracy. Without information technology, the competing demands of the public's "Do this!" but "Don't let the government do it!" would be impossible to meet.

Reinvented government (called the new public management in other countries) began in Great Britain in 1982, in New Zealand in 1984, and in American state houses in the 1980s. In Great Britain, the establishment of the efficiency unit under Minister Michel Heseltine began the process of bringing to the civil service private market accountability for results. In part, the eventual report of this unit:

> ... argued that to solve the management problem, the government would have to separate service-delivery and compliance functions from the policy-focused departments that housed them—to separate steering from rowing. Second, it would have to give service-delivery and compliance agencies much more flexibility and autonomy. And third, it would have to hold those agencies accountable for results, through performance contracts.[13]

The British government then put these theories into action with the publication of "Improving Management in Government: The Next Steps," written under the leadership of Sir Robin Ibbs. Out of this report came the creation of next-step agencies or executive agencies. These agencies were to be public sector agencies *without* public sector trappings. Next-step agencies would be run by CEOs who were to be hired from within or outside of the civil service, on a performance contract basis, and with the potential for large bonuses. The agencies would have more control over their budgets, personnel, and other management systems. The new head of each agency would negotiate a framework agreement between the agency and the relevant cabinet minister. And, perhaps most important, the heads of these agencies could be fired for not living up to their performance agreements.

By 1997, 130 British agencies had been established under the next-step framework, and these agencies accounted for about 75 percent of the British civil service.[14] Now that the next-step agencies are more than a decade old, they can boast of a considerable record of accomplishments: improvements in the processing of passport applications, savings in "running costs" (administrative costs) in the National Health Service Pensions Agency, improvements in waiting times for the National Health Service, and reductions in per-unit costs at the Patent Office.[15]

As Britain was remaking its large government bureaucracies into entrepreneurial governments, New Zealand was undergoing an even more dramatic revolution. Unlike other government reform movements, the New Zealand experience is unique for its boldness, for its continuity across political parties, and for its intellectual coherence. It is no wonder that government reform seems, at times, to have outstripped lamb as the most popular New Zealand export. In the mid-1980s New Zealand faced an economic and political meltdown of striking proportions. As the new Labour government took over in 1987, it published a postelection briefing paper described as the manifesto of the new public management.[16]

Like the Thatcher reforms in Britain, the New Zealand reforms injected the language of competition, incentives, and performance into public administration. In absolute terms these reforms were remarkable, and against the quasi-socialist record of previous governments they were even more remarkable. They called for getting the government out of those activities that could be carried out more effectively by nongovernmental bodies. They called for a clear separation of the responsibilities of ministers and departmental heads—giving the traditional civil service both more autonomy and more responsibility for results than ever before. Perhaps the most revolutionary aspect of all was the directive that *everything* that was publicly funded—even policy advice—was to be made "contestable and subject to competitive tendering."[17] To this day, cabinet ministers purchase government outputs from what used to be the bureaucracy, and the bureaucracy must often compete with other public and/or private organizations to do the work of the government.[18] New Zealand broke the public monopoly of government on governance. While officials in the United States were still asking "What is a core governmental function?", New Zealand had decided the answer was, essentially, nothing.

Reinvented government started at the national level in Britain and New Zealand, but at the state and local levels in the United States. Unlike the federal government, the state houses could not print their own money. Forced to live within their means and buffeted by tax revolts on the one hand and continued demands for services on the other, mayors and governors had no choice but to try to do more with less, even if it meant stepping on some toes. When former Mayor Ed Rendell took over the troubled city of Philadelphia in the late 1980s, he quickly recognized that either he could raise taxes, and push even more of the tax base to the suburbs, or he could cut services, and push even more of the tax base to the suburbs.[19] As a Democratic mayor, he had no choice but to take on the status quo, including the powerful public sector unions, and reinvent government. The Republican former mayor of Indianapolis, Steve Goldsmith, got national attention when he put 27 city services out to bid. In Minnesota, the governor set about dismantling the government's central control mechanisms and reconstructing them in ways that would add to, not detract from, individual agencies' missions.[20]

For American state and local officials in the 1980s, as for British and New Zealand national officials, reinventing government was the only way out of an impossible governing situation. The philosophy that evolved was more or less coherent despite beginning as an adaptation to budget crises. In America the philosophy came to be called reinventing government. In other countries it came to be called the new public management.

As this way of implementing policy became more widespread, many scholars expressed fears about where it was going, chiefly, the fear that somehow this new philosophy would undercut the rule of law.[21] However, as many a practitioner of entrepreneurial government knows, although the law itself is often very flexible, over time the administrative application of the law can introduce a degree of rigidity into the implementation of a program that seriously impedes its original mission.

In their research, Mark Considine and Jenny Lewis set out to assess the behavior of civil servants on the front lines of these reforms. Somewhat to their surprise, they found out that civil servants in newer, reformed organizations did not differ from other civil servants when it came to the importance of rules in their work. They concluded, "… [I]t also is possible that rules are always so much a part of even the most flexible public programs that they do no more than define the parameters of action and fail to define actual work strategies."[22]

Reinvented government is still government, albeit a government that attempts to rid itself of the self-inflicted wounds of the bureaucratic culture.

It is fundamentally a lot less threatening to traditional government than the next two models.

## Government by Network

As these new forms of government take shape, they do so amidst a vibrant and ongoing argument about what, exactly, is a core governmental function. In the future, reinvented government will be the chosen method of implementing government policy in those areas where it is determined that a government organization, populated by public employees, is the best way to go about the government's business. But making that determination will not be so easy, as we will see when we look at the second new governmental form—government by network.

In recent years the term network as applied to government has come to have at least three separate meanings. Networked government is often used to describe the constellation of public, private, and semipublic organizations that influence a policy world—in other words, a policy network. This use of the term network is not very new and is similar to what an earlier generation of political scientists might have called "the iron triangle" of bureaucrats, congressional staff, and interest groups.[23]

Network has also been used to describe emerging relationships between states. As the economy has become global, the need for global governance measures has increased. But international bureaucracy has proved even less attractive to states than have their domestic bureaucracies. The concept of world government is a nonstarter with all but the most sanguine futurists. Instead, as Anne Marie Slaughter and others have documented, the response to the need for international governance has been for subunits of national governments to develop relationships in which both law and administrative processes are harmonized, thus allowing for governance in the place of actual government.[24] John Peterson and Laurence O'Toole use "network" to apply to the complex, mutually adaptive behavior of subunits of states in the European Union, which, while often slow and opaque, solves an important supranational governance problem.[25]

In addition, a third way the term network comes to be used is in those instances where the government chooses to implement policy by creating, through its power to contract and to fund, a network of nongovernmental organizations. The diminished role of traditional bureaucracy in networked government caused H. Brinton Milward and Keith G. Provan to dub these forms of government the hollow state: "… [T]he hollow state refers to any joint production situation where a governmental agency relies on others (firms, nonprofits, or other government agencies) to jointly deliver public services."[26]

They go on to make the point that in spite of the prevalence of this form of government, we know relatively little about how to manage networks.[27] In fact, only in the last 10 years has the term been used with any regularity in reference to implementing policy, even though the network form is not particularly new—especially not in the United States, where nongovernmental actors have always had roles in implementing policy. Although there is very little empirical data on whether or not government by network actually increased at the end of the 20th century, the discussion of networks in the field of public administration has certainly increased.[28] One possible explanation is that government by network has been largely an unconscious choice on the part of policy makers. They have sought to create networks out of a desire to avoid traditional bureaucracies. Hence, networks have become, like reinvented government, popular implementation choices for what they are not (bureaucracy) as opposed to what they are.

In government by network the bureaucracy is replaced by a wide variety of other kinds of institutions, almost all of which have better reputations (and sometimes better performance) than government itself. In government by network, the government stops trying to do anything itself; instead it funds other organizations that, in turn, do the actual work the government wants done. An immense variety of organizations have been part of government by network. Churches, research labs, nonprofit organizations, for-profit organizations, universities—all have been called on to perform the work of the government. But while some view the emergence of this form as a "hollowing out" of the state, it pays to remember that the sum total of all this activity by different kinds of organizations is still something that the state wants done and that the state pays for. While some persist in seeing networks as a weakening of the state, networks can also be perceived as a different way of implementing the purposes of the state.

There are two major attractions of networked government: It is not bureaucratic, and it has the potential to be flexible and to innovate. Traditional bureaucracies seem to lack these characteristics. In fact, networked government has been used in the past in cases where the government valued innovation so much that it was willing to give up a certain degree of control. The most long-standing example of networked government is the famous military-industrial establishment. The offensive and defensive capacity of the U.S. military is much more than the total of its actual military assets, as we discovered during World War II. Although faced with the need for massive mobilization at the beginning of the war, President Roosevelt did not nationalize the industrial might of America. Instead, he used the government's financial and other powers to create a network of participants in the war effort. The military might of the United States rested as much on its ability to produce weaponry (a private sector function) for itself and all its allies as on the ability of its soldiers, seamen, and airmen to fight.

As we moved from World War II to the Cold War, the model remained the same. Seeking ever better weapons against the Soviet Union, the United States engaged countless corporations, universities, and private laboratories, along with their own internal research laboratories, in developing sophisticated weaponry. In the kind of controlled experiment that rarely happens in the real world, the Soviet Union, a totalitarian state, kept its weapons research within the all-encompassing bureaucracy of the Communist state. By 1989 the experiment was over. When the Soviet empire fell, we learned, among other things, that its technological and military capacity had fallen way behind that of the United States. Government by network had won; bureaucratic government had lost.

As bureaucratic government has failed in one policy area after another, policymakers have looked to implement policy through networks instead. In 1996, the landmark welfare reform bill ended more than 50 years of a welfare system that had been almost universally regarded as a failure. The old welfare system was characterized by its bureaucratic attention to detail and its insistence that applicants meet all the rules and that social workers fill out the paperwork properly. It was a closed system, run by the bureaucratic imperative and impervious to the needs of welfare mothers.

In its place, the new law sought to change the system to a work-based system. Part of that transformation was to give states an unprecedented amount of freedom to create welfare-to-work networks. These networks could consist of not-for-profit organizations (a traditional piece of the social service network), for-profit organizations, and religious organizations. In a dramatic abdication of control, the federal government as much as admitted that the state bureaucracies, which had traditionally done this sort of work, had failed and that the task of getting welfare mothers to work should be given to whoever felt they could do it.

When the government creates a network, the private sector is quick to respond. Take, for example, Lockheed Martin, a giant American corporation that almost single-handedly exemplifies the military industrial complex. Imagine how surprised people were when, in 1996, Lockheed Martin IMS (a former subdivision of the company) announced that it was going into the welfare-to-work business. From supersonic airplanes to welfare mothers?

Lockheed Martin was simply using its years of experience in government contracting to get into the latest and one of the biggest government sectors ever—social services. For many, this was a jarring development indeed. One of Lockheed's competitors for this business, Maximus, tells potential investors that social services administration is a potential $21-billion market.[29] And the owner of America Works, one of the oldest for-profit welfare companies in existence, urges local governments to set tough standards for their contracts, knowing that they will then have a greater advantage over their competitors.[30]

Networked government is not necessarily cheap and, frankly, not always very efficient, but it has two chief virtues. The first, of course, is that it doesn't look like government. But the second is that it permits experimentation and produces innovation. In other words, it allows a thousand flowers to bloom. That is why networked government tends to appear in those areas where one solution can't be expected to solve the problem. There is no one solution to getting people off welfare, getting people off drugs, encouraging children to learn, or avoiding AIDS.

While networked government is a familiar form in the world of social services, the diversity inherent in a network is likely to make networked government a staple of law enforcement and the fight against terrorism. Even before the tragedy of September 11, it was clear to many that bureaucracy was a major impediment in the fight against crime and terrorism. Pieces of the terrorism puzzle crossed an enormous number of agencies—the Immigration and Naturalization Service, the CIA, the FBI, and Customs—to name a few. Each one of these agencies grew up in a time when the world was more or less neatly divided between internal threats and external threats. The amorphous nature of terrorism, organized international crime, and new crimes such as cyber-terrorism means that the closed worlds of the intelligence agencies and the law enforcement agencies will have to change.

Cooperation tends to operate at an ideal level when an attack is anticipated or in the aftermath of one. But, as we saw in the case of the World Trade Center, finding the suspects quickly is no replacement for preventing the attack in the first place. The answer is not to combine all these different agencies into one giant agency. That would decrease rather than increase the diversity of information. The answer is to link them into a network in which each player reinforces the other in order to yield results needed *before* an attack, not after.

In spite of the advantages that the diversity of networked government presents, the fact that policy makers have used it as a sort of default mode of implementation for very difficult, even "sticky" public policy problems means very little attention is paid to what makes for successful networked government. Kenneth J. Meier and Laurence J. O'Toole studied school superintendents in Texas and found that, with other factors held constant, superintendents who participated in networks had better results than those who did not.[31] In the work of Provan and Milward on mental health networks, they point out that while resources matter, effective principal agent relationships and stability are also important to the effectiveness of the network.[32]

However, the soft underbelly of networked government is the nearly 100 percent probability that, over time, some actor in some part of the network will screw up; someone will steal money, waste money, or simply prove to be ineffective. On the other hand, overzealousness against waste, fraud, and abuse on the part of actors in the network can re-create all the pathologies and rigidities of traditional bureaucratic governments that networked government can avoid. Bruce Reed, architect of the Clinton administration's welfare reform bill, understood this problem. In a recent interview he said, "Under the new arrangement the country has to accept a greater level of risk, and states have to accept responsibility and they get more ability to experiment." When asked why the country seemed so ready to delegate the entire system and accept more risk, he said, "There was greater willingness to take that risk because the old system was so encumbered by dumb federal rules."[33]

The reason networked government looks "hollow" to many who observe it is that few people in government really understand how to manage networks. Often networks have been created to solve the most difficult governmental problems, such as creating a weapons system that does what no other weapons system before it has done, or figuring out how to end a cycle of welfare dependence that for decades had remained impervious to economic booms and economic busts. But in addition to the difficulty of the public problems, many government managers find themselves managing networks when their experience, training, and expectations have been to manage traditional bureaucracies. The management of networks is a topic that goes well beyond this chapter, but suffice it to say that creating learning communities within the network and establishing accountability without stifling innovation are two of the most serious management challenges.

## Government by Market

Reinvented government and networked government differ from traditional bureaucratic government and yet both involve a significant amount of government as we know it. In reinvented government, the public's work is done by people who work for the government; in networked government, the public's work is paid for by the government even though the work is not performed by people who work for the government. In the third emerging model of government, market government, the work of government involves no public employees and no public money. In market government, the government uses its power to create a market that fulfills a public purpose. It takes account of what economists call "externalities." (I use the term "market government" differently than have other scholars, such as B. Guy Peters, who uses it to describe "... the basic belief in the virtues of competition and an idealized pattern of exchange and incentives."[34] Most other public administration scholars, when they talk about markets and government, are usually talking about what I have referred to previously as reinvented government or networked government.)

But government by market is something very distinctive. If reinvented government is government all dressed up to look like the private sector, and government by network is government that hides behind the façade of much more popular organizations, government by market is so well disguised that most people aren't even aware that it's government in operation. Because of this, it is the model most different from traditional bureaucratic government.

Those who are old enough to remember Lady Bird Johnson (wife of President Lyndon Johnson) are old enough to remember that she waged a battle to clean up America's highways, which in the 1960s were becoming overrun with beer cans and soda bottles. By the 1970s, beer and soft drink bottles were posing serious problems for cleanliness and for landfills. The solution to this problem came from government. In 1971 the state of Oregon passed the nation's first "bottle bill." But instead of creating the Bureau of Clean Highways and hiring workers to pick up bottles, government did something unusual—it created a market. By passing laws that required deposits on bottles and soda cans, government created an economic incentive to keep people from throwing bottles out of their cars. And for the hard-core litterbugs who persisted in throwing bottles away, the laws created an economic incentive for other people to pick them up.[35]

Similarly, in the 1991 Clean Air Act, Congress decided to put a price on sulfur dioxide emissions from industrial plants. Sulfur dioxide ($SO_2$) is the primary cause of acid rain. Essentially, the government determined how much sulfur dioxide the environment could handle and then developed a trading system that allows clean plants to sell permits and dirty plants to buy permits. Most analysts feel this system has worked. In the last 30 years, emissions trading and other improvements have caused nearly a 50 percent drop in the amount of $SO_2$ in the air.[36] The "price" was high enough to encourage plants to get new equipment for cleaner air but low enough that companies could determine their own timetable for doing this and their own technology.

In retrospect, market government applied to certain environmental problems has been a big success. But only recently has this approach become politically acceptable. Professor Rob Stavins, one of the early advocates of this approach in the environmental field, recalls how, just a decade ago, environmentalists chafed at the notion of buying and selling pollution. Their reaction and the reaction of their colleagues in the government at the Environmental Protection Agency was nothing short of horror. The use of a market to control pollution was considered immoral. That reaction, reports Professor Stavins, has changed dramatically in recent years. The most ardent environmentalists will admit to the attractiveness of market government, and now people seek to apply market government in places where it may well not work.[37] The recent effort to deregulate the electricity market in the state of California is a perfect example of an attempt at market government where so much went wrong that energy executive Barbara Kates Garnik has referred to it as "the perfect storm."[38]

Market government has shaped the education reform debate through proposals to substitute vouchers to parents for the current state-funded education system. The voucher movement argues that the government can create a market in education by attaching education money to each student instead of attaching education money to public schools. This reform movement argues that government should use tax cuts and universal tuition tax credits to turn over education purchasing power to individuals. According to the argument, this would create a vibrant education marketplace and offer consumers a range of services and products that the current system does not.

A vibrant market already exists in education at the college level where parents save, borrow, and do without in order to send children to elite, expensive, private institutions. In recent years, as unhappiness with the public K–12 educational system has grown, an education market of a sort has emerged even without government subsidies. Edison schools, Bright Horizons, Nobel Learning Communities (these began as child-care providers and expanded business to include K–12 education), and others have created a new class of educators called "edupreneurs."[39] The advantages of creating a market in education are many: variety in curriculum, innovation in instructional methods, higher academic standards, weeding out of substandard schools, introduction of new technologies in the classroom, and investments in research, to name a few.

A well-functioning market is, of course, a marvel to behold. In our lifetimes, the marketplace has given the vast majority of Americans color TVs, microwaves, and VCRs. Who knows what it will bring in the next century? But the description "well functioning" is key. For those who are attempting to design markets for public good instead of private good, the problems are immense. First are the pricing problems. Too high a price on bottles clearly would have wrecked much of the beverage industry and would have caused a serious outcry from the public. (To this day the beer industry remains opposed to bottle bills wherever they have not yet taken root.) Too low a price on bottles would not have solved the public problem at all. Similarly, if the number of pollution permits were so high that they cost very little to buy, they would not have created an incentive for plants to clean up their manufacturing. On the other hand, if the number of permits were too low, the price would be so high that older plants would have gone out of business.

Second are problems in understanding the range of the market. A major failure in the California energy debacle was the deregulation of the wholesale market without deregulation of the retail market. False expectations (that energy prices would continue to go down) and unavoidable political pressures (reassuring voters that the changes would not cost them more money) ended up creating a crisis. It is not surprising that California is retreating from its experiment with markets in the electricity field.

Third is the problem of creating the right conditions for implementing market government. Using market government to achieve a public good presupposes a certain amount of honesty in the economic system and a certain level of honesty and effectiveness in law enforcement. Although market government applied to environmental problems has proven a success in the United States, not surprisingly Americans' talk about creating "market mechanisms" to implement the Kyoto Accords falls on skeptical ears in other countries. Market government works where the rule of law is well established and where law enforcement is effective enough to deter cheating. This is simply not the case in much of the world.

And fourth is the problem of inadequate information. A well-functioning market depends on high-quality information and universal access to it. There has been substantial opposition to voucher plans from teachers' unions and other inhabitants of the education status quo, but parents and others with no professional stake in the status quo have been almost as reluctant to embrace the market approach to education. Lurking behind the failure of so many voucher plans is the suspicion that somehow someone will get screwed. Buying a second grade education is simply not as easy as buying a bread-making machine. There are many sources of information about various bread-making machines, and most Americans know how to find them and understand them. But sources of information about one school's second grade versus another school's second grade are hard to come by and difficult to interpret. Good markets require good information, and, in spite of the recent trend toward testing, good information is simply not so easy to come by for most parents.

Problems aside, however, market government is a very powerful alternative to bureaucratic government precisely because it allows an unlimited number of individual adaptations to achieve the overall public good. In reinvented government, one entity—the government—is pursuing the public good. In government by network, one entity—the government—is choosing a finite number of organizations to pursue the public good. In contrast, government by market allows every individual (as in the case of bottles) or every company (as in the case of sulfur dioxide emissions) to pursue the public good as they see fit. It is, therefore, perfectly suited to America, where citizens glorify individual choice and chafe at any system that feels too controlling.

# The Challenge of Homeland Security: Two 20th-Century Responses

Terrorism is typical of many of the challenges 21st-century government will face. The problem is not located in any one nation but in a network that spans as many as 60 nations. The problem exists inside and outside the United States and therefore spans borders and bureaucratic jurisdictions. The leadership structure of terrorist organizations is ambiguous, and terrorists constantly change their methods and targets; thus the problem is immune to bureaucratic routines. The solutions to the problem exist in many disparate pieces of the government, all of which have other important, nonterrorist missions. Finally, terrorism, by its nature, is likely to be random and haphazard. Therefore it is difficult to imagine sustaining a bureaucracy dedicated solely to a problem that is likely to be episodic.

The efforts of the United States as it struggles to adapt its institutions to this new problem may well serve as the archetype for its adaptation to many other challenges of the 21st century. The model of 21st-century government laid out in the first part of this paper can help by offering a new and systematic approach to this problem. But first it will be useful to look at the initial responses to homeland security—the "coordination response" and the "bureaucratic response." Both are typical 20th-century reactions to a 21st-century problem, and thus they disappoint.

## The Coordination Response

Confronted with 21st-century problems, the first reaction of 20th-century governments has been to "coordinate." "The only turf we should be worried about protecting is the turf we stand on," said former Pennsylvania Governor Tom Ridge at his swearing in as the chief of homeland security. Governor Ridge's position was created by an executive order of the president to coordinate the government's homeland security. Executive orders can be powerful instruments, but they are no substitute for real legal authority or for real money, neither of which Governor Ridge had. He reviewed budgets submitted by agencies but could not alter them. He coordinated 40-plus government agencies with approximately 100 staff members borrowed from other agencies, but he did not have the ability to make any single one of them do what he wants.

Washington usually loves these types of high-level coordinators of policy. In fact, cooperation and coordination are among Washington's most favorite words. Coordination occurs at the top, makes for a good press conference, and doesn't require the painful process of changing the way government goes about its business. In recent years we have had a high-level coordinator of drug policy, called the drug czar, and a high-level coordinator of AIDS policy. Both have had to borrow staff and beg for money.

But this time around, even the Washington establishment, usually so tolerant of coordination, recognized that coordination as a homeland security strategy was likely to be inadequate. Former General Barry McCaffrey was the drug czar in the last years of the Clinton administration. He exchanged command of real troops in Central and South America for the coordination job. Through sheer force of personality he made a difference, and yet this quote from him about Tom Ridge's original role comes from his own, somewhat bitter, experience: "If all [Mr. Ridge] has are five people and a black sedan, he'll be a speakers' bureau for U.S. counterterrorism efforts and nothing more."[40]

The problem with coordination is that it occurs in the Cabinet room in the White House, not at the borders where terrorists are stopped. And that is why Director Ridge did not have an easy time after his appointment in September 2001. At one point, he was placed in the position of master of ceremonies to a press conference of government agencies trying to respond, and not doing so very well, to the anthrax-containing envelopes. Much of the criticism Ridge received stemmed from perennial confusion over what the White House can and cannot do. The White House cannot run operations. It lacks the legal authority and the capacity to do so. The history of White House attempts at operations, from President Lyndon Johnson picking bombing targets from the Situation Room during the Vietnam War to Ollie North's pursuit of a secret war in Central America from the Old Executive Office Building, is not a happy one.

The coordinator always ends up as simply another member of the White House staff. What the coordinator can have is the ear of the president, an often overrated asset in Washington, D.C., since presidents have only two ears and a set number of hours in the day. Also, in a government of laws, the president's wishes get translated into action only if there is a legal basis for doing so.

In the months that the Office of Homeland Security existed, people have suggested that it be strengthened in a variety of ways. One of the most common suggestions is that it be given the authority to sign off on agency budgets vis-à-vis homeland security. In fact, the experience of the drug czar's office, created in 1988 to oversee the 50-odd federal agencies that were involved in the drug war, offers a pessimistic precedent in this regard. As drug czar, McCaffrey exercised a never-before-employed provision in the law to refuse to certify a line item in the Pentagon's budget. This resulted in a showdown with the secretary of defense and a compromise, brokered by the president, which split the difference.[41] Because the executive branch can send only one budget to Congress at a time, disputes are likely to be brokered by the president or by the Office of Management and Budget (OMB).

Thus, while giving power to the coordinator to certify budgets sounds plausible, the fact that it has been used only once in the 14 years that the drug czar's office has been in effect, the fact that it resulted in an embarrassing news story, the fact that it forced the need for presidential brokering— all mean that it is a power not likely to be used with any frequency. In addition, OMB is a small but highly effective and powerful bureaucracy with 500 top-level civil servants and a deep sense that its mission is to integrate and implement the president's wishes. A second White House entity with budgetary authority would only sow confusion and complicate the extremely complicated task of creating a coherent budget. All White House policy shops interact with OMB in preparing a presidential budget; creating another, parallel office with budgetary authority in the White House is bound to fail.

In addition to giving Governor Ridge budget authority, Congress was anxious to have him come to the Hill to testify.[42] That too would have been a mistake. White House staff traditionally are covered by executive privilege, which they need in order to operate as extensions of the president and the vice president. This gives White House staff the freedom to explore ideas and options and offer the president the kind of advice he needs.

If Governor Ridge cannot run operations and cannot control budgets and isn't allowed to testify to Congress, what could he have done? Was he, as Barry McCaffrey quipped, doomed to run a speakers' bureau on homeland security? The answer is no. A White House staffer with good access to the president and an important assignment has a unique ability to effect change. That's what Governor Ridge should have done from the beginning of his tenure as the head of the Office of Homeland Security, and it looks like that is what he did in that office. The day-to-day business of tracking down al Qaeda members and anthrax letters belonged, by virtue of statute and capacity, in the agencies. But the agencies historically are ill equipped to reform themselves. Even political appointees often are captured by the long-time civil servants in the agencies, and historically the agencies are beholden to the congressional committees and interest groups, which constitute their day-to-day environment and control their budgets. Only the White House can formulate and pursue fundamental, nonincremental changes.

When former Vice President Al Gore was handed the job of reinventing the federal government, he created an enormous task force of civil servants to come up with ideas for reform. Over a period of eight years, money was saved and nearly 100 pieces of legislation stemmed from the initial report. As director of this effort, I had to negotiate among the institutions of the executive branch and the institutions, especially OMB and the National Security Council (NSC), of the Executive Office of the President. In spite of some initial tests of will with OMB, we settled into the following rough division of labor: The National Performance Review dealt with problems that required management or bureaucratic reform. We did not deal with annual statutory pay negotiations; we did not deal with congressional committees. We dealt internally with the executive branch, and once we came up with reform proposals, we went to Congress as a united administration.

Governor Ridge's office showed signs of settling into this model. While each agency of the far-flung federal government and many congressional actors might have good ideas for homeland security, only the White House can build a thorough, coherent reform plan for homeland security. When former Vice President Al Gore and his staff finished the first round of re-inventing government recommendations, we spent an entire Saturday after-noon presenting the proposals to the President and his staff. Some were scrubbed, some were amended, and most were accepted. These then became the president's agenda and, as they were enacted over the years, the recommendations changed large parts of the federal bureaucracy. Ridge needed to create the plan and then see that it was implemented. This is best done from the White House, where someone like Ridge can capture the attention of the president. The consistent exercise of pressure from the White House is important because the bureaucracy has enormous capacity to thwart change.[43]

## The Bureaucratic Response

The second response to the problem of homeland security is to create a bureaucracy dedicated to the problem. This was first advocated by former Senators Warren Rudman and Gary Hart as part of their important work on the United States Commission on National Security/21st Century.[44] This report, which got very little attention when released, will stand as one of the boldest, most creative descriptions of a major 21st-century problem and how the 20th-century government was not equipped to deal with it. But the Hart/Rudman prescription is classically 20th century in form—identify a problem and create a bureaucracy with the same name.

The Hart/Rudman prescription, which was introduced in several pieces of legislation, was to create an actual national homeland security agency that encompasses both sides of the problem, prevention as well as reaction.[45] Under the Hart/Rudman plan, the centerpiece of the new agency would have been the Federal Emergency Management Administration (FEMA) and the three agencies that deal with American borders—Customs, Border Patrol, and the Coast Guard. At that time, FEMA was a freestanding agency, Customs was in the Treasury Department, Border Patrol was in the Justice Department, and the Coast Guard was in the Transportation Department.

Some elements of the Hart/Rudman plan went a long way toward addressing some of the major problems in homeland security. For instance, in discussing the importance of the Coast Guard in this effort they focus on the border problem, noting that the Coast Guard is unique among U.S. agencies because of its ability "… to operate within, across and beyond U.S. borders."[46] But the initial instinct to create one agency to deal with a problem as broad as homeland security is inadequate to the task at hand.

Shortly after the September 11 terrorist attacks and shortly after the appointment of Governor Tom Ridge as director of the newly created Office of Homeland Security, the *New York Times* published an elaborate chart.[47] More than 150 boxes, linked in an incomprehensible jigsaw of formal and semiformal relationships, constituted a picture daunting in its complexity. One New York hostess, knowing of my experience in the federal government, thrust it into my hand as I walked into a dinner party, saying, "Is this for real?"

The natural instinct of those schooled in 20th-century bureaucracy is to organize those boxes into a comprehensible hierarchy. But reorganizing the boxes into one box or two or three under new statutes and new leaders would not solve the essential problem. The problem is the boxes themselves and the ways in which they interact or fail to interact with each other. The problem of homeland security is like many other problems we will face in the 21st century—it does not fit in one box. To the student of 21st-century government, the question is not "Where do the boxes fit on the chart?" but "How do they operate and how do they communicate with each other?"

(**Editors' note:** *In November 2002, Congress passed legislation creating a new Department of Homeland Security. Tom Ridge was appointed to serve as the first Secretary of the department in January 2003.*)

# A Case Study in 21st-Century Government: Homeland Security

## Dimensions of the Homeland Security Problem

Homeland security encompasses a wide variety of governmental missions. Almost everyone agrees that there is a continuum. According to retired Air Force Colonel Randell Larsen, the continuum ranges from deterrence to prevention to preemption, on the one hand, and moves toward crisis management, consequence management, attribution, and retaliation on the other hand.[48] The last four missions require governmental cooperation *after the fact.* Leaving aside for a moment the issues of attribution and retaliation, the homeland security problem can be separated into three broad categories:

- Reforms that will help **prevent** acts of catastrophic terrorism in the first place

- Reforms that will **protect** Americans from terrorists by preempting their actions
- Reforms that will increase the effectiveness of the **response** to any terrorist act that does occur

These are reflected in the boxes across the top of Table 4.1.

The vertical axis of this table shows the various governmental options that exist to reform the current bureaucracy. Included are five options available to policy makers. The first option, the most straightforward and probably the easiest, is to make incremental changes to already existing programs. A great deal can be done to strengthen functions and agencies that already exist. The second row on this table consists of reinvented government. It includes changes that can be made to existing bureaucracies by reorganizing them, changing the legal context and administrative cultures in which they operate, or using new technologies to increase their effectiveness. The third row consists of options that involve creating and managing networks that consist entirely of public sector organizations. The fourth row consists of networks that involve both public and private sector organizations. The final row consists of markets that government might want to create in order to meet some of the objectives in homeland security.

The recommendations set forth in the following tables in this section are illustrative of how the 21st-century government framework can be applied to national problems. They are not meant to be a comprehensive set of actions for homeland security. The challenge of 21st-century government will be to create effective portfolios of actions that incorporate reinvented government, networked government, and market government.

**Table 4.1: Governmental Options for Achieving Homeland Security**

|  | **Prevention** | **Protection** | **Response** |
|---|---|---|---|
| Incremental Change |  |  |  |
| Reinvented Government |  |  |  |
| Government by Network (public) |  |  |  |
| Government by Network (public and private) |  |  |  |
| Government by Market |  |  |  |

## Elements of a Comprehensive Approach to Homeland Security

### Incremental Steps

Understanding homeland security along these dimensions allows aspects of the problem to be matched with the most appropriate mode of action. Table 4.2 gives some examples of incremental steps that could be taken in the war on terror. Incremental steps, while clearly less headline grabbing, can be very important. Ideas for incremental changes or improvements to existing programs often come from within the bureaucracy. In fact, the tendency when any issue becomes "hot" is to repackage existing requests for more money under the latest hot topic. In the Clinton administration many budget requests were identified as environmentally necessary, and recent budget requests have been wrapped in the mantle of homeland security. OMB is ill equipped to sort out which of these make sense in terms of a national strategy for homeland security and which do not—that is an important mission for a White House office dedicated to the subject.

**Prevention:** Incremental steps include Ash Carter's suggestion to prevent potentially disastrous acts of nuclear terrorism by extending the highly successful and well-thought-out Nunn-Lugar program to Pakistan.[49] This

**Table 4.2: Examples of Incremental Changes to Existing Government to Achieve Homeland Security**

| Prevention | Protection | Response |
|---|---|---|
| Extend Nunn-Lugar to Pakistan.<br><br>Develop an effective means for tracking formal and informal money flows. | Provide consular officers abroad access to criminal and terrorist databases.<br><br>Deputize local law enforcement officers so that they can arrest criminal aliens.<br><br>Create an improved warning system for state and local law enforcement.<br><br>Issue guidelines on airline passengers' security responsibilities. | Require all medium- to large-sized American cities to invest in the all-hazard approach to emergency response.<br><br>Increase the pharmaceutical stockpile for civilian use in case of bioterrorist attacks. |

involves an incremental change to an existing program designed to prevent the development of nuclear weapons by terrorists or rogue states. Considering the discovery of documents in an al Qaeda safe house in Kabul on how to make an atom bomb, the need for enhancing this program cannot be overlooked.[50] The enhancements can be done quickly and do not involve creating a new infrastructure, although, as with many of the ideas that fall within this category, they would most likely entail extra appropriations.

The September 11 tragedies have also focused new attention on the role of money in promoting terror. In October 2001, the Bush administration announced the creation of a beefed up team to identify and track the flow of money to terrorists. This team was in the Treasury Department, under the Customs agency, and expanded an already existing team devoted to other financial crimes. As a result of the decades-long war against drugs, the government had in place the expertise for tracking money flows. Expanding this capacity was a critical but incremental step in the war on terrorism.[51]

**Protection:** Consular Services, an agency of the U.S. government found in the State Department, represents the first step in protecting our borders from unwanted individuals. The former head of the Bureau of Consular Affairs, Mary Ryan, told a Senate committee that "… consular affairs in American embassies and consulates could have stopped some of the terrorists from entering the country if agencies such as the CIA and FBI shared more information with the State Department."[52] A relatively inexpensive incremental step would be to immediately grant consular officials access to international crime and terrorist databases.

Another example of an incremental protection step that could be taken immediately would be to deputize state and local officials so that they can arrest illegal aliens, a process that is now reserved only for federal officers. The contribution to fighting terror would be immediate and obviously important. In his prior position, Governor Ridge announced a new warning system, in response to criticisms that the government's warnings on terrorism were inadequate guides to proper action by local police.[53]

Incremental steps can be quite simple and can involve very little formal government. In an op-ed, Graham Allison suggested that the government and the airlines enlist average passengers in the war against terrorists, instructing them in what to look for and what to do if a terrorist should get on the plane. The model he cites is the safety procedure card that the Federal Aviation Administration requires be placed in every passenger seat pocket.[54] Making everyone more aware and more observant is bound to save lives, especially against something as difficult to detect as terrorism.

**Response:** The government can require all medium- to large-sized American cities to invest in the "all hazard" approach to emergency response.[55] Because New York City is such a potent symbol and because it had experienced an earlier, potentially devastating terrorist attack on the

World Trade Center in 1993, former Mayor Rudolph Giuliani invested in the all-hazard approach. This involved preparing "… first responders—firefighters, police officers, EMTs, and other medical personnel first on the scene—to respond to terrorism the same way they'd respond to other disasters, such as floods, hurricanes, toxic spills, plane crashes, and fires."[56] The federal government has many ways of forcing states and localities to do what it wants. An effective, if unpopular, method is to tie a goal—in this case emergency preparedness—to some source of federal funding (highways are always a reliable option). A more popular approach is to appropriate money to help the state and/or locality achieve its goal.

And, a simple but critical action is to increase the amount of drugs available for the civilian population in case of a bioterrorist attack. Like many incremental changes, this involves new money but money that would be well spent.

## Using Reinvented Government

Reforms in the reinvented government category tend to be more fundamental and thus more difficult than incremental reforms. They often involve changing the entire orientation of an organization, beginning with its legal context and moving on to the culture in which it operates. Many of the ideas that fall into this category existed before the attacks of September 11 made homeland security a front-page topic. They are summarized in Table 4.3.

**Prevention:** When the Cold War ended, it became clear that American intelligence had to be rethought and reorganized. Critiques of the intelligence agencies, especially the CIA, have fallen into two broad categories—corresponding, not coincidentally, to the division of the CIA into a directorate of intelligence and a directorate of operations. As John E. McLaughlin, deputy director of the CIA, pointed out, the days are gone when the CIA could employ a "canned goods analyst," someone whose entire job was to understand the food processing industry of the Soviet Union.[57] Well before September 11 the CIA had downsized the Soviet office within the directorate of intelligence and had moved considerable resources to the new Office of Transnational Issues, which dealt with the cross-border nature of many emerging threats.

In a prescient book that predated the September 11 terrorist attacks by a full year, Bruce D. Berkowitz and Allan E. Goodman create a prescription for the post-cold-war intelligence world whose reforms are much more fundamental and far reaching than the mere moving of resources from one part of the organization to the other: "The intelligence community is a classic bureaucracy, characterized by centralized planning, routinized operations, and a hierarchical chain of command. All of these features leave the intelligence organization ill suited for the Information Age."[58] The bureaucratic organization of the intelligence community worked well

**Table 4.3: Examples of Reinvented Government to Achieve Homeland Security**

| Prevention | Protection | Response |
|---|---|---|
| Reinvent the intelligence agencies. | Create a new border patrol agency. | |
| Reinvent the traditional relationship between foreign intelligence and domestic law enforcement. | Develop new technologies for speedier movement of goods and people across borders. | |
| Create an entity responsible for analyzing foreign and domestic intelligence to look for terrorism. | Resurrect the international trade data systems plan.  Establish guidelines for use of racial profiling. | |

when the enemy it tracked, the Soviet Union, was also a bureaucracy and one that, in spite of its secrecy, moved in glacial and often predictable ways. But to keep up with the nonstate basis of new threats such as terrorism and the enormous changes in capacity resulting from the information revolution, Berkowitz and Goodman propose a radical "reinvention" (my term, not theirs) of the CIA.

The changes that would follow from their analysis are certainly not incremental. For instance, they challenge the need for secrecy in the gathering of intelligence as oddly out of step with the Information Age, which the intelligence community itself helped create. They also challenge the culture that reinforces compartmentalization and isolates analysts from each other and from the customers of their intelligence—policy makers.

A second critique of the intelligence agencies has focused on the tendency to rely on "signit" (signal intelligence from satellite eavesdropping, etc.) at the expense of "humit" (human intelligence, or good old-fashioned spies). According to some former CIA operatives such as Robert Baer, beginning in the late 1980s the CIA failed to replace the Middle East experts who were leaving. By the end of the 1990s we had very few or no operatives capable of penetrating the terrorist movements that had become so dangerous.[59] In addition, when it came to light that a paid informant had been involved in the murder of two people, one an American, the CIA director ordered a directive that came to be known as the "scrub" order. According to some, this review of recruits, issued with the best of intentions, had a chilling effect on the spy business—one that, in conjunction with the short-age of Arabic language experts, further impeded our ability to find out what was going on in the world.[60]

It is not at all clear that correcting any of the intelligence failures evident to many before September 11 would have prevented the attacks. In recent hearings before Congress, former CIA officer Milt Bearden pointed out that no one else in the world saw the attacks coming and that infiltrating terror-ist cells where everyone is related to everyone else is an inherently difficult task.[61] But previous intelligence failures, such as the failure to predict nuclear testing in India in 1998, and the demoralizing Aldrich Ames case, were warnings that the intelligence community needed to rethink its post-Cold War routines.

In addition to reinvention at the CIA is the need for reinvention at the FBI as well as reinvention of the relationship between the two agencies. The separation of intelligence between the FBI and the CIA resulted from the excesses of the Hoover-era FBI, which routinely kept files on political dissi-dents and peaceful protest groups. In the aftermath of September 11 it became clear that terrorism did not fall neatly within the bureaucratic and jurisdictional lines of either the CIA or the FBI and that changes needed to be made if the government was to prevent future attacks.

Most conversation about the future of the FBI revolves around chang-ing the culture of the organization from one focused on seeking indict-ments and convictions of criminals—acting after the fact—to one that could prevent criminal activity of the terrorist type—before the fact.[62] Of the governmental changes that are most difficult, changing the culture of an organization ranks at the very top. Changing the law is the first and often most important step. An important first step came shortly after September 11 with passage of the U.S.A. Patriot Act of 2001, which made it easier for the FBI and the CIA to share more sensitive information with each other.

But legal reform is only the beginning of what must be an ongoing effort to transform two very different and sometimes hostile agencies into a coherent and effective preventive force. In the past, the two agencies have been quite competent and cooperative when the source of the threat was known well enough that information collected overseas could be passed neatly from a foreign agency to domestic law enforcement. Prevention, though, requires a much more fundamental assessment of foreign and domestic intelligence. It requires ongoing and systematic analysis of both foreign and domestic data bits and an organization that can weave them into a coherent picture.

How should the government reinvent itself to undertake this chore? The emergence of terrorism as a top-level problem has not gotten rid of the need to prosecute less dramatic crimes or the need to collect more conventional kinds of intelligence. And even the generally noncontroversial elements of the U.S.A. Patriot Act have civil libertarians worried. The episodic nature of terrorism is likely to mean that ongoing attention to it will wax and wane. Thus, one option is to create an entity whose sole mission is to look for pieces to the terrorism puzzle, from Buffalo to Baghdad. One suggestion that came from a Harvard University executive session on catastrophic terrorism, held three years before the September 11 tragedy, bears repeating today. The idea was to create a national terrorism intelligence center in the FBI. As a separate organization this entity would:

> … combine the proactive intelligence gathering approach of the national security agencies, which are not legally constrained in deciding when they may investigate a possible crime, with the investigative resources of law enforcement agencies. We must have an entity that can utilize our formidable but disparate national security and law enforcement resources to analyze transnational problems. This combination should be permitted, consistent with public trust, only in a National Center that has no powers of arrest and prosecution and that establishes a certain distance from the traditional defense and intelligence agencies. The Center would also be subject to oversight from existing institutions, like the federal judiciary, the President's Foreign Intelligence Advisory Board and the select intelligence committees of the Congress.[63]

**Protection:** The first and most important priority to consider is increasing protection at the borders. The government should explore an idea that has been around for many years, creating a border patrol agency. Protection of the borders should begin outside the United States, with the agency charged with allowing people into the country. Visas are required for entry into the United States. Visas are given out at our embassies around the world where overworked consular officers, generally young diplomats trained in diplomacy rather than police work, are given the responsibility of deciding who gets to come to America and who doesn't. In recent years consular officers have been under extreme stress. The number of people wanting to come to the United States has increased dramatically, and the Congress has starved the entire State Department, including the consular corps, of funds. According to former State Department official T. Wayne Merry, "… visa work is a low-prestige poor relation to the conduct of diplomacy and always low in budget priorities. The professional consular corps is often highly competent but is badly overworked, under financed, and so few in number as to staff only supervisory positions."[64]

The first step in creating a new agency is to upgrade Consular Affairs and turn it into an agency that has the intelligence and the resources to weed out dangerous people before they even get to the United States. It should be moved out of the State Department and formed into a corps of people who combine the unique blend of diplomatic, language, and detective skills needed to detect dangerous people before they leave their countries.

The second step is to tackle the enormous problem of securing our borders against terrorists and weapons of terror while maintaining our participation in a global economy. Historically we have separated protection of the borders into two bureaucracies. One agency, Customs, is supposed to protect us against bad things; the other, the Immigration and Naturalization Service (INS), is supposed to protect us against bad people. This bureaucratic bifurcation has never worked very well. The two agencies have often feuded at the borders, even going so far as to have separate and hostile canine crews!

As international trade and travel have grown, the pressures on these two agencies have only increased. On June 29, 1995, a melee erupted at the Miami International Airport involving passengers frustrated by three-hour-long waits to get through customs and immigration checks. Long before September 11 there were calls for the creation of a border patrol agency that would combine the two services and improve the functions of the U.S. government at the borders. But this idea has been consistently fought by the agencies themselves, their congressional sponsors, and whatever attorney general and treasury secretary happen to be in charge at the time. In 1993, a proposal to create a border patrol agency created such intense division within the Clinton administration and opposition from the attorney general and treasury secretary that it was watered down to read, in the final National Performance Review report, "Improve Border Management."[65]

Protection of the borders is a core element in homeland security. What was not politically possible before September 11 will still be politically difficult but should not be impossible, for now the case is stronger than ever. For instance, Stephen E. Flynn has written persuasively of "terrorist needles in a transportation haystack." "In 2000 alone," he explained, "489 million people, 127 million passenger vehicles, 11.6 million maritime containers, 11.5 million trucks, 2.2 million railcars, 829,000 planes, and 211,000 vessels passed through U.S. border inspection systems."[66]

Problems of a similar scale exist on the people side, where international travel has increased dramatically and where the agency in charge has been plagued by decades of difficulties. In the past decade, the INS has been in one crisis after another. Globalization of the economy, cheaper air travel, etc., have meant a huge increase in the number of foreigners to the U.S.—from fiscal years 1981 to 1998 the number of annual admissions of visitors with visas nearly tripled to 30 million.[67] The INS has been unusually slow to adapt, leading two members of Congress to call it "the most dysfunctional agency in all of government," a sentiment echoed by anyone who has ever had anything to do with the agency. Unlike the Bureau of Consular Affairs, the problems of the INS cannot be blamed on lack of money because Congress has consistently increased their funding in recent years. In spite of this, they process applications by hand, having inexplicably failed to implement the electronic systems that would help them. When they do buy new systems such as their anti-smuggling electronic systems, they fail to train employees to use them. They can't keep track of their weapons or their property.

Failure on the part of the INS is not new. During the Iranian hostage crisis in 1979, the INS was able to track down only 9,000 of the 50,000 Iranian students in the United States. In 1993, the INS had no idea that Jordanian Eyad Ismoil had violated his student visa until he drove a bomb-laden truck into the World Trade Center. It is well known that the INS does not do a very good job of getting people out of the country who have overstayed their visas. The INS estimates that 40 percent of all illegal immigrants are people who come to the U.S. with visas but don't leave when the visas expire.[68] Of the hundreds of people who have been detained as suspects in the weeks since the September 11 attacks, most are being held on immigration charges. The agency reported recently that a computer network to track foreign students in the country was still being tested and wouldn't be ready for another year even though Congress had ordered it six years ago![69]

In its 2002 budget the Bush administration proposed splitting the agency into two parts, a good and long overdue idea. As this report was being written the House passed a bill to accomplish the split, and the attorney general, echoing President Clinton's famous pledge to "end welfare as we know it," vowed to "end the INS as we know it."[70] The naturalization service, which makes legal immigrants into citizens, should be kept in the Justice Department and transformed into an agency respectful of those wanting to become Americans. But the border patrol officials should be moved to a new agency where, like consular officials, they have access to real-time intelligence about who is entering the U.S. and why. As it now stands, border patrol agents are cut off from real-time intelligence, overworked, and ill prepared to stop potentially dangerous people from entering the country. Efforts to improve the technology of the agency fail, inexplicably, to materialize. We cannot preempt terrorists with the current organization.

During the Clinton administration a plan emerged to create an international trade data system. But it was killed by a combination of vested interests. One reason for its demise was the increased transparency it would give to the vast array of goods crossing American borders.[71] This plan should be reviewed, and possibly revived, in the post–September 11 world.

Finally, there is no tougher issue in American politics than racial profiling. Yet when terrorism originates in and is sponsored by certain identifiable nationalities, being forced to ignore ethnicity in protecting the borders becomes absurd. There needs to be a process whereby racial profiling is allowed, for instance, where intelligence and other tips indicate that doing so would contribute to the protection of the public. This is part and parcel of moving law enforcement away from acting after the fact to becoming part of protecting Americans by preempting terrorist acts. Penalties exacted after the fact could serve as a sufficient deterrent for using profiling to harass innocent Americans. The fact remains that either this issue must be grappled with, or it will impinge on our security or our liberty, or both.

## Using Public Sector Networks

Compared to other countries, America has a decentralized government. Most of American history has involved some form of discussion about federalism—the proper relationship between the national government, the state governments, and local governments—and deep suspicion of centralized government. Homeland security starts that conversation again. The sheer number of jurisdictions, laws, regulations, and operating protocols that makes up the American federal system is designed to defy control by any one entity, which is exactly what Americans have always wanted. So how do you improve homeland security in a system that is intentionally, indeed, passionately, decentralized? Here's where the concept of government by network, applied to the vast system of American governmental jurisdictions, comes in handy. Table 4.4 shows how this concept might help us think through the prevention, protection, and response categories.

**Prevention:** Take the issue of national identification, a problem critical to preventing terrorism. Among the many holes in our domestic defense is

**Table 4.4: Examples of Public Sector Networks to Achieve Homeland Security**

| Prevention | Protection | Response |
|---|---|---|
| Modernize the states' identification (driver's licenses) system. | Create a network among the FBI and state and local law enforcement, which would permit sharing of information on terrorist threats. | Adapt the CINC model with FEMA as the lead agency in charge of training, gaming, and command. |

the fact that we have a very lax system of acquiring identification cards, namely driver's licenses. In fact, as Shane Ham and Robert D. Atkinson point out, most American teenagers possess a fake ID in order to drink alcohol. The practice is so common as to be almost a rite of passage.[72] One solution proposed to the problem is to issue a national identification card. This would require a new, federal bureaucracy, another layer on top of existing state bureaucracies. It would also invoke images of big brother and likely would be almost as unpopular today as it has been in the past.

In contrast to creating an entirely new identification system, Ham and Atkinson propose creating a public sector network (my term, not theirs). The proposal would modernize the current system by having Congress issue guidelines and provide appropriations for standardizing driver's licenses. They propose that Congress require states to issue "smart ID cards" which contain "… a standardized hologram and digitally encoded biometric data specific to each holder."[73] In addition, they recommend that Congress set higher standards for documentation before issuing identification cards such as driver's licenses and that Congress provide funds for linking states' department of motor vehicle databases: "This would virtually eliminate the practice of ID poaching, and if tied in with a smart visa proposal, would prevent foreign visitors from obtaining driver's licenses and then hiding out in the United States after the visas expire."[74]

Thinking nationally about the problem of identification builds on the federalist system by using national power and federal money to form a network of state motor vehicle departments. While the proposal would cost more, it would not cost as much as the creation of a brand-new bureaucracy, nor would it cause the inevitable opposition that comes with the accretion of centralized powers in a decentralized state. And, it would surely increase security and help prevent terrorists from getting the legitimacy they need to operate in this system.

Forging a network like the one proposed by Ham and Atkinson has other advantages. Tighter security around driver's licenses would probably reduce the number of accidents due to teenagers driving drunk, and it would make the crime of identity theft even more difficult. Because terrorism is apt to be a sporadic and intermittent threat, when reforms are made that offer other, nonterrorist-related advantages to the society, they should be emphasized and promoted in order to secure continued political and budgetary support. That will keep existing reforms from withering on the vine—a particular problem in a society where memories are short and news cycles and political attention are even shorter.

**Protection:** Since September 11, long-simmering anger by local law enforcement toward the FBI for its traditional reluctance to share information with state and local law enforcement has come to the surface.[75] Shortly after September 11, we learned that the FBI did not share information about suspected terrorists with Michael Chitwood, chief of police of Portland, Maine, the origination point for the Logan Airport–bound hijackers. New York City officials were particularly upset by two recent episodes: They were not told about anthrax-containing letters, and they were not told about a nuclear threat to their city. The Schumer-Clinton bill (S.R. 1615), sponsored by the two senators from New York State, would permit, but not require, the FBI to share information about potential terrorist attacks with state and local police forces. It is a necessary step in creating what should be a comprehensive network of law enforcement agencies designed to improve information sharing between federal and local law enforcement agencies.

**Response:** The immediate response to terrorist acts (or any catastrophic events, for that matter) also involves all levels of government because the first people on the scene are always local police, firefighters, and medics. In the case of a bioterrorist attack, the definition of first responders, which was developed from more traditional catastrophes like fires and earthquakes, would have to change. First responders in a bioterrorist attack would very likely be nurses, doctors, and lab technicians. Only recently have we begun to consider that public health is part of national security. In terrorism-related budgets prior to September 11, the bulk of the money went to law enforcement and defense, with public health the poor relative. As the confusion around the anthrax attack in the fall of 2001 proved, the U.S. government is not equipped to respond to bioterrorist attacks. In a role-playing episode at the end of the 1990s, the Defense Department (DoD) declared the right to seize command during a bioterrorist attack.[76] Constitutional issues aside, although DoD has many capabilities, expertise in disease and contagion is not among them.

In preparing for the future and for the need to respond to totally new and unexpected forms of terror, the United States needs to build response networks that involve all levels of government and have practiced reactions to scenarios that can only be imagined. Identifying the spread of a rare disease such as smallpox on a national level, tracking its progress, acquiring and moving stocks of vaccine, communicating with the public, placing affected people in quarantine, restricting travel—the list of steps to be taken and the confusion that would result from missed steps are of nightmarish proportions. The only way to prepare is the way the military prepares: practice, practice, and more practice. But the number of entities involved is huge and each one has other, important, day-to-day responsibilities to the public. They must be rehearsed and molded into a network that, when needed, can operate as one entity.

How to do that? Right before the September 11 attacks, Lieutenant Colonel Terrence Kelly published an article in which he suggested borrowing a concept from the military—the commander in chief (CINC)—for homeland security.[77] The last major reorganization of the U.S. military dealt with the traditional divisions (and rivalries) among the services and the need to make these historically separate bureaucracies into a coherent force in battle. As a result, the regional CINC command structure in the Defense Department gives one person the power and authority to plan for and then, if necessary, command the assets of the various branches of the military (air force, marines, navy, army, etc.). Kelly was suggesting the CINC concept for a homeland security agency, a version of the coordination option discussed above but with more teeth. However, the CINC option has even more utility when applied to the need for coherent response.

FEMA should be given more resources and the formal authority to act as CINC in preparing and coordinating federal, state, and local governments to respond to all kinds of terrorist events. A modest start in that direction was made in President Bush's homeland security budget with $3.5 billion out of the $37.7 billion allotted to first responders and FEMA given responsibility for coordinating training and response.[78] But given the complexity of the task at hand, an agency (and FEMA is the most likely candidate) needs to have the resources and the authority to force other federal agencies such as the Centers for Disease Control and state and local governments into an effective response network. As the simulation known as Dark Winter proved, a smallpox attack can cause massive confusion and death.[79] In that exercise, the sticky issue of federalism arose. Former Senator Sam Nunn, who played the U.S. president in the exercise, said, "We're going to have absolute chaos if we start having war between the federal government and the state government."[80]

The sooner a CINC-like authority is vested in FEMA, the better. The creation of a first-rate response network will also fulfill an important criterion of homeland security reform mentioned above. Improving the coordination of responses to terror will improve the coordination of responses to all sorts of catastrophes, whether or not they are the result of terrorist acts. In the 1990s, FEMA went through one of the largest agency transformations in recent history. When the Clinton administration came in, several bills were pending in Congress to abolish FEMA. Thus, it became an early candidate for the Clinton/Gore reinvention efforts and, under the leadership of James Lee Witt, went from a disaster itself to a government agency that elicited applause from the public after the Northridge earthquake in California. Organizationally, FEMA is prepared for the task, but it needs a clearer mandate, both inside and outside the federal government.

(**Editor's note:** *FEMA was included in the new Department of Homeland Security as part of its Directorate of Emergency Preparedness and Response.*)

## Using Public and Private Sector Networks

As we have seen, government by network is an important concept for building greater security in a fragmented federalist system. It is an equally important concept for involving the private sector in homeland security. Table 4.5 gives some examples of how the government could go about creating networks of public and private sector institutions that would increase security.

**Prevention:** The private sector has pioneered the use of "data mining," the process of analyzing large databases to construct information, usually about sales or about market trends, that is not immediately evident from the raw data alone. This is an expensive and carefully guarded process, but it could potentially allow the government to find clues important to its mission of preventing terrorism. An early example of the use of data mining in terrorism comes from West Germany in the 1970s. A law enforcement officer named Horst Herold helped with a major breakthrough against the terrorists known as the Red Army Faction. By mining travel company, utility, and even pension-fund databases to create prescient profiles of where the terrorists were and how they behaved, Herold turned the West German federal crime office into an "unparalleled crime fighting machine."[81]

His efforts, however, were not without controversy because significant proprietary issues and privacy issues arose as a result of his breakthroughs, and the West German system he created was eventually dismantled. An important caveat to the use of data mining applies to all examples of the government by network method: When the government establishes a network involving the private sector to help do public business, it needs to protect privacy and property. These issues need to be negotiated carefully and their implementation needs to be monitored carefully. Government by net-

**Table 4.5: Examples of Public and Private Sector Networks to Achieve Homeland Security**

| Prevention | Protection | Response |
|---|---|---|
| Create a network with the private sector that would utilize modern data-mining techniques. | Create a network for protection of critical infrastructure.<br><br>Create a small agency based on the DARPA model to innovate in homeland security technology. | Develop plans for surge capacity in the public and private health-care sectors.<br><br>Create a network of emergency response teams, medical leaders, and broadcast journalists for cases of bioterrorist attacks. |

work survives ultimately on trust—trust that the public's privacy, market information, and other intellectual property of the business sector all will be protected.

**Protection:** Nowhere is this difficulty more evident than in the need to protect America's information systems from cyber attack. In May 1998, the Clinton administration issued Presidential Decision Directive 63 (PDD) on Critical Infrastructure Protection, acknowledging a new source of vulnerability to asymmetric warfare resulting from increasing U.S. reliance on cyber-based systems to operate every part of our economy. The directive created the National Infrastructure Protection Center (NIPC) in the FBI. The problem, however, has proved to be typical of many 21st-century problems in that solving it involves significant, regular cooperation from the private sector.

But the private sector has been exceedingly reluctant to cooperate. In a survey conducted by the Computer Security Institute in April 2002, 94 percent of the respondents reported having detected security breaches of their information systems in the previous 12 months, but only 34 percent reported the intrusions to law enforcement (an improvement over the 16 percent who had reported intrusions to law enforcement in 1996).[82] The lack of reporting stems from fears that the government will not adequately protect the customers or the proprietary information of private companies. This lack of trust is having, and will continue to have, severe consequences for the ability of law enforcement to protect us from cyber attacks. Senator Bob Bennett, a Utah Republican, is the sponsor of the Critical Infrastructure Information Act of 2001. According to Bennett, trying to devise a protection plan for the Internet without candid information is like "trying to run a battle, when 85 percent of the battlefield is blind to you."[83]

Thus, the network concept becomes increasingly important. For government to do its job, it must create a network in the private sector that will allow it to learn what it needs to know to deter, detect, and prosecute crime. As in the case of data mining, creating such a network for cyber security is fraught with concerns for privacy and for property protection. Nevertheless, earlier generations worked out protocols for wiretaps on telephones that served the country well while, on the whole, protecting civil liberties. The new imperative is to develop similar protocols that will allow the government to use the data in the vast databases of the private sector, including data about cyber crime, to protect us from terrorists.

As has been clear throughout this chapter, effective homeland security will require the development of many new technologies. As our experience in developing weapons over many decades has shown, innovation in technology cannot be limited to the public sector. The Soviet Union tried that and lost. William Bonvillian and Kendra Sharp have proposed creating a Defense Advanced Research Projects Agency (DARPA) for homeland security technology.[84] DARPA, best known to the public as the creator of the

Internet, is one of the most successful technology development agencies in history. Critical to the success of DARPA is the fact that government uses its money and power to enlist all manner of actors—from universities to the private sector—in the innovation process. It was once referred to as "75 geniuses connected by a travel agent," which is what is required today.[85]

**Response:** Recent trends in medicine have resulted in less capacity to deal with a surge in demand for serious medical care than ever before.[86] Innovations such as just-in-time inventory systems for equipment and drugs and the increase in outpatient care, as drug therapy has replaced surgery and hospitalization for some illnesses, mean that the U.S. does not have the infrastructure to deal with mass injuries. The absence of "surge capacity" is serious when contemplating a high number of injuries resulting from a terrorist attack involving explosives. The absence becomes even more dangerous when contemplating the number needing medical care that could arise from a bioterrorist attack, in which everything from sterile equipment and clothing to isolation wards would run out almost instantly.

It is unrealistic to expect an overburdened, increasingly expensive private health-care system to develop and maintain the capacity to treat massive numbers of victims of something like a terrorist attack. However, it is not unrealistic to expect the government to lead the private sector in developing a plan whereby the location of medical supplies, plans for their delivery, and locations for makeshift hospital beds and isolation wards would be identified ahead of time. In other words, working with both the private and the public health-care sectors, the government could create a network in every major metropolitan area that would be dedicated to the instantaneous creation of emergency hospitals. In the immediate aftermath of the attack on the World Trade Center on September 11, an emergency medical unit was set up downtown and access to Manhattan was cut off to everyone except medical personnel who knew to come into the city. This had been practiced and planned because former New York City Mayor Giuliani acted on the warning provided by the World Trade Center bombing in 1993.

Also important to the response effort are the media. For days after the September 11 attacks, most Americans were glued to their televisions. Especially in the case of a bioterrorist attack, the media have a role to play in conveying useful information and preventing panic. Dr. Matt Meselsen, an eminent biologist and expert on bioterrorism at Harvard University, pointed out that we should start thinking about a bioterrorist attack by "thinking small."[87] Creating a list of the small things that people could do to avoid spreading disease, and then working with national and local media to educate people on the likely course of a bioterrorist attack, could both save lives and prevent the panic that is often a goal of terrorists.

The importance of effective communication in responding to a terrorist attack, especially a bioterrorist attack, was emphasized by former Senator

Sam Nunn after participating in the recent Dark Winter simulation of a smallpox attack. Testifying before Congress on the lessons learned he said:

> "How do you talk to the public in a way that is candid, yet prevents panic—knowing that panic itself can be a weapon of mass destruction?" My staff had two responses: "We don't know," and "You're late for your press conference." I told people in the exercise, "I would never go before the press with this little information." And Governor Keating, who knows about dealing with disaster, said "You have no choice." And I went, even though I did not have answers for the questions I knew I would face.[88]

In the case of bioterrorism, the president of the United States of course must know what to do, but more than any politician, the public will need to hear from trained medical personnel who have useful, simple words of advice for a panic-stricken, confused public.

### Using Government by Market

Of the models of 21st-century government discussed in this chapter, government by market is perhaps the most powerful and the most difficult to use. Some examples of its use are listed in Table 4.6. Government by market is powerful because it allows for infinite innovation in accomplishing the public goals. But it does require the political will to establish the goals in the first place.

**Prevention:** For instance, since September 11 many people have commented on the fact that we have paid a price in our foreign policy for our excessive dependence on fossil fuels. Our cautious relations with Saudi Arabia, home of the vast majority of the September 11 hijackers and funding source of much of al Qaeda, have been shaped by our appetite for their oil.

**Table 4.6: Examples of Government by Market to Achieve Homeland Security**

| Prevention | Protection | Response |
|---|---|---|
| Create markets that reduce dependence on fossil fuels in order to make the United States less dependent on foreign oil. | | Create economic incentives for research into vaccines or treatments against bio-terror threats. |

At some point, we as a nation may conclude that we have paid too high a price for our dependence on foreign oil. Putting aside the serious environmental consequences of increasing domestic production to replace foreign production—increasing domestic production when there is a finite amount of domestic oil is simply not a decent long-term solution. But whether for environmental reasons or foreign policy reasons, we may decide to get serious about weaning our economy from fossil fuels.

Here is where government by market comes in. To wean the economy from fossil fuels without wrecking it, the government will have to create a sophisticated market that subsidizes the use of alternative energy sources and discourages the use of fossil fuels until technological progress moves us away from fossil fuels altogether. Market thinking on this question has not been limited to one end of the political spectrum. People as different as former Vice President Al Gore and conservative economist Martin Feldstein have thought in terms of government by market. In the summer of his 2000 presidential campaign, Al Gore proposed an energy plan that consisted of a series of tax incentives for the use of nonfossil fuels. These incentives, the largest of which was a tax credit for purchasing new hybrid-fuel automobiles, were intended to stimulate the market in alternative energy and technologies. The tax credits were also intended to phase out over a period of 10 years. Martin Feldstein has proposed a system of tradable oil conservation vouchers modeled on the successful experiment with tradable permits to reduce sulfur dioxide emissions.[89] The vouchers could be traded among households, encouraging the use of public transportation and fuel-efficient cars by those seeking to sell their vouchers and creating an extra cost for those who continue to drive sport-utility vehicles.

The advantage of government by market is that it would allow for millions of adaptations and encourage enormous amounts of innovation *if* the government had the will to set the serious national goal of reducing fossil fuel use.

**Response:** Government by market is a very efficient way of stimulating innovation. Right now, as Bonvillian and Sharp point out, with regard to our response to bioterrorism there is "… zero market incentive to develop effective vaccines or treatments for bioterror attacks."[90] We will need to develop new drugs and explore the use of existing drugs in response to a wide variety of biochemical terrorist agents. While research grants and other government-led activities may accomplish some of this, in the long run we must enlist the research capacities of the entire pharmaceutical industry. How? There are plenty of market incentives to develop drugs for breast cancer or the common cold. There are precious few incentives to develop drugs for diseases that may never appear. Thus, the government needs to explore creating some kind of a market incentive that would encourage the pharmaceutical industry to devote at least some research to this problem. Many possible options, from tax breaks to patent extensions, could be put together to create a market where none currently exists.

# Conclusion

Homeland security is the first new challenge for 21st-century government. It is not, as we have seen, a challenge that lends itself only to the creation of a new bureaucracy, nor is it the kind of challenge that can be met effectively by one man or woman sitting in the White House coordinating the government. Instead, we need to think about homeland security as a problem that knows no borders and that crosses every aspect of society and every part of every government. That means looking beyond bureaucracy to new forms of policy implementation—from reinvented governments to government by network to government by market—which can help create effective prevention, protection, and response.

We can hope that terrorism will not be a permanent feature of American life. But we don't know that and thus we must be ready. Even if it is not, we should recognize that many of the reforms we might make for purposes of preventing, protecting against, or responding to terrorism have a dual use. Many of the ideas presented here (and many others, which will doubtless emerge as this debate goes on) will bring other societal benefits. Some of the improvements we can make to help us respond to a terrorist attack— from clarifying FEMA's authority to creating networks to allow for surge capacity in our hospital systems—will be invaluable in responding to other catastrophes, whether accidental or natural. Strengthening both our borders and the ability of our law enforcement agencies to work with intelligence agencies across borders will pay enormous dividends in the war against drugs, even if we never experience another attack. And improving our system of national identification cards will prevent the premature deaths of some teenagers even if we manage to catch every terrorist before he or she obtains a fake ID.

If we start with the assumption that new threats require new organizational forms, and then adapt those forms to parts of the problem, we can build a safer society and minimize our loss of freedom. This strategy begins by recognizing that the problems of the 21st century will not fit into the organizational model of the 20th century, the bureaucracy. Homeland security is only one of those problems. To meet the new problems of a new century, we will have to continually redesign the government.

# Endnotes

1. Joseph S. Nye, David C. King, Phillip D. Zelikow, eds., *Why People Don't Trust Government* (Cambridge, Mass.: Harvard University Press, 1997).

2. Ibid.

3. Pippa Norris, ed., *Critical Citizens, Global Support for Democratic Governance* (Oxford: Oxford University Press, 1999).

4. Gary Langer, "Water's Edge: Greater Trust in Government Limited to National Security," ABC News (January 15, 2002), http://more.abcnews.go.com/sections/politics/ Daily News/poll/0120115.html.

5. See Salvatore Schiavo-Campo, Giulio de Tommaso, and Amitabha Mukherjee, "An International Statistical Survey of Government Employment and Wages," in Public Sector Management and Information Technology team/Technical Department for Europe, Central Asia, Middle East, and North Africa, World Bank Policy Research Working Paper 1771 (August 31, 1997). While admitting the methodological difficulties of comparing size of government across the globe, they conclude, nevertheless, that "a large contraction in both central government employment (relative to population) and the relative wage bill is evident in all regions, with the relative size of central government shrinking by about one-third when measured by employment and one-fourth when measured by the wage bill ...," p. 9.

6. See, for instance, the story of Governor Orriciro dos Santos of Brazil in "Fiscal Prudence Goes Local," *The Economist* (March 10, 2001), p. 35.

7. Following a report that two-thirds of the state-run firms had cooked the books and reported billions in fake profits, Zhu Rongji promised to shut down loss-making enterprises and sell off others. "China's Confident Bow," *The Economist* (March 10, 2001), p. 37.

8. For instance, a variety of social ills, from teen pregnancy to drug addiction, turned out to be highly correlated with each other and yet government programs tended to treat one pathology at a time. Homelessness was a problem that turned out to be more about mental health than housing, yet the first programs to deal with the problem were placed in the Department of Housing and Urban Development. Welfare dependency often turned out to be about transportation and the physical isolation of the poor from jobs, yet state and federal transportation agencies rarely saw this as their mission.

9. See Robert O. Keohane and Joseph S. Nye, Jr., "Introduction" in *Governance in a Globalizing World,* Joseph S. Nye and John D. Donahue, eds. (Washington, D.C.: Brookings, 2000).

10. See, for instance, B. Guy Peters and John Pierre, "Governance without Government? Rethinking Public Administration," *Journal of Public Administration Research and Theory* (April 1998).

11. David Osborne and Ted A. Gaebler, *Reinventing Government: How the Entrepreneurial Spirit Is Transforming the Public Sector* (New York: Perseus, 1991).

12. As various scholars attempt to categorize what is going on in the postbureaucratic state, they have used a variety of terms. For instance, what I describe here as reinvented government, others have described as "market-type bureaucracies." See Mark Considine and Jenny M. Lewis, "Governance at Ground Level: The Frontline Bureaucrat in the Age of Markets and Networks," *Public Administration Review,* Vol. 59, No. 6 (November/ December 1999).

13. David Osborne and Peter Plastrick, *Banishing Bureaucracy: The Five Strategies for Reinventing Government* (Reading, Mass.: Addison-Wesley, 1997), p. 25.

14. Statement of J. Christopher Mihm, acting associate director, Federal Management and Workforce Issues, in U.S. General Accounting Office, *Performance Based*

*Organizations: Lessons from the British Next Steps Initiative,* GAO/T-GGD-97-151 (Washington, D.C., July 8, 1997).

15. Ibid., p. 6.

16. Johnathan Boston, John Martin, June Pallot, and Pat Walsh, *Public Management: The New Zealand Model* (Auckland: Oxford University Press, 1996).

17. Ibid., p. 5.

18. See Tim Irwin, "An Analysis of New Zealand's New System of Public Sector Management," in *Public Management in Government: Contemporary Illustrations,* OECD Occasional Papers, No. 9 (Paris: OECD, 1996).

19. Conversation between Mayor Rendell and the author, May 1991.

20. See Michael Barzelay, *Breaking Through Bureaucracy* (Berkeley, Calif.: University of California Press, 1992).

21. See, for instance, Linda de Leon and Robert B. Denhardt, "The Political Theory of Reinvention," *Public Administration Review* (March/April 2000) in which they comment, "The 'shadow' side of the entrepreneur is characterized by a narrow focus, an unwillingness to follow rules and stay within bounds...," p. 92.

22. Considine and Lewis, op. cit., p. 475.

23. See, for instance, Paul Sabatier and Hank Jenkins-Smith, eds., *Policy Change and Learning: An Advocacy Coalition Approach* (Boulder, Colo.: Westview Publishing, 1993).

24. "The Real New World Order," *Foreign Affairs,* (5) 76 (September/October 1997).

25. "Networks and Governance in Europe and America: Grasping the Normative Nettle," paper prepared for Rethinking Federalism in the EU and the US: The Challenge of Legitimacy, John F. Kennedy School of Government, Harvard University, April 19–21, 1998.

26. H. Brinton Milward and Keith G. Provan, "Governing the Hollow State," *Journal of Public Administration Research and Theory* (April 2000).

27. Ibid., p. 1.

28. One piece of research, based on a comparison of federal law from two points in time, shows no change over time (1965–66 to 1993–94) in the use of non–state actors to implement programs. See Thad E. Hall and Laurence J. O'Toole, Jr., "Structures for Policy Implementation: An Analysis of National Legislation, 1965–1966 and 1993–1994," *Administration and Society,* Vol. 31, No. 6 (January 2000), pp. 667–686. However, a much more exhaustive analysis is needed, one which includes state-level legislation. In addition, the selection of the years 1965–1966, which included passage of much Great Society legislation, could bias the results.

29. See William P. Ryan, "The New Landscape for Nonprofits," *Harvard Business Review* (January-February 1999).

30. Interview with Peter Cove, president, America Works, April 1998.

31. Kenneth J. Meier and Laurence J. O'Toole, Jr., "Managerial Strategies and Behavior in Networks: A Model with Evidence from U.S. Public Education," *Journal of Public Administration Research and Theory* (July 2001), pp. 271–293.

32. "Governing the Hollow State," ibid.

33. Interview with the author, September 27, 2001.

34. *The Future of Governing: Four Emerging Models* (Lawrence, Kansas: University of Kansas Press, 1996), p. 22.

35. By 1987, 10 states, accounting for 25 percent of the nation's population, had passed some form of bottle bill. See www.bottlebill.com.

36. See Robert N. Stavins, "What Can We Learn from the Grand Policy Experiment? Lessons from $SO_2$ Allowance Trading," *Journal of Economic Perspectives,* Vol. 12, No. 3 (Summer 1998), pp. 69–88.

37. Interview with the author on April 26, 2001.

38. Interview with the author on April 20, 1999.

39. See, for instance, Carrie Lips, "'Edupreneurs'—A Survey of For-Profit Education," *Policy Analysis* (Washington, D.C.: Cato Institute, November 20, 2000).

40. Quoted in interview with Katie Couric, *Today Show,* September 24, 2001.

41. Bradley Graham, "McCaffrey, Cohen Settle Drug War Budget Dispute," *Washington Post* (December 13, 1997), p. A13.

42. Alison Mitchell, "Letter to Ridge Is Latest Jab in Fight Over Balance of Powers," *New York Times* (March 5, 2002), p. A8.

43. For an example of the early opposition, see Joel Brinkley and Philip Shenon, "Ridge Meeting Opposition From Agencies," *New York Times* (February 7, 2002), p. A16.

44. *Road Map for National Security: Imperative for Change,* The United States Commission on National Security/21st Century, March 15, 2001.

45. See H.R. 1156 introduced by Congressman Thornberry and S.R. 1534 introduced by Senators Lieberman and Specter.

46. Ibid., p. 16.

47. See Alison Mitchell, "Disputes Erupt on Ridge's Needs for His Job," *New York Times* (November 3, 2001), Section 1B, p. 7.

48. Paul Mann, "Technology Threat Urged Against Mass Weapons," *Aviation Week and Space Technology* (December 4, 2000), p. 64.

49. See Ash Carter, "The Architecture of Government in the Face of Terrorism," *International Security*, Vol. 26, No. 3 (Winter 2001/02), pp. 5–23.

50. See Graham Allison, "We Must Act As If He Has the Bomb," *Washington Post* (November 18, 2001), Outlook Section B.

51. Kathleen Day, "Agents to Track Money," *Washington Post* (October 26, 2001), p. A23.

52. http://www.govexec.com/dailyfed/1001/ 101201b2.htm.

53. Philip Shanon, "Color Coded System Created to Rate Threat of Terrorism," *New York Times* (March 13, 2002), p. A16.

54. Graham T. Allison, "Preventing Terrorism in the Air: A How-To Guide for Nervous Airline Passengers," *Chicago Tribune* (November 20, 2001), Section 1.

55. Lory Hough, "Terrorism in America," *KSG Bulletin* (Cambridge, Mass.: John F. Kennedy School of Government, Harvard University, Autumn 2001), pp. 17–23.

56. Ibid., p. 21.

57. Speech by John E. McLaughlin, April 2, 2001, special to washingtonpost.com/ac2/wp-dyn/A17769-2001mar30?language=printer.

58. Bruce D. Berkowitz and Allan E. Goodman, *Best Truth: Intelligence in the Information Age* (New Haven and London: Yale University Press, 2000), p. 67.

59. Robert Baer, *See No Evil: The True Story of a Ground Soldier in the CIA's War on Terrorism* (New York: Crown Publishers, 2002), p. 95.

60. See Seymour M. Hersh, "What Went Wrong: The CIA and the Failure of American Intelligence," *The New Yorker* (March 18, 2002), pp. 34–42.

61. Steve Hirsch, "CIA Performance Disputed as Congress Plans Hearings," *Global Security Newswire* (April 1, 2002).

62. Dan Eggen and Jim McGee, "FBI Rushed to Remake Its Mission: Counterterrorism Replaces Crime Solving," *Washington Post* (November 12, 2001), p. A1.

63. Ashton B. Carter, John M. Deutch, and Phillip D. Zelikow, "Catastrophic Terrorism: Elements of a National Policy," a report of the Visions of Governance for the 21st Century Project (Cambridge, Mass.: Harvard University, 1998), www.ksg.harvard.edu/visions.

64. W. Wayne Merry, "How Visas Can Perpetrate Terror," *Washington Post* (September 28, 2001), p. A39.

65. Al Gore, *Creating a Government That Works Better and Costs Less: Report of the National Performance Review* (Washington, D.C.: Government Printing Office, September 7, 1993), p. 151.

66. Stephen E. Flynn, "The Unguarded Homeland: A Study in Malign Neglect," in James F. Hoge, Jr., and Gideon Rose eds., *How Did This Happen? Terrorism and the New War* (New York: Public Affairs, 2001), p. 187.

67. Mary Beth Sheridan, "Tougher Enforcement by INS Urged," *Washington Post* (September 18, 2001), p. A15.

68. Ibid.

69. Kate Zernike and Christopher Drew, "Efforts to Track Foreign Students Are Said to Lag," *New York Times* (January 28, 2002), p. A1.

70. CNN, April 25, 2002.

71. See Jane Fountain, *The Virtual State* (Washington, D.C.: Brookings, 2002), for a description of this program and the politics that killed it.

72. Shane Ham and Robert D. Atkinson, "Modernizing the State Identification System: An Action Agenda," *Progressive Policy Institute Policy Report* (Washington, D.C.: Progressive Policy Institute, February 2002).

73. Ibid., p. 1.

74. Ibid., p. 6.

75. Kellie Lunney, "FBI Promises to Share More Information with Local Law Enforcement," www.govexec.com, downloaded November 14, 2001. Michael Cooper, "Officials Say U.S. Should Have Shared Tip," *New York Times* (March 5, 2002), p. A11.

76. Laurie Garrett, "The Nightmare of Bioterrorism," *Foreign Affairs,* Volume 80, No. 1 (January/February, 2001).

77. Terrence Kelly, "An Organizational Framework for Homeland Defense," *Parameters* (Carlisle Barracks, Autumn 2001).

78. Bill Miller, "$37.7 Billion for Homeland Defense Is a Start, Bush Says," *Washington Post* (January 25, 2002), p. A15.

79. Tara O'Toole, Michael Mair, and Thomas V. Inglesby, "Shining Light on 'Dark Winter,'" *Confronting Biological Weapons,* CID 2002:34 (April 2002), pp. 972–983.

80. Ibid., p. 982.

81. Ian Johnson, "Another Autumn: A Top Cop Won Fame and Blame for Profiling in the 1970s—New Terrorist Hunt Recalls 'Red Army' Campaign, Bitter Debate on Privacy —the Fears of 'Glass People,'" *Wall Street Journal* (December 10, 2001), p. A1.

82. "Cyber Crime Bleeds U.S. Corporations, Survey Shows: Financial Losses from Attacks Climb for Third Year in a Row," press release, April 7, 2002, the Cyber Security Institute, San Francisco, Calif.

83. Matt Richtel, "New Economy," *New York Times* (December 3, 2001).

84. William Bonvillian and Kendra V. Sharp, "Homeland Security Technology," *Issues in Science and Technology,* Vol. 18, No. 2 (Washington: Winter 2001/2002), p. 43.

85. Ibid.

86. See, for instance, Joseph A. Barbera, Anthony G. Macintyre, and Craig A. DeAtley, "Ambulances to Nowhere: America's Critical Shortfall in Medical Preparedness for Catastrophic Terrorism," Discussion Paper 2001-15 of the Belfer Center for Science and International Affairs (Cambridge, Mass.: Kennedy School of Government, Harvard University, October 2001).

87. Remarks by Dr. Meselson at Undermining Terrorism, a conference at the John F. Kennedy School of Government, Cambridge, Mass., May 3, 2002.

88. Testimony of Senator Sam Nunn before the House Government Reform Committee Subcommittee on National Security, Veterans Affairs, and International Relations, July 23, 2001.

89. Martin Feldstein, "Oil Dependence and National Security: A Market-based System for Reducing U.S. Vulnerability," *The National Interest* (Fall 2001).

90. Bonvillian and Sharp, op. cit.

# PART II

## Networks and Partnerships in Action

# CHAPTER FIVE

# Using Virtual Teams to Manage Complex Projects: A Case Study of the Radioactive Waste Management Project

Samuel M. DeMarie
Associate Professor
Department of Management, College of Business
Iowa State University

*This report was originally published in August 2000, revised November 2003.*

# Introduction

Time constraints and other factors, such as travel costs and the availability and high cost of specialized human expertise, have created an increased demand for organizations to explore the use of advanced new—virtual—technologies. These technologies offer a wide range of tools that allow team members to communicate and work as if they were colocated when they are actually geographically dispersed.

Just as the personal computer revolutionized the workplace throughout the 1980s and 1990s, recent developments in information and communication technology are forging the foundation of another new workplace. This workplace is largely unrestrained by geography, time, and organizational boundaries; it is a *virtual* workplace, where productivity, flexibility, and collaboration may reach unprecedented levels.

One of the most promising organizational structures to emerge from this new workplace is the *virtual team*. Virtual teams are groups of geographically and/or organizationally dispersed collaborators that are brought together to address a specific task or ongoing function, and whose members' primary mode of interaction is through a combination of communication and information technology.[1] Virtual teams rarely, if ever, meet face-to-face. They may be established as temporary structures, existing only to accomplish a specific task, or occasionally are more permanent when used to address ongoing issues, such as strategic planning. Further, membership is often fluid, evolving according to changing task requirements.

While virtual teams offer many potential benefits, such as reducing downtime and travel costs, organizations must learn more about how, when, and where to implement them in order to turn potential gains into realized gains. This study examined an actual government organization and its complex efforts to improve its efficiency and effectiveness through creating and managing virtual teams.

## Research Setting and Methodology

This research was conducted in a field setting. It focused on actual teamwork being conducted by workers associated with the Department of Energy's Radioactive Waste Management Project at Yucca Mountain, Nevada (RWMP). Actual employees of the various organizations working on the RWMP that had been assigned to work as part of a virtual team were studied. Individuals who regularly work as virtual team members on the RWMP come from a variety of professions including research scientists, engineers, middle managers, clerical staff, and community relations experts.

The RWMP is a highly complex project that is designed to assess the ultimate suitability of a site at Yucca Mountain, Nevada, to store nuclear waste. The Department of Energy is in charge of the RWMP. The Yucca Mountain site is approximately 100 miles northwest of Las Vegas, Nevada, in a sparsely populated desert environment. Specific information about the site and the work being done at the RWMP can be found at http://www.ymp.gov/.

The project includes seven separate government contract entities, two Department of Energy offices, two prime contractors, and approximately 40 significant subcontractors. A total of more than 2,500 people are assigned to the various areas of the RWMP. These employees are spread across the various organizations mentioned above and are located in six different states stretching from California to Washington, D.C. The complex scientific evaluations involving experts across multiple disciplines that characterize the majority of the work being done at the RWMP require collaboration among specialists spread across the United States, making it a perfect setting to investigate virtual teamwork.

The breadth of employee expertise involved in the RWMP is impressive and unique. The organization requires experts from scientific fields such as nuclear physics, geology, plant and animal biology, and various environmental sciences to collaborate in assessing the risks associated with long-term storage of nuclear waste. It also involves engineers from a whole host of backgrounds including the specialty areas of nuclear, mechanical, structural, civil, and electrical, to name a few. Because the subject matter of the project is one that engenders high public interest and sometimes controversial and impassioned interpretations, the RWMP also must employ media and public relations professionals to ensure that accurate information is provided to all stakeholders. Finally, the complex communications network required to connect and support the work of these employees, and the very serious need for security in issues related to the handling and storage of nuclear materials, required collaborations among a team of information technology specialists.

The primary data collection method used in this study was structured, open-ended field interviews. These interviews, for the most part, were recorded and transcribed word for word. In three cases, the interviews were actually conducted in text form by using a series of e-mail messages. These data were supplemented by archival data (primarily in the form of press releases and printed news stories), and to a more limited extent by observational data (in the form of meetings on-site with managerial personnel). Field interviews were chosen because the topic of virtual teamwork is a recent phenomenon that has not been thoroughly researched. In addition, interviews provide flexibility and often lead to richer insights on topics that are not well understood. For these reasons, interviews were deemed more appropriate than a structured survey for this project.

There were several important considerations in selecting interviewees. A primary concern was to select individuals who were knowledgeable about and had firsthand experience with the issue of virtual teamwork. Only organization members who were currently participating as a member of a virtual team were included in the pool of interviewees. Members of both the administrative and managerial staffs of the primary managing organization (MO) were instrumental in identifying personnel who had experiences most relevant to this study. Final selections of interviewees were made based on the participants' range of experiences in team settings at the RWMP, and the willingness and availability of individuals.

Another important concern was the need to obtain a sample that represented different perspectives of the issues surrounding virtual teamwork. To accomplish this, interviewees were selected from multiple managerial levels, functional backgrounds, and geographical locations. The final group of interviewees included scientists, engineers, managers, administrative staff, and media specialists. This group also represented four different managerial and administrative levels of the RWMP organization.

The sensitive nature of this government project made it necessary to guarantee complete anonymity to participants. It also required that interviews be focused on the process of virtual teamwork as opposed to the content of the teams' work. Thus, references to specific areas of expertise and information that could possibly be used to compromise security were deleted. The final group of interviewees included 16 people. They either participated in and/or supervised a total of 78 separate teams; of these, 34 teams met the definition of being virtual teams (i.e., they included members who were not colocated). Each interviewee was associated with at least one virtual team.

## The Technology Infrastructure

All members of the RWMP organization were provided a personal computer that was connected to a network through a common server platform. Most of these personal computers were selected from a single vendor through a centralized purchasing program. Each computer was configured to accommodate custom applications and usage criteria provided by each user. The software system used to coordinate communications over the network was Lotus Notes. The interviewees continually stressed that this common network platform was invaluable to their day-to-day work. In fact, several people mentioned that work seemed to come to a halt on occasions when the network system was not functioning. Team members use the Lotus Notes platform for much more than e-mail. It provides bulletin board type postings, scheduling for meetings, archiving hundreds of imbedded databases, and some highly specific applications.

The wide range of scientific disciplines involved in the project led to a large number of application programs in the overall system. It seems that each discipline has evolved a set of applications that are customized to their particular needs. Many of these application programs were not designed to interface with other systems/formats. Thus, the overall information system was highly complex and somewhat unique to this organization. The system support personnel seemed to be highly competent and have designed both security and ease of use (as much as possible) into the network system.

Virtual team members also regularly use telephone conferencing and videoconferencing in dedicated conferencing facilities. At the time of the study, the organization members did not have desktop video-conferencing available to them. Several individuals mentioned that this technology could be beneficial to their work and that they believed the organization was considering adding it to the existing system. When asked about the frequency of use of the various technology tools, members reported that e-mail and Lotus Notes databases were used every day. Teleconferences were used weekly on average, with videoconferencing used less frequently, ranging from one to three times per month.

# Virtual Teams: A Case Study of the RWMP

## Teams in Use at RWMP

It was difficult to ascertain the exact number of teams operating at the RWMP at any given time. Administrative records, in terms of typical human resources data, were kept only on teams that had an expected long-term duration, for approximately one year or more. Many of the virtual teams described by the interviewees did not meet this criterion in that they were formed on an ad hoc basis to meet a pressing need and disbanded when their work was completed. In fact, over 40 percent of the virtual teams studied were assembled for a period of less than 12 months. Organizational members called some of the teams that were designed with a shorter life span "task forces" or "ad hoc committees." By combining data given by managers from several parts of the organization, it was estimated that between 900 to 2,000 virtual teams were operating on any given day at the RWMP.

As the interviews progressed, it became apparent that three different kinds or archetypes of virtual teams were used most commonly at the RWMP. Table 5.1 provides an outline of the team archetypes, which include administrative teams, cross-functional project teams, and task force teams. The teams are delineated according to their work scope, membership char-

**Table 5.1: Team Archetypes at the RWMP**

|  | Administrative Teams | Cross-Functional Project Teams | Task Force Teams |
|---|---|---|---|
| **Scope of work** | Monitoring and assessing progress towards overall RWMP goals | Complex projects requiring multiple areas of expertise | Special projects contained within one department or discipline |
| **Approximate team size** | 5-8 | 6-12 | 3-7 |
| **Membership** | Across multiple units | Across multiple units | Within a single department/unit |
| **Members' home locations** | Geographically dispersed across 2-4 sites | Geographically dispersed across 3-6 sites | Colocated, or spread across 2-3 sites |
| **Meeting frequency** | Regular intervals: monthly/quarterly | Regular intervals and as needed: weekly/bi-monthly | Primarily as needed: daily to weekly |
| **Primary communication media** | • Face-to-face<br>• Video-conferencing<br>• E-mail<br>• Phone conferencing | • E-mail<br>• Phone conferencing<br>• Video-conferencing | • E-mail<br>• Face-to-face<br>• Phone conferencing |
| **Primary goals** | • Cross-unit coordination<br>• Resource allocation<br>• Inter-organizational communications and relations | • Cross-functional assessment of complex choices concerning materials or design of facilities and their long-term impact | • Assessments that usually become input into later, more complex cross-functional projects |
| **Planned duration of teamwork** | Ongoing | Six months to two years | Three to nine months |
| **Biggest challenges** | • Managing multiple constituencies and conflicting interests<br>• Establishing a hierarchy among resource allocations | • Determining which data are most critical<br>• Facilitating communication across disciplinary specialists | • Meeting aggressive deadlines |

acteristics, level of geographic dispersion, communication practices, primary goals, planned duration, and biggest challenges. Each of the three archetypes is briefly discussed below.

### Administrative Teams

The administrative teams were primarily designed to monitor overall organizational progress across the various areas of the RWMP and to allocate financial and human resources. These teams were moderate in size (falling in between the other two archetypes), ranging from five to eight members. The membership represented multiple organizational units and tended to be geographically dispersed across two to four locations. The makeup of these teams was less fluid than the other types in that membership rarely changed once it was established.

Administrative teams met on a regular schedule, the most typical frequency being either monthly or quarterly. This meeting frequency was lower than the other team archetypes. Meetings of these teams were predominantly face-to-face, although they sometimes accommodated a member who could not attend by using videoconferencing.

Administrative teams were assumed to be ongoing for the life of the RWMP. Despite the assumed duration, occasionally these teams were disbanded or substantially reconstituted. One of the administrative teams investigated herein was disbanded during the course of this study when the organizational reporting relationships were significantly changed due to a restructuring initiative. This team was later replaced by one that more closely matched the new organizational structure.

The primary goals of the administrative teams included cross-unit coordination and planning, resource allocation, and inter-organizational communications primarily concerning effective community and media relations. These teams' biggest challenges tended to center around issues related to estimating the time required to complete ongoing work in the various scientific areas, allocating adequate resources to ensure that the overall project could meet targets determined by the Department of Energy, and managing communications with the general public and press.

### Cross-Functional Project Teams

Cross-functional project teams were assembled to deal with highly complex scientific issues. An example of this would be assessing the environmental impacts of proposed site developments. A team dealing with this issue required animal biologists, plant scientists, geologists, hydrologists, and climatologists, among others. These teams tended to be the largest teams involved in the RWMP, ranging from six to 12 members for those included in this study. Team membership was geographically dispersed, ranging from three to six separate home locations. Cross-functional team membership was highly fluid, with members being added as new issues were uncovered and dismissed as their portion of the work was completed.

Cross-functional project teams met weekly and bi-monthly on average. These teams favored asynchronous communications (primarily e-mail with attached documentation) when possible. The complex nature of the tasks often created interdependencies among the various experts. For example, some members needed input from other members' work product before they could begin to assess issues in their specialty. In other cases, several experts needed to work together and integrate their data and analyses to create rigorous assessments.

For the most part, these teams were formed with a planned duration, the completion of a specific assessment. However, several of the teams included in the study completed their original charge only to be recharged with additional assignments related to assessing new issues that were uncovered during their original work. Thus, in practice, many of these teams became ongoing entities that continuously dealt with evolving issues related to the complex nature of their work. In fact, three team members interviewed for this study reported that they did not believe that their teams' work would ever be completely done.

Cross-functional teams' biggest challenges related to resolving conflicts among the various expert members. The complex nature of the tasks often created conflicting interpretations. Assessing the likelihood of alternative interpretations in a rigorous manner was difficult and often led to emotional interactions among team members. Achieving a level of consensus while at the same time providing appropriate recognition of dissenting views became a daunting task in several teams.

## Task Force Teams

Task force teams were assembled to deal with issues contained within one discipline or functional area. A task force team, for example, might evaluate a choice of materials to assess their structural properties. These teams typically are made up of members from a single department or organizational unit. Task force teams tended to be smallest in terms of numbers of members, ranging from three to seven. Because of the small size and limited scope of their tasks, these teams often were colocated, or involved members from only two or three home locations. Because of their relatively close proximity, task force team members used face-to-face communications more frequently than members of the other team archetypes did. Team members also reported a high level of e-mail usage, sometimes e-mailing information to someone who was located only a few paces away.

Task force teams dealt with fairly specific issues and thus were disbanded once they completed their mission. Many of these teams were formed to provide critical input to cross-functional teams dealing with more complex topics. When this was the case, the task force teams were given relatively short time frames to complete their assignments. Almost all interviewees mentioned the aggressive deadlines as a cause for concern.

Task force teams were the most informal in terms of their meeting schedules. Because most, if not all, members were colocated, they would communicate as needed to facilitate the work at hand. Some interviewees reported communicating face-to-face several times a day with task force team members. In addition, most of the teams had a regularly scheduled weekly meeting to assess overall progress and deal with unexpected issues that may have come up.

The biggest challenge that task force teams faced was meeting aggressive deadlines for completion of their work. Most interviewees understood why the deadlines were necessary, especially when other teams were waiting on results to complete other projects, yet many felt that they could have been more thorough had they been given more time. The time pressure that members felt may also have been related to the number of different teams that each individual was assigned to. Most interviewees reported that they believed they were assigned to too many teams and that this affected their ability to perform up to their full potential.

## Motivations for Virtual Teaming

A foundational assumption guiding this study was that virtual teamwork would provide real organizational benefits beyond those associated with traditional teamwork. In fact, many writers have espoused a wide range of advantages that organizations might achieve through virtual teamwork.[2] The potential advantages afforded by virtual teams include:

1. Increasing productivity by enabling simultaneous in addition to sequential work;
2. Improving work quality by providing members continuous access to the latest and best information;
3. Increasing the pool of potential team members by allowing members to participate from their home office (or even their homes in the case of teleworkers);
4. Decreasing organizational costs by avoiding travel costs and downtime;
5. Efficiently training and socializing new team members by using an online record of ongoing work; and
6. Increasing the impact of teamwork by capturing the work electronically so it can be accessed by other segments/members of the organization as needed.[3]

Thus, a primary aim of the study was to evaluate if in fact the focal organization did benefit from virtual teamwork, and alternatively if there were hidden costs and/or barriers to overcome in implementing virtual teams. Table 5.2 provides some simple questions to test whether your organization might benefit from virtual teamwork.

**Table 5.2: Might Your Organization Benefit from Virtual Teamwork?**

| If you answer "yes" to all of the questions below, then your organization should seriously consider implementing virtual teams in the future. |
| --- |
| 1. Are your employees geographically dispersed?<br><br>2. Is travel time limiting the productivity of key employees?<br><br>3. Do you regularly use teams to tackle important projects? |

## Benefits Achieved

It was very difficult to get members of the virtual teams to assign a measurable metric to the benefits that virtual teamwork afforded. Most members did, however, express the view that their particular teamwork would have been impossible without the ability to regularly connect with distant members. In relation to the six potential benefits of virtual teamwork just described, five seem to have been achieved to some degree at the RWMP.

### Increasing Productivity

Interviewees consistently reported that the work done in virtual teams tended to be a more efficient use of their time than work done in face-to-face teams. It seems that communicating primarily through the network interface with virtual team members required teammates to carefully consider most communications. Over time this led to more efficient interactions. Additionally, the virtual team setup strongly encouraged team members to break work assignments down into sequential and independently manageable units. This allowed members to schedule their particular workload at times that were convenient, given their other commitments. This also allowed virtual teams to avoid one of the biggest complaints associated with traditional teamwork at the RWMP, which was time wasted at team meetings discussing issues that did not affect all members.

### Improving Work Quality through Access to the Latest and Best Information

Benefits related to work quality were seen to be somewhat indirect. Members of teams that relied on timely updates from other units of the

**Table 5.3: Benefits Achieved and Problems Encountered by Virtual Teams**

| Benefits Achieved | Problems Encountered |
|---|---|
| Increasing productivity | Communication difficulties |
| Improving work quality through access to latest and best information | Overload of assignments |
| Increasing the pool of potential team members | Ambiguities surrounding reporting, evaluation, responsibilities |
| Decreasing organizational costs associated with travel and downtime | System downtime due to upgrades and inconsistencies across locations |
| Increasing the impact of teamwork by capturing the work electronically | |

project felt strongly that they benefited from the design of the information infrastructure that allowed access to Lotus Notes databases in a manageable format. They believed that the use of the network computer system to archive up-to-date information had helped to improve the overall quality of work by immediately updating members when critical new data became available.

### Increasing the Pool of Potential Team Members

A majority of virtual team members commented that the communications facilities afforded by the common computer network allowed them to bring specialized expertise into their team projects that otherwise would not have been available if team membership had required regular travel to face-to-face meetings in a central location. This is a critical advantage at a project such as the RWMP where a wide range of scientific specialists are required to interact with people outside of their regular professional environment. There also is some evidence that members with highly specialized skills were used more productively by eliminating a large percentage of their travel requirements.

### Decreasing Organizational Costs Associated with Travel and Downtime

It was not possible from the interviews to derive an accurate estimate of the amount of cost savings related to decreased travel and downtime. However, most interviewees believed that the savings were substantial. Related to this, several virtual team members suggested that some critical work may have been impossible to complete or severely delayed had key specialists in high demand been forced to travel to team meetings. Thus, members suggested that the largest cost savings might have come from avoiding delays rather than from the actual reduction in travel-related expenses.

### Increasing the Impact of Teamwork by Capturing the Work Electronically

A consistent theme throughout the interviews was that the organization seemed to benefit from various teams putting the output from their efforts into an accessible location and a manageable format on the information network. In most cases, this meant creating databases on the Lotus Notes system. Nearly all (more than 90 percent) of the teams studied regularly used databases on the network to communicate their progress to organizational stakeholders.

### The Exception

The one area where the RWMP did not realize any of the potential advantages associated with virtual teamwork was "efficiently training and socializing new members by using an online record of ongoing work." In fact, most members felt that virtual teamwork made the training and socialization of new members more difficult. This may be at least partially attributable to the relatively infrequent use of videoconferencing and the lack of desktop video facilities, although members did not believe that increased online video interactions would have significantly improved training and socialization of new members.

## Problems Encountered

While virtual teamwork did provide some significant advantages to the RWMP, virtual team members also identified significant challenges and problems encountered with this kind of interaction. In fact, in a minority of cases (less than 20 percent), members believed that the problems encountered may have totally offset the gains afforded by virtual teamwork.

### Communication Difficulties

Difficulties encountered in communication were a common theme throughout the interviews. Virtual team members found it frustrating that messages often were misunderstood or not received by important constituents, which understandably led to inefficiencies in workflow. Areas that were identified as causing communication difficulties included: e-mail slang and informalities, technical jargon, confusion concerning teleconferencing protocols, and the lack of an up-to-date listing of constituents (including members and non-members) to include in the distribution of information.

E-mail has become a ubiquitous component of the workplace and was in fact the most frequently used means of communication among virtual team members at the RWMP. While e-mail provides many benefits in terms of convenience, cost and accessibility, it also has some downsides. It seems that as people become more familiar with e-mail communications, they tend to use more informal language, abbreviations and slang terms. The more informal the language becomes, the more likely that the content of the message may be misunderstood.

Beyond just language choice, because e-mail is a text-based communication, it does not include the non-verbal cues that make face-to-face communication so rich and effective. Thus, it is difficult to portray tone, emphasis, and humor in e-mail communications. Virtual team members across almost all teams cited cases where a misunderstanding related to an e-mail communication hurt team productivity.

Similar to language choice in e-mail messages, virtual team members also cited the use of technical jargon as a barrier to effective communications. Most teams in this organization are cross-functional and involve specialists from multiple professional backgrounds. Each discipline has its own set of commonly used and widely understood abbreviations, acronyms, and buzzwords. This kind of technical jargon became troublesome in interactions with members from another discipline, and often resulted in communication difficulties because team members did not understand the terminology common to areas outside of their own specialty.

Another frequently cited problem was the lack of explicit protocols to use in conferencing situations. Members expressed frustration at both teleconferencing and videoconferencing because communications became awkward when people were unsure of how and when to speak up and be recognized. This led to situations where two people talked "on top" of each other and other times when long periods of silence occurred when members tried to allow others the chance to participate. Several members reported that these kinds of protocol difficulties were the main reasons why conferencing was used infrequently.

Finally, virtual team members cited ambiguity about whom to include in communications as another significant problem that inhibited effective communication. Virtual team membership in the organization was more variable than in face-to-face teams, especially in the case of task force and cross-functional project teams. Team members were not always kept informed as to the addition or removal of team members. Related to this, many of the virtual teams worked on projects that had an almost immediate impact on other parts of the organization. In some cases, the teams themselves did not fully appreciate how their work would affect the other parts

of the organization. Thus, they may have inadvertently left important constituents out of the communications loop. Both of these conditions led to
situations where individuals (both members and non-members) did not
receive critical information in a timely manner.

## Overload of Assignments

Virtual teams allow organizations to use their personnel more efficiently by avoiding downtime associated with travel and scheduling face-
to-face meetings. There is a downside to using people more efficiently,
however; it usually entails increasing the number of assignments given to
each individual, which was in fact the case at the RWMP.

Virtual team members consistently identified unrealistic workloads
given to members across multiple team assignments as a significant barrier
to team success. Interviewees in this study averaged 3.8 team memberships,
and some supervisors identified people under their direction who belonged
to as many as eight separate teams. Without exception, interviewees felt
that conflicting team responsibilities impaired their ability to perform at the
levels expected of them. Unrealistic workloads, in terms of multiple team
assignments, increased members' feelings of stress and burnout.

## Ambiguities Surrounding Reporting, Evaluation, Responsibilities

A unique challenge associated with the RWMP was that teams often
included members from several different parent organizations. As such, it
was not uncommon for a person's direct supervisor to have little or no
involvement with that person's RWMP team assignments. Similarly, designated team leaders often had little or no input into a person's home organization evaluation of performance. While this challenging setup was
necessary to assemble the range of specialized expertise required by many
of the teams, it caused confusion among team members when trying to pri-
oritize assignments. Several interviewees reported that the most critical
work they performed for RWMP earned them little recognition within their
home organization in terms of advancement opportunities and salary raises.

In a related area, coordinating the actual work of the virtual teams in
some cases proved most difficult. Members felt that the reporting requirements of the team (i.e., whom to report to and what specific information to
report) were not clearly communicated and seemed to change on a fairly
frequent basis. A similar situation existed *within* some of the virtual teams.
Members reported that they were unsure at times about who was responsible
for administrative issues such as team minutes and following up to make sure
that members were on track with assignments. Members, almost unanimously, believed that team performance could be improved by making the
formal responsibilities of each team member more explicit.

**System Downtime Due to Upgrades and Inconsistencies Across Locations**

The final problem area identified by virtual team members was related to frustrations associated with interacting with the actual communications system. Most interviewees reported significant time lost because of problems using the technology, ranging from the overall system being off-line to problems with individual hardware and software configurations. While the computer network was reported as being mostly reliable, members did identify instances when the system was not operating at times critical to meeting work deadlines. Interviewees suggested that some sort of backup or redundant system architecture would have facilitated their teams' productivity. Several interviewees also cited instances where incompatibilities in the hardware and software across multiple member home locations led to significant delays. The differences among the various site infrastructures at times made it difficult or impossible for critical team members to meet deadlines for important work. Most members, however, did suggest that a major computer upgrade initiative at the RWMP within the last 18 months had corrected many of the long-standing incompatibility issues. However, a key problem remains, because the wide diversity of applications used across the various units makes incompatibility issues an inevitable outcome as existing applications are upgraded or new ones are added.

# Lessons Learned and Recommendations

In many ways, the RWMP has broken new ground in the area of virtual teamwork. By necessity, it has integrated professionals in multiple disciplines and across many locations into teams. Like any venture into an uncharted area, it has had to learn from trial and error. In Table 5.4, the most important lessons learned from these complex organizational challenges and the resulting recommendations are summarized to help organizations attempting similar initiatives.

## Lesson 1: Face-to-face interaction should not be totally replaced.

Perhaps the strongest message that came from the interviewees was that high-tech tools, including videoconferencing, could not totally replace the advantages of in-person face-to-face communications. Virtual team members reported that some initial face-to-face meeting was necessary to establish the high levels of interpersonal trust required for effective teamwork. This issue of trust is one that frequently seemed to be discounted, but should not be overlooked. Team members on teams that did not have at least one in-person

**Table 5.4: Lessons Learned and Recommendations from the RWMP**

| Lessons Learned | | Recommendations |
|---|---|---|
| Lesson 1 | Face-to-face interaction should not be totally replaced. | Launch virtual teams with in-person meetings to help establish trust that provides the basis for productive working relationships. |
| Lesson 2 | Training is critical to team success. | Invest in training related to both team dynamics and effective use of conferencing technologies. |
| Lesson 3 | Virtual teamwork tends to increase members' workload more than anticipated. | Limit team assignments and plan for learning curve effects related to team formation and changing team membership. |
| Lesson 4 | Technology must be compatible and reliable. | Keep systems as simple as possible. Do not rush to add new features if they provide marginal benefits. Select vendors that provide high quality support relationships. |
| Lesson 5 | Technical assistance must be competent and available. | Do not underestimate the value of providing adequate technical support people. State-of-the-art systems require outstanding support personnel. |

meeting believed that their productivity and the overall quality of the team's work suffered. Several virtual team members also suggested that an ongoing occasional in-person meeting regularly scheduled (quarterly or annually) could help with coordinating and communicating future directions for the team.

This finding may be at least partly due to the fact that teams were reluctant to use the videoconferencing systems available. They found these systems awkward to manage since they required technical personnel to operate them. If the organization was to provide desktop video systems in the future, these strong feelings may be moderated to some extent. Desktop video systems allow video interaction without requiring special facilities and outside technical assistance. However, given the strong feelings expressed, it is doubtful that even high-quality desktop video systems could totally replace the value that members attributed to in-person face-to-face meetings.

**Recommendation 1: All new teams should be launched with a significant face-to-face interaction.**

These launching meetings need to focus on establishing team goals, setting milestones, clarifying the roles to be filled by each member, developing meeting schedules, and setting norms and standards for team communications. If possible, a schedule for future on-site meetings should be established. These meetings can be quarterly, semiannually, or annually depending on the task environment and the degree of geographic dispersion among the team members. For teams that are widely dispersed, additional face-to-face meetings may be impossible to schedule. If this is the case, the initial meeting should be extended into a format that allows for some social interactions in addition to dealing with organizational issues. These teams should also strongly consider scheduling regular videoconferencing sessions or implementing desktop video communications if possible.

## Lesson 2: Training is critical to team success.

Virtual team members consistently expressed the viewpoint that additional training could improve team productivity. Interviewees identified two areas in particular where training could provide significant benefits: team communication dynamics and the use of new technology tools. Somewhat surprisingly, a majority of virtual team members believed that training in the mechanics of effective teamwork could provide a common body of knowledge that would greatly improve team communications. A slightly smaller number of team members cited training in the use of new technology as having the potential to provide gains in team efficiency and effectiveness. Members noted several instances where basic training related to new software applications would have allowed their team to avoid some obstacles to their work.

Virtual team members frequently expressed frustration at the difficulties of managing communications across the electronic media. Several team members cited situations where they had insights to contribute, but refrained from joining a discussion because they were unsure about the proper method of gaining the attention of their peers. Members were reluctant to appear rude or overbearing. These situations involved both telephone and videoconferencing. Other asynchronous methods of communications, such as e-mail and bulletin boards, did not produce the same frustrations for obvious reasons.

Members believed that their team could have benefited from discussing and establishing norms for team members to follow in obtaining and yielding the floor during real-time conferencing sessions. While this seems to be a simple and possibly obvious solution, none of the teams in this study had conducted a session to set norms and protocols for team interactions prior to attempting real-time conferencing. Several teams had, however, come to an informal understanding of preferred methods for gaining the floor and identifying oneself, only after experiencing a series of sessions with unsatisfying interactions. Virtual team members, almost unanimously, suggested that their team could have saved much time and effort had these issues been formally discussed early on. They also suggested that once established, norms and protocols should be recorded and that members must be held accountable for adhering to them.

**Recommendation 2: Virtual team members should be required to complete formal training in the area of team dynamics and the effective use of conferencing technologies.**

Much training in this area focuses too heavily on the technical issues of how to operate the systems. To be effective, this training should emphasize interpersonal communication skills and how to overcome the challenges that conferencing technologies pose for effective teamwork. Many organizations underestimate the value of training people in the area of team dynamics and methods. Assigning a group of people to a common project does not make them a true team. Effective team members need to understand what it is that makes teams successful and unsuccessful. Finally, the training must be consistent for all organization members so they can draw from a common body of knowledge during the formation of new teams.

Specific training in the actual use of communication and information technology is also critical. Many organizations seem to underestimate the training necessary to allow members to effectively use specific new software applications and upgrades to existing applications. This often leads to a situation where team members underestimate the value of their technology tools because they have not learned the range of possibilities offered by the new tools. Basic training in the benefits afforded by new applications and upgrades can provide a surprising return in increased productivity.

**Lesson 3: Virtual teamwork tends to increase members' workload more than anticipated.**

Virtual teams are relatively easy to assemble. They allow organizations to avoid much of the inconvenience and cost associated with traditional teamwork. Several team members expressed the view that the convenience and cost efficiency of *forming* virtual teams frequently resulted in supervisors underestimating the workload necessary to *participate* in the teams. A majority of the team members that participated in this study felt that they belonged to too many teams and that their combined teamwork responsibilities exceeded reasonable expectations. Supervisors in the study supported this view by expressing concern about workers performing below expectations due to being overburdened.

It may be that the RWMP as a whole simply has a challenging workload and aggressive schedule, and, in fact, some interviewees supported this insight. However, there was a consistent message in the interviews that suggested that the challenges associated with virtual team assignments were seriously underestimated. Interviewees believed that supervisors must closely monitor the burden associated with multiple team assignments and fight the tendency to underestimate virtual team responsibilities if they hope to avoid burnout among employees.

**Recommendation 3: Do not underestimate the time it takes to develop a team into a high-performing organizational unit.**

Effective virtual teams do not just happen. They take a tremendous amount of time and effort to coordinate and manage. Much of this time and effort occurs soon after a team is formed; it is similar to the concept of a learning curve. Members must learn the personalities and work styles of their team members and establish norms, protocols, goals, and milestones. People who join a new team must plan for this drain on their time and schedule their other commitments accordingly. Supervisors must also recognize the effects of the learning curve and resist the temptation to assign high-performing employees to multiple new team assignments. Finally, changing the makeup of a virtual team also has some commonly underestimated costs. As existing members leave and new members join, all team personnel must acquaint themselves with the new people, and help to educate the newcomers concerning team norms, standards, history, and goals. If possible, team membership should remain stable to ensure higher levels of productivity and lessen the chance of overburdening members with off-line work.

## Lesson 4: Technology must be compatible and reliable.

Virtual team members consistently expressed frustration at time lost to technical problems. Some team members went as far as to say that technical problems more than offset the advantages that the communication technologies afforded. Despite the fact that most members acknowledged that the organization had improved over time in managing and maintaining its technology infrastructure, most interviewees believed that technical problems remained a significant concern.

Some level of technical problems is probably unavoidable. That is, the organization may have to actually experience a requisite number of technical problems before it can develop effective ways to solve those problems and ultimately prevent similar problems from occurring. Several members expressed the view that new technology (including system upgrades) should be tested on a subset of the organization prior to widespread adoption. This kind of solution may not be possible, however, when changing (upgrading) the system infrastructure.

### Recommendation 4: Keep systems as simple as possible.

Make sure that your systems are adequate to your teams' requirements, but do not overload team members with bells and whistles that they are not likely to use. Each new application or feature added to existing systems seems to exponentially increase the likelihood of technical problems and system downtime. Carefully assess the potential benefits of upgrades and new applications. Those that offer only modest advantages may not be worth the potential problems that they might bring about. Similarly, whenever possible, deal with vendors that have a reputation for excellent technical support. Vendors who actively track customer problems and develop close working relationships with their customers have access to a wide range of experiences from other organizations. It is possible that some other customer organization may have already found a solution to the problem that you are encountering. Vendors can help to bring those solutions to your organization in a timely and less painful manner.

## Lesson 5: Technical assistance must be competent and available.

Related to the previous point, several interviewees believed that the RWMP had seriously underestimated the level of technical support necessary to facilitate such a complex organization. Common complaints seemed to focus on two viewpoints—that technical support people were not available when needed and that some technical support people lacked the qualifications to deal with difficult problems. Interviewees who had resource allocation responsibility also felt that determining the appropriate allocation for support personnel was extremely difficult. Several interviewees believed that they had underestimated the technical support necessary to facilitate new investments in both hardware and software systems.

### Recommendation 5: Do not underestimate the value and necessity of competent technical support personnel.

Many organizations spend a tremendous amount of resources on purchasing state-of-the art technology only to undermine the value of these technical tools by not providing adequate support to implement and maintain them. In most cases, organizations would be better served by using slightly out-of-date technology that is adequately supported if their budgets do not allow for first-class support of new technology.

## Summary

It is interesting in this world of rapidly changing new technologies that virtual team members primarily recognized the "softer side" of organizations as providing the largest potential impact. Very few interviewees expressed the need for newer or better technology. Alternatively, issues such as the need for more in-person face-to-face meetings, the establishment of communications protocols, the support and maintenance of existing technologies, and increased training for team members were consistently identified as high priorities. Organizational leaders may be able to learn from these insights. Many organizations seem to have a bias in resource allocation toward investing in new hardware and software. While these investments often are necessary, some organizations could provide greater return for their investment by focusing on the softer issues discussed here.

# Endnotes

1. Townsend, Anthony, Samuel DeMarie, and Anthony Hendrickson, "Virtual teams: Technology and the workplace of the future." *The Academy of Management Executive,* 1998, v12, i3, pp. 17-29; Geber, Beverly, "Virtual teams," *Training,* 1995, v32, i4, pp. 36-40.

2. See, for example, Lipnack, Jessica and Jeffrey Stamps, "Virtual teams: The new way to work." *Strategy and Leadership,* Jan-Feb 1999 v27, i1, pp.14-20; Duarte, Deborah L. and Nancy T. Synder, *Mastering Virtual Teams,* 1999, San Francisco: Jossey-Bass.

3. Grenier, R., and G. Metes, *Going Virtual,* 1995, Upper Saddle River, NJ: Prentice Hall.

# CHAPTER SIX

# Communities of Practice:
# A New Tool for
# Government Managers

William M. Snyder
Managing Director
Social Capital Group

Xavier de Souza Briggs
Associate Professor of Public Policy
Harvard University

*This report was originally published in November 2003.*

# Introduction

*"Here the focus is on grassroots innovation efforts where innovating community groups have the opportunity to come together and share how they have solved problems.... It's like a virtual center of excellence, where all the partners are experts."*

*"This approach helps build buy-in from people who will implement the approaches, versus saying, 'Oh here comes another dictate from Washington.' These are our own problems and we should design our own solutions."*

Transformative changes in the world—driven by globalization and a sweeping knowledge revolution—are creating challenges too complex for traditional structures and management methods to address. This is clear in the private sector but may be even more important in the realm of public problem solving, where government, nonprofits, and businesses increasingly work together. The complexity of today's challenges and associated performance expectations requires a commensurate capacity for learning, innovation, and collaboration across diverse constituencies. But action learning—the kind that leads to real impact on important public problems—calls for organizational arrangements that we are only beginning to envision and create. Existing models of teamwork and collaboration, while useful, are hard-pressed to overcome persistent barriers: bureaucratic inertia, fear of change, and turf-minded managers, among others. And many change efforts are much too dependent on charismatic champions whose exits spell the demise of promising innovation.

Conventional government bureaucracies—designed to solve stable problems for established constituencies through centrally managed programs and policies—are hampered by important limitations in this environment. While scale and functional specialization still offer important benefits, and while centralized coordination and enforcement of standards also have a role to play, the old structures are not enough. Many of our most urgent social problems—in education, community safety, the environment, job creation, affordable housing, healthcare, and more—call for flexible arrangements, constant adaptation, and the savvy blending of expertise and credibility that requires crossing the boundaries of organizations and sectors.

Private-sector firms—both multinationals and start-ups—are embracing network-based forms of organizing to build new capabilities, accelerate innovation, and increase agility (Nohria and Eccles, 1992; Dyer and Nobeoka, 2000). Nonprofits, too, are organizing more frequently as cross-sector networks of organizations that partner together to address complex civic issues (Keyes et al., 1996). Governments must also learn to leverage the power of networks, both internally (across agencies and sub-units) and externally (across levels of government, across sectors, and across important constituencies). But doing this work presents important challenges that outrun much of the private sector's experience. What's more, many of the most important players display "collaboration fatigue." Process alone, and the promise of better governance, is not enough to win their commitment.

Let us go back to first principles. The most important business of government is governance. In democratic societies, particularly where civic engagement is desperately needed, effective models of governance must be able to *meaningfully* engage organized public interest groups, private-sector parties, and citizens at large to tackle matters of civic concern (Barber, 1985; Putnam, 1993; Fung and Wright, 2003).

Unfortunately, while scholars and other opinion leaders have made a compelling case for more engagement and more structure, the effort to develop, document, and test new structures and new norms is still in its infancy. Furthermore, it is particularly unclear, in an era defining "civic" all too often as "local," what role, if any, the federal government should play.

That is, the crucial challenges ahead are less about the "whether" of broader engagement than about the when and how. This chapter describes how collaborative action-learning networks—here called "communities of practice"—can combine disciplines, interests, and capabilities across boundaries to take on national priorities. Though much of the action is local, the federal government plays a lead role in sponsoring and structuring the work. The chapter mines rich case studies that show the model in action and offer specific examples of breakthroughs and pitfalls.

This chapter addresses three key questions:

- What are communities of practice, and how should we distinguish them from transaction- or advocacy-oriented networks and traditional organizational structures?
- When and where should federal government managers develop communities of practice to address strategic priorities, particularly those that cross boundaries within and across agencies?
- How can you create and manage these informal, action-learning structures? How do you get them launched, support their growth, and help them achieve desired results?

We illustrate these points in the context of a core set of four federal case studies (with occasional references to others). These cases illustrate how federal agencies can cultivate these structures and bring them to scale to address national priorities.

Our findings and recommendations are drawn from an in-depth analysis of a "revelatory" (Yin, 1989) set of cases. These include a federal initiative, sponsored by senior staff in Vice President Gore's National Partnership for Reinventing Government, which began in 1998, that launched three communities of practice. These communities focused on three urgent national issues: children's health and school readiness; public safety; and workforce development. They were called Boost4Kids, SafeCities, and 21st Century Skills, respectively. Each network consisted of 10 or more local, multi-stakeholder groups from cities across the nation. In addition, we report on a fourth case, a community of practice sponsored by the Federal Highway Administration (FHWA), which focuses on reducing highway fatalities. The FHWA case is based primarily within one agency, as opposed to the other three cases, which featured intensive cross-agency collaboration. In all four cases, linkages between players across sectors and levels of government were crucial.

Cultivating high-performing communities of practice—as opposed to mere "interest roundtables" or affinity groups—presents a formidable management challenge to the federal government and other stakeholders such as businesses, foundations, universities, local and state governments, and non-profits. The good news is there are working examples of such networks today—in all sectors, at all levels—including successful ones in which the federal government has played an instrumental role.

A "community of practice" is a particular type of network that features peer-to-peer collaborative activities to build member skills as well as organizational and societal capabilities. Education and public safety communities of practice generally involve organizations from the private and nonprofit sectors, even when they are primarily sponsored by public agencies. Organizations and researchers use a variety of terms to describe similar phenomena, such as "learning networks," "knowledge communities," "competency networks," "thematic groups," and others (Wenger, McDermott, and Snyder, 2002, pp. 239-240).

The analysis of these cases suggests three recommendations for what the federal government can do to spur improvements at the local level on a national scale.

1. *Sponsor and support communities of practice to achieve national outcomes that require ongoing innovation and action-learning.* There is now no other entity as well placed as the federal government to provide such sponsorship and support. Key roles and structures required to help communities of practice succeed include agency sponsors to provide strategic focus, seed funding, and institutional legitimacy; community coordinators to develop a learning agenda, build the community, and lead outcome-oriented initiatives; and agency champions and support staff to bridge formal-unit barriers, coach community initiatives, and liaise with sponsors and stakeholders.

2. *Align community goals with the agency strategic imperatives and policy mandates.* Many communities of practice are simply loose networks of professionals who have no aspiration to influence policy or build new organizational capabilities beyond individual professional development. But the cases described here show that well-supported communities of

practice can be powerful engines for achieving strategic goals. Alignment actions include linking the community's learning agenda with
agency objectives; leveraging community capability outcomes by consistently implementing them in formal service-delivery units; and partnering with communities of practice to accelerate the dissemination of
good ideas and enhance policy development.

3. *Leverage the unique position of the federal government to broaden the
scope and scale of pilot initiatives.* Wherever there are urgent socioeconomic imperatives that require building and sharing new capabilities,
there are opportunities to leverage communities of practice to achieve
results faster. National priorities such as homeland security and school
improvement are important, high-profile areas to consider—and so are
specific strategic objectives for every federal agency, whether in the
Army to promote professional development for newly minted company
commanders, the Federal Highway Administration to reduce traffic
crashes, or a multi-agency initiative to establish and implement federal
e-government standards and methodologies. The same goes for scale: If
10 cities find a way to connect faith leaders and police departments—
and reduce gun violence and urban conflict in the process—why not
provide an infrastructure that over time helps 1,000 cities nationwide
do the same thing? The opportunity here is to leverage a relatively small
investment in infrastructure and senior executive attention to catalyze
peer-to-peer learning networks on a national scale and thereby achieve
results not otherwise possible.

# Understanding Communities of Practice

## What Is a "Community of Practice"?

Communities of practice steward the knowledge assets of organizations
and society. They operate as "social learning systems" where practitioners
connect to solve problems, share ideas, set standards, build tools, and
develop relationships with peers and stakeholders. These structures are considered informal because they cannot be mandated from the outside. An
essential dimension of a community of practice is voluntary participation,
because without this a member is less likely to seek or share knowledge;
build trust and reciprocity with others; or apply the community's knowledge in practice. Members' willingness to learn and relate together is what
drives value in communities. This is not to say external sponsors and stakeholders cannot guide or influence a community—in fact, they have important
roles to play. But the nature of the sponsor relationship is qualitatively dif-

ferent from a traditional reporting relationship. It is more like a strategic alliance, in this case with an informal, knowledge-based structure.

As knowledge structures, communities of practice complement the function of formal units, such as departments or cross-functional teams, whose primary purpose is to deliver a product or service and to assume accountability for quality, cost, and customer satisfaction. A salient benefit of communities, in fact, is to bridge formal organizational boundaries in order to increase the collective knowledge, skills, and professional trust and reciprocity of practitioners who serve in these organizations (Wenger, et al., 2002). Communities of practice are a particularly appropriate structural model for cross-agency and cross-sector collaborations because they are inherently boundary-crossing entities. A community's effectiveness depends on strength in all three of its core structural dimensions: its domain, community, and practice. (See Figure 6.1.) The "domain" refers to its focus and identity, the "community" to its member relationships and interactions, and the "practice" to its methods and learning initiatives.

## Domain

The domain of a community of practice includes the key issues or problems that practitioners wrestle with or consider essential to what they do. Airline pilots discuss advances in flight technologies and ways to adjust to new security requirements; petro-geologists talk about rock formations and where to find oil reserves; and teachers share their thoughts and experiences about lessons plans and ways to adapt them for different students. In all these cases, the issues are ones that elicit members' passion for their work. A professional's vocation is not an abstract, disinterested experience. A community's domain is often a deep part of members' personal identity and a means of talking about what their life's work is about. As a member of one community enthused: "[We can] get to a point ... where we change the psychology and thinking and culture of the country about what we can do for kids and families." Community leaders perform a stewardship function for stakeholders, as well as members, by ensuring the profession's integrity, standards, and efficacy. Of course, members of communities of practice may focus exclusively on their own selfish, internally focused interests, even when these contradict or violate the needs and interests of stakeholders and society. Such narcissism ultimately hurts members themselves—as was true for members of many traditional guilds in the late 19th century, whose insulation from changes surrounding them accelerated their demise. Communities, like any group or organization, require effective leadership and inquiry-oriented, engaged relationships with stakeholders to assure an integrity and capacity for growth that serves both members and society.

In some cases, it is particularly challenging to set the boundaries for a domain. Some domains—the field of psycho-neuro-immunology is a readily

## Figure 6.1: Structural Elements of a Community of Practice

- Three basic dimensions define a community of practice: domain, community, and practice
- Its purpose is to cross organizational, sector, and geographic boundaries to foster learning and innovation in specific topic areas
- Its effectiveness depends on strength in all three dimensions, and this evolves over time
- Key characteristics of community of practice are:
  - a focus on building and sharing knowledge among practitioners vs. delivering a product or service to customers
  - a reliance on informal phenomena such as passion, relationships, and shared experience, as opposed to dependence on formal rules and job descriptions

**Sponsorship and support**
- Sponsorship: Federal government or agency mandate; involvement of cross-sector sponsors at local, state, and national levels; funding for staff and travel
- Professional and logistical support: coaching community leaders, acting as liaison with sponsors, providing communications infrastructure, logistics for meetings, etc.

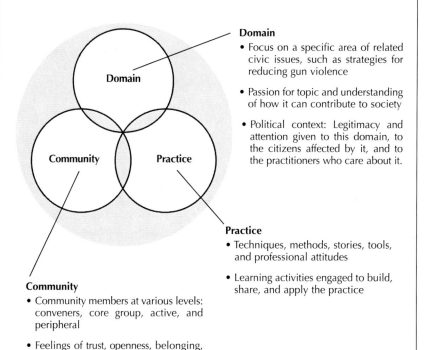

**Domain**
- Focus on a specific area of related civic issues, such as strategies for reducing gun violence
- Passion for topic and understanding of how it can contribute to society
- Political context: Legitimacy and attention given to this domain, to the citizens affected by it, and to the practitioners who care about it.

**Practice**
- Techniques, methods, stories, tools, and professional attitudes
- Learning activities engaged to build, share, and apply the practice

**Community**
- Community members at various levels: conveners, core group, active, and peripheral
- Feelings of trust, openness, belonging, and commitment to others in network

apparent example—include a varied mix of disciplines to match an emerging cluster of problems. Communities must carefully gauge what is the requisite variety of perspectives needed to address messy problems. In one community we studied, practitioners were divided on the question of whether it made sense to combine a focus on distance learning with more specific issues related to workforce development. In another community, members asserted that a variety of perspectives was essential to the community's effectiveness—even as they sought support from agency sponsors who wanted to narrow the focus. As one member argued: "It is the right thing to keep everything in the mix—including issues about health, education, safety, nutrition, and transportation—because they are so interrelated when it comes to helping kids."

## Community

In the context of the federal government, communities of practice require collaborative relationships among federal officials from various agencies, and from a diverse array of stakeholders and partners—including state and local agencies, business, universities and schools, hospitals, foundations, citizen coalitions, and nonprofits. Optimally, the membership mirrors the diversity of perspectives and approaches relevant to leading-edge innovation in the field and reflects the varied professional interests and demographic characteristics of practitioners. In thriving communities, members appreciate the range of contributions their peers can make: "I feel I'm in the company of other dedicated professionals. The energy level, trust, and creativity are higher because you know others are at high levels of capability. That's been extremely valuable to me."

Community members participate at various levels of involvement—including community leaders, active participants, and peripheral members who only participate occasionally. Leadership by an effective community coordinator and core group is essential.

Members' mutual feelings of trust, openness, belonging, shared commitment, and common values provide the foundation for mutual learning among diverse members. As one member said: "It is important to meet each other and build relationships and talk to each other and learn from each other. If we were just voices on the phone, we would not be so comfortable with each other." This sense of community is at the heart of communities' success. The reason successful communities of practice do not mandate participation is because building collective trust, reciprocity, and shared values is not something that you can require from the outside, any more than you can force someone to feel passionate about something they simply do not enjoy.

## Practice

Practice is used to denote both methodologies and skills. It includes both codifiable "best practices" that can be documented, as well as the tacit skills of an expert—a heart surgeon, for example, or a good plumber. Practice also connotes the implicit notion that true expertise involves continuous learning, as expressed in the phrase "practicing the piano." Hence, elements of a practice include its repertoire—tools, methods, and stories—as well as learning and innovation activities. The elements of SafeCities' "practice," for example, included methods for using Geographic Information System (GIS) mapping techniques to determine high-crime areas that need more attention.

In addition to the GIS mapping example, the elements of the practice repertoires of the communities described here included methods for building local coalitions, running after-school programs, linking education to job training, tracing illegal guns, and using "rumble strips" to reduce highway fatalities. Each of the networks coordinated a varied mix of learning and innovation activities to build, share, and apply knowledge related to their shared practice. These activities differed along several dimensions—face-to-face and virtual; formal and informal; public and private. Further, activities were orchestrated to take place at various rhythms—listserv announcements came weekly, teleconferences were semi-monthly or monthly, visits occurred occasionally throughout the year, e-mails and phone calls were ongoing, and the whole group gathered about once a year. This ecology of activities—which served various functions and occurred at different rhythms—provided value on multiple levels. Moreover, it increased the communities' "presence" in members' lives and reinforced the sense of belonging and identity that were the foundation for knowledge-sharing and collaboration activities. One member reinforced the importance of a mix of activities: "We should combine these various elements of cutting-edge ideas, research evidence, and best practice, along with the local context about how to implement best practices in real cases."

The dimensions of domain, community, and practice are, of course, highly interrelated. For many "emergent" communities, the domain has not been well defined, and therefore the professional repertoire is spotty or uneven. Moreover, if the domain is not compelling, it is less likely to attract motivated and talented members, or ones who want to learn and work together. Conversely, even if members are talented and enjoy working together, if they cannot define a compelling learning agenda to address and do not have case problems to work on or tools they want to build together, then the community is unlikely to get traction.

## When, Where, and Why Do You Create Them?

Agencies and government managers are becoming increasingly conscious that the challenge of keeping up with strategic challenges is mostly about building, sharing, and applying capabilities—at organizational, group, and individual levels. (The plethora of business books published since 1990 on learning and knowledge is just one indicator of the recognition of knowledge, learning, and innovation as the drivers of strategic performance today.) Effectively managing the production and delivery of high-quality products and services is, of course, necessary; but it isn't nearly sufficient in today's management environment (Kotter, 1996). Organization leaders must do "adaptive" work, not only "technical" work, to keep up in a turbulent environment where new technologies are changing how work gets done, demographic shifts are roiling talent pools, and market demands are increasingly dynamic (Heifetz, 1994). The challenges that are most likely to require an adaptive approach are those that are unfamiliar, complex, and require a combination of disciplines to address. Often, an organization's most important strategic challenges fit these criteria. This is why it is important for federal managers to manage two types of complementary structures serving distinct purposes: *formal units*—teams, projects, and business units—that support product and service delivery; and *informal structures*—communities of practice—that steward learning and innovation activities to build professional skills and organizational capabilities.

Adapting to new strategic realities requires learning and innovation, and that is why an increasing number of agencies are sponsoring communities of practice (Wenger and Snyder, 2003). Communities of practice complement traditional structures by stewarding both codifiable tools and frameworks (contained in documents and other media that you can store in a website) as well as the "non-codifiable" dimension that includes professional skills and complex organizational capabilities for which standard policies and procedures cannot substitute (Snyder, 1996, pp. 30-34).

Federal managers should consider community-based initiatives in situations such as the following:

- *Building and disseminating a new capability*—such as homeland security.
- *Increasing current capability levels*—for example, improving school system performance so "no child is left behind."
- *Integrating a new dimension to current capabilities*—such as e-government applications to government purchasing and citizen-service processes.
- *Attracting, retaining, and developing talent*—including professionals in various disciplines and levels of expertise—and particularly as the government, like organizations in every sector, faces massive losses of baby-boomer staff (in many agencies, 40 percent of employees will be eligible to retire in 2005).

## Building New Capabilities

The mission to ensure homeland security, for example, presents an enormous capability-building challenge for 11,000 cities and 3,000 counties nationwide. Local cities and counties must now establish the capacity to prepare, prevent, and respond to unfamiliar threats of unprecedented danger—bio-terrorism, dirty bombs, suicide attacks, and other potential dangers. How can we build local security capabilities all across the country quickly and effectively? How can we combine and coordinate the multitude of disciplines and organizations—such as businesses, agencies, schools, universities, hospitals, fire and police—and connect across local, state, and federal levels where needed? How can we build a sufficient practice repertoire that must include new databases, protocols, technologies, simulations, standards, case studies, and research?

The homeland security problem is much like the gun-violence problem faced by SafeCities, only with increased complexity and uncertainty. But from a knowledge perspective, the challenge is the same: building local capability quickly; leveraging the best capabilities available at various levels of government; and creating mechanisms for innovation, knowledge-sharing, and collaboration among groups within and across cities.

Traditional mechanisms will get us part of the way there. Mandates, policies, and standard procedures should be defined and implemented— but, as usual, the catch is executing plans and intentions at the local level in order to achieve desired outcomes. Every town has its own idiosyncrasies and limitations that may or may not align with the best-laid plans; any complex capability requires adaptation to implement at the local level—not to mention the right motivation, skills, and resourcefulness to make it work.

Communities of practice are effective mechanisms for building and disseminating capabilities because they address the "local" (or "situated") (Lave and Wenger, 1991) nature of knowledge—as well as issues related to skill and will. When you are engaged with peers struggling with the same issues as you face, and when you can put a human face on agency bureaucrats and experts who participate in your community, it becomes less daunting to take on a challenge you have never faced before.

Communities of practice also provide a living repository for ideas, information, best practices, directories of experts and resources, and the rest of the requisite repertoire that civic leaders will need. The amount of information to absorb just to keep up with an established professional discipline can be overwhelming (Davenport and Beck, 2001). Member relationships provide a network for finding out quickly which information is most important to pay attention to and where to get the knowledge you need "on demand," instead of piling it up on your desk or storing it in an obscure folder somewhere in your computer's hard drive "just in case."

## Increasing Current Capability Levels

In many cases, the problem is not to build a new capability, but rather to raise up an established capability to a new level, or even simply maintain it. The new emphasis on improving schools' ability to enable all children to succeed—that is, children of every socioeconomic status, ethnic background, and special need—has raised the national standard for public schools and illustrates a case where the challenge is to raise a current capability to a new level.

The federal government could convene and cultivate a community of stakeholders at the national level. Such a group could provide cross-sectoral stewardship for the array of initiatives and policy mandates being applied to increase school performance levels. This group might consider how communities of practice could be used within and across districts to promote innovation and peer-to-peer knowledge sharing. For example, it could sponsor a pilot initiative to spur student success by promoting the professional development of school leaders and classroom teachers.

Consider briefly how such a group might frame the school leadership crisis we face today. School leaders, particularly principals, are now widely seen as perhaps the most critical lever for school improvement (because they have much influence on teacher effectiveness, which in turn drives student success). There are 90,000 principals in the nation, and approximately 40,000 will be eligible to retire in 2005. Moreover, the schools most in need of effective principals, urban schools in poor districts, are the ones that suffer most from high levels of turnover and underdeveloped leaders. Schools of education generally do not prepare graduates sufficiently for the distinctive challenges of leading urban schools. While formal education and training is essential, the most reliable methods for developing effective urban principals—as is true for any professional—are informal learning activities that occur during internships and on the job. These include coaching and counseling by mentors and co-consulting, visits, and mutual encouragement among peers and colleagues (Fink and Resnick, 2001).

The Department of Education, in collaboration with cross-sector partners at various levels—including foundations, corporations, and nonprofits focused on this work—could lead a collaborative initiative in this area. Such a group could sponsor pilots that demonstrate how school districts can cultivate and leverage local peer-to-peer learning networks that accelerate the development of effective school principals. The approach could also be used to help superintendents learn together about leading transformative change initiatives in districts that need to radically improve performance with scarce resources and restrictive union contracts. Finally, the approach applies just as well to teachers learning to organize a curriculum and manage a classroom.

## Integrating New Capability Dimensions

Communities of practice are also effective for integrating new dimensions into established capabilities. For example, many agencies have been mandated to incorporate a variety of e-government capabilities to reduce operational costs and to increase citizen access and convenience. (President Clinton issued a Presidential Memorandum in 1999 to this effect.)

The Office of the Secretary of Defense, the Defense Acquisition University, and the United States Navy, for example, launched a community of acquisition program managers (called PMCoP for "Program Management Communities of Practice") to provide online access to performance-support materials that help accelerate the production of high-quality weapon systems—an area with tremendous potential for savings. The community includes over 3,000 government and defense-contractor procurement acquisition professionals who serve in all three military services. They present new practices (such as "evolutionary acquisition" and "performance-based contracting" and "reverse auctions"), share ideas, and ask and answer questions via face-to-face meetings, video conferences, listserv discussions, and an online repository. These activities help members build and share vetted tools, methods, lessons learned, and application examples. Community participation enables acquisition professionals to solve problems faster and supports the professional development of an increasing flow of new personnel (just as the implications of baby-boomer demographics are kicking in).[1]

Another cross-agency community, the e-Regulation Community of Practice ("e-Reg"), was launched in the fall of 2001 to develop electronic filing and records management systems by sharing member experiences related to different software and application systems. It was sponsored by the "Knowledge Management Working Group," which was led by pioneering executives from the General Services Administration and the Navy—Shereen Remez and Alex Bennet—who were then part of a cross-agency group of Chief Information Officers called the CIO Council. The community included approximately 30 professionals in various disciplines, including information technology, knowledge management, and records management. They represented a number of departments—Defense, Interior, Agriculture, and Transportation—as well as agencies, including the Federal Energy Regulatory Commission, the General Services Administration, the Securities and Exchange Commission, the Nuclear Regulatory Commission, and others. William Bennett of the Federal Energy Regulatory Commission (FERC) was the lead coordinator for the group, which met every two months (with various informal exchanges in between) to share experiences, demonstrate tools, talk about standards, and work together on projects to accelerate the implementation of a government-wide mandate to convert record-keeping from a primarily paper-based system to an electronic one.[2]

## Attracting, Retaining, and Developing Talent

Every agency in the federal government—like organizations nationwide—is faced with a demographic time bomb that threatens to decommission nearly half their employees between now and 2010. One way that communities of practice build organizational capabilities is by providing professionals a forum for learning; for testing ideas and innovations; and for building relationships and a sense of professional identity with colleagues. This informal sense of belonging among practitioners and associated opportunities for professional development are the most reliable hallmarks of organizations that attract, retain, and develop top talent.

A particularly striking example of a community devoted to professional development is the CompanyCommand.com community. The focus of this community is professional development for U.S. Army company commanders, a leadership position that is responsible for 120 to 250 soldiers and a $10 million budget—a role that can only be mastered by experience. This community envisions every company commander in the Army participating in an ongoing, vibrant conversation with peers and other experts about leading and building combat-ready teams. Determined to find a way to accelerate the learning process and provide encouragement and support for leaders in an extremely challenging and crucial role, a small group of experienced company commanders cultivated a community of over 1,500 past, present, and future company commanders worldwide. Members use a public website to get access to vetted tools; hear (and tell) stories about their experiences; read updates on development opportunities and new resources; and find others to get help or share interests. Community coordinators have been able to leverage the expertise of former commanders, connect "silos of excellence" among members, and accelerate the "time to talent" of isolated leaders in demanding roles. The power of community participation is particularly visible as members support their peers when they are serving in active battlefield conditions.[3]

## Tools for Running a Community of Practice

Vital, strategic communities of practice orchestrate a constellation of complementary learning activities to promote professional development for members. These activities enable members to build tools and methodologies and moderate an online knowledge base at the organizational level. The experience of communities described in this research illustrates how a healthy community can promote effective learning, which in turn builds strategic capabilities that enable the organization to achieve outstanding results. Community members connected in a variety of ways—generally in self-initiated, informal activities, both public and private. This participation generated new ideas, diffused promising practices, and forged new professional relationships. As a result, cities improved their after-school programs, schools and businesses gained flexibility to enhance workforce skills, faith leaders united with police departments to reduce gun violence, and state highway departments cut down on traffic crashes.

The learning mechanisms used by all these communities were essentially the same. These are the same types of activities used by mature communities of practice in the private sector. Each of the activities—including face-to-face meetings, teleconferences, visits, projects, listserv exchanges, and website moderation—contributed a unique dimension to the overall network participation. (See Figure 6.2.) A review of the constellation of learning practices used in these cases provides an instructive and robust template for implementing such communities in any context.

- **Face-to-face conferences** built trust and fostered a sense of joint enterprise that increased productive participation in all learning activities.

> "I really appreciated the face-to-face meeting. It is expensive to bring us together; but when hearing about a project, it is important to see the person to know their level of enthusiasm; and it gives you a chance to sit down over sandwiches and share ideas that may not be on the agenda."

> "We have more in-depth discussions about coalition building in person, versus over the telephone, because you need time for people to process the ideas and some of that takes place overnight—you need a couple days to sit and talk about it."

> "I think you need an initial meeting to bring people together because so much of this work is relationship based. Then you can use technology from there."

- **Teleconferences** provide for low-cost, interactive problem solving, idea generation, and "on-demand" executive education. Monthly or semi-monthly teleconferences featured expert speakers and interactive discussion of problems and solutions among partners.

> "On the calls we have guest speakers and then Q&A, and people talk about their own programs. You're able to ask questions and bring up issues."

> "The teleconferences paint a verbal picture of what's working and allows you to ask questions. You can read about the best practice, but talking about it with peers gives it more life and vitality and helps you more fully leverage what there is to learn."

**Figure 6.2: Networks' Ecology of Learning Activities**

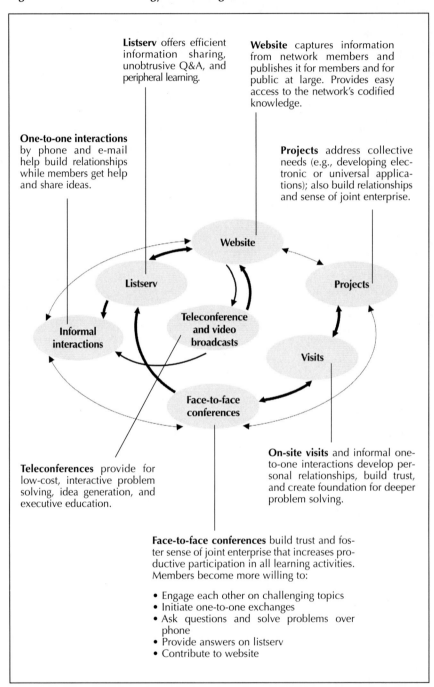

**Listserv** offers efficient information sharing, unobtrusive Q&A, and peripheral learning.

**Website** captures information from network members and publishes it for members and for public at large. Provides easy access to the network's codified knowledge.

**One-to-one interactions** by phone and e-mail help build relationships while members get help and share ideas.

**Projects** address collective needs (e.g., developing electronic or universal applications); also build relationships and sense of joint enterprise.

**Teleconferences** provide for low-cost, interactive problem solving, idea generation, and executive education.

**On-site visits** and informal one-to-one interactions develop personal relationships, build trust, and create foundation for deeper problem solving.

**Face-to-face conferences** build trust and foster sense of joint enterprise that increases productive participation in all learning activities. Members become more willing to:

- Engage each other on challenging topics
- Initiate one-to-one exchanges
- Ask questions and solve problems over phone
- Provide answers on listserv
- Contribute to website

"Our satellite broadcast on 'one-stop' jobs-education centers had hundreds of downlinks and was a powerful way to demonstrate how different agencies were working together."

- **Special face-to-face meetings** were organized to learn about special topics. For example, the 21st Century Skills network held a meeting for members in Austin, Texas, to learn more about how one of the members had organized industry clusters to promote skill development and job placement in industries such as hospitality and financial services. The Boost4Kids community coordinators organized a training session at the Atlanta office of the Centers for Disease Control to learn more about GIS methodologies. Various partners followed up by applying GIS mapping techniques to improve local results. For example, the coalition in Athens, Georgia, used GIS to focus outreach efforts in areas where they were mostly likely to find kids qualified to get health insurance. (Later, the SafeCities coalition also learned about GIS methods, which were helpful in that context as well.)

"We decided that we should learn more about GIS, and this has been a very helpful initiative."

- **Projects** address collective practice-development needs (e.g., crime-mapping methods) and also build relationships and a sense of joint enterprise.

  For example, a project undertaken by a sub-group of Boost4Kids members called the "California Caucus" (including members from three California counties) combined efforts to develop a universal, electronic application for various social services, as well as new program-evaluation approaches. The 21st Century Skills network made plans for an ambitious project to develop a national "electronic learning library."

"In California, our three counties had an all-day workshop together where we carved out three general areas, and each county took responsibility for a project or initiative to develop a universal electronic application for all these social services benefits [that are split up now by siloed agency programs]."

"The Skills Network is seeking support for projects, including one to create a world-class, public-domain, electronic "Learning Library"; and to establish a "Learning Distribution System" for delivering learning to counties nationwide, especially to underserved populations."

- **On-site visits and informal one-to-one interactions** develop personal relationships, build trust, and facilitate deeper problem solving.

"Fort Wayne went to Highpoint to see how to make partnership [including players such as the mayor's office, police department, faith community, district attorney, FBI, local businesses, and others] real. People don't learn by reading books; they learn by doing things and seeing it in practice."

- **Federal agency-champion visits** to local partner communities helped agency champions learn more about partners' local goals and challenges and get help at state and federal levels. Champions helped a number of Boost4Kids participants break through long-standing barriers to innovate for improved results. Examples include: The Boost4Kids coalition in Hawaii increased utilization of a federal nutrition program; Georgia leveraged funds better to increase health-insurance enrollments for kids; Michigan resolved a regulatory dispute to get increased funding for Head Start programs; California achieved a breakthrough on an electronic application; and Iowa gained access to data on births to support new mothers and babies.

  "Our champion can call the state commissioner of insurance. This is high priority for families and kids, so we have met with the governor on down to bring these people to the table."

  "Having the federal people come here made a big difference for us locally–it helped us build trust, develop a relationship, exchange ideas, and feel more open to ask questions."

- **One-to-one interactions by phone and e-mail** help build relationships while members share ideas and get help they need.

  "I'm comfortable calling another police chief about 'chiefly matters' such as how they get funding; how to sell ideas to city managers; pitfalls when talking to the community—or about downsides that you may not hear on the teleconferences."

  "I have called partners in cases where I know they have done something that we're trying to do."

- **Websites** captured information from partners and published it for all network members and for the broader public. The website provided easy access to the network's codified knowledge.

  "We use the website as a place to put information after we talk; also to learn more about issues and to get follow-up information from meetings, for example, minutes and contact names.... It also lets you go into various

# Network Activity Vignette

The monthly teleconferences were the main convening forum for these far-flung networks. Teleconferences were held every two to three weeks, and they focused on a particular topic, such as after-school programs or methods for increasing enrollment of kids in a health insurance program. Conveners and network members identified topics together. Conveners arranged speakers, handled setup and scheduled logistics, facilitated discussion, and managed follow-up (such as documenting discussion and posting items on a listserv or website). Participants included partners, federal champions, and charter members—generally there were about 20 people on a given call. Participation was driven by interest in the topic and by members' desire to keep up with new ideas and connect with other members.

Here's an illustration of a network teleconference: It is 1 p.m. EST on Thursday, April 27, and 24 members of the Boost4Kids Network are joining their monthly teleconference. This month the topic is "Outreach to Youth." Members of the Baltimore coalition are the featured speakers. Audrey and her colleagues describe Baltimore's approach to a city-wide after-school initiative. They explain how Geographic Information System mapping techniques were used to compare locations of after-school activities and incidents of teenage crime. They tell participants how they can access and coordinate diverse funding streams to help get programs started, and how to measure program results. Partners from Vermont and Georgia describe their own successes and problems they had yet to solve. Federal champions from the General Services Administration and the White House offer help on getting more information on after-school programs and pointers for getting press coverage.

Information on resources mentioned during the call was later posted on the network's website. Several partners were encouraged to look again at their own after-school efforts and were motivated to explore new ways to improve them. Soon after, the Palm Beach coalition contacted the partners in Baltimore to get their help. After a number of consultations, Palm Beach adapted the Baltimore model to fit their own situation, and subsequently launched an ambitious county-wide after-school initiative. Their goal was to reduce crime rates and improve graduation rates just as successfully as their Baltimore peers.

states and see what they're doing. For example, you can learn about Louisville's mapping experience or go to a dedicated mapping website and learn more about it. This gives me background before calling my partner in Louisville to learn more."

"[Our] website has an increasing amount of information listed by topic; educators can go there and find information on job banks."

"The website is incredibly helpful for building capacity in our community by providing access to cutting-edge information and ideas."

- **Listservs** were highly effective for efficient information sharing, unobtrusive Q&A, and peripheral learning.

"Pam and Bev [community coordinators] send out valuable information about grants, meetings, papers, resources—and the listserv goes to selected external groups as well as Boost4Kids members—and to many people beyond them on sub-lists that they have created."

"After the calls, we can ask follow-up questions on the listserv."

### Summary—Community of Practice Activities

The various learning activities provide for multiple ways to connect and learn—formal and informal, public and private, virtual and face-to-face. They constitute a learning ecology where various interdependent activities complement each other.

The teleconferences provide the heartbeat of the community—regular, easily accessible ways to keep up to speed on hot topics and hear what others are doing. The website provides a mechanism for catching up on resources or finding contact names or resources mentioned during the calls, while the listserv reminds members of what's coming up and highlights related news in the field such as new grant opportunities or partner accomplishments. Agency-champion and peer visits as well as informal back-channel conversations are ways for members to get help in areas where they want to learn and innovate—often following up on ideas or experiences they hear about from others. Informal conversations among member peers and with the community coordinator, combined with ongoing coordinator canvassing, help identify future topics for teleconferences and collective projects for the community or project teams to pursue. The face-to-face meetings provide a crucial foundation for all these activities. They provide a forum—"where we can break bread together"—to meet people in person and find connections. These personal relationships weave the community together and help build trust and mutual commitment. The overall constellation of learning activities enables practitioners—from a striking variety of disciplines, sectors, and locales—to discover and leverage their shared passion for improving civic well-being.

## How Do Communities of Practice Get Results?

Communities of practice provide a social context for building and sharing ideas and experiences together, and for getting help from colleagues to put them into practice. The link between community participation and performance can be framed in a simplified model that posits causal links between (Snyder, 1996):

a. The community context (relationships, trust, reciprocity, shared values)
b. Collective learning (formal and informal)
c. New professional skills and organizational capabilities (codifiable and tacit)
d. Improved results

Figure 6.3 depicts this model.

An example from the SafeCities case illustrates these linkages.

- **Community context:** A SafeCities convener invited the police chief from Highpoint, North Carolina, to speak at the SafeCities launch conference. Members were interested to hear how Highpoint had cut

**Figure 6.3: What Are the Benefits of Networks?: A SafeCities Example**

| Community Context | Learning Activity | Knowledge Gained | Results |
|---|---|---|---|
| **❶** Convener invited police chief from Highpoint, North Carolina, to describe how they reduced gun violence significantly through both rehabilitation and enforcement efforts that focus on the city's most violent individuals | **❷** Chief Quijas presents case study to all network partners who attend launch meeting in Washington, D.C. **❹** Indiana and Michigan partners visit Highpoint to see program in action | **❸** New ideas and interest—and know who to contact to learn more | |
| | **❺** Indiana and Michigan partners adapt Highpoint model for local application | **❻** Indiana and Michigan partners have methods, skills, and initiative to implement new violence-reduction strategy | **❼** Implementing local versions of Highpoint model, with goal to achieve significant reduction in gun violence as demonstrated by Highpoint |

firearm homicides in half through a combination of rehabilitation and enforcement efforts that focused on the city's most violent individuals.

- **Learning activity:** Chief Quijas presented his case to network partners at the launch meeting in Washington, D.C. Members buttonholed him later during informal conversations to learn more, and they asked if they could visit to see the work firsthand. Subsequently, Indiana and Michigan partners visited Highpoint and observed its programs in action. Both coalitions then adapted the Highpoint model for application in their own locales. It was important for key players from the coalitions back home to talk face-to-face with Quijas and his partners. The police chiefs, mayors, and faith leaders from different towns met their peers and learned more about how the Highpoint model really worked; and they learned about the pitfalls to expect along the way.

- **Knowledge gained:** Indiana and Michigan community members developed new ideas and motivation as well as "know who"—who to contact to learn more.They gained methods, skills, motivation, and external legitimacy (via a successful example and strong federal agency encouragement) to implement an innovative violence-reduction strategy.

- **Results:** Implementation takes time, and generally there are bumps along the way—and results generally lag even when an intervention is implemented well. When data was collected for this chapter, no definitive results were yet available. Nevertheless, the goals in both Indiana and Michigan were to achieve significant reduction in gun violence on the same order of magnitude as the 50 percent reduction achieved in Highpoint.

The main purpose of the initiatives presented in this chapter was to improve results—healthy and educated kids, reduced gun violence, and a stronger, better-employed workforce. There are three main ways in which these communities made contributions at local, state, and federal levels:

- Increased access to information, methods, expertise, and resources
- Provided more influence with stakeholders to bust barriers and build support
- Heightened attention and initiative to try new approaches

### Increased Access to Information, Methods, Expertise, and Resources

The array of network activities described here—including teleconferences, champion and peer visits, face-to-face case presentations, listserv announcements, website documents, and various informal interactions—all provide information about methods, expertise, and resources that members were much less likely to know about otherwise. For example, several SafeCities members asked for contact information from the police chief in Redlands, California, after he presented his exemplary community-policing initiative. But as one member later reported, she was unlikely to have contacted him if she had not made the personal contact on the teleconference. In fact, she was unlikely to have heard about it in the first place. Police chiefs, like most busy executives working in turbulent environments, are consumed with solving immediate problems. Moreover, without the personal contact, you are less likely to trust the source or have any hope for help adapting the idea to your unique context (Szulanski, 1996).

- Partners learn about new programs and funding opportunities through teleconferences and champion recommendations.

  "We got a grant for character-based education to divert youth from the criminal path that we wouldn't have heard about or qualified as well for if not for SafeCities."

- Federal "agency champion" visits help partners address problems at the state level and get answers quickly about where to focus efforts to implement new ideas.

  "When Pam [agency champion] tells us it's not a federal problem, then we don't spend three months waiting. We went through 10 different suggestions to find the denominator for the number of kids insured—and did it much quicker than we could have done otherwise."

- SafeCities' meetings and teleconferences reduce time for new mayors in Fort Wayne and Inkster to get up to speed on leading practices.

  "We learned how community policing works, and now we have renewed a moribund community-policing program and stepped it up.... The Network gave us a quick window on best practices from around the country."

### Provided More Influence with Stakeholders to Bust Barriers and Build Support

It matters to know that if you try a new approach, you'll get the support of key influencers along the way—both logistically and politically. Members were motivated to try harder to solve local problems—or ones involving state agencies—because they knew they had the support and credibility that federal officials could provide. They were impressed by how hard the federal coordinators and champions worked for them, and this gave them motivation to try just as hard at the local level. They knew they were not alone, and seeing the power of increased federal support on local and state players, they were encouraged to work harder to cultivate these relationships on their own.

- Federal champions helped ensure that partners got requested help from agency officials on gun tracing and in the process built a new relationship at the federal level.

  "Our champion's intervention influenced federal policy people to learn more about how to be responsive to local communities."

- Members of the 21st Century Skills community gained prestige, national prominence, and increased local stakeholder support for their innovation efforts.

  "When we were selected we got a press conference and editorial in the newspaper. This has made it a lot easier to get meetings with elected officials, who now see us as a major player and see our work as important. High-level university officials are more likely to listen to us and answer our phone calls."

### Heightened Attention and Initiative to Try New Approaches

Knowing about an innovation is not the same as seeing it or hearing a participant describe in passionate and proud terms what they're doing and what they're achieving; or getting the details about the challenges they faced and how they overcame them. Network participation gives members a chance to meet others who are in the same boat; who have the credibility only a peer can have; and who have succeeded at doing things some never thought possible. It is not merely models and methods that count, but also the passion and encouragement of peers to try a new approach—peers who will listen to your woes during false starts, cheer your successes, and offer help when you ask. Civic initiative isn't easy. There are frequently conflicts among diverse constituencies and nay-saying by bystanders who criticize from the sidelines. A national network of innovating peers is a welcome home base and source of renewal for continuing the charge.

- Successes of partners in the areas of parolees, gun tracing, involving faith leaders, and after-school programs increased peers' attention to new approaches and willingness to implement them.

  "The Highpoint visit added ideas and motivation to an initiative that we had been planning for a year. Once the mayor visited, he wanted to do it.... Participation in the network has helped us venture into these unknown waters not alone."

# The Federal Experience with Communities of Practice

The four case histories described here—three are a related set of cross-agency, intergovernmental communities, and one was sponsored by a single agency—provide a "thick description" (Geertz, 1973) of why we need to cultivate communities of practice to address today's challenges, what they do to operate and accomplish results, and how federal agencies can sponsor and support their development. The cases provide insights related to both theory and practice, and outline the unique role the federal government can play. These cases address a number of key issues:

- Why communities of practice are so effective—and why they should be used to complement and enhance conventional initiatives and policy mandates
- What communities can do to foster learning and innovation among members and increase capabilities that enhance strategic results
- How sponsoring federal agencies can focus communities on strategic issues without killing the internal leadership initiative that drives them

Many of the models and methods that these networks discovered and developed over time were not known when the first one, Boost4Kids, was started. The theory of the case about the nature of cross-agency communities is thus particularly robust because it was shaped primarily through practice—and especially because this practice evolved in the context of three separate cross-agency initiatives, each of which took advantage of what the others were learning along the way.

A key feature of the action-learning structures that emerged was how rooted they were in local priorities, which in turn drove a process that spurred cross-agency collaboration among federal players. The initiatives did not rely on cumbersome, top-down interagency collaboration—for example, around service integration—to build or sustain momentum. On the contrary, helpful interagency work—streamlining and more—emerged in response to learning among the networks and coaxing from sponsors and community coordinators.

## Boost4Kids

### History

Boost4Kids began as a variation on a standard technical assistance model, where a selected group of local "performance partners" would get special attention and policy waivers from "federal champions" from a variety of agencies. Several senior officials, including Pam Johnson and Beverly

## Boost4Kids

**Domain:** Boost4Kids focused on what it called "results for kids," including a number of interrelated outcomes such as school readiness, health insurance, nutrition, healthy behaviors, and child abuse. There is a great deal at stake in this area. At the time, California alone had a million children without health insurance. Of these, 750,000 were eligible for insurance covered by federal programs, but could not gain access to the right channels. The costs to children, to their families, and to society of untreated illnesses such as lead poisoning, asthma, and other ailments far outweigh the cost of preventative treatments covered by health insurance.

**Community:** The Boost4Kids Network included a wide range of federal agencies in addition to various foundations and nonprofits. Participating agencies included the Departments of Agriculture, Defense, Education, Health and Human Services, Housing and Urban Development, Justice, Labor, and Transportation; the Environmental Protection Agency, the National Partnership for Reinventing Government, the Office of Management and Budget, the Consumer Product Safety Commission, the Social Security Administration, the Federal Geographic Data Committee, and the Interagency Forum on Child and Family Statistics. Outside partners included the Annie E. Casey Foundation, Hitachi Foundation, the Institute for Educational Leadership, National Civic League, The Finance Project, and the State of Missouri.

Each member participated in the context of a "performance partnership" that consisted of a local community, a state, and a federal partner; each was assigned a federal agency champion to work with the partnership to help measure results and cut red tape. Local members came from all over the nation, including:
- **California:** Contra Costa, Placer, and San Diego Counties
- **Florida:** Pinellas and Palm Beach Counties
- **Georgia:** Athens Family Connection and Houston County
- **Hawaii:** Good Beginnings Alliance
- **Iowa:** Cass, Mills, and Montgomery Counties, State Empowerment Board
- **Maine:** Communities for Children
- **Maryland:** Family League of Baltimore City, Inc.
- **Michigan:** St. Joseph County
- **North Carolina:** Charlotte-Mecklenburg Resolves II
- **Vermont:** Vermont Regional Partnerships

**Practice:** The Boost4Kids Network included:
- Geographic Information System (GIS) tools and methods for identifying strategic sites for after-school programs and focused efforts to find kids who had no health insurance
- Templates for electronic, "universal" applications that allowed families to apply for multiple, related family services without getting bounced around from agency to agency to fill out dozens of forms

- Best practices for improving access to federal nutrition programs and for enhancing school readiness programs for kids, including better ways to use Department of Transportation funds to get young children to day-care facilities
- Ways to strengthen outreach to at-risk youth to encourage them to join after-school programs

Godwin, sponsored by a special office organized by Vice President Gore—called the National Partnership for Reinventing Government (NPR)—helped identify special needs for each partner and linked the coalition members with appropriate officials in the various agencies. The purpose was to help local, multi-stakeholder civic groups get results and, in the process, to help agencies learn more about how to design and manage their programs to achieve greater impact nationwide.

The impetus to form the Boost4Kids Network came from leaders at several levels, including local, state, and federal. At the federal level, the initiative was an outgrowth of ongoing work by the "Reinvention Office" sponsored by the Office of the Vice President. While the office had focused since 1993 on the internal operations of agencies (streamlining paperwork, improving customer service, etc.), in later years it went beyond the federal government boundaries. In 1998, the State of Oregon asked NPR officials for program changes that would help them leverage federal dollars better to deliver healthcare benefits in the state. The partnership—later called the "Oregon Option"—was a great success. At the local level, another element of this catalytic combination was emerging. Dr. Robert Ross, director of Health and Human Services in San Diego County, was documenting how onerous federal regulations got in the way of healthcare results at the local level.

Vice President Gore's 1998 seventh annual "Family Reunion" brought together families and those that work with them to discuss and design better ways to strengthen family life in America. Dr. Ross was asked to speak at this national conference on healthy families. He presented his accomplishments at the local level, and then used his opportunity on the national stage to decry the federal constraints that prevented him from going further.

Dr. Ross described how San Diego County had cut overhead, streamlined administrative processes, and instituted progress measures. These efforts had freed up resources to serve children and families and improved results significantly. But he argued that the federal government was holding up further reforms. He held up an 800-page tome (called "the phone book") of application forms required by various federal and state agencies and

## The National Performance Review

The history of the organization that spawned three of the networks featured in this chapter actually begins in 1993. That year, President Bill Clinton established the "National Performance Review" (NPR), headed by Vice President Gore, as a major cross-agency initiative to streamline government structures, procedures, and regulations in order to create a government "that works better and costs less" (Gore, 1993). While the NPR office, made up of dozens of full- and part-time staff on loan from various agencies, achieved significant operational savings, its scope was focused on improving internal agency results related to operational efficiency, customer service, and employee empowerment (Kettl, 1998).

The NPR organization was nevertheless an important innovation in federal government—something like a "skunk works" (Peters and Waterman, 1982) for improving the cost and quality of internal government services. But many of the greatest opportunities for "really reinventing government in the context of lasting governance ideas" lie in crossing the sector boundaries of public institutions and civil society (Kettl, 1998). During NPR's first year, David Osborne, co-author of the influential book *Reinventing Government* (Osborne and Gabler, 1992), acted as a senior advisor to the NPR initiative. In 1994, he met with a group of 20 leading innovators from a variety of agencies to talk about how the federal government could encourage state and local cross-sector coalitions to take on more responsibility for the design and implementation of federal programs.

Although it is beyond the scope of this chapter to describe in detail the nature of the NPR office itself, it is fair to say that none of the cross-agency, intergovernmental communities of practice described in this chapter would ever have been launched without it. Moreover, even where federal teams and agencies supported the communities, the energy, skills, and influence of key players in the NPR office were crucial to their success.

explained that these were the forms a typical at-risk family of four—with a disabled father who had lost his job and a mother seeking employment and insurance for her kids—would need to complete in order to get the assistance they needed.

Ross explained that since the 1930s, when human services programs were first created, there had been 60 years of policy and program development spurred by demographic change, social upheaval, and political movement. As a result, local cities and counties were now constrained by an impossible tangle of highly targeted, unconnected programs and restrictive budget allocations. These make it difficult to treat children and families as whole persons in a social context, not as a "3717 kid" or "40A3 family"—known only in terms of the legislative program for which they qualify.[4]

Dr. Ross asserted before Vice President Gore and assembled audience that the current regulations were a rat's nest—overlapping, unconnected, and burdensome—and that they wasted funds and limited the ability of local agencies and non-government groups to help people in need. He challenged the federal government to find a way to reduce the red tape and help local groups get results.

Something had to change, he said, or nearly one million kids at risk each year in California alone would not get the health insurance they needed, with drastic consequences in both human suffering and eventual financial costs.

The federal officials attending the conference got Dr. Ross's point. They understood that the San Diego County situation was not unique. Furthermore, the Oregon Option experience suggested a practical way to make progress. In fact, NPR officials had already begun working with state officials in California and Hawaii to build on the Oregon success. But Ross's call raised the bar: How to accelerate the process?

The NPR group decided to recruit a larger group of results-oriented local cross-sector coalitions nationwide to participate in an "innovation network" where each participating group—and its state partners—would get the Oregon Option treatment. NPR officials would coordinate a network of officials from various federal agencies to work with the local coalitions to reduce paperwork and overhead expenses, and to channel funds and expertise more effectively to improve results. Federal agencies, in turn, would learn more about how to design programs and policies to have maximum leverage.

A steering committee that included federal champions from various agencies and NPR conveners[5] was formed. In February 1999 they published an invitation in the Federal Register and recruited "family-services coalitions" to join a national network of social innovators. Ultimately, 75 local groups applied and 13 were selected, based on criteria that included a track record of multi-sector collaboration, partnership with state agency officials, and a commitment to learn and innovate to achieve improved outcomes.

Boost4Kids was born. Its charter goals included:

- Cut red tape and streamline services to get better results for our nation's children
- Achieve specific targets and results identified by performance partners
- Create better models for cross-government delivery of services for children
- Identify and resolve barriers at the federal, state, and local levels
- Learn promising practices to better manage for results and maximize resources

The original Boost4Kids network model was a kind of hub-and-spoke design, with the NPR office serving as the hub that brokered relationships between federal agencies and local coalitions—helping identify opportunities locally and then brokering assistance from appropriate federal agencies. For example, the State of Hawaii requested a waiver from the Department of Agriculture to disperse funding for its school-nutrition program so it could reach more of the neediest kids in the state. The NPR office helped them find the right person to talk with to find a solution. Figure 6.4 presents the Boost4Kids community network structure.

But once the network was formed, conveners, federal champions, and the performance partners all discovered additional ways the network could create value—essentially by moving from a hub-and-spoke model to one that actively facilitated peer-to-peer links as well. For example, when they began meeting each other in the initial teleconferences, members were very impressed with their peers and expressed interest in learning more—peer-to-peer—about what others were doing to improve results for kids in health-care, school readiness, and other areas. Likewise, once the federal agency champions started working with partners to solve specific problems, they found out how helpful it was to hear what other agencies where doing to address a common constituency. For example, how did local problems affecting nutrition programs also show up in related transportation, health, and school readiness programs? Each program was housed in a separate agency, but clearly there were opportunities to learn across agencies about how to improve their collective impact, while reducing bottlenecks and overhead costs.

What started as a souped-up, cross-level variation on a conventional technical assistance model began to evolve into a peer-to-peer model linking all the participants together. Partners learned from their peers, agency officials learned from each other, and all participants—agency officials, NPR conveners, and partners—took collective responsibility for learning about and innovating ways to improve results for kids. This was more than a network for getting individual coalition (local) problems fixed. It was a community of practitioners with mutual interests in learning and innovating together for their collective benefit and, beyond that, the nation's. This model coalesced in a very concrete way when network participants met face-to-face as a group about six months after the initiative was launched.

The initial Boost4Kids face-to-face meeting took place in Nashville in June 1999, in conjunction with Vice President Gore's Family Reunion 8, and was funded by the Hitachi Foundation. The gathering included a reception for members and coordinators to meet informally as well as a formal day-long meeting. Network members established their purpose, identified issues, and discussed goals. Issues identified in Nashville became topics for biweekly teleconferences.

"Meeting network partners face-to-face significantly increased trust to share electronically and over the phone."

**Figure 6.4: What Is the Overall Community Network Structure?**

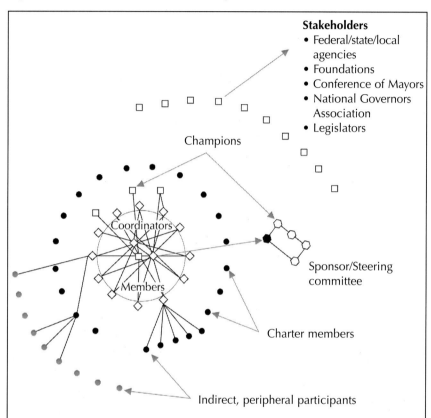

- 2 to 3 federal agency coordinators facilitate network activities, link with agencies, and provide support functions (coach other coordinators, develop technology, liaise with sponsor, etc.)
- 13 members—each a local, cross-sector coalition focused on a particular domain (such as workforce development)— who participate in conferences, projects, visits, listserv, etc.
- Agency champions provide technical assistance and intervene to help solve problems for members
- 60 "charter members" who participate through listserv and website
- Steering committee guides network development; includes sponsor, co-ordinators, support team, and federal agency champions
- Peripheral participants are colleagues of partners and charter members; network members pass along information and ideas that are posted on listserv or website
- Stakeholders include federal/state/local agencies and other groups who support or influence members and who could be influenced by their ideas and proposals

## Accomplishments

- Boost4Kids community coordinators organized a workshop on Geographic Information Systems and how to use it to target kids who needed health insurance. As a result, members increased enrollment in their local communities and reduced associated administrative expenses.

  "The GIS training helped us move forward more quickly, because we got answers about laws related to confidentiality and talked with other Boost4Kids partners about how they dealt with it. It's a real capacity issue for us to address these issues; there's more motivation and direction when other sites are involved."

- Members heard about a model after-school program implemented by the Baltimore partner on a teleconference and then developed the idea with help from experienced practitioners in Baltimore—this led to improved after-school programs for elementary and middle schools in members' cities and regions.

  "Stakeholders in our community think it's a big deal to be selected to Boost4Kids, and this gives us more credibility. The school district came to us recently regarding an after-school program idea. They asked for our help designing it and put our name on it as a way to encourage participation."

  "Before Boost4Kids, there was interest in mobilizing local coalitions to improve nutrition and insurance results, but there was nothing happening. Without Boost4Kids, we would not have achieved these improved results. We took full advantage of the opportunity; we leveraged it to the max."

## What Happened to Boost4Kids?

In 2000, Boost4Kids almost moved to the Department of Health and Human Services (HHS), but the department could not fund a coordinator (full- or part-time). The network continued to meet, with much of the focus on finding a sponsor to support one full-time equivalent (FTE) to continue in the role of network coordinator. After several promising discussions with officials at HHS, the funding initiative fell through. The department could not define or staff a job with the appropriate responsibilities. In any case, as the agency negotiated with Boost4Kids members to understand what level of support they needed, it was clear that a condition would be that the members focus much of their energy on one of its featured programs. Members were glad to focus on the objectives of this program, which were to increase access to healthcare and reduce health disparities. There was some tension during these negotiations nevertheless. While the healthcare objectives (for both adults and children) were important elements of Boost4Kids' mission, they did not align with the network's unique focus on the combination of factors influencing children's well-being.

Boost4Kids met one last time in conjunction with a related HHS conference, with travel paid by a nonprofit organization that had been involved in the network during the previous year and a half. Though the conference meeting was very successful and a number of plans were made to continue to learn and work together, the absence of a dedicated coordinator and agency sponsorship was sorely felt and several leading participants regretfully opted out soon after. This further deflated overall participation and eventually the network petered out.

### Lessons Learned

- **Leadership (sponsor):** Usefulness of a catalytic event, such as the highly visible, compelling case made by Dr. Ross to mobilize action with the support of high-level federal sponsors.
- **Leadership (coordinator):** Key role of the community coordinator as a linchpin that keeps the community going—perhaps even more important than a high-level agency sponsor, given the value members attributed to their peer-to-peer learning and potential for collective influence in their field.
- **Practice:** Power of peer-to-peer learning as a mechanism for building and sharing capabilities—complementing the traditional function of federal technical assistance as well as the unique NPR focus on "barrier-busting."
- **Community:** Widespread interest among local community coalitions to link with state and federal partners and discover new ways to innovate for results.
- **Domain Legitimacy:** Value of the national "brand name" to increase support at the local level. For example, in one city the school principal became much more collaborative once the local coalition was selected by the Vice President's office as a Boost4Kids member.

## SafeCities

### History

The SafeCities and 21st Century Skills Networks built on the Boost4Kids model. Both arose, like Boost4Kids, out of discussions held in national forums—on the topics of public safety and workforce development, respectively. SafeCities launched about a year after Boost4Kids, and 21st Century Skills about three months later. The experience of both groups leveraged the Boost4Kids model, and the experiences and lessons learned from all three accelerated the evolution of the model over time.

# SafeCities

**Domain:** The SafeCities network focused on reducing gun violence, addressing issues such as gun-tracing methods, community-policing strategies, after-school programs, crime mapping tools and methods, and how to involve faith leaders.

**Community:** Federal partners included the Department of Justice's Office of Community Oriented Policing Services (COPS), the Executive Office for U.S. Attorneys, the Office of Legal Policy, and the Office of Justice Programs; the Department of The Treasury's Bureau of Alcohol, Tobacco and Firearms; the High Intensity Drug Trafficking Program of the Office on National Drug Control Policy; the Office of Management and Budget; and the National Partnership for Reinventing Government.

SafeCities local members include a variety of local coalitions in cities and regions nationwide: "Weed and seed" sites (funded by the Department of Justice) in Eastern Michigan and Atlantic City, New Jersey; SafeCities Partnership in Fort Wayne, Indiana: the King County (Washington) Violent Firearms Crime Coalition; Violence Prevention Coalition in Los Angeles; Springfield (Massachusetts) Violence Prevention Task Force; Safe City USA in Fort Worth, Texas; Centinela Valley (California) Juvenile Diversion Project; and police departments in Louisville, Kentucky; Miami, Florida; and Highpoint, North Carolina. Local SafeCities coalitions included community groups, law enforcement officials, mayors, public health officials, leaders of faith and business communities, and educators—and each has a federal point of contact to help achieve their goals.

**Practice:** SafeCities practice-development activities focused on tools and methods related to a number of gun-violence-reduction approaches that the Justice Department established as particularly effective for preventing gun violence.

- SafeCities teleconferences and visits to local communities described how to establish a broad, active local coalition that works with state and federal agencies and fosters collaborations among multiple constituencies and municipalities at the local level. There were several calls and visits, for example, to promote improved collaboration among police chiefs, mayors, and faith leaders (particularly those in high-crime areas who traditionally had weak ties with city authorities).
- Learning more about the principal sources of illegal guns and developing a comprehensive plan to interrupt sources of sales and distribution—including methods for identifying both high-volume storefronts and individual sellers.
- Approaches related to various prevention activities, such as community-policing strategies, after-school programs, and understanding how to deal with the linkages between domestic violence, substance and alcohol abuse, and gun violence.

- Methods for responding to illegal gun use, such as crime mapping and data collection and analysis of crime scenes, aggressive prosecutorial strategies (that facilitate collaboration of district attorneys at local, state, and federal levels), and the design of local gun-possession laws.
- How to improve the interaction between at-risk youth and law-enforcement professionals, creating educational marketing initiatives and increasing access to after-school programs.
- Finally, SafeCities members organized a significant effort to establish behavioral anchors that described high and low levels of competence for each of the principal gun-violence-prevention strategies. The purpose was for each agency and local membership coalition to be able to assess strategic capabilities in concrete terms—even if there were no reliable and relevant statistics available. For example, one city may do quite well at organizing a local coalition but have a severe deficiency in the area of aggressively prosecuting offenses.

The catalyst for SafeCities had been Attorney General Janet Reno's 1998 "Mapping Out Crime" report, which recommended the formation of a "peer-to-peer network." At first, it was not clear how many of the elements of the Boost4Kids model that SafeCities should adopt. For example, the community coordinators thought that the domain would focus on a much more limited area—in this case, techniques related to crime mapping—rather than on a broader domain defined in terms of social impact (as was Boost4Kids', which was defined simply as "results for kids"). Further, they considered convening the network primarily through an on-line technology forum, without regular teleconferences and other "live" ways to interact. At this point, Boost4Kids was considered an independent experiment rather than a model for others to build on and replicate in other domains.

About this time, the NPR was reflecting more broadly on inter-organizational approaches to innovation, particularly ones that could bridge the boundaries between federal, state, and local governments. Several NPR leaders connected with peers working in an innovative federal program in the United Kingdom sponsored by the Prime Minister's office, called the Social Exclusion Unit. The UK initiatives have focused on areas similar to NPR's—including "children and young people," "reducing reoffending," and "barriers to employment"—and are also run as partnerships with local authorities and voluntary organizations. The UK's Social Exclusion Unit thus includes initiatives that closely parallel the U.S. interagency community domains.[6]

The point of these programs, much like the NPR communities of practice discussed in this chapter, was to convene agencies and organizations across levels and sectors in the UK that had a role to play in these areas. The federal conveners in the Prime Minister's office organized meetings, coordinated the learning agenda and various activities, and helped link members from various constituencies and organizations to facilitate innovative solutions and improved results.

At about this time, the NPR group invited several outside speakers to talk to them about relevant organizing frameworks in the private and public sectors. One model, for example, applied a type of "center of excellence" approach to public service—proposing that a cross-agency entity like NPR connect innovating local groups, capture and filter ideas, and then disseminate them—with the expectation that local groups would report back on their results. (This model was something like the original Boost4Kids "hub-and-spoke" model, with an added dimension of performance accountability from local partners to Washington conveners.) Another model (proposed by the first author) was closer to the peer-to-peer model toward which Boost4Kids seemed to be organically evolving. In this model, the role of the convener functioned as a combination community organizer, activity coordinator, and knowledge broker. It emphasized the importance of voluntary membership in learning communities and did not grant the convener administrative jurisdiction or authority over participant actions and results. The network sponsor and conveners could of course emphasize results as a key focus and make it a criterion for participation. But the guiding principle for participation was more like one used in voluntary associations than the approach used in many organizational centers of excellence, where members are formally staffed to specific roles and regularly evaluated on their performance outcomes.[7]

These ongoing discussions highlighted and legitimized key elements of the Boost4Kids Network and influenced the SafeCities conveners to reframe their design along these lines. The SafeCities coordinators thus broadened their domain to focus on a compelling social issue—in this case, "reducing gun violence," and ditched the idea of limiting interactions to an online forum in favor of an emphasis on live peer-to-peer knowledge sharing and collaboration. They all recognized that police chiefs, mayors, and others were unlikely to participate actively in an online forum. They also followed the Boost4Kids start-up process. They began by convening officials from relevant federal agencies and developing a shared vision for what the network would be about and how they would work together. They adapted Boost4Kids' recruitment and selection documents and processes. In November 1999, 10 communities were selected—about the same number as Boost4Kids and based on similar criteria:

- Comprehensive prevention and enforcement strategies
- Commitment to achieve improved outcomes
- Measurement of results

- Participation of key stakeholders, including federal, state, and local law enforcement; education, faith, and other community leaders

The announcement of the SafeCities Network coincided with publication of FBI's crime-rate statistics, which showed significant variation across cities in areas related to gun violence and violent crime. One goal of SafeCities was to reduce these disparities and bring all cities up to the level of the best-performing ones.

During their initial introductory teleconference, members discussed how the group would work together and what issues they would like to address. Members were glad to share ideas over the phone, but strongly argued that they should all meet face-to-face—coordinators, agency champions, and partners—to get to know each other and build the kind of trust and familiarity that would facilitate sharing ideas and mutual efforts to act on them.

In addition to what they were hearing from participants, the SafeCities coordinators were emboldened by the success of Boost4Kids' face-to-face meeting. They were also encouraged by what they had learned about how private-sector organizations had developed similar types of networks. They agreed to sponsor a conference for participants, and designed it according to key dimensions of a community of practice. They made plans to meet in March 2000 for a face-to-face meeting in Washington, D.C. Members would learn more about federal agency resources, get to know each other, and make plans together about what issues to address and how best to promote learning and improve results across sites. The first SafeCities conference agenda focused on:

- What is SafeCities? (domain)
- What does SafeCities do? (practice)
- How does SafeCities work and who is part of it? (community)

The conference included an evening reception and "fair" for members to meet each other and federal agency champions informally—plus many other opportunities over two days to learn about federal agency and foundation-sponsored programs and grants, hear an exemplary case study on reducing gun violence, define objectives, and get to know each other.

SafeCities coordinators Pam Johnson and Michael Seelman began the conference with background on communities of practice, and then framed the conference agenda in terms of the three basic dimensions of communities—topic *domain,* *community* membership, and *practice* tools and methods. During the conference members identified issues related to reducing gun violence (domain); got to know each other (community); and talked about practical methods they could use to reduce gun violence (practice).

> "We used a wonderfully elaborate technology during our meeting in Washington which helped us identify our top 10 issues as a group and come up with goals and objectives and kinds of projects to work on together."

**Figure 6.5: Building Complex Capability to Reduce Gun Violence Nationwide**

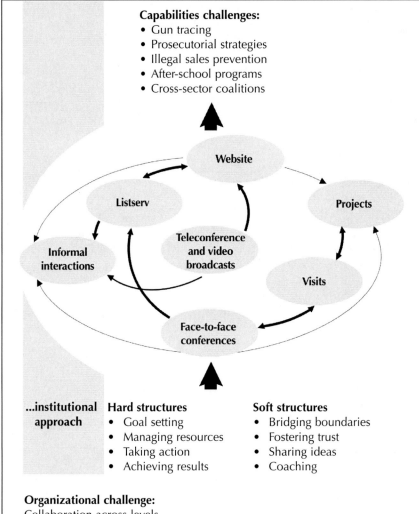

**Capabilities challenges:**
- Gun tracing
- Prosecutorial strategies
- Illegal sales prevention
- After-school programs
- Cross-sector coalitions

Website

Listserv

Projects

Teleconference and video broadcasts

Informal interactions

Visits

Face-to-face conferences

**...institutional approach**

**Hard structures**
- Goal setting
- Managing resources
- Taking action
- Achieving results

**Soft structures**
- Bridging boundaries
- Fostering trust
- Sharing ideas
- Coaching

**Organizational challenge:**
Collaboration across levels
- Agencies: Justice and Treasury agency sub-units: FBI, ATF, etc.
- Levels: agencies and governments (local, state, and federal); U.S., state, and local district attorneys
- Cities: started with 11 cities, aspiration to grow nationwide

**Results:**
- Joint efforts between police and faith community spread to new cities
- Collaboration between ATF, FBI, U.S. Attorneys, and local law enforcement
- Catalyzing a new cross-sector coalition in one city and reinforcing others

Network members identified issues and four main outcomes: 1) identify causes and solutions of gun violence, 2) build partnership at federal, state, and local levels, 3) develop a national strategy that includes prevention and enforcement, and 4) share ideas and strategies inside and outside the core network members. They outlined a design for how network members would learn together—including teleconferences, champion and partner visits, and a website. The issues they identified during the conference sessions became topics for their biweekly teleconferences. The conference was a great success. The expert speaker from Highpoint, North Carolina, was so impressed with the quality and energy of participants that he asked if he could join, which he did (as an "honorary" member).

The conference was instrumental in coalescing members around a shared agenda, and building trust and reciprocity. The SafeCities teleconferences became more active and members were more forthcoming about selecting topics and offering to speak to the group about their experiences. The importance of fostering "community"—a sense of mutual trust, shared identity, and belonging—became more apparent as an important structural condition for success. (Wenger, et al., 2002, pp. 33-37) The SafeCities experience reinforced the value of peer-to-peer learning and helped demonstrate how it could complement and leverage the power of cross-level collaborations among federal champions, state officials, and local coalition members.

A meeting of several SafeCities coalitions in Fort Worth, Texas, illustrates how strongly members valued opportunities for peer-to-peer learning. The coalition members from King County, Washington, and Miami, Florida, visited Fort Worth to learn more about their highly successful public advertising campaign against gun violence. Participants in the meeting included a number of senior officials, including the King County sheriff, Miami's police chief, the mayor and police chief from Fort Worth, and a contingent of others from all three cities. Michael Seelman, the SafeCities coordinator from Washington, helped to connect the key players and consulted with them about how to prepare for and structure the gathering. He had organized an earlier teleconference that featured the Fort Worth experience, which was the catalyst that motivated the Seattle and Miami groups to visit in person.

While the focus was on the Fort Worth experience, Miami also presented its successes with youth programs, and King County explained how they had organized a remarkably diverse coalition of over 30 municipalities in the Seattle area. One measure of the value members' attributed to the visit was the time and expense senior officials and others invested to travel to Fort Worth and spend a day together talking shop. Another was the evidence of how much they learned. For example, King County Sheriff Reichart, a nationally recognized leader in the law enforcement field, took prodigious notes throughout the meeting. He highlighted this to his peers at

## SafeCities Vignette

It is 1 p.m. EST on Wednesday, April 12, and 29 members of local coalitions nationwide are joining their monthly teleconference. They are all members of the SafeCities Network—a community of practice focused on reducing gun violence and sponsored by a steering committee consisting of several collaborating federal agencies. This month the topic is "faith-based community strategies."

Faith leaders from Fort Wayne, Indiana, and Highpoint, North Carolina, are the featured speakers. They describe how groups of faith leaders in their cities have achieved dramatic reductions in gun violence through collaborations of local faith organizations and police departments. Reverend Jordan from Fort Wayne describes the evolution of a collaborative effort that began in 1992 after a highly publicized accidental shooting of a teenager participating in activities at a local Boys' Club. Jordan began holding meetings between gang leaders and city officials to talk together about how to stem the rising tide of violence in the city. These gatherings—which featured gang leaders giving presentations and putting on skits to communicate the importance of recreation alternatives and mentors for teenagers—were very successful. The meetings led to the development of a citywide "Stop the Madness" program and to later collaborations that included an alliance of churches, the police department, and community leaders.

Reverend Fails of Highpoint describes how faith leaders and the police department collaborated to reduce citywide violence by focusing on "the baddest of the bad"—individuals on parole or probation most likely to commit violent crimes. Their approach included faith leaders, school principals, social services agencies, and community leaders—as well as the chief of police, district attorney, and representatives from the FBI, ATF, and state- and federal-level prosecutors. The Highpoint model featured a "good cop, bad cop" approach that focused as much on helping these people find jobs and stabilize their lives as on aggressive law enforcement methods. Speakers field questions regarding how to get faith leaders and their congregations involved. The partner from Los Angeles describes a program in which clergy helped gather information on gun violence from congregation members, and a partner from Louisville talked about their clergy's effort to pass firearm legislation and distribute trigger locks. Partners request the phone numbers of speakers and are encouraged to intensify or begin explorations of ways to involve the faith community to reduce gun violence. That summer, faith leaders from Inkster, Michigan, accompanied their mayor and police chief on a visit to Highpoint to learn how to develop their own program.

A follow-up initiative leveraged the lessons learned in the April 12 call. In October, a satellite broadcast reached over 50 sites nationwide and featured Reverend Jordan talking about youth violence and a new initiative to develop a training academy for faith leaders on topics such as crisis response and community policing.

"The faith community conversation was really useful. We have many churches in our community, but we haven't been sure about how to involve the faith community. Fort Wayne talked about how after a tragic experience they got ministers involved. We wanted to know how to involve them without waiting for a tragic experience. The Fort Wayne example encouraged me to dig for more examples," said a community member.

the meeting's conclusion saying, "I've taken pages and pages of notes, and I almost never take notes!" The mayor of Fort Worth held a press conference to publicize the event as evidence of Fort Worth's leadership and active efforts to continue to learn and innovate. Finally, perhaps the best measure is what happened afterwards. The King County coalition stepped up their recruitment of support by local business organizations—as exemplified by the Fort Worth coalition—and began its own publicity efforts to raise awareness of ways to reduce gun violence. This experience illustrates the power of a relatively small investment at the federal level to catalyze significant efforts by local players to learn and innovate for national goals.

## Accomplishments

- Federal points of contact visited partners to learn about their goals and challenges and in various cases helped them build their local coalitions and get support at state and federal levels. Examples: Miami police department strengthened relationships with federal partners in the Bureau of Alcohol, Tobacco, and Firearms, and U.S. and state attorneys' offices; Fort Wayne champion visit brought press attention and galvanized local coalition; visits to Springfield and Inkster help identify new strategies in areas of gun tracing and community courts.

   "Our champion's intervention influenced federal policy people to learn more about how to be responsive to local communities."

- Peer-to-peer visits among SafeCities members helped transfer knowledge, spur innovation, and build network relationships. Mayors, police chiefs, and faith leaders from both Fort Wayne and Inkster went to visit Highpoint, North Carolina, to learn about innovative strategies for community policing and integrating parolees back into the community; the Highpoint partner learned as well from questions the partners asked— for example, about opportunities to improve after-school programs.

   "The Highpoint visit added ideas and motivation to an initiative that we had been planning for a year; once the mayor visited, he wanted to do it. Now we have renewed a moribund community policing program and stepped it up."

   "We have developed relationships with partners from Inkster and Fort Wayne who have come and visited. Now we call each other directly [without facilitation by the coordinator], and this includes contacts between members in like roles, such as ministers who are talking to each other."

## What Happened to SafeCities?

SafeCities enjoyed a much smoother and more successful transition when the administration changed than did the other two cross-agency communities. SafeCities continued to have a full-time coordinator who was staffed by agency executives in the Department of Justice and supported by other agency champions. The staffing and support for the community coordinator was crucial to SafeCities' ongoing success. SafeCities continued its monthly teleconferences and pursued an ambitious project to develop capability measures related to strategic competencies for reducing gun violence—such as gun tracing, crime-scene evaluation, building local coalitions, and so forth. They also organized a satellite conference on preventing youth violence and an initiative to help faith leaders support local crisis response and community policing activities. In May 2001, members gathered for a face-to-face meeting to share experiences related to their various initiatives, talk about collective opportunities for projects and visits, and learn from presentations by various federal agency officials and non-government experts.

At the May 2001 meeting, Justice Department officials announced that funding for SafeCities (essentially the cost of one FTE, some travel, and occasional use of a phone bridge) would end in April 2002—and that a new program, called "Safe Neighborhoods," would begin. Although Safe Neighborhoods would provide funding for various local initiatives, the 30 members in attendance, including those from participating federal agencies as well as local ones—were very disappointed to hear the news. While they welcomed additional funding for local initiatives, they were adamant that the value of SafeCities participation went far beyond what federal funds alone could provide. It gave members opportunities to learn how to leverage current levels of resources in powerful ways that had few or no incremental costs—such as better ways to implement community policing or apply gun-tracing methods. SafeCities members were not asking for program money, but rather the continued opportunity to share ideas, innovate, and collaborate across local, state, and federal levels—including multiple agencies and constituencies at each level—to find better ways to reduce gun violence. SafeCities was working, and no grants program could replace the unique opportunities for innovation and impact that it provided.

After the announcement, Michael Seelman, the SafeCities coordinator, followed up with agency executives to help integrate some of what he called "the DNA of SafeCities" into the Safe Neighborhoods program. The name of the new program itself indicated the interest of program leaders to build on SafeCities' success. But the complex chemistry that made SafeCities so successful had few precedents in government at that time, and it was not obvious how best to build on its success or integrate key elements into the new program. Seelman listed a few of the most important elements of the SafeCities DNA: engaging local coalitions, recruiting support by agency champions, and stewarding a systemic array of proven gun-violence-reduction practices. Perhaps the most difficult element to understand or codify programmatically was how to cultivate and maintain the peer-to-peer exchanges of ideas, encouragement, and practical support.

In the spring of 2002, the SafeCities steering committee determined that it was time to conclude its role as the convener for the SafeCities community. Justice Department resources were now focused on the Safe Neighborhoods program and active agency champions could no longer focus on member coalitions. The SafeCities conveners in the Justice Department met with U.S. attorneys working on Safe Neighborhoods initiatives to brief them on how to leverage established relationships with leading local coalitions from the SafeCities community. Soon after, one of the U.S. attorneys applied a key element of the SafeCities DNA: He helped to organize a local summit that convened a coalition including the mayor's office, faith leaders, police, and community leaders.

In April 2002, SafeCities members said good-bye to each other during a final teleconference and thanked the community coordinator, sponsor, and agency champions. Although the group no longer gathers as a whole, individual members continue to enjoy the professional relationships they established, and Justice Department participants at both the coordinator and executive levels have continued to introduce the SafeCities DNA into other areas.

## Lessons Learned

- **Leadership (steering committee):** Importance of having a steering committee to coordinate agency champions and help encourage and develop champions' ability to participate and contribute effectively.
- **Leadership (coordinator):** Key role of the community coordinator to arrange speakers, coordinate peer-to-peer and agency-champion visits, respond to inquiries, send out information on the listserv; facilitate teleconferences, liaise with sponsors and stakeholders; document notes from activities; supervise website development, and so forth. We can learn much from Seelman's experience as SafeCities' full-time coordinator. He demonstrated how much value a skilled coordinator can create if given the time and support.
- **Community:** Seeing the importance of full participation from all sectors—for example, those who are generally underrepresented in this domain, such as faith leaders and businesspeople in urban areas; also, realizing the value of including diverse municipalities in regions where municipal boundaries are hard to differentiate (as in King County) and crime patterns cross these boundaries.
- **Practice:** Power of site visits to foster peer-to-peer learning about complex practices—such as working with ex-offenders—and the impor-

tance of structuring these informal learning events to realize the full value of the opportunity.

- **Practice:** Learning about the value of "behavioral anchors" for measuring capabilities—even during the development process. Discussions about how to define and describe high, medium, and low levels of strategic competencies in action facilitated peer-to-peer learning, identified areas on which to focus collective work, and provided a baseline for assessing the influence of the community on member results over time.

## 21st Century Skills

### History

As SafeCities was being launched, a third network—called 21st Century Skills and focused on workforce development—was getting ready to launch. In January 1999, Vice President Gore had convened a leadership group from business, organized labor, education, and government to develop a set of recommendations for their peers that would ensure a prepared and thriving workforce in the 21st century. The report outlined five broad recommendations, including a recommendation advocating community-based partnerships that would cross multiple sectors and focus on clear, measurable goals for lifelong learning and skill development across a community. This last recommendation was an implicit proposal to create the 21st Century Skills Network. (This recommendation, in fact, stemmed from the committee's awareness of the successful Boost4Kids example).

By this time, the template for organizing a network was well established. A steering committee of agency champions was convened in February 2000. Ten local coalitions from around the nation were recruited and selected in April on the now-standard criteria—innovative, collaborative at state and local levels, and results oriented. (An added "no loser" policy meant that other applicants could also participate in some activities, though with less attention from coordinators and federal champions.) Members introduced themselves and their initiatives in early teleconferences, and then in June 2000, about 40 members from partner communities met face-to-face for a launch event in Washington, D.C. Given the lessons learned from Boost4Kids and SafeCities about the value of meeting early on face-to-face, the 21st Century Skills community planned a face-to-face conference up-front as a way to launch the community. At the launch, members had formal and informal opportunities to get to know each other better, prioritized issues to explore and projects to focus on, and met with senior-level agency officials to discuss better ways to leverage local, state, and federal expertise and resources for results.

The 21st Century Skills built on the launch template established by its sister communities. A computer-mediated polling system was used at the conference to facilitate the brainstorming and selection of issues the community would address. The community coordinator, Lynn Kahn, brokered a connection with another initiative she had been facilitating—a group of assistant secretaries from various agencies such as Labor, Education, and Housing and Urban Development—who were collaborating on a workforce-related program. The assistant secretaries were invited to participate in the conference and meet their counterparts working at the local level. Network members later reported that the opportunity to connect with senior agency officials was a highlight of the event.

> "Everything they put together was helpful. We discussed issues, formed groups, had lunch, drank wine, and went to the White House for a tour. It made us feel important, and Lynn was scurrying around to make sure we talked to the right people."

The 21st Century Skills Network was born. Its charter goals included:
- Increase the number of Americans with 21st Century skills and high-skill, high-wage jobs;
- Close the skills gap;
- Promote lifelong learning;
- Address barriers at the federal, state, and local level to increase the flexibility and effectiveness of resources; and
- Obtain technical support and share best practices and lessons learned across communities.

## Accomplishments
- Champions work with community members to learn about their goals and challenges, to help them build their local coalitions and get support at the state and federal levels. For example: Laurens County, South Carolina, gets help working with state and federal partners to improve alignment of funding streams to meet local program-implementation needs, and the Colorado partner gets stronger support at the state level for distance learning and other adult-education initiatives.

> "This network gives us connections to people in Washington who are listening and willing to see what they can do about our problems."

- Members help each other during formal interactions on calls and in meetings and through informal interactions to learn and innovate to improve results. The Maine partner got help from partners on ways to co-locate a one-stop job center with a community college; the Florida

## 21st Century Skills

**Domain:** 21st Century Skills focused on issues related to workforce development and education, such as distance learning, curriculum design, job vacancy surveys, and how to organize a local skills summit around industry clusters. Although most members agreed that the synergies among education and workforce development issues justified the range, others felt that the domain should have been sub-divided to provide increased focus for knowledge sharing and collaboration activities. On the one hand, this contrasts with the experience of Boost4Kids, which insisted on a broad and somewhat complex domain related to the tangle of "results-for-kids" issues; on the other hand, it differs from the SafeCities community, which chose a relatively specific outcome-based domain: reducing gun violence.

**Community:** The 21st Century Skills' federal partners included members from the Lifelong Learning Interagency Strategy Group, with representatives from the U.S. Departments of Labor, Education, and Commerce, facilitated by the Vice President's National Partnership for Reinventing Government; it also included the assistant secretaries of executive agencies with Workforce Investment Act (WIA) responsibility. This allowed for cross-government coordination and resolution of policy and legislative issues.

Participating members in local coalitions included business leaders, chamber of commerce presidents, university vice presidents, city planning officials, and members of workforce development boards, citizen activists, community college deans, and others. Local coalitions included:

- **Colorado:** The Colorado Collaborative; Southeast Business Partnership
- **Florida:** The Broward Alliance
- **Massachusetts:** Pioneer Valley Planning Commission, Plan for Progress
- **New York:** Broome-Tioga Workforce Development Board; Network of Education and Community Organization (NECO) and State University of New York, Plattsburgh
- **Ohio:** Columbus and Franklin County United Way/Employment Vision Council
- **Oklahoma:** Office of Workforce Development, The City of Oklahoma City
- **Pennsylvania:** The Northern Cambria Community Development Corporation
- **South Carolina:** Laurens County School-to-Work and Lifelong Learning
- **Tennessee:** The University of Tennessee Agriculture Extension Service
- **Texas:** Greater Austin@Work Alliance
- **Utah, Colorado, Ute Mountain Ute Tribe, Navajo Nation, Southern Ute Tribe:** Southwest Educational Telecommunications Consortium

Partnership members included community-based partnerships, local governments, networks of local or state and local governments, and state or local workforce development agencies.

---

**Practice:**

- Shared methods for increasing participation among students in distance learning programs, as well as tips for designing curricula and methods for promoting adult peer-to-peer learning
- Shared templates and methods for using the results of job vacancy surveys and training evaluation models
- Insights and methods learned from site visits and related presentations about how to organize "skills summits" to promote a highly skilled workforce and effective placement mechanisms in a range of local industry clusters

---

partner got help from Colorado on how to track credit for distance learning services to students from different school districts; Florida, in turn, helped Colorado learn to manage the availability of mentors to distance learning students who call for help.

"I contacted another partner about accountability related to distance learning. I described our approach and he told me ideas I hadn't thought of; then I helped him come up with ideas that he hadn't thought of in a completely different area."

"Just getting access to the 12 other coalitions with their expertise and resources is something we would never have access to from where we are."

- Community members begin to establish collective benchmarks that define high-level capability in the field of education and workforce development.

"Information sharing is very valuable because even if I don't apply it, it helps me assess the relative sophistication of my programs with 12 other highly collaborative communities. Together we are establishing a benchmark, which spurs me to work harder to keep my projects up to snuff."

## What Happened to 21st Century Skills?

21st Century Skills was still starting up when the administration changed. The NPR coordinator managed to find a champion at the Department of Education (ED), but agency officials there did not understand well what they had inherited. They tried pushing the network to focus on ways to implement the administration's focus on school improvement, but this was only one part of what the network was about (as was the case of Boost4Kids in relation to the HHS program). They had one face-to-face meeting, at which members articulated their learning agenda and explained their methods

## The October 12 Call: "Distance Learning"

Approximately 20 network members are on the call. Elliot Massie, a world-renowned expert on distance learning, is the invited speaker; he outlines some of the key issues related to distance learning and adult education and then fields questions from participants. Massie explains that there is a growing need to develop high-quality, publicly available content now that technical barriers to learning have become relatively low.

- A participant provides links to several websites and organizations that could help in this area.
- Another question on ways to address motivation issues in distance learning elicits ideas from partners about helping adult learners to appreciate the value of what they are learning.
- A member asks how to help teachers of distance learning classes learn to develop compelling multimedia classes with effective lesson plans. Two other partners respond with ideas and a link to a website with more ideas and an 80-hour tutorial on the topic.

Ideas and information developed during several teleconferences such as this one contribute to content posted on the website and provided the foundation for a longer-term project to create a world-class, public-domain, electronic "Learning Library" that includes training modules, lesson plans, and best practices related to closing the digital divide and skills gap.

of interacting. ED officials could not provide the multi-agency sponsorship the network needed. There had always been a tension among members between focusing on issues related to education (such as distance education in rural settings) and issues directly related to workforce development (such as funding restrictions on technical training to support employment in local manufacturing plants). Without a convener who could rally the participation of multiple agencies, especially both Education and Labor, the network as conceived could not succeed. Moreover, aside from the strategic misfit, ED could not provide the level and skill of coordination and support that the network required. Afterwards, members tried to organize a project-planning conference on their own, but without active coordination and support they were not able to keep the momentum.

### Lessons Learned
- **Leadership:** Power of engaging senior executives across relevant agencies (in this case, assistant secretaries and other sub-cabinet officials with responsibility for the Workforce Investment Act) and connecting them

with local civic leaders to facilitate stronger shared understanding of policy options and implications.

- **Leadership (sponsor):** Importance of a sponsor who appreciates the full dimensions of the community's purpose and does not attempt to force-fit administrative policy priorities on a community whose domain is not so narrowly defined.
- **Leadership (coordinator):** Importance of a coordinator who can focus consistently on working with the network and liaising with agency champions; when this role is overburdened, activities do not get sufficient attention to create full value for members.
- **Domain:** Challenge of getting the domain scoped correctly—not too broad, not too narrow—and having time and support to work out the domain boundaries—especially because it is the foundation for all the work that the community members do together.
- **Community:** Value of having a strong contingent of businesspeople in the mix—ones who are assertive about their expectations of the federal government and willing to leverage political power to get increased attention from agencies to understand the local impact of federal policies.

## Federal Highway Administration Rumble Strips Initiative

### History

In 1998, a team headed by Mike Burk at the Federal Highway Administration (FHWA) saw an opportunity to help the agency meet an important strategic goal to reduce traffic crashes by 20 percent over 10 years.[8] Burk and his team believed they could do this by cultivating a community of practice to address a perennial problem: diffusing a proven innovation across all 50 states that had been effectively implemented so far in 15, but was spreading very slowly to others—despite its compelling record of reducing injuries and saving lives. The community was called the "Rumble Strips Community" because its domain was about issues related to proposing, planning, deploying, and documenting the beneficial results of rumble strips that alert drivers when they are in danger of running off the road. (Rumble strips are the washboard-like indentations at the side of the road that create a loud noise and palpable vibrations when run over by a car.)

The agency had stacks of reports and brochures documenting the research and explaining why, when, where, and how to plan and implement rumble strip installations. But safety engineers at FHWA felt helpless to communicate the information engineers and decision makers needed so it got their attention, told them what they needed to know, and motivated them to act. Burk's specialty was knowledge management, and he knew enough to know that information dissemination alone would not solve this

## Federal Highway Administration—the Rumble Strips Community

**Domain:** Reduce traffic crashes by applying "rumble strips" on the sides of roads to prevent run-off-road injuries and fatalities. Identify and promulgate what rumble strips can do to prevent traffic crashes, how to justify the investments, and ways to measure the impact.

**Members:** Targeted members are safety engineers in all 50 states; also includes safety engineers at federal level and participants from various sectors: academic, business, and citizen—such as cyclist groups.

**Practice:** Templates for making the business case for rumble strips, case studies and research on results, discussion forums on specific issues such as how to mitigate the negative impact for cyclists, a directory of practitioners that helps members find who can help, information on various types of rumble strips, and pros and cons.

problem. He decided to try building a community among safety engineers at FHWA and the states to tackle the problem. He had learned that such structures were considered an essential social infrastructure for any initiative with the intention of diffusing ideas and innovations. The old methods were not working, so he decided to try it.

### Members

The target members of the highway safety community that Burk and his team wanted to reach were state Department of Transportation (DOT) staff engineers from all 50 states—but the community also included federal safety engineers nationwide as well as governmental decision makers, researchers, and citizens. The core group of the community consists of federal engineers from the Safety Business Unit of FHWA. They are supported by the agency's internal Knowledge Management (KM) support team. During the community's start-up phase, Jim Growney, an FHWA engineer in Albany, New York, was allocated half-time to serve as the community coordinator. Growney took on the role because he felt a strong personal commitment to leverage the community-of-practice approach in order to accelerate efforts to build and share knowledge related to rumble strips. Since the start-up period, Growney spends about one day a week coordinating the community's activities. He moderates the online discussions, fields questions, and connects people over the phone. He also liaises with executive sponsors and the KM team and generally helps the community thrive as a context for learning and achieving its goal of accelerating the diffusion of rumble strips nationally.

Members have participated in the community largely online, using a facility designed by the agency's internal KM support team, led by Burk. Members discuss topics in the rumble strip online forum, and contribute and access relevant reports, brochures, and presentations in a shared repository. A directory of community members from government and industry provides information about members' areas of interest and expertise. Members can keep in touch by going to the community website and by subscribing to the repository and discussions via e-mail.

Participation by constituencies across sectors and disciplines is encouraged in order to promote broader support for deploying rumble strips and in hopes of spurring innovative approaches. In one case, a sub-community of cycling enthusiasts became quite active and challenged the highway engineers and policy makers to find ways to make rumble strips less troublesome to cyclists, who ride primarily on the sides of the road where rumble strips are located. The exchanges were sometimes heated and it took a while before members on different sides built trust, but eventually the input of cyclists led to a new appreciation by engineers of the unintended consequences of the strips and motivated them to create new designs that would mitigate the problems for cyclists.

It is not a trivial problem to recruit participation from busy professionals who are dispersed nationwide and staffed in various organizations at different levels. The FHWA KM team and the community coordinator actively promoted membership through a number of channels: They notified all state DOTs, promoted the community at the annual conference of the Transportation Research Board (the largest assembly of technical transportation officials), published brochures on rumble strips on the FHWA website and the Rumble Strips Community homepage, and registered the site with Internet search engines.

## Accomplishments

The Rumble Strips Community made a concerted effort to test their hypothesis that the community would accelerate the diffusion of rumble strips nationwide and thus reduce injuries and fatalities. As for any rigorous effort to make a community's influence visible, Burk and the community's leadership group used both qualitative and quantitative measures—and collected data that would help connect community activities with results.

- One quantitative measure of community activity was the number of visits to the Rumble Strips website, which received 60,000 hits during its first month and settled at about 1,200 visits a month. The knowledge base and online forum was used primarily by state DOT staff, but also included visitors from academia and engineers from other countries.

Other quantitative measures documented the impact on injuries and fatalities and associated socioeconomic costs. FHWA staff used research from states such as Wyoming and Pennsylvania to argue that rumble strips prevent approximately 100 crashes in a typical state, which equals a reduction of about 50 injuries and .66 fatalities. The team cut these efficacy numbers in half to be conservative. They estimated that the socioeconomic savings of implementing rumble strips one year earlier than expected (due to the activities of the Rumble Strips Community) would represent a savings of $2.56 million dollars in associated costs. (Such dollar estimates, of course, cannot adequately measure the costs of human suffering.) This compares to the community's cost of one FTE to coordinate all community activity.

- Quantitative numbers help anchor the community's report on results, but qualitative data such as stories from members are required to connect causes and effects. In his report on the Rumble Strips Community, Burk cites two sample interviews with members who were asked about the value of community participation. An engineer with the Wisconsin Department of Transportation explained how the community helped him get better information on implementing rumble strips: "We'd call state by state and see what they were doing. We were also not sure who to contact. This way, the contact information is on the website." Burk also reported that an Ohio DOT administrator said "the rumble strip portal helped her finalize plans for a number of specialty highway safety applications. [She stated:] 'We also used data from the site to help develop Ohio's current policy on rumble strip use.'"

- Finally another accomplishment of the community—on a "meta level"—has been to provide a model for communities in other domains, which are also sponsored by the internal FHWA KM group (as well as to communities beyond FHWA). Since the visible success of the Rumble Strips Community, the FHWA has sponsored communities of practice in a number of areas, including environment and planning, air quality, high-performance concrete, and transportation asset management.

### Lessons Learned

There are three principal lessons learned from the FHWA's Rumble Strips Community experience that Burk's report highlights: the importance of leadership, a compelling domain, and making results visible.

- **Leadership:** The FHWA KM report states that while coaching, support, and seed funding from the KM team was helpful, "strong leadership by community facilitators has been a critical success factor for the Rumble Strips Community." The report goes on to quote the community coordinator who says: "These sites don't run themselves.... Plus, a specialist must be involved in online conversations to answer questions and direct users to the information they're looking for; otherwise, the portal loses credibility."

- **Domain:** The Rumble Strips Community not only aligned itself with an important strategic agency objective—reducing the number of automobile crashes and related injuries and deaths—it also focused its attention even more narrowly on a particular subset of issues: reducing run-off-road crashes by implementing rumble strips. Getting the domain scope right is very important for attracting the right combination of people with passion and a desire to work and learn together. Moreover, the community got the support of stakeholders in the agency and states because its focus aligned so well with their strategic objectives.

- **Results:** The Rumble Strips Community helped to spawn other communities and garner continued support for its own work because it made a concerted effort to measure its influence on results and make these visible to stakeholders inside and outside the agency. For example, Burk's report is featured on the website of a federal government Special Interest Group on the topic of communities of practice. (See www.km.gov.)

## Reflections on Case Studies

The cross-agency networks' various denouement stories describe a sort of reverse cascade that mirrors the sequence of bootstrapping start-ups as they launched. An overview of the endgame for all three of the cross-agency networks shows how crucial the role of a federal convener—including the network coordinator, agency champions, and an overall sponsor—was to their success.

Although the common factors in their demise are most striking, there were variations on this theme across the networks. Boost4Kids lost their coordinator immediately when the negotiations with HHS fell through; 21st Century Skills had help for a while, albeit a relatively unavailable coordinator; and SafeCities enjoyed coordinator funding for another year and a half. In every case, however, the bottom line was that even with highly talented and motivated members achieving compelling results, without a dedicated coordinator the networks died. Six months before Boost4Kids was broken up, one of its members stressed how important the coordinator role was: "I don't think we'd be here without Pam and Bev [the community coordinators]. They play the role that we play at the state level: to find information, give us ideas, follow up on ideas and requests, and generally keep things moving."

Three features of the initiatives described here are especially noteworthy: the basic structure of the networks, their quasi-evolutionary nature (or structured evolution), and members' voluntary participation. It is also worth noting two roles that have particular influence on the ability to sustain and scale such initiatives: the role of the sponsor and of a "meta community" made up of coordinators and support team members which facilitates learning about the processes for cultivating successful communities of practice.

## Community Network Structure

The first key element—the community network structure—has been emphasized throughout the case descriptions. Key elements of the network structure include cross-level access and collaboration, peer-to-peer communication, and the size of the networks—about 10 coalition partners and 30 core participants in total. (While the FHWA network included more participants, the media for interaction were more limited—primarily via their online forum and individual phone calls to the coordinator, their relatively small face-to-face meetings, which included a core group of staff engineers based in headquarters.) This structural foundation was essential to solving problems in new ways, accelerating and enhancing learning among all participants, and reinforcing a joint commitment to innovate for improved results.

## Quasi-Evolutionary Development

The voluntary and evolutionary nature of the networks is closely related, and both are crucial to success. McKelvey defines a "quasi-evolutionary" process as one in which both conscious design and organic evolution are combined as highly interdependent developmental forces (McKelvey, 1977). (In fact, he argues that every organization evolves this way—even if the relative emphasis on each varies.) This evolutionary characteristic applies both at the network level itself, as well as to the "meta" evolution of the network design across all three networks over time. (This "meta" level of design evolution is also apparent at FHWA, where the KM group has sponsored the development of a number of communities, building on their experience with the Rumble Strips Community.)

This contrasts with the engineering approach commonly used to design formal business units with standardized systems and procedures. Leaders must be much more cautious about defining learning objectives for communities upfront, until the members have time to work out which issues are on the critical path and are most compelling to the group. Loading up the community with ambitious projects early on can produce the "job redundancy" effect, as in: "I already have a full-time job, and I'm here to learn and innovate in areas that feed my development and my work—but not by taking on onerous projects I haven't got time for." Moreover, many of the parameters appropriate for specifying very clearly in teams and business units, such as externally defined objectives, boundaries, roles, and performance expectations, do not apply well to communities. This is not to say these don't exist, but rather that they are inherently fuzzier and more dynamic. There is an expectation that they will adapt to local conditions and be defined through negotiations among members and between members and sponsors—with the option, as volunteers, to pitch in with gusto or hang out on the periphery. SafeCities, for example, had an objective to "reduce gun violence," but there were always questions about how to measure this result, much less where to set specific objectives. The SafeCities community did set a goal to define and document behavioral descriptions of its strategic capability goals—but there was only a small team—all volunteers—for this initiative. Although the work was very productive, it did not progress nearly as fast as it would under the sponsored auspices of a project team. The benefit was that the community members owned the process. Had SafeCities continued, it would have provided an excellent test bed for experimenting and continually improving the instrument.

## Voluntary Participation

The voluntary nature of these networks was also crucial, because participants did not report to the convener; rather, they joined of their own accord. Even more important than this structural feature, the ethic of voluntary participation was key to the spirit of mutual trust, reciprocity, and joint commitment—and to members' willingness to speak out on important issues. At the 21st Century Skills conference, for example, business leaders and college deans showed up alongside nonprofit leaders who were more directly dependent on support from federal programs. They spoke as one, however, about what changes they needed from the federal government to streamline processes and do more to coach states on how to effectively leverage funds and to adjust policies to take into account local conditions. In the context of the 21st Century Skills community, even nonprofit members were less likely to be cowed by an imperious federal official. Much of the power of the networks would erode if they lost the self-initiated participation of diverse constituencies—including those with no dependence on federal largesse.

Much of the learning that occurred—via teleconferences, visits, informed phone calls, and e-mail—depended on peer-to-peer trust and reciprocity. Voluntarism in any context is a fundamental condition for collaborative creativity and learning. Pay, performance management, and other extrinsic incentives and controls are weak levers for influencing people to offer their best ideas, admit when they're stumped, or go out of their way to help someone else. (That said, the prospect of greater leverage and influence is a real incentive and one that members certainly thought worth pursuing.) Network participants were expected to share ideas, experiment with innovations, identify problems, and ask for help. But who would know if they held back? The greatest resource of these networks was their passionate commitment to innovation, collaboration, and striving for improved results. Imposing external requirements that could not be negotiated with members would not work—as was demonstrated in several cases during the denouement of the three cross-agency communities.

## Overall Initiative Sponsor

For cross-agency communities, it appears that a high-status, powerful source of sponsorship is important. This may be an artifact of the federal government culture that generally impedes collaboration across agency silos. Presidential orders and legislative mandates seem to spur initiatives across agencies. The mandate that requires agencies to convert to electronic record keeping, for example, has helped increase interest and participation in the e-Reg Community of Practice. But that community does not have nearly the level of support that the NPR cross-agency communities had—and if it did, members say they could be making much more progress.

## The "Meta-Community" That Fostered the Communities' Evolution

The continuing replication, innovation, and successful execution of these networks were due in part to a kind of "meta-network" that had evolved among the conveners. Their "domain" in this case was network development and coordination. Coordinators and support staff would talk across networks—both in formal meetings and informally. (They all had desks in the same office). They talked about various elements of their emerging practice, including engaging diverse stakeholders during local visits, recruiting the right speakers for teleconferences, capturing useful information for dissemination, and solving bottlenecks with federal and state agencies. They also talked about problems and future challenges, such as finding continued funding for the community coordinator role (and whether to continue to position it at the federal level); enlisting more consistent and active support from champions in federal agencies; fostering better collaboration among agencies in their work with local coalitions; scaling these pilot initiatives; and getting stronger, more visible support from senior executives and political appointees. (We also see signs of a meta-community in the FHWA case, primarily consisting of members of the KM support team and coordinators of the several communities they support. Also, at the federal government level, there is the kernel of a meta-community consisting of leading coordinators (such as Bill Bennett at FERC) and KM support staff from various agencies—including those specifically interested in communities of practice—under the auspices of the KM.gov group.)

In sum, the cases described here provide a unique illustration of the role of federal leadership—and the benefits at federal, state, and local levels—from cultivating cross-sector, cross-level communities of practice. The "theory of the case" is that these communities are a linchpin for moving from centralized government to distributed, citizen-engaged governance groups that assume greater responsibility for socioeconomic outcomes at the state and local levels. Finally, the cases raise important questions about replicability, sustainability, and scale. These issues are second order, however, compared to a more fundamental one: What are the basic steps agency executives can take to cultivate strategic communities of practice?

# How Federal Agencies Can Cultivate Communities of Practice

## Foundation Building

Communities evolve through a series of developmental stages. There are five development stages during the community of practice life cycle. (See Appendix I for a detailed discussion of developmental stages of communities of practice.)

The first step in launching a strategic community-of-practice initiative is to establish a sponsorship and support structure to steward the overall community initiative. Agency executives should begin by assessing how a community of practice can contribute to their strategic objectives. This often means convening formal and informal conversations to talk about the relationships between communities of practice, capability building, and improving results.

Steps for establishing the strategic context and stewardship structure include:

- Organize and educate (informally as well as formally) a sponsor board that includes a high-level sponsor and steering committee members who will be instrumental to implementation.
- Identify where to focus the community initiative—through an executive review of strategic priorities or by engaging a broader group of stakeholders in collective conversations to identify hot issues to focus on.
- Recruit leaders to assume sponsorship and support rules:
  - Select and orient agency champions
  - Establish sponsor board functions
  - Staff one support professional (or more) to coach community leaders and liaise with sponsor board
  - Recruit and develop community coordinators (could be one or several for a community, depending on size and intensity of activity; full- or part-time)

Of course, it is not necessary to have all these roles formally established to get started. But when these initiatives are successful, they typically rely on influential and skilled people actively filling sponsorship and support roles (Wenger, et al., 2002, pp. 206-216). (Of course, there are many communities of practice that meet members' needs and never show up on the radar screen—and prefer it that way. The focus here is on strategic communities of practice taking on important agency and national challenges.)

In the civic context, communities of practice often form in response to some catalytic event that increases attention to a strategic civic issue and gets the attention of sponsors.[9] For example, the SafeCities network was spawned at a national meeting in 1999 where Vice President Gore agreed to convene a commission to respond to Attorney General Janet Reno's "Mapping Out Crime" report, which set new goals to reduce gun violence nationwide.

In fact, in all three interagency communities featured in this report, national forums on specific issues led to the formation of the communities. They helped to catalyze interest and energy by bringing diverse and passionate stakeholders together in high-profile events, with a sponsor who had the influence and prestige to motivate groups to act. In the FHWA case, it was a new strategic objective to reduce traffic crashes by 20 percent in 10 years. The community saw how it could build and diffuse a capability to make a significant contribution to that goal.

When executive-level sponsors play a strong role in catalyzing a community of practice, it is especially important to set appropriate executive-level expectations regarding what level of investments of time, attention, and money will be required to achieve anticipated results—and over what time frame. Ideally this is done collaboratively with network members—but if the network has not yet been organized, then executives should seek expert advice about setting expectations and determining what staff support will be needed. In the three interagency communities described here, an executive group—composed of a range of stakeholders related to each domain—defined the issues to address, and then community members were selected based on their interest in tackling those issues. In the FHWA case, while the strategic objective had been set by executives, middle-level managers took the initiative to organize a community on a topic area both tightly aligned with the agency strategy and compelling to safety engineers.

## Key Roles in Creating Communities of Practice

There are several key roles relevant to cultivating strategic communities throughout the community development process—though specific interventions change as communities evolve. Key roles include the sponsor, steering committee, support team, agency champions, and the community coordinator. Each role is briefly described below.

## Sponsor

The sponsor performs a number of essential functions to help communities launch, mature, and gain influence and legitimacy in their domain.

- Articulating a vision of a community-based approach to building capabilities for driving performance and achieving strategic objectives
  - Vision may include a constellation of communities addressing an array of capability areas—as in FHWA, where several communities are operating today, or in organizations such as DaimlerChrysler[10] and the World Bank, which have over 100 active communities
- Providing policy direction and ongoing reviews (generally annual or semi-annual) to assess community progress and developmental needs—types and levels of participation, accomplishments and results, development issues, and proposals for further development
- Allocating funding for coordination and support staff and for projects, travel, and other resources
- Championing the initiative among stakeholders to build support

*Sponsor issues:*

- For the interagency communities of practice described in this report, the support of the Vice President's office was extremely important for both symbolic and practical reasons. When an agency official—federal, state, or local—gets a call from the Vice President's office, they generally respond promptly. Moreover, such a high-level office has greater capacity to facilitate cross-agency collaboration and is less likely to take a perspective that is limited by parameters of agency-specific programs. As one member said: "The Vice President's office is better than any agency as a convener, because it's more flexible to represent people versus low-level agency sponsorship, where it may become focused on their policies and programs; this is more open and has a cross-agency perspective."

  The Vice President's overall sponsorship provided back-home legitimacy for members and helped to ensure that agencies would be responsive to requests for adaptations in policies and programs. It also influenced state and local officials to support the agenda of local coalitions, which in many cases had been weak or non-existent.

  But there is a downside to high-level support from politicians and appointees—it lasts only as long as the sponsor stays in office. And even when newly appointed officials are sympathetic to the methods and purposes of these initiatives, they often do not have enough background knowledge or experience to continue supporting them. The FHWA case suggests that such initiatives may gain staying power when sponsorship and support processes become institutionalized in a department or agency—for instance, by an internal Knowledge Management office as well as by technical infrastructure and processes that establish collaboration expectations with states and citizens. (Even at the agency level, however, we have seen such offices get disbanded soon after the arrival of a new agency head.)

## Cross-Agency Steering Committee

The steering committee provides strategic guidance for the network's development. For the cross-agency communities, the steering committees consisted of the sponsor, federal agency champions, community coordinators, and internal KM or consulting staff. Steering committees were especially helpful because they provided a transitional structure for institutionalizing cross-agency collaboration and collective support for network learning and innovation initiatives. The committees generally met about once a month. Champions and coordinators would discuss how well the champions' agencies were supporting their own participation, what issues they had been working on, and what results they were getting. Interestingly, because the issues raised by these communities did not fall neatly into one program or agency, the activities raised officials' awareness of their own need to collaborate in order to create value for citizens. In fact, these committees provided a model for an informal—though clearly intentional—structure that can serve as a highly effective forum for interagency collaboration.

Steering committee tasks include:
- Reviewing agency champion support and effectiveness
- Institutionalizing agencies' ability to support networks
- Identifying implications of lessons learned for cross-agency collaborations
- Providing or brokering resources

"The steering committee seems to be important for feeding back changes at the federal level to influence agency policy. It is helpful to have high-level commitment and involvement in agencies, but easy to lose their attention."

*Steering committee issues:*
- The main steering committee issues are cross-agency coordination and sufficient commitments of senior staff time and attention. There are few effective government-wide, systematic mechanisms to ensure agency collaboration. (Homeland Security may be the exception that proves the rule—it aims to foster collaboration, but only by combining agencies under one authority structure.) Kamarck (2002) and others have argued, nevertheless, for an approach that relies on cross-agency networks—rather

than on a massive structural consolidation—to leverage complementary agency capabilities and encourage knowledge sharing among them. Given the power of established hierarchies in government agencies, it is difficult for cross-agency initiatives to be influential and sustainable without creating a concrete structure or establishing an explicit policy mandate and support by agency executives and political appointees.

- The agency collaborations seen in this set of case studies were driven largely by compelling appeals from members of the communities of practice who pointed out the waste and lost opportunities at the local level when agencies did not cooperate. Community members were in a unique position to help agency officials see the unintended negative consequences of uncoordinated, overlapping, siloed programs that did not consider the real-life context of problems at the local level. Ultimately, as these initiatives go to scale, a growing network of communities may gain sufficient external influence to motivate legislators, political appointees, and agency staff to collaborate across agency silos in ways that have failed historically. Until then, the cross-agency networks, in particular, seem to depend on high-level influence to bridge obstructive agency boundaries.

## Support Team

The support team supports the launch and development of communities of practice by providing services at an overall initiative level (which may include anywhere from a few to hundreds of active communities). Support team functions include educational activities, initiative planning and coordination, coaching for community leaders, managing infrastructure (especially technology), and acting as a liaison among communities and with sponsors to facilitate ongoing learning and alignment.

The support team may consist of one or more full- or part-time members—staffed internally or contracted externally. Skills include those related to organization development, information technology, and strategy, as well as the emerging field of "knowledge management" (a term used to refer to a mix of people, process, content, and technology issues related to building, sharing, and applying knowledge).The team may be based in a specified unit—a Knowledge Management department, for example, or the office of the CIO or HR director—or it may operate as an ad hoc virtual team whose members report to the sponsor and steering committee.

The NPR support team was instrumental in promoting the replication, innovation, and successful execution of the cross-agency, intergovernmental communities. The support staff (several of whom also acted as community coordinators) worked together to develop an array of elements related to their emerging discipline. Support team members also addressed problems related to institutionalizing and scaling up the initiative, such as finding continued funding for the coordinator role (whether staffed inside or outside the federal government); enlisting more consistent and active support from champions in federal agencies; fostering better collaboration among agencies to respond to the local coalitions; scaling the pilot communities; and getting stronger, more visible support from senior agency executives and political appointees.

Wherever there is a significant community-of-practice initiative that is getting results, inevitably there is also a strong support team—whether it is a public, private, or nonprofit initiative. Mike Burk and his colleagues at the FHWA provided the support team function out of the Knowledge Management office, and they have helped launch a number of communities since the initial success of the Rumble Strips Community. The NPR office sponsored a team of senior staff that brought together a broad range of skills and stakeholder relationships, which enabled them to organize a very complex, cross-agency, cross-sector, cross-level initiative while continually reviewing results and innovating along the way. (In the NPR case, support team staff played several additional roles—including community coordinator, agency champion, and steering committee membership. It is not uncommon for skilled staff to play multiple roles; with the right skills and flexibility, this approach can promote overall agility and adaptability.) Community-of-practice initiatives are still very new for organizations, and there is much to learn in the early going. Support team staff can accelerate movement up the learning curve while promoting innovations along the way.

Support team tasks include:
- Educating government executives (formally and informally), as well as coordinators and others participating in the community initiative
- Developing an overall initiative plan for activities, players, and resources
- Providing coaching and logistical support to help communities get launched
- Liaising with sponsors and community leaders to review both successes and shortfalls for purposes of continuous improvement

*Support team issues:*
- It is a challenge to find an adequate mix of skills and expertise to staff a support team.
  - Communities of practice are a distinctive organizational form, and to date, few managers or organizations have much experience cultivating them in intentional and systematic ways. Moreover, these initiatives are complex—covering issues related to strategy, structure, technologies, performance measures, staffing, shared values, and leadership style. Sponsors should not underestimate the importance of

professional advice and support to help ensure that early initiatives succeed as basis for leveraging that experience more broadly.

- Change initiatives in organizations do not succeed without significant attention to leadership and other organization development issues. Technology-based initiatives such as EPS (Enterprise Planning Systems), for example, rarely fulfill their vendor's promises without accompanying structural, procedural, and behavioral changes. Communities of practice are no different—they are not a silver bullet unto themselves—and this is why access to skills in a range of disciplines is important.

• Another key issue for the support team—and related to its expertise—is its credibility and legitimacy with senior executives and other stakeholders whose support is critical for success.

- Community initiatives present new ways of working, learning, and collaborating. The cross-agency communities, for example, demonstrated the value of connecting officials across agencies in areas of common interest—such as workforce development. Support team contributions were crucial in these instances, but it was unlikely that they could have made so much progress without strong professional credibility and support from high-level sponsors. For example, Lynn Kahn's executive relationships and reputation were crucial to convene a group of assistant secretaries and link them with the the 21st Century Skills coalition, while facilitating collective conversations about program and policy development.

• Finally, the support team must build a repertoire of tools to help expand the initiative and incorporate lessons from experience.

- The support team can strengthen its influence by leveraging its experience to create tools, frameworks, cases, and other artifacts that can help sponsors and communities get up to speed quicker. It is easier to do this when members develop their own community to keep up to date on lessons from the field and available skills and technologies. Support team members at FHWA, the Navy, Army, GSA, and many other agencies have organized a knowledge management community for this purpose.

## Agency Champions

In this case, a compelling dimension of the value proposition for members was direct access to influential officials in various federal agencies. Agency champions were designated to work with the communities to help members build capability and solve problems. The champion role presents a unique opportunity for officials in various federal agencies to work directly with citizen coalitions in the field who directly face the problems agency programs are designed to address. Agency champions and local civic leaders work together to adapt programs to fit local conditions and consider longer-term policy changes as indicated. Champions have a unique opportunity to learn how their programs work in practice and to incorporate what they learn in the strategic thinking and program designs of the agency.

Agency champion tasks include:
- Helping partners solve problems and build collaborative relationships with officials at local, state, and federal levels
- Providing a trusted federal point of contact for local community members
- Acting as a creative, solution-focused problem solver that leverages perspectives and resources across agencies to "get to yes"

An agency champion is an enthusiast, innovator, recruiter, convener, and advocate.

"Communities need cross-agency help and this isn't in anyone's job description; but champions don't always have support, authority, and time to play this role."

"As a federal champion, I learn so much by working directly with a community."

*Agency champion issues:*
- Because these roles are relatively informal, it is particularly difficult for agency champions to maintain time and attention allocation to community needs as administrators change and policies change.
  - There may not be much to do about this in the short term, but it is worth noting that the turnover of political appointees makes it difficult to invest one's professional reputation in roles that may not last after the next election.
  - The champion role is a challenging one. It requires strong technical expertise to understand how to respond to requests for waivers or policy changes, change-management skills to deal with bureaucratic inertia, and facilitation skills to negotiate priorities with network members. It is not necessary for any one champion to have all these skills—but it is important to know what is required and find a way to access the skills needed.
  - Finally, a cadre of agency champions is especially critical for cross-agency communities, but may also be important in agencies where community initiatives cross several intra-agency department boundaries.

## Community Coordinator

Community coordinators orchestrate activities, connect members, shepherd initiatives, and help to solve problems. They are crucial to communities' vitality and ability to achieve desired outcomes. Examples of functions they provide include:

- Organizing activities such as face-to-face meetings and teleconferences
- Guiding and facilitating network projects—for example, setting up GIS training, building a website, and developing capability measures
- Coordinating with state and national stakeholders (such as state government officials and foundations) and the federal steering committee for support and sponsorship
- Weaving relationships among partners and with experts and external stakeholders
- Moderating the listserv and website repository
- Planning ahead for the community's long-term development—addressing issues such as major projects, leadership, and growth

The skill of a community coordinator can make or break a community's success. Generally, for a community of 30 active members in a strategic area, the coordinator is ideally staffed half-time or more. The most successful of the NPR coordinators, Michael Seelman in the Justice Department, was nearly full-time, as was the coordinator for the Rumble Strips Community. Even when the coordinator has less time to devote, as was the case with Bill Bennett, the coordinator of the e-Reg Community, he can nevertheless be instrumental to the community's progress and accomplishments (albeit at a lower level of activity).

It is not only the time and commitment of the coordinator that is crucial, but their level of technical and interpersonal competence. The social competencies are particularly important, because in many communities—especially technical ones—social skills are harder to find.

The coordinator must play a variety of roles, including broker, boundary-spanner, connector, recruiter, and energizer for the community. As one cross-agency community member said: "There has to be someone whose sole responsibility is to keep the network going, to bring the issues to the table.... It has to be someone with connections and with access to decision makers who will return their calls and respond to requests to come to the table."

It is not necessary for the coordinator to be an expert in the field, but it helps to know enough to appreciate who should be involved, who should talk to whom, and to have legitimacy with members who feel it is important to know the business. In the cross-agency communities, the array of disciplines represented in each was so wide that no one person could be an expert in all of them in any case. But Seelman, for example, knew enough about the domain to recognize which members had mutual interests or where to point them to community resources. They can also do well by recruiting key core-group members to substitute for their own lack of technical expertise.

*Core group of members*

Often the community coordinator role is taken by two or more members who share responsibilities. But even when there is one person playing the role, the coordinator depends on a core group of members to help set and revise the agenda over time, cultivate participation, and vet the priorities for practice-development initiatives. The core group may be as few as three, but it is generally four to eight members who are considered thought leaders, or connectors, or who provide action-oriented leadership for the community of practice.

CompanyCommand.com, for example, has a phalanx of nearly 10 core-group volunteers to keep its 1,500-plus community participants humming.

Communities of practice differ from formal teams because they do not require equal commitments of time and resources from all members. Because members' involvement is voluntary, it varies widely, depending on members' interests and time. Even "lurkers" are welcomed—they help spread the word through their own networks. Nonetheless, there must be a core group to help provide a focus for the community, organize events, attract participation, and give legitimacy to the group as "the place to be" to find out about cutting-edge initiatives and practices—and to connect with leaders in the field.

> "I don't think we'd be here without Pam and Bev [the community coordinators]. They play the role that we play at the state level: to find information, give us ideas, follow up on ideas and requests, and generally keep things moving."

> "A good coordinator is a facilitator who can draw people out and encourage them to give and receive information. They also act as a knowledge manager. Whenever we have a call, they do minutes and provide follow-up information on phone numbers and websites."

*Coordinator issues:*
- For strategic communities of practice to succeed, it is essential to establish staff roles that are designed to coordinate cross-agency collaboration. The Department of Education sponsorship failed in part because it could not provide such coordination, and Boost4Kids' demise was inevitable once it was clear that HHS could not define a salary position for a job that had no precedent in the agency.
- Given their function as a broker and liaison with sponsors, it is important for coordinators to have the understanding and cross-agency relationships required of the role—again, this was missing in the cases of both Education and HHS.

- Establishing staff roles is one thing, funding them is another. The coordinator role, as we have seen, is essential. Funding for travel is key because occasional face-to-face meetings are so important—both for conferences and site visits. Many participants at the local level are volunteers or are working for nonprofits on shoestring budgets. Furthermore, even minimal financial support makes a strong symbolic statement—it demonstrates to participants that this initiative is seen as an important national priority, and it recognizes the significant contributions that participants make.

"The network needs attention, dedicated staff, and needs some funding to make sure it lives on, not only for conveners and the website, but also travel funds for members to improve cross-cutting collaboration."

# Conclusion: An Emerging Role for the Federal Government as Sponsor of Community Initiatives

## Recommendations

The cases and analysis outlined here open up new questions about how community-based initiatives and traditional organizational structures should interrelate. What is the role of federal agencies in promoting communities of practice that seek to build capabilities to address national priorities—in domains that address the landscape of governance issues: education, economic development, health, housing, public safety, environment, culture, and others? We have argued that the federal government has a number of instrumental roles it can play—as a sponsor, champion, community coordinator, and support team—to cultivate communities that achieve results at both local and national levels. Overall, we propose three high-level recommendations that address key success factors for a broad community-based strategy to build civic capabilities for socioeconomic results:

- Sponsor and support communities of practice to achieve national outcomes that require ongoing innovation and action learning
- Align community goals and agency strategic imperatives and policy mandates
- Leverage the unique position of the federal government to broaden the scope and scale of pilot initiatives

These recommendations presume that government executives will see community-based capability-building initiatives as consistent with agency program strategies and the fundamental role of government to serve the public. They also assume that agency officials are ready to commit to an evolutionary development process that shares an increasing level of governance responsibility with locally based citizen coalitions.

For some, these community-of-practice structures may stir up the specter of a "hollowed-out" government. Kamarck (2002: 11) quotes H. Brinton Milward and Keith G. Provan, who refer to network-based governance structures as the "hollow state," which they define as "... any joint production situation where a governmental agency relies on others (firms, nonprofits, or other government agencies) to jointly deliver public services" (Milward and Provan, 2000). The emergence of network-based governance approaches, however, need not augur the end of government. To the contrary, government institutions provide crucial convening forums for working out nation-level issues that merit new legislation, national programs, and coordinated standards and protocols; and, of course, no other entity is positioned to negotiate international relations and provide national defense. Nevertheless, government officials may argue that cross-sector, cross-level network structures will hollow out agency mandates, undermine public-service initiatives, and weaken the fabric of civil society.

There are several ways to address these concerns: by seeing the emergence of communities of practice as an evolutionary process, not a cataclysmic revolution; by distinguishing the knowledge-building and knowledge-sharing functions of these communities with the primarily transactional focus of product- and service-delivery units; and by understanding that collaborative, boundary-crossing networks need not mark the loss of government's public-service identity and influence, but rather serve as an expansion of both.

## Implementing Communities of Practice

### Evolution of Role over Time

The development of communities of practice—individually or collectively—is an evolutionary process, not a revolution. Control over specific functions should be ceded as network structures demonstrate ownership, capability, and transparency of results. As we have seen, the federal government has crucial roles to play in this process—as national catalyst, sponsor, legitimizer, resource provider, and safeguarder (enforcer of critical public-trust protections, such as in vital regulations and standards).

### Understanding Functional Distinctions of Learning and Transacting

The government must understand its role along dimensions of both transacting and learning—and the complementarity between them. Communities of practice operate amidst an ecology of institutions, both formal and informal. They complement formal institutions by crossing boundaries and fostering learning and innovation. They contribute to a cross-hatching structure that combines a focus on service delivery with the capacity to cross boundaries to discover and diffuse innovations—what Wenger and colleagues refer to as a "double-knit" organizational structure (2002, pp. 18-21).

In such a multi-dimensional system, formal political and service delivery organizations are still held accountable for using resources to get results related to social outcomes—they are *resource management structures*. In this role, they set strategic direction and policies, manage conflicts, and embody public values. Meanwhile, the communities of practice are responsible for building and sharing information, ideas, skills, methods, and influence to enable organizations to get things done—they are *capacity-building structures*.

Emphasizing accountability without building capacity is unlikely to deliver radically improved results. Executives need to design and manage each type of structure to do what it does best. Managers and organization members need to assure resources are applied to get results. Meanwhile, communities of practice must steward the learning activities and knowledge assets in their domain. Understanding and developing these structures as distinct, complementary entities helps strengthen and magnify their combined impact.

These complementary structures are woven together as much by members as by management policy. Members belong to both accountability and knowledge structures—they are "multi-members"—but the mode and focus of participation is different in each. Ultimately, we need more of both—accountability and capacity—and multiple ways to interweave them.

## Philosophical Commitment to Participatory Governance

Is the federal government ready to support systematic development of strategic communities of practice? As communities of practice go to scale and gain political power, are legislators and policy makers ready to deal with them, at local, state, and federal levels? These networks will attenuate agencies' control over program design and implementation, even as they increase control over results by spurring collaboration, innovation, and diffusion of good ideas and proven practices. But radically participative management approaches are more—not less—difficult than traditional ones. Many conflicts, disappointments, and mistakes are inevitable along the way. Executive sponsors must feel strongly enough about the potential of these approaches to commit their time and energy without knowing for sure what it will take to succeed.

The challenge of sponsoring such networks, however, is not merely about a commitment of time and energy, but also a matter of mind-set. How willing are federal officials and network partners to negotiate roles and relationships as equal partners with a common mission? When federal officials participate in these networks effectively, they do so as partners; they cede unilateral control (or the semblance of it) over how policy gets determined and how public monies can be spent. It is not legitimate for federal officials to behave as privileged actors because they have special access to expertise, funds, and influential senior executives. The local players must be treated as equal partners in a larger governance system that serves and engages all citizens. This is a crucial mind-set to establish in order to elicit the foundation of trust, reciprocity, and shared values that will facilitate knowledge flows and collaboration across agencies, sectors, and levels. Current institutional silos are embodied not only in the informal elements of the organizational culture, but also in the formal structures, systems, and procedures by which federal officials are typically constrained. The SafeCities initiative to pilot capability benchmarks, for example, was hampered by agency restrictions preventing them from appearing to certify these benchmarks as an official policy position of the Justice Department.

Indeed, the quasi-evolutionary nature of cross-agency communities of practice described here is not simply an artifact of sponsors' initial unfamiliarity with these structures. In fact, these communities, like all living things, tend to evolve and mature over time—even if leaders believe they know what they want from the start. Intentionality can get in the way, in fact, if it overrides the unique, context-dependent path and pace of a community's evolution. You can't get there simply by methodically creating a logical design and then implementing it.

The evolution of Boost4Kids' emphasis on peer-to-peer learning might not have happened had executives stuck to their initial concept; and the FHWA Rumble Strips Community might not have worked so hard to improve rumble strip designs and gain the support of cyclists' advocacy groups. This is why the development process for communities is "quasi-evolutionary." The community's evolution depends on many factors, and these are constantly in motion for several reasons: the relevant knowledge base is dynamic, members come and go voluntarily, and there is no definitive set of roles, procedures, and project milestones you can determine from the beginning. As in any exploration of new ideas and new relationships, there are bound to be surprises along the way. The best approach is a an "emergent strategy" (Mintzberg and Waters, 1985) that depends on preparation, not prediction, as an organizing principle (Ackoff, 1983). This is why we refer to efforts that support the development process as ones of "cultivation," not management.

Finally, we should note that no matter how actively and capably the federal government supports the launch, growth, and diffusion of communities of practice, they cannot succeed without strong, dedicated network members. The majority of local and state partners in these networks were truly of national caliber. They were carefully selected for their distinctive commitments to innovation, collaboration, and results. But we should not take this condition for granted. Much of the value of participation for both local partners and federal agencies was the opportunity to work with innovative, action-oriented local coalitions who had much to share—both challenges and innovative proposals—and who were ready and willing to apply new ideas to achieve outstanding results. Although the federal role is crucial to the broad scope and national scale of these networks, this partnership arrangement cannot work unless both parties are ready to dance.

The promise of these communities of practice presents a challenge as steep for state and local agents as it is for their federal colleagues. After all, how many cities and regions nationwide have cross-sector stewardship groups that are as well organized, highly capable, and willing to deal with the messy conflicts and Byzantine local politics endemic to any real-life civic development initiative? Yet, we will need such groups at all levels— local, state, and national—to build a national governance capacity capable of taking on the 21st century challenges and opportunities before us.[11]

# Appendix I:
# A Stage Model—Understanding
# How Communities Evolve

Communities of practice, like all living things, grow through distinct phases of development; thus it is best to understand the challenge of cultivating strategic communities in terms of the specific activities, methods, and tensions that occur in each developmental stage. Typically, community development stages include the following (Wenger, et al., 2002, pp. 68-70):

1. *Discovery:* identifying strategic issues to address—those that align with both strategic objectives and members' interests—such as reducing gun violence or automobile crashes
2. *Coalescing:* convening members to develop an action-learning agenda and building their collective commitment to pursue it together
3. *Maturing:* building on knowledge-sharing, clinics, and co-consulting activities—toward collaborations on innovation and application projects; growing beyond the initial group
4. *Stewarding:* establishing a prominent role in the field and taking stewardship for addressing leading-edge issues at scale
5. *Legacy:* beyond success, what's next—institutionalization as a formal organization; letting the community dissolve once the issues lose salience; segmenting the community into sub-areas as issues become more differentiated

The five-stage community development model (see Figure 6.A.1) is, of course, schematic. It is based on a common pattern seen in many communities, but it varies for any particular community. Community development is generally not a linear progression—rather it often fluctuates; communities move ahead, slip back, rest a while, and sometimes leapfrog a stage.

Although intentional, well-supported community initiatives may progress from the first to third stage in three to nine months, some will move faster and others may satisfy their needs well enough at stage two. Some move too quickly to stage three—driven by pressures to show visible results or to grow quickly—and thus overlook key developmental issues and end up regressing or losing steam altogether. A number of contingencies influence the quality and speed of a community's evolution: the complexity of its practice, the level of familiarity and shared experience of members, levels of sponsorship and support, member proximity and the quality of available communication facilities, leadership (including various types—thought leadership, coordination, brokering, etc.), and others.

The three cross-agency communities described in this report operated long enough to reach stage two or three, as defined here. The FHWA com-

**Figure 6.A.1: Developmental Model of Communities of Practice**

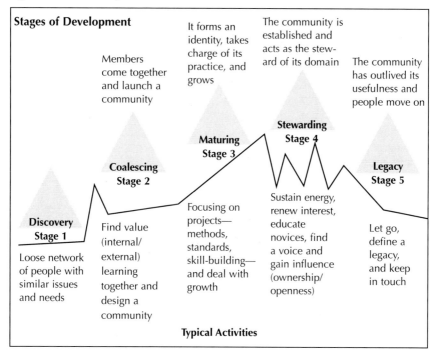

**Stages of Development**

Members come together and launch a community

It forms an identity, takes charge of its practice, and grows

The community is established and acts as the steward of its domain

The community has outlived its usefulness and people move on

**Stewarding**
**Stage 4**

**Maturing**
**Stage 3**

**Coalescing**
**Stage 2**

**Legacy**
**Stage 5**

**Discovery**
**Stage 1**

Loose network of people with similar issues and needs

Find value (internal/external) learning together and design a community

Focusing on projects—methods, standards, skill-building—and deal with growth

Sustain energy, renew interest, educate novices, find a voice and gain influence (ownership/openness)

Let go, define a legacy, and keep in touch

**Typical Activities**

munity seems to be operating at the "mature" level, with indications of stage 4 stewardship—it acts as a hub for developing a national practice. The stages model helps us see important achievements in progress and to anticipate what could be done if the community became even more influential.

## Stage 1: Discovery

The purpose of the discovery process is to "find out whether there is a there there." The "there" in this case refers to compelling issues that will attract a core of leading practitioners, a community of members who want to learn and work together, and an emerging practice of skills and techniques that promise to build skills and solve new problems.

*Key management tasks:*
- Identifying strategic objectives that require building and disseminating organizational capabilities, fostering innovation, or attracting and developing talent

- Considering what types of communities to cultivate
- Beginning to recruit community leaders—coordinator and core-group members who can take on stewardship of the community

In each of the cross-agency networks featured here, it was striking how easily the Vice President's office was able to attract top coalitions in each domain nationwide—especially when they offered no money; only an opportunity to connect with federal champions and peers to help them solve problems and learn. In fact, the only recruitment activity was to post an announcement in the Federal Register. This testifies to the recruitment power of an influential sponsor. Getting the right people in the room, particularly the core group of participants, is crucial to success. The danger here, however, is that the conveners depended too much on the prestige of their office and didn't do enough to go out and beat the bushes to find the best possible mix of partners in the first round. One thing they did well was gauging how many partners they could manage for each network—any more than 10 highly active coalitions and 30 members would have been too many for the conveners to serve. Also, a larger group would make it difficult for members to build a relatively quick sense of common ground and mutual trust.

In the FHWA case, the sponsors built on a relatively strong informal network among safety engineers at federal and state levels. In this case, it was more a matter of coalescing a latent community so it could take more intentional, collective stewardship of the practice—reducing traffic crashes.

*Key management tasks:*
- Establish methods for recruiting, selecting, and assimilating partners, steering committee, and champions
- Define clear roles for agency executives that minimize time required but leverage their influence
- Set aside sufficient time during recruitment and start-up by developing a shared vision and expectations for participation
- Get sustained participation by senior agency executives

## Stage 2: Coalescing

At this stage a community comes together. Members get acquainted, form relationships, and get a sense of whether this is a club they want to belong to. Do these people have the skills, connections, experience, and willingness to work together? Members brainstorm issues and develop a shared learning agenda, and they talk about ways to connect and learn together—meetings, teleconferences, a listserv, etc. They might also assign responsibility to one or more members to help coordinate their activities and serve as a central point of contact for members and outsiders. At this stage, the community's practice development is primarily about helping members build skills and solve immediate problems. Members may present cases, conduct "clinics" in which they consult to each other, and pay mutual visits.

Common pitfalls at this stage are moving too quickly to launch ambitious projects in order to catalogue knowledge assets or build new tools; or relying too much on online media for member interactions. The cross-agency communities of practice in this case avoided all of these pitfalls. Their emphasis was on peer-to-peer interaction, with early opportunities to meet face-to-face. They identified a learning agenda based on collective interests and priorities, not according to some rigid agenda or outsider mandate.

Another trap the four communities avoided was depending too much on public activities and not emphasizing enough the one-to-one, informal communications that solve specific problems, strengthen personal relationships, and address issues that members may not be ready to deal with publicly. For example, the cross-agency communities placed much value on assigning partners to specific federal champions, encouraged off-line problem solving, and arranged to visit sites in person and to learn more about their specific, local needs. The FHWA coordinator also plays the role of knowledge broker for members distributed across 50 states. In all four cases, as well as in the other agency communities of practice mentioned, the coordinators have done an excellent job of weaving together both formal and informal, public and private activities.

*Key management tasks:*
- Assess the extent of federal agency support required for a specific community and make necessary allocations and preparations
- Meet with community members to commit to joint capability objectives and related performance goals
  - Also talk about how to assess whether capability goals are met—and how to link these accomplishments with related strategic performance outcomes
- Set up a schedule for occasional reviews and mechanisms for liaising more informally along the way

## Stage 3: Maturing

At the maturing stage, members begin to plan joint projects—Boost4Kids' members worked together to develop an electronic application and SafeCities' members worked on capability benchmarks. Community members also began thinking about growth—either growing their own membership or splitting off sub-communities defined by region, topic, roles, or other dimensions that made sense. SafeCities organized a satellite broadcast that reached over 50 cities, and in at least one case catalyzed the formation of a local coalition while strengthening others. Members from all three interagency networks acknowledged that they would need to meet face-to-face to work out complex issues—conceptual, practical, and social—in order to collaborate effectively on ambitious projects. This is the time to consolidate the community's experience of its values, culture, and shared goals—and do this before growing so quickly that the community loses the collective sense of belonging that is at the heart of such networks.

The Boost4Kids and SafeCities networks were on the verge of moving into stage 3 activities (See Figure 6.A.2). This was particularly true of SafeCities when, in its second year, SafeCities launched a collective effort to establish capability benchmarks in areas known to be top levers for preventing gun violence. Boost4Kids had also begun typical stage 3 projects: They arranged a joint training session for members on GIS, and a sub-group of three Boost4Kids partners in California worked together on a project to develop an electronic, universal social services application. But initiating such projects takes much time from a coordinator, and they demand a level of commitment from members that is hard to develop without more face-to-face meetings among the project leaders. Finally, a commitment to such projects requires equal commitment from federal partners who can provide assurance that these efforts will not be wasted; that once completed they will have a strong chance of getting implemented.

A danger at this stage is the eagerness to grow quickly—due to core-group aspirations or fueled by outsiders who see an opportunity to meet their own objectives. (The latter is particularly dangerous because when network efforts are driven from the outside, they can lose initiative, and sponsors will have "killed the goose that lays the golden eggs.") The NPR conveners held a number of discussions about "going to scale," but were cautioned about growing too fast before the networks had consolidated their development at stage 2. They needed to establish a solid basis of coaching and sponsorship before raising the bar in terms of size and activity. (As it turned out, the sponsorship was not sustained.)

*Key management tasks:*
- Talk with community leaders about what projects to launch and what additional staff, travel funds, or infrastructure is needed to support the growth and depth of community initiatives
- Begin more systematic efforts to document the value the community creates and make these benefits visible. As the community requires more staff, travel, and related dollars, it will become increasingly important to demonstrate value—and especially in the face of

**Figure 6.A.2: Description of SafeCities Activities as It Moved from Stage 2 to Stage 3**

| | Stage 2: Coalescing | Stage 3: Maturing |
|---|---|---|
| **Typical Activities** | • Define domain focus so it has tangible value for members and their organization<br>• Develop member relationships and trust<br>• Develop ways for members to help each other by sharing tips and solving problems | • Identify and prioritize domain issues based on stakeholder as well as member interests<br>• More rigorously organize the practice and fill in the gaps |
| **SafeCities** | • Topics with practical usefulness were the focus; regular documentation of value in reports submitted to conveners<br>• Face-to-face meetings—as a network and during partner visits—were especially helpful for developing trust and personal relationships; visits by points of contact fostered openness and commitment<br>• Teleconferences provided forum for sharing ideas and offering help; face-to-face meetings and visits were better for in-depth problem solving | • Began to identify a proven set of gun violence reduction strategies and measure partners' relative strengths and weaknesses—as basis for setting learning agenda<br>• Started efforts to expand participation; for example, held satellite broadcast for over 50 cities<br>• Made ongoing efforts to organize practice resources on the website; more yet to capture, annotate, and edit based on members' and external experts' collective experience and expertise |

inevitable administrative shifts. Even if current executives don't ask for it, do it anyway—both as insurance for the future and as a learning opportunity—using feedback on results to adjust the focus of activities.

• Encourage participation by members and commitment from stakeholders—inside and outside the agency, both line and staff—to support community initiatives to apply strategic capabilities, not only build and share them. (While individual members can apply new knowledge in their work, applying new organizational capabilities—such as e-commerce, for example—depends on support from the line organization.)

- Help community leaders think about their growth strategy—where to grow, how much, and how fast—and what resources in terms of staff, travel, and infrastructure will be needed to support the growth

## Stage 4: Stewarding

At the stewardship phase, communities take on a publicly visible role as project leaders and standard-setters, establish a world-class forum where practitioners can connect and collaborate, and function as influential advocates for relevant policy changes. At this point, the community serves not only the needs of its members, but also those of surrounding organizations and society. They take active steps to link their efforts with established institutions and negotiate mutual alignment to increase the community's positive influence in the world.

Stewarding also means picking up on the growth theme begun during the maturing stage. While the community grows during the maturity stage, at stewardship, the community becomes even more strategic about where to grow and how far. Community leaders and sponsors may consider their vision of the ideal scope and scale of the community. Thus, the Rumble Strips Community knew right away it wanted to influence results in all 50 states. While the cross-agency communities began with 10 city pilots, their aspiration was always to grow nationwide. During the stewardship phase, communities begin more systematic efforts to pursue such growth strategies.

Typical community activities at the stewardship stage include establishing itself as a preeminent source of expertise and influence to achieve a specific objective (e.g., reduce gun violence); developing strong relationships with stakeholders (such as local, state, and federal agencies, legislators, and foundations); building world-class network tools and online resources; documenting their influence on results; and cultivating long-term, high-level sponsorship.

The Rumble Strips Community had many of the hallmarks of a stewardship-stage community. It took on a very specific, long-term strategic objective, well established in its field. It systematically marketed its initiative to all relevant members of its core audience—safety engineers in the federal and state governments (while also reaching out to stakeholders in other sectors). It established a robust social and technical infrastructure for connecting people and collecting (and managing) the best available content in the field (research, methods, directory of practitioners, calendar of events, etc.); the social infrastructure included funded roles for a community coordinator as well as a support team to provide coaching and technical assistance. Finally, the community took responsibility for developing ways to assess its contributions over time—a crucial commitment if it expects to sustain funding and support in the future.

*Key management tasks:*
- Support community legitimacy as a preeminent source of expertise in its field
- Work with community leaders as strategic partners to explore how to leverage capabilities more effectively inside the organization and in its markets
- Help community to develop self-funding mechanisms to sustain its growth and project-development aspirations
- Support community initiatives to institutionalize its capabilities—for example, setting standards in the field for capability benchmarks, professional certification, etc.

## Stage 5: Legacy

The legacy or "transformation" stage can take several forms. It may simply mark the demise of the community as the topic morphs or loses relevance, members lose interest, or sponsorship evaporates. The community may not die out completely, but rather return to a lower level of activity—say the coalescing stage (or even the ad hoc, informal state typical during the discovery or "potential" stage). Alternatively, the community may split up along the lines of sub-topics, roles, or regions. The legacy stage may also mark the transition of a community into a more formal organization—a consulting group, for example, or a functional department in an organization. Finally, the community may reinvent itself and reframe what its domain is about as issues evolve. For instance, automotive engineers may decide to focus on electric motors rather than gas-powered, and begin all over again to discover the right diversity of skills, practices, members, etc.

It is common that communities of practice skip to the legacy stage whether or not they attain stages 2 to 4. In this case, all three cross-agency communities went from positions somewhere in the area of stage 2, and then directly to the "legacy" stage when they disbanded sometime after the administration changed. Their legacy includes their accomplishments, ongoing professional relationships, and the visibility and influence the networks have had as exemplars of national communities of practice.

Another model of transformation might have been a formalization of the networks as a new type of program. This didn't happen, although the Justice Department did name a new program "Safe Neighborhoods," which may in part have been a nod to SafeCities' successful efforts to engage local civic action groups in reducing gun violence. In the end, even if they had stabilized at the stage 2 level, the communities might have continued to have considerable influence. It is not clear, however, that members would have been satisfied with this. Network members were strong-willed and had high aspirations, and it is likely they would have lost interest had they not felt they were on a path toward the generativity and influence of a stewardship community.

*Key management tasks:*
- Negotiate and advise the community on how to manage the transition to new community topics or to new affiliations with formal organizations—at local, state, or federal levels, both governmental and nongovernmental
- Help community find new sponsorship and support if they are vital and productive but in danger of collapse because they will lose crucial seed funding

## Developmental Challenges

While the role of executives is important for strategic communities at all stages, this is particularly true as they are getting launched (from stage 1 to 2), and as they cross a threshold from the coalescing stage (where the focus is mostly internal among members) to the maturing stage, when the community becomes more focused on its role to build organizational capabilities and influence progress in the field.

All three cross-agency networks attained different degrees of stage 2 development, but all faced a steep challenge to move to stage 3. The developmental transition from stage 2 to 3 is truly a phase-change accomplishment. At this point, the knowledge assets and relationship capital of the community can be leveraged into projects, advocacy, and distributed membership with a much broader influence. The move to stage 3 can mark a significant expansion of the initiative. In this case, it could mean growing from one network of 10 to 20 or more networks of 10, with regional networks covering the nation and effectively building toward a stage 4 strategic capability to "influence the psychology and thinking of [the] nation" in their domain.

The position at the cusp of the transition from stage 2 to 3 is particularly delicate. Sponsor support is especially critical at this point. Depending on what level of support the network gets, it may enter a vicious or virtuous cycle of development—either a demoralizing regression or a transformative advance. A relatively small, incremental investment can have an inordinate impact on participant commitments, the production of new knowledge, innovation rates, and the growth of capabilities. These outcomes, in turn,

drive increased interest, additional sources of funding, and growing influence on a broadening scale.

But this transition from stage 2 to 3 depends on key investments, and
because sponsorship for communities of practice is so unfamiliar—and
because the causal relationship between investments, capability, and the
impact on results is not easy to track, few sponsors today are willing to
make significant investments. The tragedy of this is that often it takes a relatively small investment, such as a single FTE, to move a community from
a weak stage 2 to a vital stage 3 community, which then attracts additional
sources of funding and support.

Private-sector firms that have sponsored dozens of communities over
nearly a decade have seen patterns in community development related to
investments of members' time and energy, staff support, and sponsor commitment. The presence or absence of a sponsor's incremental investment
can affect a community's development spin, spurring a reinforcing cycle
that can be either vicious or virtuous (see Figure 6.A.3).[12]

## The Effects of Incremental Investments and Cycles of Development

*Vicious cycle: Spinning wheel without support:*
* Insufficient sponsorship for funds, legitimacy, and influence

**Figure 6.A.3: Comparison of the Effect of an Incremental Investment on the
Development of a Community of Practice**

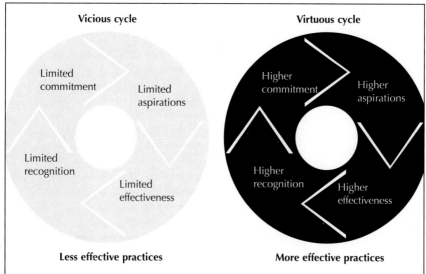

- Tenuous trust and sparse professional network with many missing links
- Spotty access to information, influence, and expertise; redundant overheads among local agencies
- Limited effectiveness and weak stakeholder support, ad nauseum

*Virtuous cycle: Increasing energy getting results:*
- High level of sponsorship fosters legitimacy, influence, and initiative
- Increased levels of trust and collaboration
- More building and sharing of information and expertise
- High impact on results, increased stakeholder support, and so forth

Thus, a relatively small investment at local, state, and federal levels can transform weak, ad hoc networks (both local and national) into powerful, self-sustaining communities of practice that achieve extraordinary results. It is remarkable how small an investment is required to catalyze 30 very busy, leading innovators from 10 cities nationwide to spend several hours a month learning new ways to solve problems, diffuse effective practices and lessons learned, and build stakeholder support and investments in local initiatives. The initial investment in these networks was only one full-time staff person. How often does the federal government get that kind of return on investment, leveraging the creative power of 30 local partners and an array of collaborating agencies for the price of one government staff member?

# Appendix II:
# Going to Scale—The Evolution
# of Communities of Practice

## Understanding Going to Scale

Once an agency or cross-agency community has been established and has demonstrated its ability to support results, sponsors may consider increasing investments to enable the community to address the full scope and scale of the issues included in its domain.

The federal government is in a unique position to cultivate an influential system of communities of practice that embrace a variety of problem or issue domains that span the nation. The challenge is to know what type of overall structure, as well as specific design elements and mechanisms, will allow the federal government to best leverage its unique assets. These assets include institutional legitimacy; knowledge and financial resources; infrastructure; influence over policy making, program design, and implementation; and a central role with sufficient scope and scale to serve as convener for organizing efforts in many domains nationwide.

The National Partnership for Reinventing Government conveners of the three networks discussed in this chapter were particularly interested in growing the scale of the networks, consistent with their national perspective. Despite some misgivings about going too fast, participants saw much value in going to scale, both in terms of their own learning as well as their ability to influence national and local results.

> "I'd like to see this go international. I'd like to talk to a bobby in London who doesn't carry a gun, or a policeman in Rome or Madrid. We have shared problems. They've got gun violence in the UK. You're more likely to be a victim of gun violence in London than New York City. And we've got officers here afraid to go to certain parts of our community."

> "There will come a point as this grows to scale that we will establish a critical mass to change the psychology and thinking and culture of the country about what we can do for kids and families."

Agency executives may also consider applying a community approach to an active program they are already rolling out. For example, Scanlon (2003) reports on a massive HHS campaign to get commitments from 3,000 communities nationwide. The case describes an approach much like a political campaign or systematically planned social movement. It reports how a group in HHS applied "social marketing" and highly visible events in local communities to get stakeholder commitments to address health access limitations and treatment disparities among diverse socioeconomic populations. The case does not address the practices that local communities will need to develop—such as coalition building; GIS mapping; analysis of patterns of access/disparity gaps; and alliance agreements between hospitals, clinics, employers, and social services agencies.

A community-of-practice approach could address the challenge to build capabilities in local communities. It could also spur the dissemination of best practices and innovations across a constellation of local communities who agree to form a community of practice together. In fact, HHS considered just this. As Boost4Kids was looking for an agency sponsor under the new administration, they began negotiations with HHS to take on the 100% access/0% disparity challenge as one of the key strategic objectives of the community. Had the alliance been implemented (HHS could not commit the staff, as it turned out), it would have been a terrific action-learning experiment to show how an intercity community of practice focused on healthcare could complement a social marketing campaign to increase attention and diffuse methods related to national healthcare objectives.

The three cross-agency communities, in particular, outline a powerful mechanism for going to scale while retaining the success factors observed in initial groups: local legitimacy and momentum; practitioner connectedness; learning and innovation; and visible contributions to civic outcomes. (Other communities described here also operate at a large scale, including the Rumble Strips, CompanyCommand.com, and Procurement Program Management communities—but the potential scale in those cases is not nearly as large as the cross-agency communities, which—like the HHS initiative—could include 3,000 county regions nationwide (and, eventually, cities on an international scale[13]). The cross-agency examples further suggest what a national rollout of these initiatives might look like—where equivalent network configurations exist at national, state, and local levels:

- *State networks:* Members of Boost4Kids' "California cluster" discussed a future scenario under which they would serve as the core group for starting up a state-based replication of the Boost4Kids model. Both the Vermont and Georgia coalitions were part of state-based networks with goals similar to Boost4Kids—also functioning as knowledge sharing and collaboration forums. Many problems that local coalitions faced were state related, not federal. The development of state-level networks could be a powerful lever for a national new-governance model.
- *Local networks:* The coalitions themselves operated as networks at the local level. Generally, their explicit focus was on specific project-based collaborations rather than on knowledge sharing and ongoing innovation. But a local coalition's commitment to learning is essential if

diverse constituencies are going to achieve a shared understanding of relevant issues and build new relationships across long-standing divides.

*The "going to scale" problem statement:*
How do you significantly increase the scale of a community of practice initiative without losing core elements that members considered important—personal relationships, direct access to well-connected federal officials, and special recognition and access to learning opportunities?

Although network members hoped these initiatives would have national impact, they were generally averse to growing much beyond their original numbers. They, like the NPR sponsors, were unsure how to expand a model that depended so much on personal relationships and direct access to senior officials in the federal government.

> "We're very loathe to see bigger as better. When programs expand, they expand into oblivion, so how to expand the sphere of influence without expanding the program? The strength of the program is that it is relatively small, with one-on-one relationships with each other and people in Washington."

> "I am fearful that expansion beyond 13 will make it difficult to have dialogue; I don't want to go to lecture-hall mode where it is information dissemination and not a dialogue or small enough to build relationships."

There are a number of considerations relevant to scaling networks from local to global levels. The challenge is to frame the problem not merely in terms of increasing the size of the initiative, but rather by *expanding and replicating its current structure and context both horizontally and vertically—horizontally by going across regions and vertically by creating second- and third-order "communities of communities."* The point is to find ways to keep the essential functions of the network—influence, access, peer-to-peer learning with leading practitioners—while constructing a system of networks that can scale to a national level.

## A Federalist Model for a National "Community of Communities"
The ability to scale these networks from single instances to a system of such networks on a national level could mean leveraging a "fractal" design. Fractal structures are characterized by sub-structures that have similar design features, such as the undulating edge of a coastline or the pattern of a river's tributaries that appear similar when sampled at various lengths (Wheatley, 1994, pp. 80-86, 130-133). Large networks, for example, often have major hubs with many links among them as well as with smaller hubs.

These smaller hubs, in turn, are linked to each other and to still smaller clusters—and so on. Each size hub looks similar—each has the same ratio of nodes and satellite links. (See Figure 6.A.4.) Applying such a design principle, it is possible to create a small-community feeling while extending a network at local, state, and national levels. In this case, it is possible to grow a "community of communities" in which each level of sub-communities share basic characteristics: a similar set of focal issues, shared values, and a common practice repertoire.

In network analysis terms, the fractal approach applies the advantages of "scale-free" networks (Matlis, 2002; Watts, 2003). In scale-free networks, a

**Figure 6.A.4: A Fractal Model for Going to Scale—Cultivating Communities at Local, State, and National Levels**

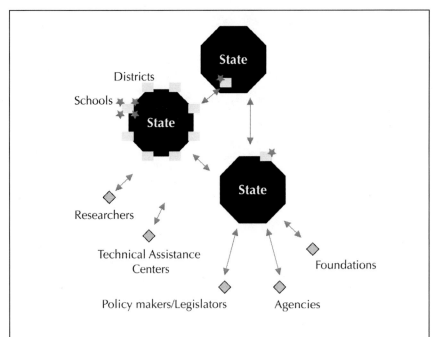

Cultivate communities at multiple geographic levels: nation, states, districts, and schools

Define cross-hatching community domains by:

- Roles—e.g., professional development for principals/teachers
- Methods—e.g., technology in schools
- Curriculum—e.g., math and literacy methods
- Context—e.g., urban schools

unique fractal configuration is repeated over and over. This is not merely a randomly dispersed network that exists at a national scale. Rather, the component networks—at each level—take on a specific configuration that prepares them for a clear path to replication.[14] At the lowest level (the initial "first order" network that includes approximately 10 local coalitions, as in the case of the cross-agency communities described in this chapter), there is a coordinator for every 10 or so local coalitions. Moving "horizontally," additional community networks can be created—each with their own coordinator and 10 or so local coalition partners. As these additional networks accumulate, a higher-level (now moving "vertically") second-order network of coordinators emerges (as it did in the NPR case; and as it has in the context of a Special Interest Group made up of community coordinators who are leading communities based in various federal agencies[15]). This second order of network coordinators helps ensure that the first-order networks are led effectively, and that they take advantage of opportunities to leverage shared investments—say in a training program, satellite broadcast, or website. They can also help network members enjoy the same influence and access to officials at various levels as the original NPR groups did. Meanwhile, network benefits are maintained, including opportunities within each network to build professional relationships with other innovators, to share ideas, and to get help and encouragement for implementing new approaches.

As the overall "network of networks" grows, the ratio of the number of connecting nodes to the number of hubs stays the same. (See Figure 6.A.5.) It is always about 10—at each level. Whenever the number of individual baseline networks reaches about 10, then a new second-order network is launched. For example, if there are 10 SafeCities community networks nationwide (each of which has 10 or so local coalition partners), there would be a single second-order network of coordinators representing the 10 networks. If another five baseline networks get started, they would organize their own network of coordinators. At some point, there may be enough second-order networks (say three to five) to justify a third-order network.

In this way, a fractal network of networks could link hundreds of individual networks at different levels of aggregation. Across levels, various networks might collaborate on projects such as the development of a measurement instrument or policy recommendation. Other role-based groupings may emerge—mayors leading citywide initiatives, for example, or executive sponsors at the state and federal levels.[16]

The key insight of this design is that crucial features of these networks can be maintained, no matter how many participants join—as long as the basic configuration, organizing principles, and ratio of links to nodes is maintained. This fractal scaling approach allows the power of both the overall network and the influence at local levels to increase significantly. Networks can take several steps to maintain the essential nature and benefits of

**Figure 6.A.5 An Evolution Toward Increased Network Instances at a National Scale**

**Stage 1:** 3 NPR networks—SafeCities, Boost4Kids, and 21st Century Skills—operating in 34 cities or regions. Options:

- Consolidate development of current networks at next level of maturity
- Create "meta-network" for current network conveners on topic of how to foster networks and leverage knowledge for results
- Build active, informed involvement of sponsor and stakeholders to support growth and further strategic development of these networks

**Stage 2:** Spawn regional chapters of current networks

- Share knowledge assets and publicize successes by inviting charter members and non-members to satellite broadcasts, website, and annual conferences
- Staff network conveners to guide and develop regional networks; conveners join a growing meta-network focused on how to foster successful learning networks
- Garner increased attention and support from state, local, and federal agencies, foundations, and nonprofit organizations

**Stage 3:** Add new networks and continue to spawn regional chapters until covering both national scale and broad scope of socioeconomic issues (public safety, families, workforce, environment, etc.)

- Build technology infrastructure, templates, and software to facilitate network formation
- Continue devolution of policy and program administration to local level
- Launch "executive networks" of mayors who want to develop their clients as "intelligent communities" that cultivate a constellation of local coalitions on various topics

a single network while scaling up. For example, they can facilitate trust and sharing across networks by organizing occasional large-scale events (annual conferences, satellite broadcasts, etc.) where members throughout the broader set of networks attend. The payoff for creating such an extensive, multi-tiered network is that it provides a magnificent learning laboratory to identify emerging issues and test proposals in practice with motivated sites. This natural laboratory leverages innovations and replication efforts throughout a national network of local coalitions who are ready and willing to share results quickly and convincingly with peers and stakeholders, and who can then help to translate these quickly into better policies and improved results.

The key challenge for skeptical pilot-community members is not "how will I get influence without direct contact," but rather "can I trust that a broader 'community of communities' can serve our local purpose as well as it does a national purpose?" The answer is, of course, "It all depends." Mostly it depends on the networks at all levels—local, state, and national— to establish a culture of trust, reciprocity, and shared values (i.e., social capital). This is the critical success factor for going to scale. And it highlights the importance of a kind of meta-community that helps the network gauge the pace and methods of growth, and the need for a strong sponsor board to provide help along the way. Sponsorship is especially important for the large-scale events that will be required as additional activities in the ecology.

Scaling is itself a "second-order" problem and a long-term challenge. The first step, of course, is to launch pilot initiatives to see what a community-based approach can do to promote agency objectives. These early experiences and related lessons learned and staff capabilities provide a robust foundation for growing and scaling the initiative over time. Finally, as the theory of communities of practice would suggest, agencies are more likely to learn quickly about launching and scaling community-based initiatives by forming a community of practice on the topic itself—one that includes key players such as executive sponsors, support team members, and successful community coordinators.

## Role of Federal Government in Going to Scale

These considerations for scaling community-of-practice initiatives beg the question of whose role it is to lead the charge. For a variety of reasons, the federal government is uniquely positioned to help foster the evolution of nation-scale community-of-practice networks through five principal mechanisms: 1) leveraging infrastructure efficiency; 2) promoting agency learning and alignment; 3) diffusing learning and innovation across states and nations; 4) establishing standards for measuring performance outcomes; and 5) modeling an approach for diffusing ideas and methods that can be used at state and local levels.[17]

1. *Leveraging infrastructure efficiency*
   - Serve as broker (or direct source) of investments in shared infra-structure for communities of practice that are addressing an array of domains (education, economic development, health, housing, public safety, etc.) nationwide. Social and technical infrastructure investments include online facilities, support staff, strategic part-nerships with vendors, conference planning, etc.

2. *Promoting agency learning and alignment*
   - Foster opportunities for learning among various agencies and between them and local and state constituencies. Community-of-practice initiatives enable local coalitions to learn more about agency policy and programs, while agencies learn more about the impact of programs at the local level. This multi-directional learning activity creates opportunities to improve policies and programs, as well as partnership agreements to implement them effectively.
   - Engage senior agency and congressional staff and representatives to shorten the policy development and improvement cycles based on experience in the field.

3. *Diffusing learning and innovation across states and nations*
   - Leverage the legitimacy and visibility that the federal government can provide to local and state initiatives. Make much of its ability to give initiatives the aura of a "national priority"—especially with brand approval of high-level cabinet and executive office affiliations.
   - Facilitate international exchanges through established federal mechanisms for connecting internationally, such as offices and ini-tiatives managed by the State Department, Department of Commerce, U.S. military services, and others.

4. *Establishing standards for measuring performance outcomes*
   - Measuring results is key to the sustainability, scale, scope, and speed of innovation initiatives. Measures that make communities' influence on results visible are as instrumental for gaining peers' interest as they are for gaining sponsors' attention and investments (and these two are not unrelated). As already mentioned, the issue is *how* to measure, not whether. The federal government can help research, legitimize, and provide ongoing renewal for measure-ment approaches. It can also provide a way to publish results—per-haps something like a Bureau of Census version of the JD Power Quality reports—as a way of communicating the "state of the nation" in terms of civic capabilities within and across cities and regions.

- Maintaining national measurement standards is a traditional role for the federal government in many areas, such as air quality, weather, demographics, disease, and economic indicators. Establishing a strong foundation for measures of civic capabilities (in areas such as education, health, and economic development) would help to spur innovation and direct resources to innovators who were best able to achieve results.

5. *Modeling an approach for diffusing ideas and methods*
   - Model cross-agency, cross-sector, cross-level, participative governance approaches, and demonstrate this on a highly visible national scale as a way to influence and guide governments at state and local levels (as well as international). Provide a forum for "meta" learning across various networks—establishing a home base for learning about the skills, tools, methods, frameworks, and lessons learned that can help leaders at any level launch successful community-of-practice initiatives.

## Going to Scale: Options

For agencies that are ready, there are a number of mechanisms for building a scaled-up community-of-practice initiative that achieves impact at both local and global levels. Briefly stated, here are options to consider:

- *Establishing a foundation* of strong shared vision and values, including cross-community commitments to social norms and a collective vision of what their domain is about.
- *Multi-membership:* Members join first at the level of local baseline networks (the equivalent of "demes" in the place-based model of community governance in ancient Greece). But as the ecology of networks evolves along topic or role dimensions that span geographies, members may participate in communities at multiple tiers (the equivalent of the tribe, which includes 10 demes, or the Council of 500, which includes 50 representatives from each tribe) in ways that help interweave relationships in the broader community. (In fact, civic leaders may participate in communities of practice across domains—for example, both workforce development and public safety—and thus help connect themes, people, and practices across various dimensions.)
- *Shared technical infrastructure:* Communities of practice benefit from at least a minimal communications and knowledge-capture infrastructure, including a website, listserv, etc., for posting and commenting on local achievements, questions, news, etc. Ideally, such an infrastructure is designed for easy access and use both within and across networks. Longer term, it makes sense to use a common set of infrastructure facilities and tools to facilitate interoperability problems and reduce behavioral hurdles to users—learning how to use multiple tools, remembering passwords, etc.
- *Events at various levels:* Events can be designed to include communities across regions and at multiple tiers—local, regional, national. They may also be organized to include communities focused on different domains to encourage cross-pollination of ideas and to weave relationships that facilitate the flow of insights and methodologies across communities of all types. These events may be either face-to-face or virtual (using satellite technology, for example); synchronous or asynchronous (e.g., using computer-mediated discussion forums, or a grand tour in which members of various communities participate in a sequence of peer-to-peer visits across communities in various localities).
- *Subdivide along various dimensions:* geography, topic, role, and others. Topical and role-based subgroups provide a way to connect members across regions—strengthening the overall fabric and connectedness of the entire network.
- *Logistical support infrastructure:* Helps with local event planning, identifies resources, and coordinates projects at local levels and beyond.

- *Creating a "brand":* Participation is a recognized achievement, even if you are not the only group of its kind. Many members of the cross-agency communities mentioned the power of the brand of the network as having a positive effect on their credibility and influence at the local level.
- *Subsidiarity:* Where problems can be solved locally, they are. When they need regional or national attention, members can escalate the issues through mechanisms they develop within and across participating chapter communities. Local communities are likely to have much more influence and credibility for issues they raise to the federal level because they have been vetted by a representative group before being escalated.
- *Timescale:* Finally, the evolution of such a structure needs to be paced at the timescale consistent with building social relationships, not according to political impetus to demonstrate results immediately. Reconciling this with the realities of political life is invariably tricky. It is important to ensure that first-order communities have achieved a sufficient level of effectiveness and cohesion to build on. Many e-commerce start-ups during the dot-com era failed because they sought to make big revenues too quickly. We have learned, in that context and others, that it is important to focus on "community before commerce" in order to establish a foundation for sustained growth. This lesson applies to communities who grow too fast before they are ready for the sake of making a dramatic impact.

# Appendix III:
# Communities of Practice as
# a Type of Collaborative Model

It is important to identify the basic structural elements of communities of practice as a basis for thinking about how to replicate, expand, and develop them further. What is the unique nature of this type of network? How do the main structural dimensions—domain, community, and practice—help to distinguish communities of practice from other types of networks? Finally, what does such a structural analysis tell us about how to assess their health and effectiveness—and help craft interventions for improving the vitality of community-of-practice networks?

In recent years, there has been an explosion of research and practical initiatives related to various types of networks. Network theory has drawn comparisons between patterns in social networks and those found in nature (for example, neural networks in the brain) and man-made systems (such as power grids and the Internet). Research applications have led to the development of mathematical and computer-based analyses that can identify structural elements such as "weak ties," "structural holes," and "rich hubs" (Watts, 2003). Generally, however, these rigorous theoretical works on network theory do not provide practical applications of their models to organizational case studies. The work by Robert Cross and colleagues (2001) is an exception.

Organization research and consulting have demonstrated the transactional efficiencies and knowledge-based advantages of interorganizational networks in the private and nonprofit sectors (Nohria and Eccles, 1992; Keyes, et al., 1996) and increasingly in the public sector (Agranoff, 2003; Kamarck, 2002). Meanwhile, more attention has been paid to interpersonal networks as mechanisms for communication, dissemination of ideas, and finding help to solve problems (Gladwell, 2000; Borgatti and Cross, 2003; Wellman, 1999). This work overlaps with organization research on professional networks, which, as mentioned earlier, are called by various names, such as "knowledge networks," "learning communities," and "communities of practice." Detailed research in this area is quite new, and there has been very little done to date related to applications in the governmental and civic sectors.

Communities of practice are distinctive as networks in large part because members feel a *communal commitment to steward practice development in a knowledge domain*—say, java programming, thoracic surgery, or "results for kids." Such a community focuses on compelling issues ("*a knowledge domain*") that practitioners care about; cultivates a community of thought leaders, peers, and apprentices who want to connect with each other (*"communal commitment"*); and builds the tools and methods that practitioners use, while also capturing case studies and the stories they tell (*"steward practice development"*).

These key features of communities of practice—issue *domains, community* members, and shared *practices*—provide a framework for distinguishing at a structural level two broad types of networks—"discursive" and "community"—which are defined in terms of the relative degree of communality or mutuality in the network:

1. Members of *discursive networks* do not share a strong collective identity among themselves. This resembles something like a "six degrees of separation" model, where one member knows somebody who knows somebody, etc.—without necessarily sharing any particular set of common values or interests.

2. Members of *community networks* share a sense of belonging and communal identity—such as a veterans association chapter, members of the local "dance community," or an online discussion group talking about ways to treat diabetes.

A more common way to categorize networks is by their functions. The "discursive-community" distinction is emphasized here because it highlights a fundamental structural distinction between communities of practice and the more familiar notion of networks. Networks may play a number of functions. Transaction networks trade goods, services, and "transactional" information (such as a job lead or investment opportunity); advocacy networks lobby for common causes; communities of interest enjoy shared interests and affiliations; and communities of practice build and share knowledge together. Transaction functions related to goods and services at either retail or wholesale levels depend greatly on network relationships.

When network roles are highly heterogeneous and the focus is on making transactions, there is little emphasis on building skills and capabilities together. In community-oriented networks, by contrast, the emphasis is on connecting people as a collective. In communities of interest, this means people with shared affiliations (for instance, college alumni) or interests (talking about mystery novels) (Wenger, et al., 2002, p. 42). The hallmarks of a community of practice that make it distinctive are that members both recognize themselves as a community and have a collective commitment to share and steward a practice. They are people who *write* the mystery novels, not merely fans who like to read them.

In practice, there are fuzzy boundaries between these types. Many networks display both "discursive" and "communal" qualities Communities of practice generally have a layer of "peripheral" members who are loosely attached to the more active core of participants—and therefore are less likely to have a collective sense of belonging. Conversely, conventional discursive networks will often have pockets or hubs where participants do feel a sense of mutuality—whether along lines of commerce, affiliation, or practice. Networks might also concurrently serve multiple functions, although generally they emphasize one kind or another. If a community-of-practice network, for example, becomes too transactional, then members may be less generous sharing time and expertise with each other—thinking, perhaps, there should be a direct quid pro quo.[18] But different types of networks can also be complementary. Members of a community of practice can become insular or "provincial"; their relationships with others in more discursive networks help to remind them of outsiders' views and provide leads to new ideas that expand a community's learning agenda.

The collaborative learning networks described here most resemble the "community of practice" model. Yet, they also show signs of activity that could be thought of in terms of the transaction or advocacy functions of networks (for example, getting access to senior officials who allocate funds or talking together about ways to influence agency policy).

Managed well, a network can perform multiple functions and take advantage of the complementarities that are possible. Transactional and advocacy interests invite knowledge-sharing connections; and a communal sense of identity and belonging among practitioners can facilitate transactions and joint advocacy initiatives that rely on trust and reciprocity. The danger for community-of-practice networks, as stated, is that commerce and advocacy will crowd out community- and knowledge-building activities. John Hagel, an authority on the e-commerce revolution, concluded that many of the dot-coms failed because they put "commerce before community." In the end, community members need to have a nuanced appreciation of a community's overall purpose, member interests, and its stage of development in order to balance the configuration of functions it can play (Harmon, 2001).

# Appendix IV:
# Notes on Research Methodology

The research approach to the three NPR-based cross-agency cases described in the report was primarily qualitative, with significant participative observation and action-research dimensions as well. The first author was a consultant to the three cross-agency communities and participated in conversations with coordinators and members that influenced the communities' design and evolution over time.

- Primary research included approximately 75 interviews with community members and federal agency coordinators, champions, and sponsors.
- Extensive interview notes and initial findings were summarized in three separate documents—each focused on a particular community—Boost4Kids, SafeCities, and 21st Century Skills. These reports were read and vetted by community coordinators and participants, who offered corrections where appropriate and discussed the reports with the first author in teleconferences and face-to-face meetings.
- Participation in activities supplemented formal interviews. These activities included conversations and presentations at face-to-face meetings and teleconferences, as well as formal and informal conversations with members and coordinators.
- Additional research included reviews of website materials; artifacts such as the original recruitment letters in the Federal Register; teleconference notes; listserv announcements and exchanges; presentation slides from face-to-face meetings; materials on local initiatives provided by members; member reports on accomplishments sent in to the federal coordinators; reports from academics, internal reviews (including material in a book written by Lynn Kahn, one of the coordinators); and analogue organizations (such as the Social Exclusion Office in the UK).

Qualitative methods were used to gain a "thick description" of these cases and to help to identify themes and patterns to explore when quantitative data were insufficient. Tables and other displays of primary interview and archival data were created to identify themes and provide supporting evidence. (These are available in documents created in preparation for this chapter.)

Research on the internal agency communities (such as the Rumble Strips Community, the Program Management Community of Practice (PMCoP), and CompanyCommand.com) and additional cross-agency communities (such as the e-Reg Community) was conducted in the context of a separate study that included over 20 interviews with members, consultative conversations and presentations, and reviews of internal community reports on activities and results.

# Endnotes

1. Thanks to Noel Dickover for providing a synopsis of the Program Management Communities of Practice, upon which this brief description is based. See also: http://www.dau.mil/communities.asp

2. Thanks to William Bennett for providing a synopsis of the E-reg community of practice, upon which this brief description is based. See also: Wenger and Snyder (2003) at http://www.km.gov

3. Thanks to Pete Kilner and Nate Allen for providing a synopsis of the Company-Command community of practice, upon which this brief description is based. See also: http://www.companycommand.com/

4. Lynn Kahn, a member of the NPR team, reports revealing statistics that support Ross's point: "Fifteen agencies have responsibility for food safety; 144 major federal programs support children and families; and 154 federal offices have employment and training programs.... States and localities have the same problems.... Florida addresses juvenile crime with 200 activities spread across 23 state entities...." (2003: 98). Margaret Dunkle conducted the study that helped to substantiate Ross's argument. She documented how tangled is the plethora of siloed federal, state, and local programs that provide social services to families in need. See: http://www.childrensplanningcouncil.org/photopages/understanding_systems/showphotos3.asp.

5. The term "convener" is occasionally used in this chapter to refer to NPR community coordinators, particularly in reference to those who played multiple roles (such as Pam Johnson, Beverly Godwin, and Lynn Kahn), including community coordinator, agency champion, and internal consultant (also called "support team" in this chapter).

6. http://www.socialexclusionunit.gov.uk

7. Center-of-excellence programs in organizations are increasingly gravitating from a hub-and-spoke model, where the center captures best practices and disseminates them to the field, toward a peer-to-peer, community model that facilitates peer-to-peer exchanges among practitioners and collective responsibility for stewarding innovation (Moore and Birkinshaw, 1998).

8. This review of the Rumble Strips Community closely follows a report by Michael Burk, who was a principal organizer and heads up FHWA's Knowledge Management office. The office provides a common technical infrastructure for FHWA communities of practice, and members of the KM office have served as the support team for a number of them. His report is available at: http://www.km.gov/stories/FHWA_Rumble-Strips.doc

9. Many successful local civic coalitions have been spurred to action by a crisis. For example, the highly effective 10 Points Coalition for reducing juvenile violence was started in Boston when a gang member killed another during a funeral (being held for still another gang member). In another case, a civic coalition was formed in Silicon Valley during the 1990s when hard times hit the high-tech industry. Another in Cleveland was spurred when the Cuyahoga River caught on fire.

10. A leader of a community-of-practice initiative at DaimlerChrysler related that a local civic coalition in his town, Kirchheim unter Tech, riled the local city council to such an extent that the council attempted to undermine the group's credibility in the town. But the citizenry stood up to them and further increased the influence of the civic group and its various project-focused sub-groups.

11. Kahn, the lead coordinator for the 21st Century Skills Community, builds on her experience to describe a governance model characterized as "democracy as a living system." She argues that "[i]n the 21st century, the basic building blocks of government are learning networks joined together as communities of practice to improve results in a spe-

cific domain and cement in place the missing feedback loop between local results, national success and government policy. In places large and small, in all domains of democracy, this combination can achieve what hierarchy alone has failed to do—get results people care about" (2003: 158).

12. Thanks to Nathaniel Foote for this figure, which summarizes an aspect of his analysis of performance drivers for communities of practice at McKinsey & Co. (published in Wenger et al., 2002: 165.)

13. The Ayuda Urbana community of practice (www.ayudaurbana.com) was originally sponsored by the World Bank and includes a number of mayors and deputies from the capital cities of Central American and Caribbean cites. They address a variety of topics, such as urban slums and infrastructure (Wenger et al., 2002: 229). Another international case is one that included over 100 cities in developing countries worldwide that came together to reduce the human and financial costs of natural disasters (http://www.unisdr.org/unisdr/ radius/leaflet.htm).

14. Examples of organizations that have used fractal structures to foster learning and innovation in large global communities include ones organized by Shell Oil petroleum engineers and McKinsey and Company consultants (Wenger et al., 2002: 126-128).

15. A number of community leaders of agencies in the federal government participate in a "meta-community" for community-of-practice leaders in the federal government. They have organized what they call a "Strategic Interest Group (SIG)," that has organized relevant documents and posts a calendar of events in an online repository used by a broader group interested in "knowledge management applications" (http://www.km.gov/cop/cop.html).

16. This model of radically participative democracy correlates with the original Western model of democracy that evolved in Athens 2,500 years ago, where 140 "demes" of citizen leaders governed at the village level; the demes were organized into 10 "tribes," each of which in turn chose 50 representatives from various member demes to participate in a governing Council of 500 members. Finally, an assembly body, open to all citizens, participated in the most important decisions of the state, including whether or not to go to war (Manville and Ober, 2003: 68-76; 103-104). This multi-tier governance network constitutes the original model of Western democracy—and provides a working model for the federated fractal model described here. Only in this case, the overall framework is organized by communities of practice as well as place—where practice-based communities can help to recover many of the original dimensions of a radically democratic model of governance that was developed in ancient Athens and has been an inspiration to nations of the world ever since.

17. In recent papers on the role of the federal government with respect to network forms of organizing, both Agranoff (2003) and Klitgaard and Treverton (2003) outline several functions that the federal government is uniquely positioned to provide: information clearinghouse, civic legitimacy, communications infrastructure, and overall convener (with both a national scale and a scope that covers the full terrain of civic-practice domains).

18. Putnam (1993) distinguishes two types of reciprocity—"direct," where the quid pro quo is expected, and "generalized," where no immediate trade is expected; nor is it expected in relation to a specific person. This latter type of reciprocal relationship corresponds to an expectation that "what goes around comes around," and is a hallmark of a culture that has a high level of "social capital."

# Bibliography

Ackoff, R.L., "Beyond Prediction and Preparation," *Journal of Management Studies,* Vol. 20 (1983), pp. 59-69.

Agranoff, R., "Leveraging Networks: A guide for public managers working across organizations" (Arlington, VA: IBM Center for The Business of Government, 2003).

Barber, B.R. *Strong Democracy: Participatory Politics for a New Age* (Berkley: University of California Press, 1985).

Borgatti, S., and Cross, R., "A Social Network View of Organizational Learning: Relational and Structural Dimensions of 'Know Who'," *Management Science* (2003).

Cross, R., Parker, A., Prusak, L., and Borgatti, S., "Knowing What We Know: Supporting Knowledge Creation and Sharing in Social Networks," *Organizational Dynamics* Vol. 3, No. 2 (2001), pp. 100-120.

Davenport, T.H., and Beck, J.C., *The Attention Economy: Understanding the New Currency of Business* (Boston: Harvard Business School Press, 2001).

Dyer, J.H., and Nobeoka, K., "Creating and Managing a High-Performance Knowledge-Sharing Network: The Toyota Case," *Strategic Management Journal,* Vol. 21, No. 3 (2000), pp. 345-367.

Fink, E., and Resnick, L.B., "Developing Principals as Instructional Leaders." *Phi Delta Kappan,* Vol. 82, No. 8 (2001), pp. 598-606.

Fung, A., and Wright, E.O., *Deepening Democracy: Institutional Innovations in Empowered Participatory Governance* (London: Verso Books, 2003).

Geertz, C., *The Interpretation of Cultures* (New York: Basic Books, 1973).

Gladwell, M., *The Tipping Point* (Boston: Little, Brown and Company, 2000).

Gore, A., *Creating a Government That Works Better and Costs Less: Report of the National Performance Review* (Washington, D.C.: Government Printing Office, September 7, 1993).

Hagel, J., and Armstrong, A., *Net Gain: Expanding Markets through Virtual Communities* (Boston: Harvard Business School Press, 1997).

Harmon, A., "Getting 'Amazoned' and other Fantasies; Eek! What have E-consultants Wrought?" *New York Times* (May 13, 2001), Section 3, p. 1.

Heifetz, R., *Leadership Without Easy Answers* (Cambridge, MA: Belknap Press, 1994).

Kahn, L.S., *Results at the Edge* (Oxford: University Press of America, 2003).

Kamarck, E.C., "Applying 21st-Century Government to the Problem of Homeland Security" (Arlington, VA: IBM Center for The Business of Government, 2002).

Kettl, D.F., *Reinventing Government: A Fifth-Year Report Card* (Washington, D.C.: Center for Public Management, The Brookings Institution, 1998).

Keyes, L., Vidal, A., Schwartz, A., and Bratt, R., "Networks and Nonprofits: Opportunities and Challenges in an Era of Federal Devolution," Housing Policy Debate, Vol. 7, No. 2 (1996), pp. 201-229.

Klitgaard, R., and Treverton, G.F., "Assessing Partnerships: New Forms of Collaboration" (Arlington, VA: IBM Center for The Business of Government, 2003).

Kotter, J.P., Leading Change (Boston: Harvard Business School Press, 1996).

Lave, J., and Wenger, E., Situated Learning: Legitimate Peripheral Participation (New York: Cambridge University Press, 1991).

Manville, B., and Ober, J., A Company of Citizens (Boston: Harvard Business School Press, 2003).

Matlis, J., "Scale-Free Networks," Computer World, (November 4, 2002).

McKelvey, W., "Quasi-Natural Organization Science," Organization Science, Vol. 8, No. 4 (1997), pp. 352-380.

Miles, M.B., and Huberman, A.M., Qualitative Data Analysis (Thousand Oaks, CA: Sage Publications, 1994).

Milward, B.H., and Provan, K.G., "Governing the Hollow State," Journal of Public Administration Research and Theory (April 2000).

Mintzberg, H., and Waters, J. A., "Of Strategies, Deliberate and Emergent," Strategic Management Journal, Vol. 6 (1985), pp. 257-272.

Moore, K., and Birkinshaw, J., "Managing Knowledge in Global Service Firms: Centers of Excellence," Academy of Management Executive, Vol. 12, No. 4 (1998), pp. 81-92.

Nohria, N., and Eccles, R. C., (Eds.), Networks and Organizations: Structure, Form, and Action (Boston: Harvard Business School Press, 1992).

Osborne, D., and Gabler, T.A., Reinventing Government: How the Entrepreneurial Spirit Is Transforming the Public Sector (New York: Perseus, 1992).

Peters, T.J., and Waterman, R.H., In Search of Excellence: Lessons from America's Best-Run Companies (New York: Harper & Row, 1982).

Putnam, R. D., Making Democracy Work: Civic Traditions in Modern Italy (Princeton: Princeton University Press, 1993).

Putnam, R. D., Bowling Alone: The Collapse and Revival of American Community (New York: Simon & Schuster, 2000).

Scanlon, J.W., "Extraordinary Results on National Goals: Networks and Partnerships in the Bureau of Primary Health Care's 100%/0 Campaign" (Arlington, VA: IBM Center for The Business of Government, 2003).

Snyder, W.M., "Organization Learning and Performance: An Exploration of the Linkages Between Organization Learning, Knowledge, and Performance" (Ph.D. Dissertation, University of Southern California, 1996).

Szulanski, G., "Exploring Internal Stickiness: Impediments to the Transfer of Best Practice within the Firm," Strategic Management Journal, Winter Special Issue (1996), pp. 27-43.

Watts, D.J., *6 Degrees of Separation: The Science of a Connected Age* (New York: W.W. Norton & Company, 2003).

Wellman, B., (Ed.), *Networks in the Global Village: Life in Contemporary Communities* (Boulder, CO: Westview Press, 1999).

Wenger, E.C., and Snyder, W.M., "Communities of Practice: The Organizational Frontier," *Harvard Business Review*, January-February (2000), pp. 139-145.

Wenger, E., McDermott, R., and Snyder, W.M., *Cultivating Communities of Practice: A Guide to Managing Knowledge* (Boston: Harvard Business School Press, 2002).

Wenger, E., and Snyder, W.M., "Communities of Practice: Facing Complexity in Government," Paper presented at the Knowledge Management in Government Conference, Washington, D.C., April 14 (2003), (www.km.gov).

Wheatley, M.J., *Leadership and the New Science* (San Francisco: Barret-Koehler, 1994).

Yin, R.K., *Case Study Research: Design and Methods* (Newbury Park, CA: Sage Publications, 1989).

# CHAPTER SEVEN

# Leveraging Networks to Meet National Goals: FEMA and the Safe Construction Networks

William L. Waugh, Jr.
Professor of Public Administration,
Urban Studies, and Political Science
Andrew Young School of Policy Studies
Georgia State University

*This report was originally published in March 2002.*

# Understanding Networks

The transformation of governance in the United States has been characterized by more than a shift of responsibility for public programs from public agencies to institutional arrangements involving public agencies, nonprofit organizations, and private firms. "Third party government"—in which public programs are contracted out to nongovernmental, nonprofit, or private organizations, or privatized—is not the only change in how national policy goals are being pursued. In some policy arenas in which the federal government lacks authority to pursue national policy goals directly, the goals are being pursued through the cultivation of formal "partnerships" and less defined relationships with nongovernmental organizations in areas in which the federal government lacks authority to pursue those goals directly. One of those policy arenas is that involving the encouragement of safe construction in the United States.

The movement for safe construction involves networks of public, private, and nonprofit organizations working individually and in concert through a complex array of formal and informal partnerships, collaborations, and supportive arrangements, as well as through their independent activities. The federal government, through the Federal Emergency Management Agency (FEMA) and other agencies, has some regulatory authority relative to building standards and practices, but primary responsibility for regulating construction lies with state and local governments and the building industry itself. In order for the federal government to encourage safe construction, it must leverage the various networks that are working to strengthen building standards and to encourage the adoption of specific disaster-resistant construction methods. To reduce property losses from disasters, FEMA has been promoting stronger building standards and codes when it has authority, encouraging the adoption of stronger standards by those with authority, supporting those who are working for the adoption of stronger construction standards, providing assistance in developing stronger standards and safer construction practices, and simply encouraging the efforts of other agencies and individuals who are engaged in activities that further the effort. In essence, FEMA has been working within a complex array of networks by a variety of means to advance the cause of safe construction.

The development of networks in policy arenas is not new. In 1997, Lawrence O'Toole noted the emergence of networks as an important aspect of public administration, and there is increased attention to the unique characteristics of such arrangements. They can have a profound effect on policy making and policy implementation, complicating the processes and the politics. Many of the networks are based on relationships that are hierarchical, such as multiple delivery systems for contracted services. But, many of the networks are based upon more non-hierarchical relationships, and those present unique challenges for public officials and administrators. They may also present unique opportunities. Fragmented authority within the American federal system makes it extremely difficult to accomplish national policy goals when the federal government lacks regulatory authority or cannot offer attractive incentives to encourage compliance. While Congress and the president frequently can provide incentives for compliance, they cannot easily preempt state and local authority, even when the ends are generally agreed upon. Nonetheless, federal influence has been extended in a number of policy areas through involvement in intergovernmental and public/private "partnerships" and other multi-organizational efforts. Interdependence, shared goals, and strong interest in finding solutions to problems have encouraged collaboration among independent public, nonprofit, and private actors.

FEMA is charged with reducing losses because the costs of disaster recovery are rising rapidly for the federal government, and it has found common cause among other public, private, and nonprofit agencies. The insurance industry is concerned about its own exposure to losses, particularly when they could have been prevented or at least limited. The building industry is interested in changes in construction practices to reduce losses as long as the changes do not reduce sales. And, the public supports safer construction and lower insurance costs as long as they do not add too much to the price of homes and businesses. Despite consensus on the seriousness of the problem, state and local governments need incentives to adopt and enforce wiser land-use regulations, stronger building standards, and stronger building codes, and builders and property owners need incentives to implement effective disaster-resistant building practices. FEMA has been leveraging the safe construction networks to achieve those ends.

## Intergovernmental and Inter-Sector Networks

The safe construction policy arena is not unique. Increasingly there are policy arenas in which federal or state authorities lack effective authority to control policy decisions. Responsibility for the decisions necessary to achieve the policy goal resides in many hands. Watershed management, for example, is one such arena. Local governments, farmers, commercial fishing interests, recreational interests, the U.S. Army Corps of Engineers, the U.S. Environmental Protection Agency and its state counterparts, the U.S. Fish and Wildlife Service and its state counterparts, and a variety of other public, nonprofit, and private interests have interests in the use of water and in its quality. Interdependence encourages cooperation, but does not assure agreement on policy. Even among the government agencies involved, responsibility and authority are diffused. Resolving pollution and other water problems requires consensus, not just majority approval, on remedial actions. With-

out consensus, levels of cooperation and regulatory compliance are likely
to be much lower.

O'Toole described networks as:

> ...structures of interdependence involving multiple organizations or parts
> thereof, where one unit is not merely the formal subordinate of the others
> in some larger hierarchical arrangement. The institutional glue congealing
> networked ties may include authority bonds, exchange relations, and
> coalitions based upon common interest, all within a single multiunit struc-
> ture. In networks, administrators cannot be expected to exercise decisive
> leverage by virtue of their formal position (p. 45).

O'Toole went on to suggest that networks are more common in policy
arenas in which issues are complex or ambiguous. The lack of direct control by a government agency encourages network approaches, as does the
need to accommodate a variety of programs in a particular policy area.
Managers often cannot control those on whom they depend for goal
achievement and, therefore, they must bargain in order to meet performance goals. Indeed, as O'Toole concludes, "giving directives may actually
weaken influence" (p. 48). Building trust is all important.

Beryl Radin and colleagues found the same sort of arrangement in dealing with rural development. The George H. W. Bush administration in 1990
charged the U.S. Department of Agriculture with creating rural development
councils to coordinate the federal and state programs that address such
diverse issues as jobs, economic development, and education. The expectation was that the councils would involve federal officials, state officials, local
government officials, tribal representatives, and private sector representatives. What developed were networks unique to each state. The fuzzy boundaries of "development" meant that the goals were interpreted differently in
each state, approaches reflected the state-local sociopolitical culture, and a
different mix of programs and actors were involved in decision making. Success was dependent upon the effectiveness of interorganizational and interpersonal relations. Mutual dependency encouraged resolution of conflicting
goals. Collaborative problem solving became the dominant pattern of interaction. The arrangements were characterized by multiple power centers,
overlapping responsibilities, many sources of resources, and a free flow of
information. Because of the lack of hierarchical structure, coordination
tended to be a problem (Radin et al., 1996: 149-154).

In terms of the structures of networks, Myrna Mandell and Toddi Steelman
describe them in the following manner:

> A network structure is typified by a broad mission and joint and strategi-
> cally interdependent action. The structural arrangement takes on broad

tasks that reach beyond the simultaneous actions of independently operating organizations. There is strong commitment to overriding goals, and members agree to commit significant resources over a long period of time. There is a high degree of risk involved. Examples of this type of network include a variety of community building efforts and economic development programs (2001: 5).

They go on to suggest that the defining characteristics for the relationships are: 1) the "members' problem orientation and commitment to goals," 2) "the intensity of the linkages and the breadth of effort," and 3) "their complexity of purpose and their scope of effort" (2001: 5).

In short, the nature of the linkages is determined by the extent to which the members share a common perspective on the problem being addressed and are committed to those broader goals, the strength and closeness of the linkages among the members and the openness of the structure to participation, and the complexity of the mission in terms of the need for collaborative problem solving and the scope of the collaboration. Common perspectives on the problem and commitment to its resolution will characterize strong networks. Strong and close relationships among the members, but with an openness to new participants, and joint processes for problem solving and other actions are also necessary. The networks would not be characterized by a narrow purpose being pursued by a small group of members with limited collaboration in problem solving. Nor would they be characterized by contractual relationships, formal processes of interaction, and limited sharing of resources and information. They are characterized by personal trust, respect, and cooperation. Informal rules are more important than formal ones.

Mandell and Steelman also conclude that the management of networks is different from management in more traditional contexts. It is less oriented to lead agencies and executive control. They suggest that "[b]uilding new management skills in which the role of the manager relies more on communication skills and building areas of trust is seen as a critical strategy of building effective networks" (2001: 17). The interrelationships are complex and messy. Network building, in terms of encouraging participation and commitment and cultivating the relationships, is a critical task. A common history and common organizational culture can help, but there is likely to be considerable diversity in perspectives, motivations, and resources.

The relationships that have to be cultivated and maintained may range from short-term linkages to serve common ends to long-term partnerships based upon broader congruence among organizational goals and objectives. As Myrna Mandell and Robert Agranoff have characterized them, the relationships may be:

- "Linkages or interactive contacts between two or more organizations.

- Intermittent coordination or mutual adjustment of the policies and procedures of two or more organizations to accomplish some objective.
- Ad hoc or temporary task force activity among organizations to accomplish a purpose or purposes.
- Permanent and/or regular coordination between two or more organizations through a formal arrangement (i.e., council, partnership, etc.) to engage in limited activity to achieve a purpose or purposes.
- A coalition where interdependence and strategic actions are taken, but where purposes are narrow in scope and all actions occur within the participant organizations themselves or involve the sequential or simultaneous activity of the participant organizations.
- A collective or network structure where there is broad mission and joint and strategically interdependent action. The structural arrangement takes on broad tasks that reach beyond the simultaneous actions of independently operating organizations (i.e., action may include, but reaches beyond, linkages, coordination, task force or coalitions)" (Mandell, 1999: 5-6).

As the following analysis will demonstrate, the safe construction network involves all of these kinds of relationships. Indeed, multiple networks are in operation (see Agranoff and McGuire, 1999). Consequently, to advance its own goals, FEMA has to navigate among the major actors and encourage momentum in the desired direction. "Management" may be the wrong term to describe the process because it implies hierarchy and at least some control. The agency has to cultivate formal partnerships when possible, informal linkages when agency goals coincide with those of another organization, coalitions when there is mutual agreement on goals and means, temporary linkages when they contribute to goal attainment, and collective action when there is agreement on a broad mission and the efforts of many are needed. It is a complex task environment that requires special skill and patience. FEMA may find it more advantageous to use contractual relationships to advance its agenda, as well (see Milward and Provan, 2000). In essence, FEMA, as well as other actors, may serve as leaders, supporters, catalysts, and cheerleaders with different roles in each network. Turf battles, inflexible procedures and rules, and hierarchy are to be avoided. Support within the organization for external network building is critical because of the time and resource demands on managers (Agranoff and McGuire, 1999: 25-28).

## The Safe Construction Networks

At the federal level, the Federal Emergency Management Agency is encouraging safe construction through formal and informal partnerships, collaboration, and the cultivation of relationships based upon shared responsibility within at least several networks of public, private, and nonprofit organizations. FEMA has developed relationships with building firms. It has encouraged the adoption of stronger building codes through the Disaster Resistant Communities and Project Impact programs. It has also provided support and encouragement to the Blue Sky Foundation of North Carolina, which works with developers and builders, and the Institute for Business & Home Safety (IBHS), which represents the insurance industry, as well as to other organizations of similar purpose. At the same time, public, private, and nonprofit organizations are soliciting FEMA's support for their efforts to generate new standards for building and land use through model home programs, building code integration, research and development on safe construction practices, and other activities.

In some cases FEMA is guiding and coordinating specific programs to create safer construction practices, in other cases FEMA is providing financial resources for efforts directed by other organizations, and often FEMA is simply lending encouragement and offering advice. Within the Project Impact communities themselves, FEMA has some influence because it is providing money and technical expertise. Lacking direct authority over state and local governments and nongovernmental partners, FEMA offered them a stake in the outcome of the mitigation effort (see Daniels and Clark-Daniels, 2001: 53). However, FEMA has had to develop trust in its own intentions, maintain a focus on the common purpose, and, especially, avoid heavy-handed methods to achieve its goals.

The context within which FEMA is operating is a national network involved in the reduction of property losses and human casualties and suffering due to environmental hazards through the adoption of safe construction measures. Prior to Hurricane Hugo, which struck the Carolinas and traveled up the East Coast in 1989, the insurance industry in the United States had suffered no billion-dollar disasters. Since Hugo, the insurance industry has experienced a series of multi-billion-dollar disasters. When Hurricane Andrew crossed Florida in 1992, it left $30 billion in damage, killed 61 people, and cut a 30-mile swath across the peninsula. Approximately 49,000 homes were left uninhabitable, 180,000 people were homeless, and only nine of the 6,600 mobile homes were left habitable (Morrow, 1997; Waugh, 2000: 78-79). The recovery effort continues today. South Florida had some of the strictest building codes in the nation, but, as Hurricane Andrew demonstrated, communities had very poor code enforcement. Nine insurance companies failed in south Florida following Hurricane Andrew because they were overwhelmed by claims. They had not anticipated the devastation caused by poor construction, and they found themselves with too many policyholders and too little reserves to handle the claims (Kunreuther, 1998: 4-5). Florida suffered heavy property losses again with tropical storm Alberto in 1994 and with back-to-back

Hurricanes Erin and Opal. The need to reduce vulnerabilities was manifest, and mitigation became the focus of state disaster policy.

The Northridge, California, earthquake in 1994 caused $20 billion in damage and killed 57 people. Freeway overpasses collapsed; 112,000 buildings were damaged; and the infrastructure, including water and utility lines, was seriously damaged. Nonetheless, retrofitted overpass supports and homes built after the adoption of newer building codes fared far better than those built earlier (Godschalk, 1999; Waugh, 2000: 69). The Northridge experience reinforced the need to focus on mitigation at the national level. The relatively minor damage done by an earthquake in the Seattle area in 2001 demonstrated the value of mitigation efforts. The prediction by seismologists of a 67 percent chance of a major earthquake in northern California in the next 30 years has given some urgency to the effort to reduce vulnerabilities (FEMA, 1998).

Hurricanes Hugo and Andrew were followed by other super storms, and the Northridge earthquake was only one of a number of major earthquakes during the 1990s. Cycles of super storms and powerful earthquakes are not new, and there is scientific evidence to suggest that more powerful forces will strike the United States in the foreseeable future. Population increases and dense development along the hurricane-prone Gulf and East Coasts and in the earthquake-prone states have put more people and property at risk. It is extremely expensive and getting more expensive to fund disaster recovery, and insurance is not always available to property owners. The economics of disasters provided impetus for change at the national level. Fortunately, there are ways to reduce the risk and limit the losses. Better construction standards and land-use regulation can significantly reduce losses of life and property. The remarkably low losses from the 2001 earthquake in the Seattle area demonstrated the value of mitigation efforts like Project Impact. The mantra of FEMA in the 1990s was that "one dollar spent on mitigation saves two dollars in recovery." Mitigation is clearly the cost-effective policy choice.

# The Goal: Reducing Property Losses and Protecting Lives

Reducing property losses and protecting human lives from environmental hazards are quintessential government goals, although some might prefer that the financial burden be borne by property owners or others with vested economic interests. The goals are supported by the insurance industry, the mortgage banking industry, the building industry, and the general public.

*This house was torn apart by the flooding of the nearby Clear Fork Creek, W.Va.*
Photo: Leif Skoogfors/FEMA News Photo

The agreement, however, is in principle rather than practice. While the reduction of risk is accepted as important, people want to live on the beach, in the mountains, next to the river or lake, and in other aesthetically pleasing locales. They choose views or access to water, snow, or woodland, and are willing to pay for them. As a consequence, there is a strong demand for property in hazardous areas, and thus strong pressures for developers and builders to build. Moreover, public officials want to make the developers and property owners happy and they want development to generate tax revenues. It is not that no one cares about the growing risk; rather, it is that so many different individuals and organizations contribute to the problem that it is difficult to stop the process. High-income property owners are too often willing to assume the economic risk of building in hazardous areas, even though such development might increase the risk to other property owners and to the larger community. Low-income residents often have little choice but to live in high-risk areas, such as on floodplains, because the land and housing is less expensive and there may be less concern about their safety.

Flood-prone property, often defined in terms of 100- or 500-year flood risk, may not flood frequently enough to dissuade developers, builders, and property owners from assuming the risk of loss. Or, it may flood frequently after years or decades of relative quiescence. The risk alone is insufficient to discourage undesirable land uses. Federal, state, and local government officials may not be able to force property owners to reduce risk by moving them to less hazardous environs. While buyouts were the most common mitigation tool in recent major flooding along the Mississippi River, the purchase of flood-prone property has been controversial even when property owners have voluntarily sold or traded their land and buildings. Local officials have not always kept flood-prone property free of development when given the opportunity through buyouts. It has also been legally contentious when property owners have chosen to resist those efforts.

The question is how to regulate such development when there are strong pressures to build in hazardous areas and the federal system prevents, or at least inhibits, effective control over the actors and processes that drive development. Primary responsibility for regulating land use and construction standards lies with local officials. Development is fed by builders and developers, and presumably driven by prospective homeowners and local officials who wish to expand tax bases. How can building and land use be regulated to reduce the risk from environmental hazards? How can mitigation policies and programs be encouraged?

Adopting and enforcing building codes appropriate to the community and encouraging builders and property owners to implement measures to further strengthen structures to withstand wind, flood, and seismic forces would greatly reduce the loss of life and property from environmental hazards. However, new technologies and materials introduce new risks. As the American Institute of Architects concluded in a report on failures of "long span" construction, architects and builders are under pressure to use light materials and exotic designs and to keep costs as low as possible. To reduce costs, little redundancy is built into supports and other systems. Also, it is extremely difficult for general contractors and government inspectors to monitor complex projects with hundreds or even thousands of contractors and subcontractors (Waugh and Hy, 1996: 254-255). Building codes decay over time as builders seek variances to the standards. Local governments have a difficult time enforcing building codes when the salaries of inspectors are low and there is a lot of turnover in personnel. Maintaining training levels, even with state support, can be difficult. Moreover, in the aftermath of a disaster, there is strong pressure on local officials to issue building permits quickly and with minimal review of building design and materials. There have literally been disasters in which property owners have sought building permits before their burned homes quit smoldering.

Voluntary compliance does not work, according to a 1993 report by FEMA. The report went on to recommend requiring compliance for all property funded or guaranteed directly or indirectly by the federal government, including property financed through loans insured by the Federal Deposit Insurance Corporation. Tax credits, tax-free bonds, and grants might be used to encourage compliance, and noncompliance should negate eligibility for disaster assistance. But, the expectation was that local preferences would prevail. Therefore, selling mitigation is the answer.

## Mitigation

Mitigation efforts are those activities that prevent a disaster from occurring or reduce the likelihood that it will occur and, if a disaster does occur, reduce its effects. In short, mitigation strategies prevent or lessen the effects of disasters. Mitigation strategies can be classified as structural or nonstructural. Structural mitigation techniques include building dams, levees, seawalls, and containment ponds to hold water or slow its flow; building storm shelters to protect residents from high winds; and building containment buildings to hold in hazardous materials. Nonstructural mitigation techniques include adopting and enforcing building standards and codes, land-use regulation, zoning ordinances, tax incentives to reduce risk, and public education to encourage risk reduction. Public officials are often predisposed to choose one approach over the other, as evidenced by the reliance on dams and levees along major waterways in the United States, but there is growing support for nonstructural approaches today. Buyouts of flood-prone properties and using natural wetlands to absorb flood waters is preferred over building dams, levees, and seawalls.

Mitigation programs may be voluntary or mandatory. Voluntary programs generally rely on individuals, organizations, and communities to recognize the dangers posed by hazards and to reduce their exposure to the risk. Public information concerning hazards and how to avoid them and information on safe building practices educate the public, builders and developers, and officials so that they can reduce risk to themselves and to those for whom they are responsible. Reducing taxes or insurance rates for those homeowners who install storm shutters or adopt other risk-reduction measures has also been recommended (Petak, 1998). However, voluntary programs only work if individuals, organizations, and communities decide that the risk outweighs the benefits. Mandatory programs use the threat of punishment to encourage risk reduction. Financial penalties and even criminal prosecution can be used to discourage undesirable behaviors. Nonetheless, some individuals, organizations, and communities may risk punishment rather than change their behaviors. Regulation has been the most common mandatory approach, with punishment for those who do not comply with the regulations, but it is not always easy to follow through with the punishment. For example, studies of floodplain management generally find that people will not limit development on floodplains without strict regulations and the threat of punishment (Cigler, 1996). The punishment for those failing to comply is to withhold disaster assistance following the next flood. However, it is extremely difficult for federal and state officials to deny communities help in the aftermath of disaster and the glare of television lights.

While there is certainly support for mitigation in theory, there is great resistance to regulations that limit the use of private property. The resistance is rooted in American political culture (Waugh, 1990; Waugh and Sylves, 1996). Private property is sacred. Powerful interest groups oppose disaster mitigation programs, such as building codes and land-use regulations, because they put constraints on the use of private property. Developers and builders may oppose stronger standards and safer construction practices even if they are reasonable, because acceptance might encourage more changes. At the same time, professional organizations, such as the International Association of Fire Chiefs, actively promote hazard-reduction regulations and lobby state legislatures and local officials for their adoption. Organizations of professional engineers, architects, and other building experts have actively lobbied for safer building designs, and professional emergency managers have lobbied for more effective mitigation programs. What is important in terms of the adoption of safe construction measures is that the power of special interest groups tends to be stronger at the local level, rather than at the state or federal level, and control over land-use decisions and building standards is most often local.

Nonetheless, some communities do recognize the need to control development in order to protect lives and property. Indeed, studies of building code adoption indicate that professional groups and individual experts can have a significant influence on local officials' decisions to adopt appropriate codes (see Waugh and Hy, 1996: 257). Educating officials about risk seems to work. Impetus for code adoption, as well as other risk-reduction measures, is also enhanced because local officials can be held personally responsible for failing to address known hazards. While federal and state officials are generally protected from legal liability because of the principle of sovereign immunity, local officials can be held liable for their action or inaction when they are exercising their own discretion. Nonetheless, controlling the behavior of individuals may be difficult for local officials. The courts have not always accepted the necessity of restricting the use of private property even to protect the property owner and the community from hazards. The "takings" issue can be a legal quagmire for officials who wish to reduce the risk to life and property by restricting or preventing development in hazardous areas (see Platt and Dawson, 1999; Waugh, 2000: 175).

While support for mitigation is weak in the absence of a clearly definable risk, major disasters tend to make mitigation a priority. Since the 1989 Loma Prieta earthquake, the city of San Francisco has evaluated its plans and expanded its mitigation programs. The city passed over $1 billion in bond issues for mitigation programs and integrated its hazard mitigation plan with the city's general plan to guide development and operations (Godschalk et al., 1998: 261-262). There were conflicts with FEMA over local priorities, particularly in terms of retrofitting the city hall to be more earthquake resistant. Local officials prefer discretion in the selection of priorities, and federal officials generally prefer specific kinds of programs that are more easily monitored.

State governments have also implemented mitigation programs. As a condition for receiving federal disaster assistance, states are required to develop mitigation plans and to respond to a list of recommendations developed by an Interagency Hazard Mitigation Team of state and federal experts. Following the 1989 Loma Prieta earthquake, the state of California adopted an earthquake mitigation plan, *California at Risk: Reducing Earthquake Hazards 1992-1996*. The plan outlined priorities, schedules, funding, and specific hazard-reduction initiatives and recommended actions to improve hazard identification and monitoring and to improve the state's land-use planning and regulation, among other things. State funding was provided for hazard analysis and planning. Following the 1994 Northridge earthquake, the state of California's Office of Emergency Services (OES) and FEMA issued their Interagency Hazard Mitigation Team report, which recommended specific mitigation strategies, including compliance with the 1991 Uniform Building Code and additional public education efforts. The state mitigation strategy issued in 1995 outlined priorities including addressing the vulnerabilities of educational and medical facilities, even moving some schools to safer ground (Godschalk et al., 1998: 237-244).

Similarly, the state of Florida implemented mitigation programs following Hurricane Andrew in 1992. Andrew caused $25 billion to $30 billion in damage, and the recovery process continues over 10 years later. Miami-Dade County produced a hazard mitigation plan in order to receive disaster assistance. Projects funded under FEMA's Section 404 Hazard Mitigation Grant Program were slowly implemented, some as late as 1996. Many of the projects were for storm shutters and other improvements needed to make buildings more wind resistant. The Interagency Hazard Mitigation Team's report focused primarily on the building codes in south Florida. While the codes were relatively strong, compliance was poor because much of the construction was done by unlicensed contractors; there were too few building inspectors to monitor construction adequately; the building inspection process was ineffective; the structural design and wind standards were poor; the standards for manufactured homes, including mobile homes, were inadequate; and the standards for window design were poor. Local governments had not adequately monitored construction and enforced building codes. Builders had not regulated themselves as expected. And, residents had not complied with codes when residential structures were renovated (Godschalk et al., 1998: 116-119). There had been strong pressure for development and very little attention to the vulnerability of the structures being built. Relying on voluntary compliance with codes by builders and property owners simply did not work.

In March 1993, the Florida state building code was changed. The new code required the 116 mph national wind speed standard that accommodates gusts and wind pressures; protection, such as shutters, for windows and doors in new homes; review of structural plans by a structural engineer; concrete columns in single-story houses; and more roofing inspections. Miami-Dade County also increased the number of building inspectors from 16 to 43 and roofing inspectors from four to 31 (Godschalk et al., 1998: 120).

The state of Florida established a trust fund to finance recovery and mitigation programs that were not covered by federal funds. Miami-Dade County passed a sales tax to generate revenue for recovery and mitigation projects. Also, the state created the Florida Hurricane Catastrophe Fund, which provides reinsurance coverage so that insurance companies would not fail in the next catastrophic storms, and the state Emergency Management Preparedness and Assistance Trust Fund, which places a surcharge on residential and business property insurance policies to fund emergency management, disaster planning, and mitigation projects (Godschalk et al., 1998: 122). FEMA approved Florida's State Mitigation Plan in May 1994. "Immediate priority" was given to mitigation programs for critical systems, the loss of critical infrastructure, shelter strategy, repair and retrofitting structures, protecting the outside envelope of buildings, and intergovernmental mitigation efforts (Godschalk et al., 1998: 150). "Highest priority" was given to standards for manufactured homes and state buildings, building code enforcement, a common building code, local land-use planning, relocation and land acquisition, and the process for issuing building permits (Godschalk et al., 1998: 150).

Unfortunately, while the biggest danger from hurricanes is usually storm surges, most of Florida's mitigation efforts focused on wind resistance. To address the storm surge problem would require greater restrictions on building on and close to the beaches, and there would have been great resistance to such restrictions in south Florida (Godschalk et al., 1998: 135, 146-147). The new Florida Building Code, which went into effect on January 1, 2002, increased wind-resistance requirements and required measures to deal with wind-blown debris. The measures to make windows less vulnerable to flying debris include shutters and impact-resistant glass (Twisdale, 2001).

Clearly, local and state governments can and often do act to reduce the risk of environmental hazards. Major disasters provided needed impetus, including financial support, for the effort. Problems emerge when there are strong political pressures to ignore hazards, too little scientific knowledge about the hazards, and/or too little technical knowledge about how to mitigate the hazards. For example, recent coastal flooding in the Pacific Northwest due to the El Niño phenomenon has revealed the remains of forests buried by giant tsunamis ("harbor waves") caused by earthquakes and landslides off the coast of Washington State and Oregon. Coastal communities are implementing mitigation plans to reduce the likelihood of property damage and the loss of life, as well as implementing warning systems, in preparation for the next large tsunami to hit the coastline (Waugh, 2000: 68, 70).

## Building Codes and Safe Construction

States and/or communities may adopt building standards and building codes to ensure residential and commercial structures meet minimum standards. Building standards specify the materials that can be used in the construction of homes, businesses, and institutional structures. The standards are based upon such criteria as strength, durability, flammability, and resistance to water and wind, and the appropriateness of designs for the environment. Building codes are sets of regulations adopted by states and/or communities that specify the kinds of building materials and designs that are appropriate for particular locations. Codes include general standards to reduce the risk of fire and/or damage from earthquakes or other kinds of disaster and specific measures to reduce the potential damage from wind or other hazards. Building codes set standards for the substructure (below ground), superstructure (above ground), and infrastructure (interior, principally plumbing and electrical systems) of buildings. Codes specify minimum standards for wiring, trusses, beams, and other design and construction details. Codes may differ according to the building use, expected occupancy (including whether special populations—e.g., the disabled or children—may use the building), and other factors. Building codes do not always include fire codes.

There are a number of model building codes that are used in the United States, including the following:
- National Building Code (NBC)
- Uniform Building Code (UBC)
- International Building Code (IBC)
- Southern Building Code (SBC)

Some states have adopted statewide codes and require enforcement by counties and municipalities. According to IBHS, there are no statewide residential building codes in 21 states and no state commercial building codes in five states (as of December 2001). Others recommend that local governments adopt codes or leave it up to local governments to do so or not. Peter J. May (1997) has categorized the orientations of state governments to building regulation as minimalist, enabling, mandatory, or energetic. Minimalist states have no codes or have them only for some situations. Enabling states authorize local governments to adopt and enforce codes, but do not require it. Mandatory states have state codes and require local enforcement, but do not strictly oversee enforcement. Energetic states both require local enforcement of codes and monitor local compliance with that requirement. The orientation to building regulation, according to May, is related to the state's political culture, including the influence of interest groups. May's categorization of the states is detailed in Table 7.1.

**Table 7.1: State Groupings for Building Regulation**

| Categories of States | | | |
|---|---|---|---|
| **Minimalist** | **Enabling** | **Mandatory** | **Energetic** |
| Alabama | Arkansas | California | Alaska |
| Arizona | Georgia | Florida | Connecticut |
| Colorado | Idaho | Indiana | Kentucky |
| Delaware | Iowa | Maryland | Michigan |
| Hawaii | Louisiana | Massachusetts | Montana |
| Illinois | Minnesota | Nevada | New Jersey |
| Kansas | Nebraska | New Mexico | New York |
| Maine | West Virginia | Rhode Island | North Carolina |
| Mississippi | | Utah | Ohio |
| Missouri | | Virginia | Oregon |
| New Hampshire | | Washington | Tennessee |
| North Dakota | | Wisconsin | Vermont |
| Oklahoma | | | Wyoming |
| Pennsylvania | | | |
| South Carolina | | | |
| South Dakota | | | |
| Texas | | | |
| **N=17** | **N=8** | **N=12** | **N=13** |

*Source: May, 1997: 75.*

What the data indicate is that half the states do not have statewide building codes and do not require that their communities adopt codes. While some states do require strong codes and require serious enforcement by local authorities, much is left up to local officials. It is not just a case of needing to encourage state officials to make appropriate building standards and codes mandatory and forcing communities to adopt and enforce the codes. The responsibility for land-use decisions and related issues, such as building standards and zoning, often resides at the community level based on constitutional provision, rather than by statutes that are more easily changed. Residents and officials from rural areas often have different views on land-use and building regulation from their more urban and suburban counterparts. In short, it's not always an easy matter—politically or legally—for state officials to preempt local prerogatives. Sometimes state officials do recognize the need to reduce the risk to their constituents, and significant improvements can be made. Indeed, officials in South Carolina have adopted the new International Building Code after long resisting the idea of having a statewide code (i.e., South Carolina has moved into the "mandatory" category since May's 1997 study).

It should also be mentioned that the adoption of building standards and codes, in and of itself, does not ensure that residential and business structures will be protected from hazards. At best, there is a time lag between the adoption of a building code and its impact on local residential and commercial property. Codes are usually enforced only for new construction. Moreover, as was found when Hurricane Hugo struck South Carolina in 1989, some communities had building codes but no inspectors. Other communities had untrained or ill-trained inspectors and grossly inadequate code enforcement. Communities are faced with the question of whether to require retrofitting of old buildings to reduce the risk from high winds, flood, and/or earthquake, and such retrofitting can be very expensive. Mandating retrofitting, in fact, can have very negative consequences for the community. High costs can cause property owners to abandon old structures and to tear down structures needing extensive retrofitting and replace them with new structures that meet the code (which may mean eliminating low-income housing and replacing it with moderate- to high-income housing or tearing down historic buildings). Old business districts might never recover financially. Such was the case in Oroville, California, following a 1975 earthquake (Olson and Olson, 1993).

In Oakland, California, following the Loma Prieta earthquake in 1989, the city identified the structures, mostly built of unreinforced masonry, that might be considered dangerous and attempted to mandate retrofitting of those properties. Officials were met with considerable resistance from property owners. Realistically, the cost of retrofitting would have been prohibitive for some property owners, and the alternatives—abandonment of

## Examples of Construction Methods to Reduce Property Losses

**Wind damage can be reduced by:**
- using hurricane clips or straps to connect rafters and trusses to the walls of a home;
- strengthening the connection between building walls and foundation;
- reinforcing garage doors;
- using head and foot bolts to strengthen doors;
- using structural adhesive to strengthen connections between roof sheathing (plywood cover) and rafters;
- using shatter-proof glass and/or shutters to protect windows from wind-blown debris; and
- adding a safe room to protect family members from tornadoes and other high winds.

**In addition to the base flood elevation required by the National Flood Insurance Program, flood damage can be reduced by:**
- raising electrical service panels and the air conditioner two to three feet above the base flood election;
- adding a waterproof veneer to the home;
- having openings in foundation walls so that floodwaters can flow through, thereby reducing the likelihood that the water flow will cause a collapse of the foundation and the structure;
- adding flood shields to doors; and
- installing sump pumps to pump out water.

**Earthquake damage can be reduced by:**
- bolting the walls of the home to the foundation;
- strapping water heaters and other appliances securely to walls;
- strengthening hanging light fixtures;
- strapping bookcases and shelves to walls;
- putting heavy objects on lower shelves; and
- using flexible connectors for gas and electrical appliances.

**Fire damage can be reduced by:**
- using mesh or screens to keep flames and sparks out of chimneys, attics, crawl spaces, and other openings, including under porches;
- using nonflammable materials in roofing, shutters, and other building materials; and
- using fire-resistant landscaping around the structure.

*Source: USAA, 2001.*

the property or simply tearing it down—would not have been in the best interest of the community. The compromise arrived at by a coalition of economic development advocates (i.e., property owners and builders), seismic safety advocates, and historic preservation advocates was to require the abatement (retrofit) of those structures posing the most risk to residents and encouraging the abatement of others. Soon thereafter, it became economically feasible for many property owners to retrofit their structures. The coalition recommended not requiring retrofitting for all the old buildings in town, because to do so would have destroyed the character of the downtown. Therefore, some structures are still vulnerable to earthquakes and dangerous for residents (Olson, Olson, and Gawronski, 1999). The lesson is that eliminating all risk is not possible and may not be economically feasible. The best that can be expected is that residents understand the risk and learn to live with it. But, when the level of acceptable risk exceeds what might be considered reasonable, they should be strongly encouraged to prepare for the disaster that is likely to come.

Public purchase of property on floodplains, in landslide areas, or in any other kind of hazardous area can also be controversial, although some communities have chosen to take property out of the market when property owners die or the property has been severely damaged and significant reconstruction would be necessary. Using bought-out properties as parks and recreational areas with minimal development is a popular mitigation strategy.

Building standards may also include specific construction methods to reduce losses from wind, fire, flood, earthquake, and other hazards. Many of the disaster-resistant building and landscaping practices may eventually be incorporated into local building codes. For example, the new code in the state of Florida requires windows to be resistant to wind-blown debris and doors to be strengthened. New technologies and building practices are promoted as enhancements to current building standards and may be incorporated into construction as they are accepted by the building industry. Acceptance of new practices is much faster if prospective homeowners demand more disaster-resistant residences.

# FEMA and Mitigation

Mitigation became the focus of FEMA's efforts in the mid-1990s. The National Mitigation Strategy was issued in December 1995 and called for greater "partnership" between the federal government and state and local governments in the reduction of hazards. Disaster mitigation efforts have since expanded under Sections 404 and 406 of the Stafford Act of 1988

(FEMA, 1997). Section 404 of the Stafford Act created the Hazard Mitigation Grant Program, which provides funding for mitigation projects. The Volkmer Amendment in 1993 improved the cost-sharing arrangement and increased the amount of federal money available for mitigation projects. The grant program is funded at a level equal to 15 percent of the federal money spent on public and individual assistance programs, minus administrative expenses, for a disaster. Proposed projects have to be consistent with the overall mitigation strategy for the area, and the grants can cover up to 75 percent of the cost of the project. Section 404 of the Stafford Act provides similar financial support for mitigation projects for government and non-profit agencies, including such activities as debris removal following the disaster.

The mission of FEMA prior to implementation of the Government Performance and Results Act (GPRA) tended to be defined in terms of outputs rather than results. The agency reported numbers of training programs and students, interagency contacts and agreements, presidential disaster declarations, dollars paid out in disaster assistance, and so on. In 1997, when FEMA's goals were expressed in terms of overall results, the orientation of the organization to other federal agencies and to state and local governments changed significantly. The new strategic goals were to: 1) protect lives and prevent the loss of property from all hazards; 2) reduce human suffering and enhance the recovery of communities after disaster strikes; and 3) ensure that the public is served in a timely and efficient manner (FEMA, 1997). Each of the goals had performance measures—e.g., a 10 percent reduction in risk to human life and a 15 percent reduction in the risk to property by FY 2007—and five-year strategies as required by GPRA. The most recent set of performance goals is very similar, although the second goal is now to "prevent or reduce harm and losses from future disasters through mitigation efforts" (GAO, 2001: 1). The emphasis is clearly on mitigation. FEMA lacks authority to address all of the threats to life and property by all hazards, and it necessarily has to enlist the participation of partners to do so. Not all of the risks relate to construction, although the disaster experiences of the 1990s strongly suggest that nonstructural mitigation measures (e.g., building codes and land-use regulations), as well as some structural mitigation measures, can significantly reduce losses.

In the 1990s, FEMA's organizational structure changed from one characterized by the separation of national security or civil defense programs and its state and local programs. James Lee Witt, then director of FEMA, reorganized the agency around the four functions of mitigation, preparedness, response, and recovery to better integrate programs and to reflect the philosophy of an "all-hazards" emergency management paradigm. With the need to develop new instruments to achieve its national goals, the agency's role changed dramatically. The new strategic plan was appropriately named the "Partnership for a Safer Future," and the necessity for developing partnerships with state and local governments was acknowledged early in the document (Waugh, 1999). While FEMA had had programs that involved partnerships with other public, private, and nonprofit organizations, such as a collaboration with the National Association of Home Builders (NAHB) in the 1980s to encourage safer construction practices, the new pursuit of partnerships encouraged a more open agency. The results expected of the agency also encouraged a focus on mitigation rather than recovery. An early product of that reorientation was a video and educational materials on wind-resistant construction in hurricane-prone areas entitled "Against the Wind." FEMA, NAHB, the American Red Cross, The Home Depot, and the Georgia Emergency Management Agency cosponsored the effort in 1993, and more videos have since been produced. After 1995, the focus on partnerships greatly expanded.

## The Federal Government and Safe Construction

In terms of building regulation, the federal government does have some regulatory power. For example, following the Hurricane Andrew disaster in 1992, when as many as 18,000 manufactured housing units (mobile homes) in south Florida and Louisiana were damaged or destroyed, legislation was enacted to require that manufactured housing in high-wind areas meet stricter wind standards. Since July of 1994, manufactured homes sold in Hawaii and 25 counties along the coasts of Alaska, Louisiana, Florida, and North Carolina are required to withstand winds of 110 mph. Manufactured homes sold in another 91 counties in Alaska, Texas, Louisiana, Mississippi, Alabama, Florida, Georgia, South Carolina, North Carolina, Virginia, Massachusetts, and Maine must be able to withstand winds of 100 mph (McConnaughey, 1994). The regulations are based upon the federal government's authority relative to interstate commerce, because manufactured housing is moved from one state to another.

Many federal agencies do have less direct roles in the regulation of building and the encouragement of safe construction practices. The U.S. Department of Commerce, through the National Institute of Standards and Technology (NIST), tests building materials and encourages the adoption of uniform building codes; the U.S. Fire Administration promotes fire safety; the Consumer Product Safety Commission regulates standards for products sold to consumers (including flammable products that might increase fire risks in residences and businesses); and the U.S. Department of Labor enforces standards to protect the health and safety of workers. The U.S. Department of Health and Human Services regulates safety issues in health care facilities; the Department of Housing and Urban Development regulates safety issues in HUD-financed buildings; the Federal Aviation Administration regulates safety in airports; the General Services Administration regulates safety in federal buildings; and the Department of Veterans Affairs regulates safety in its health care facilities. Other federal agencies have direct and/or indirect roles in ensuring appropriate building codes are followed in the construction of federal facilities and facilities built with federal money (Hy, 1990: 242-243). There are federal responsibilities to address workplace safety and corruption or malfeasance in construction projects. There are also federal programs, in addition to Project Impact, that encourage attention to hazards and the need to mitigate them.

## FEMA and Safe Construction

Hazard reduction through the encouragement of safe construction has been pursued through FEMA programs such as the National Flood Insurance Program (NFIP), the Firewise program to reduce wildfire losses in urban-woodland interfaces, and a variety of other programs. The promotion of "safe rooms" by FEMA is intended to reduce human casualties from windstorms. NFIP is the most far-reaching of these efforts.

### The National Flood Insurance Program (NFIP)

Over 12 million households are located in flood-prone areas in the United States, and those areas cover 150,000 square miles (FEMA, 1998), almost the size of the state of California. Over 19,000 communities with almost 4.4 million policyholders participate in NFIP, which provides economic incentives to communities that adopt land-use regulations for floodplains. The incentives are discounted flood insurance rates to the residents of those communities that adopt such measures as restricted development, elevated construction, and flood-proofing buildings in floodplains. Failure to join NFIP and to adopt at least minimal hazard-reduction measures disqualifies communities and their residents from receiving federal disaster assistance following floods. FEMA's estimate of flood loss reductions in FY2000 due to mitigation efforts is $1 billion (GAO, 2001: 3).

NFIP provides economic and political incentives to reduce the risk of flooding, including reducing the use of building designs and standards that may increase flood losses. The federal government is the final guarantor of flood insurance because the insurance industry itself is unable to provide coverage when flood events affect very large areas or flood insurance may be prohibitively costly for property owners. The numbers of communities in each Community Rating System (CRS) class are indicated in Table 7.2.

As Table 7.2 indicates, the number of communities enrolled in NFIP is growing. The number of communities that have improved their CRS classi-

## The National Flood Insurance Program

The National Flood Insurance Program was created in 1968 following dev-astating floods and the rising costs of disaster relief. The program is designed to make federally backed flood insurance available in communities that agree to manage their floodplains to reduce flood losses. The Federal Insurance Administration, within FEMA, administers the program. NFIP has reduced flood losses by almost $800 million per year, and homes built to NFIP stan-dards have 77 percent less damage per year. "And, every $3 paid in flood insurance claims saves $1 in disaster assistance payments" (FEMA/NFIP, 2001).

The Community Rating System (CRS) was added in 1990 to encourage local flood mitigation efforts. Under the National Flood Insurance Reform Act of 1994, it became a means of rewarding local efforts by providing dis-counted flood insurance rates based upon community CRS points. Points or credits are given for implementing specific mitigation measures, such as: 1) public information, including advising the community about the hazard and providing data to insurance agents; 2) mapping and regulations, including mapping and regulation of areas under development; 3) flood damage reduction, including relocating or retrofitting flood-prone structures and maintaining the community's drainage systems; and 4) flood preparedness, including having warning systems and dam safety programs. Technical assis-tance is provided by FEMA and other agencies. The activities are verified by the Insurance Services Office, Inc. (ISO), which grades communities for fire insurance and now is responsible for implementing the Building Code Effec-tiveness Grading Schedule for the insurance industry.

There are 10 CRS classes. Class 1 requires 4,500 or more points and provides a discount of 45 percent. Class 5 requires 2,500 to 2,999 points and provides a discount of 25 percent. Class 10 communities, with 0 to 499 points, receive no discount. Communities located in non-SFHA (Special Flood Hazard Areas) receive a maximum of 5 percent discount if they have at least 500 points. SFHA communities are located wholly or partially on floodplains and have a significant risk of flood loss. Communities must do elevation certificates for all properties built on the floodplain after the CRS application and, if they are designated repetitive loss communities, they must have repetitive loss projects in those areas subject to frequent flooding.

fication is strong evidence of the adoption of flood mitigation programs. However, most of the communities are categorized as Class 10 and do not qualify for flood insurance discounts. NFIP has experienced problems in terms of property owners buying flood insurance following a major flood, largely in response to government pressure to buy insurance, and then

**Table 7.2: National Food Insurance Program Communities**

| Class | Number of Communities | | Discount |
|---|---|---|---|
| | April 2000 | October 2001 | |
| Class 3 | 0 | 1 | 35% |
| Class 4 | 0 | 2 | 30% |
| Class 5 | 3 | 12 | 25% |
| Class 6 | 20 | 33 | 20% |
| Class 7 | 83 | 134 | 15% |
| Class 8 | 341 | 362 | 10% |
| Class 9 | 460 | 394 | 5% |
| **Total** | **907** | **938** | |

*Source: FEMA/NFIP, 2001.*

letting their policies lapse. FEMA has contracted for a study of NFIP with particular attention to these kinds of issues. In addition to discounted flood insurance rates, communities participating in NFIP can also qualify for other federal assistance, including the Flood Mitigation Assistance Program, the Hazard Mitigation Grant Program, and U.S. Army Corps of Engineers projects.

NFIP has not been without critics, however. They argue that NFIP encourages the development of floodplains because property owners are assured that they can get insurance coverage and thus reduce their losses. NFIP also may suggest that floodplains can be safely developed when the wiser course may be to prohibit development altogether. Moreover, the threat to deny disaster assistance to property owners who develop known hazardous areas, such as coastal zones prone to flooding due to storm surges, has not deterred such development. Indeed, federal and state programs often encourage development because they fund the infrastructure, such as roads and bridges, that makes development economically feasible. The infrastructure itself lures prospective buyers and generates demand for homes and businesses.

### Project Impact

Project Impact is a logical extension of the principle stated by former FEMA Director Witt that "all mitigation is local." It also reflects the shift from FEMA's reactive approach to disasters in the 1980s and early 1990s to a more proactive approach to managing hazards and reducing their poten-

## Project Impact

The Disaster Resistant Community Initiative, which came to be known as Project Impact, was begun in the summer of 1997. As the FEMA brochure states, "The goal of Project Impact is to reduce the personal and economic costs of disasters by bringing together community leaders, citizens, and businesses to prepare for and protect themselves against the ravages of nature." Through the program, the federal government was to act as a catalyst, helping citizens and communities deal with the hazards that might cause loss of life and/or property. The four phases of Project Impact were: 1) "building community partnerships, 2) assessing risks, 3) prioritizing needs, and 4) building support and communicating what you are doing." Recommended actions for individuals included adopting measures to reduce the risk of fire, flood, and other damage to their homes and buying flood insurance. Recommended actions for businesses included complying with fire and building codes and buying flood insurance. Recommended actions for government officials included reviewing building standards and codes, ensuring that codes are enforced, and adopting new standards where needed to increase disaster resistance (FEMA, 1998).

At the national level, Project Impact has recruited public, private, and nonprofit sector partners to assist FEMA and participating communities. The private partners include such firms as the Associated Builders and Contractors, which helps with promoting the program; Michael Baker Jr., Inc., which determines whether homes are in floodplains; Dewberry & Davis LLC, which provides community education and hazard awareness programming; ESRI, which provides geographic information on hazards; Fannie Mae, which offers loans to homeowners to finance mitigation measures; the International Code Council, which is developing and encouraging the adoption of building codes; KeepSafe and the Portland Cement Association, which are promoting the building of safe rooms; and Wall-Ties & Forms, Inc., which is promoting aluminum forms for the construction of concrete homes and safe rooms. Other private partners help promote the program and encourage the adoption of disaster-resistant construction and disaster preparedness (FEMA, 2001).

tial effects. The focus on reducing property loss through disaster-resistant communities, rather than simply providing recovery monies following disasters, is central to the agency's strategic plan (see GAO, 2000). The program is designed to permit communities to set their own priorities for hazard-risk reduction. The initial challenges are to organize the projects well enough so that maximum public participation will be encouraged, reasonable priorities will be set based upon the risk assessment, and the organization can sustain itself and operate over time. Clearly it is necessary for local participants to understand and be committed to the goals of Project Impact. It is not the intent simply to create a committee of local government officials to run the project, as might be done for other community efforts. Broad public participation, including the business community, is needed if the communities are to develop consensus on goals and objectives. Public/ private partnerships are expected to be one of the cornerstones of the program. FEMA's roles are to provide technical assistance, financial support, and connection with the other Project Impact communities to encourage cross-fertilization. Local politics, interorganizational conflicts, and public apathy have to be overcome, and energetic and capable coordinators are essential to the maintenance of commitment and the recruitment of new partners.

FEMA is developing partnerships at the national level to assist Project Impact communities, particularly in technical areas such as risk assessment, and the communities themselves are developing partnerships with local businesses, community organizations, universities and colleges, and other institutions to generate and support local mitigation efforts. The partnership with Fannie Mae is to provide loans for homeowners to finance mitigation measures. The partnership with the International Code Council (ICC) is to support the efforts of that organization to develop and encourage the adoption of effective building codes. The ICC membership includes the major building code and standard-setting organizations: Building Officials and Code Administrators, International Conference of Building Officials, and Southern Building Code Congress International (FEMA, 2001). The American Red Cross' Disaster Resistant Neighborhood initiative is also connected to FEMA's effort.

In terms of Project Impact's attention to disaster-resistant construction, the list of recommended mitigation measures includes wildfire-, wind-, flood-, and earthquake-resistance measures. A lengthy checklist of such measures is included in the program's guidebook (FEMA, 2001).

In 1997, the Disaster Research Center at the University of Delaware began an assessment of Project Impact's seven pilot communities. Other Project Impact communities were added to the study in subsequent years. The assessment of the first year of the program concluded that there were start-up problems in terms of the availability of funding and the uncertainty that funding would be available for subsequent years despite the stated intent of FEMA to provide funding for five years. The creation of the community "partnership" or network was contingent upon the energy and effectiveness of key personnel. According to Kathleen Tierney, turnover in key personnel can be critical and can threaten the continuity of efforts. The learning curve for officials who did not participate in the initial kickoff of the Project Impact community was steep. While newly elected and appointed officials could be added to the program, they lacked the understanding and commitment of those officials who were engaged at the beginning. There is also a critical need for an energetic and effective Project Impact coordinator. Grassroots organizing and local capacity building were critical, and someone has to organize and, at the same time, maneuver within the local political system (Disaster Research Center, 1998).

In terms of the relationship between community partners and FEMA, the report pointed out the importance of federal guidance, connection with other Project Impact communities, and reliable funding. Initially, some community leaders feared that funding might end before the five-year period was over, and that fear tended to lessen the initial level of commitment. Nonetheless, community participation in Project Impact stimulated change in terms of a longer-term view of hazards and the threats they pose, and some communities were successful in finding private and Community Development Block Grant funding to supplement FEMA funding. The involvement of colleges and universities and other professional groups was a notable benefit, as well. The expansion of community participants made it possible to leverage a variety of new resources. The next steps would be to move from single mitigation projects to building disaster resilience into other local programs, including economic development programs, and to encourage building-standard development and code adoption (Disaster Research Center, 1998).

The assessment of the second year of the pilot phase focused on the status of mitigation efforts in Project Impact communities, including the adoption of building codes for new construction and for retrofitted structures and upgrading the communities' CRS ratings. Overall, there was a 15 percent increase in the "types of mitigation actions that had been adopted" (Disaster Research Center, 2001: 3). Communities were trying more kinds of activities. Smaller communities, in particular, were making progress in defining their risks, and the fastest increases in mitigation programs were among the communities with the poorest records prior to joining the Project Impact program. Community involvement had increased, as well. Greater access to government expertise and the increased involvement of community organizations helped the smaller communities in particular. The authors conclude that "[i]n summary, within two years, the seven pilot communities have completed 20 new assessment and mitigation activities and are working on an additional 56 projects.... It does seem highly unlikely that this level of activity would have taken place without the infusion of financial and technical resources from Project Impact" (Disaster Research Center, 2001: 8). In terms of partnership building, by the end of the first year the communities averaged 26 partner agreements, with most being local or nongovernmental. By the end of the second year, the communities averaged almost 47 partners with an average of 35.4 local and nongovernmental partners (Disaster Research Center, 2001: 10-13).

Maintaining and growing the partnerships was viewed as a critical process, with an emphasis on recruiting local business partners. Integrating Project Impact goals into community development and other policies and programs was slow, and knowledge of the programs, including the meaning of the term "mitigation," was growing. The report drew no conclusions regarding the effectiveness of administrative structures. Most of the communities had hierarchical structures but decentralized decision processes, reflecting the active involvement of community groups and other agencies in the program. The willingness of participants to collaborate, to donate time and other resources, and to invest themselves in the projects suggests that the less formal aspects of the Project Impact relationships were most important to them. As in the assessment of the first year of the pilot phase, the assessment of the second year concluded that the coordinator was a critical player in terms of maintaining momentum, recruiting partners, and assuring that the focus on mitigation activities was not lost (Disaster Research Center, 2001: 26).

Local goal setting, the location of the project, and community participation were considered essential issues by the participants. The location of the project in an emergency management office was seen as a problem, particularly if the office was attached to an emergency response agency. The preference was for locating the Project Impact program in the city or county manager's office. Relationships with some state emergency management offices and some FEMA regional offices were also viewed as problematic. Some communities also were bothered by the need to spend money quickly, particularly when projects were approved late (Disaster Research Center, 2001: 27-30).

# Components of the Safe Construction Networks

In addition to pursuing policy goals through its own programs, FEMA has used a variety of partnerships and looser collaborations to achieve policy goals. Two of the closest relationships at this point are between FEMA and the Blue Sky Foundation of North Carolina and the Institute of Business & Home Safety (IBHS). The missions of both organizations are focused on building standards, and IBHS also has a "fortified home" program that demonstrates safe construction techniques. FEMA has also been involved with numerous model home programs, some sponsored by the U.S. Department of Agriculture through the Agricultural Extension Service and the U.S. Department of Energy through the Consortium for Advanced Residential Buildings, and some sponsored by state government, public utilities, and other organizations.

## Blue Sky Foundation

The Blue Sky Foundation of North Carolina focuses on the building industry role in safe construction practices. As a nonprofit foundation, it relies on funding from FEMA and other agencies and organizations. It also serves as an intermediary between FEMA and builders and developers, providing training and education on safe construction practices and encouraging the adoption of stronger building standards.

Most of the funding for Blue Sky projects has come from FEMA, through the North Carolina Division of Emergency Management in the form of proj-

### Blue Sky Foundation of North Carolina

The Blue Sky Foundation of North Carolina began in 1997 with the goal of reducing loss of life and property due to storms and other kinds of hazards. The nonprofit corporation was an offshoot of the Blue Sky Project that was created in 1995 by the town of Southern Shores, North Carolina. The impetus for the creation of the foundation was a series of major hurricanes and other windstorms that struck the state in the 1990s. Sustainable development through safe construction and appropriate land use are the focus of the foundation's programs. Blue Sky sponsors conferences, training programs, public forums, and workshops on hazard-resistant construction practices. It also sponsors research on best practices in safe construction (Blue Sky Foundation, n.d.).

*The hurricane straps seen here are an example of how a structure can be reinforced to survive severe winds.*
Photo: Dave Saville/FEMA News Photo

ect grants. The foundation conducts conferences, including a Markets for Mitigation Forum held in August of 2001, and produces educational materials to encourage builders and developers to adopt safe construction methods. The foundation's efforts have been given momentum by the state mitigation and recovery efforts following Hurricane Floyd in 2000, and it has strong ties to the North Carolina Division of Emergency Management. The foundation has also developed a close working relationship with the Institute for Business & Home Safety and supports that organization's Showcase and "fortified home" programs. Most of the foundation's current projects involve identifying and encouraging best practices. Blue Sky's website lists IBHS and FEMA publications on best practices, and the foundation is developing new research initiatives to address the need for structures resistant to technological hazards, including terrorism, as well as natural hazards (Markle, 2001).

The Blue Sky Foundation has an important role in bridging the gap between FEMA, IBHS, and other organizations that promote safe construction, and the building industry, which tends to be very wary of attempts to regulate construction practices. The building industry's preference is to rely on market forces and wait for a demand for safer construction to develop. But, if all builders are required to meet the same standard, no one is at a competitive disadvantage. Builders and developers are resistant to new standards that they, in turn, have to sell to prospective buyers. On the other hand, if there is a market for hazard mitigation measures, such as roof straps, they will address that demand. The Blue Sky Foundation does promote such building practices as the use of structural adhesives and hurricane strapping to make buildings more resistant to high winds.

## Institute for Business & Home Safety (IBHS)

The Institute for Business & Home Safety is broadly focused on encouraging safer construction. Its programs include disseminating information about building codes and disaster-resistant building practices, as well as information to the insurance industry on loss reduction and risk. The building code efforts aim to provide accurate information to insurance companies about risk and to property owners so that they can ensure their property is in compliance with the code.

FEMA is working with IBHS on the development of an integrated building code, integrating the standards of the several major building codes in the nation, and increasingly on safe construction practices. IBHS's "fortified home" program has several model homes in the Tampa Bay area of Florida, and FEMA is providing financial support for some of the effort. Disaster mitigation features include wind- and fire-resistant roofing, impact-resistant windows and shutters, more secure connections between homes and their carports and porches, stronger entry and garage doors, and fire-resistant landscaping (USAA, 2001). IBHS has a demonstration project "on the elevation/ reconstruction of a repetitive loss home" in Ruskin, Florida. The project was begun as a partnership between FEMA and Hillsborough County, and the home was rebuilt to be two feet above Base Flood Elevation. IBHS joined the effort to address wind hazards, as well as the flood hazard. IBHS and FEMA are partnering in a project in Holmes Beach, Florida. FEMA is funding most of the reconstruction to meet IBHS's Fortified Criteria and FEMA's Coastal Construction Manual guidelines. Other collaborations are anticipated (Sciaudone, 2001).

FEMA necessarily has a focus on making low- and moderate-income housing more disaster resistant, because such housing tends to be more vulnerable to damage and because the agency has an obligation to the public to address broad social needs. IBHS can focus on marketing more up-scale disaster-resistant homes to consumers who can more easily afford the added expense of disaster-resistant features. IBHS, the Blue Sky Foundation, and FEMA also have working relationships with the Florida Association for Safe Housing (FLASH) to encourage building code integration. Much of the effort has concentrated on wind resistance, but the inclusion of fire and flood measures, as well as earthquake-resistant measures in places like Charleston, South Carolina, that have significant seismic risk, are being considered.

## Institute for Business & Home Safety

The Institute for Business & Home Safety, formerly the Insurance Institute for Property Loss Reduction, was created by the insurance industry to "reduce deaths, injuries, property damage, economic losses and human suffering caused by natural disasters" (IBHS, 2001). IBHS's members are insurance and reinsurance companies. The institute's priorities are: 1) consistent building codes, including drafting codes, targeting opportunities to encourage code adoption, and gathering data on disaster losses; 2) its "Fortified ... for safer living" program to encourage builders and homeowners to build disaster-resistant homes; 3) retrofitting homes to reduce losses, including impact-resistant windows and shutters; 4) the Community Land Use Evaluation form for planners to rate land-use practices, including consideration of hazards; and 5) converting the institute's paid-loss database to a geographic information system.

PROTECT
YOUR HOME
AGAINST
HURRICANE
DAMAGE

INSTITUTE FOR BUSINESS & HOME SAFETY

IBHS's new facility in Tampa, Florida, is in the city's Museum of Science and Industry. When completed, the facility will house the National Center for Natural Disaster Safety, which will serve as an educational facility to encourage attention to natural hazards and how to prevent or reduce their effects, a training facility for building professionals, and a research library.

## Other Safe Construction Efforts

There are other federal efforts to encourage better construction practices. For example, the U.S. Department of Agriculture, through the Agricultural Extension Service (AES), has been encouraging communities, builders, property owners, and students preparing for the building professions to embrace energy efficiency as a criterion for building. AES programs are increasingly embracing the concepts of sustainability and disaster resistance, as well. The 113 Calhoun Street Sustainable Living Center is a partner in the Charleston, South Carolina, Project Impact program and serves as a model for disaster-resistant elements in retrofitted historic homes.

"FEMA provided the majority of the bricks and mortar funding for the renovation of the project here [113 Calhoun St.] supported by SC Sea Grant [South Carolina Sea Grant Consortium] and Clemson [University] Extension" (Judge, 2001). The center is a renovated historic home, and the foundation that operates it is a partner in Charleston's Project Impact program. The center demonstrates methods for melding historic preservation, energy efficiency, and disaster resistance in a community in which retrofitting old structures is a major concern.

The U.S. Department of Energy (DOE) also is involved in model home building through the Consortium for Advanced Residential Buildings (CARB). The Mercedes Homes project in Melbourne Beach, Florida, involves construction of town homes. The project is sponsored by DOE as a model of energy efficiency and should be complete in 2002. The Department of Housing and Urban Development and, later, FEMA became sponsors as disaster-resistant elements were included in the homes. Better construction methods can increase both energy efficiency and disaster resistance. There are also model homes financed and operated by utilities, building materials manufacturers, and other private concerns, some in collaboration with CARB, that also encourage disaster mitigation.

Some of the listed model home projects (see the appendix, "Selected Model Home Programs") have received FEMA funding and support. FEMA's Region IV office has construction specialists who monitor safe construction efforts in the region and provide assistance when the projects are consistent with FEMA's goals. Nonprofit programs to encourage disaster-resistant construction, as well as energy efficiency and other improvements, are good marketing tools because they are more accessible to homeowners and builders than centralized facilities and can reflect local building needs. The State Farm House in Deerfield Beach, Florida, was part of that community's Project Impact effort. Deerfield Beach turned over responsibility for the house, an educational center, to the State Farm Insurance Company.

FEMA's "safe room" program is also related to the safe construction efforts. "Safe rooms" are being promoted principally to reduce the loss of life from tornadoes and other severe windstorms. Private firms have developed model "safe rooms" based upon FEMA's specifications. The Project Impact program in Louisville/Jefferson County, Kentucky, has "safe rooms" in its model homes, and the program in Warren County, Kentucky, has actually created a "safe room fire station." The Alvaton Fire Station facility is a shelter for the community.

Obviously efforts are under way by other agencies to encourage safer construction and wiser land use. The Florida Department of Insurance, for example, has a model home in Pensacola. The state of Florida has encouraged retrofitting of commercial properties through its "Open for Business" program. Money has been earmarked to encourage small firms to implement energy conservation measures. The money saved by the energy retrofits has been used to provide no-interest loans to businesses so they can implement hazard-reduction measures. City workers have donated their time after hours to help the small firms develop business continuity plans, as well.

# Leveraging the Safe Construction Networks

Catastrophic property losses during the 1990s have given impetus to the promotion of safe construction. The movement includes a number of major public, private, and nonprofit actors arrayed in several networks pursuing related but significantly different priorities. In general, the efforts have focused on: 1) encouraging the development of a market for safe construction so that buyers will insist on wind-, fire-, flood-, and earthquake-resistant homes and businesses; and 2) getting state and local officials to assist by requiring compliance with appropriate building standards and codes and by adopting appropriate land-use regulations.

It is difficult to separate the efforts into neat categories, but they have included a wide range of major actors. FEMA is addressing the need for safe construction through Project Impact, the National Flood Insurance Program, the Firewise Program, the Safe Room Program, and other efforts such as the model home programs. IBHS is addressing the need through its "fortified home" program and its efforts to integrate building codes and encourage their adoption. The Blue Sky Foundation is addressing the need through its research and education programs and promoting the efforts of both FEMA and IBHS. Other organizations, ranging from the Florida Association for Safe Housing to the Agricultural Extension Service, are also engaged in the effort to encourage safer construction. These efforts are also being tied to the movements for "smart growth" and "sustainable development." FEMA is one of several major actors—sometimes leading, sometimes supporting, and sometimes following—but the agency has more technical and financial resources than the other actors.

FEMA has a strategic goal of reducing property losses significantly, and the promotion of safe construction is one of the principal means to that end. FEMA's efforts include:

- The Project Impact program, which provides technical assistance for hazard reduction in member communities;
- NFIP, which requires flood-resistant construction on floodplains;
- Participation in the International Code Council's effort to integrate building codes;
- Support of the Association of State Floodplain Managers' efforts to encourage flood-proofing of new and retrofitting of old homes;

- The promotion of "safe rooms" to reduce the loss of life from tornadoes, including research ongoing at Texas Tech University and Clemson University; and
- Partnerships with the Blue Sky Foundation, IBHS, and other organizations to encourage safe construction practices and affordable disaster-resistant designs.

Project Impact community efforts can involve a mix of projects from building code adoption and land-use regulation to building or retrofitting homes for fire and flood resistance and from more limited disaster-resistance building methods to safe rooms.

FEMA has had to develop working relationships within a number of networks involved in promoting safe construction. Those relationships and networks are illustrated in Figure 7.1. FEMA has direct regulatory control over communities involved in NFIP. The flood insurance program requires that communities implement floodplain management measures, including land-use regulations and building standards, in order to qualify for discounted flood insurance and for disaster assistance following future floods.

FEMA has considerable influence with its partners in the Disaster Resistant Community or Project Impact program. The reliance of Project Impact communities on FEMA's financial support and technical assistance provides considerable leverage, although, as the Disaster Research Center assessments concluded, local participants greatly resent it when FEMA officials are too heavy-handed in their promotion of the agency's preferences. The partnerships require sensitivity to local priorities. The Project Impact participants also require more personal attention by FEMA officials. The relationships have to be cultivated and maintained.

The efforts to integrate building codes into one comprehensive and effective code are being driven by the International Code Council, which includes representatives of the major building code and standard-setting bodies. In this case, FEMA may largely serve a supporting role in terms of providing technical expertise and financial support.

Lastly, FEMA is actively involved in promoting the development of safer construction practices. Through the Blue Sky Foundation's training and education programs, IBHS's "fortified home" program, and, increasingly, through Agricultural Extension Service and other model home programs, the agency promotes the adoption of disaster-resistant building methods. The relationship with the Blue Sky Foundation is more of a principal-agent arrangement, with FEMA funding fueling the foundation's programs. The partnership with IBHS is based more on mutual interests, although they do have significant differences in priorities.

The need for a multi-level approach to hazard reduction is manifest. Development on the coasts, near woodlands, on floodplains, and in seis-

**Figure 7.1: The Safe Construction Networks**

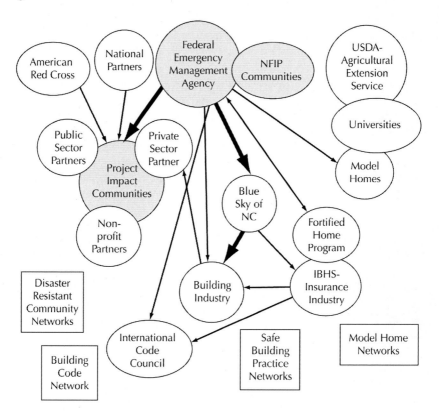

mically active zones is expanding rapidly, and the consequence is increased exposure of people and property to wind, flood, and seismic hazards, as well as to other environmental hazards. A seemingly obvious solution is to restrict development in hazardous areas and prohibit development entirely in the most hazardous areas. To some extent that can be done through land-use regulation, including mandatory programs such as the National Flood Insurance Program and state coastal zone management programs. Buyout programs for repetitive loss properties can reduce some of the exposure, as well. To the extent that some losses cannot be anticipated because of limited knowledge of hazards, there will continue to be significant losses. An answer to that problem is to change how we build homes and businesses to ensure that they are disaster-resistant to the greatest

## FEMA's Relationships with the Safe Construction Networks

**National Flood Insurance Program (NFIP) Communities Network**
  Strong influence, regulatory control, contractual relationships

**Project Impact Community Networks**
  Strong/moderate influence, resource role, formal partnership relations

**Building Code Network**
  Moderate/weak influence, supportive role, formal relationship

**Model Home Networks**
  Variable influence, supportive role, less formal relationships

**Safe Building Practice Networks**
  Weak to moderate influence, educational/supportive role, partnerships
  and ad hoc relationships

extent feasible. Cost will continue to influence building practices, but there are relatively inexpensive ways to make structures less vulnerable to wind, flood, fire, and earthquake.

Working through existing networks to promote safe construction is necessary. Broad participation encourages agreement on ends and means and compliance with policy choices. But, working through networks does present some challenges. The assessments of FEMAs Project Impact reflect the unique nature of networks. As Mandell and Steelman argue, networks require a different kind of management. In this case, disaster resistance provides the common mission, although some local participants still find the term mitigation confusing, and some state and federal participants are uncertain about local priorities and policy choices. The effort is seen as long term. There is risk in terms of the commitment of resources if the effort is terminated, as government programs frequently are. Collaborative problem solving, open decision processes, and innovative approaches are encouraged. The formal partnership agreements are less important than the commitment and involvement. Indeed, some of the Project Impact partners have not been active participants. The role of the coordinator is critical in terms of communicating the goals of the program, facilitating interaction, and building trust among the participants, not in terms of executive control and decision making. It may also be the case that FEMAs regulatory role through NFIP creates distrust. The response of Project Impact community participants was that FEMA officials were trying to foist certain kinds of projects on them rather than accept local priorities and proposals. The building industry, as well, may be slow to respond to recommendations because of concern that they may become regulations   the   slippery slope   of policy making. Gentle nudges, some funding, or some research assistance may be more effective than a more aggressive approach.

The problem FEMA may experience in working within the networks is that it is more difficult to measure success in these diffuse terms than it is to measure more direct program impacts. The success of disaster-resistant programs, for example, is difficult to measure until they have been put to the test in a disaster. Capacity in the abstract will always be suspect until tested, and excess capacity may be a waste of resources (Waugh, 1999). Measuring the strength of inter-organizational linkages, individual and group commitment, non-monetary contributions, and spillover effects is difficult. Nonetheless, the cultivation of effective networks to accomplish necessary tasks is worthwhile. Broad public involvement in the networks assures commitment to the ends and consensus on the means. Citizens and community groups bring local perspectives that government officials do not have and, as Frank Fischer argues (2000: 148), a sociocultural rationality that is lacking in decision processes dominated by technical experts. The real goal is to create a culture of mitigation or disaster resistance because the success of the effort is dependent upon sustained individual, family, and community compliance.

How might the FEMA efforts through Project Impact, the Blue Sky Foundation, IBHS, and the other organizations be compared? Certainly the efforts are interrelated. The grassroots nature of Project Impact may assure that it has a long-term impact and has the greater potential to create a culture of disaster resistance. Whether the Project Impact communities are developing a momentum of their own that will continue if FEMA support is terminated is an issue that should be examined. The model home projects in Florida that were products of Project Impact are connected with other disaster-resistant construction projects, as well as with energy efficiency and affordable housing projects. The local priorities of the Project Impact communities may prove invaluable in terms of generating innovative approaches to disaster resistance, including new safe construction measures. Tying the efforts to   smart growth   strategies and sustainable development plans would provide more momentum.

Working within the network is a challenge for FEMA, and it does require a less aggressive, more collaborative style of leadership. Indeed, the critical variable is the leadership. FEMAs representatives in the network, like Project Impact coordinators and other network managers and leaders, have to have strong interpersonal skills, uncommon patience, and considerable political acumen in order to interact effectively. They must also have energy to invest in the inter-organizational processes. Just as the boundaries of organizations become fuzzy, the boundaries of work relationships become fuzzy. The network is a high-maintenance set of working relationships.

In most respects, it is easier to interact with an organization like IBHS that has a clear mission and its own resources. The relationship can be mutually beneficial as long as the goals are similar and the areas of cooperation can more easily be negotiated. A difference that FEMA does have with IBHS is that FEMA has to give priority to making affordable housing more disaster resistant. The effort has to result in reducing the vulnerability of middle- and low-income housing. IBHS, on the other hand, has to create marketable technologies to reduce vulnerability, and that may mean a focus on high-income housing. Nonetheless, FEMA and IBHS do have common interests that can be pursued in partnership.

The relationship with the Blue Sky Foundation is more of a principal-agent relationship. FEMA can largely define the terms, although maintaining a close working relationship is very useful. The Blue Sky Foundation can focus on almost any kind of disaster and any aspect of construction. It can be a convenient and effective conduit for FEMA, IBHS, or any other safe construction program. It is limited in terms of geography and its staff and resource base, but it is flexible and responsive.

# Conclusions

Safe construction is a policy goal that is easy to define. There is broad support within government at all levels, the insurance industry, the mortgage industry, and even the building industry for strengthening building standards and making construction more disaster resistant. The social and economic costs of disaster recovery are powerful arguments for a mitigation approach. What is lacking is public demand for safe housing. People still want to live in hazardous areas and build at the lowest cost possible. They will pay for more floor space and amenities, but they will not pay much more for safety features hidden in walls and ceilings.

Governments can address the problem of housing vulnerability by strengthening building standards and by adopting and enforcing appropriate building codes and land-use regulations. This is the solution for reducing the vulnerability of new construction. But, stronger regulations and wiser planning may do little to reduce the vulnerability of old construction. Also, population growth and other factors increase risks. As hazards are better understood, different mitigation strategies may be required. Hazards themselves may change. Geophysical and meteorological disasters tend to run in cycles, and we may experience more frequent and more powerful disasters in the future. In short, the risk is growing  hazards are changing. The challenge is to be prepared for whatever changes may come. Therefore, the cultivation of a  culture of mitigation  is the wisest solution, and that requires developing market demand for safe construction.

FEMA has been reasonably successful in encouraging safe construction through direct and indirect means. There are important lessons to be learned from FEMAs experience in promoting safe construction through the various networks. Clearly, the experience has demonstrated that traditional administrative approaches are insufficient and that more collaborative and comprehensive approaches may be more effective in the long term. The following  lessons  are drawn from FEMAs successful and less than successful efforts:

**Lesson 1:** Mitigation should be the policy priority for property loss reduction. Maintaining a consistent and comprehensive focus on mitigation assures a clear mission.

**Lesson 2:** The cultivation and maintenance of network relationships requires long-term effort. Relationships are built upon trust, and trust is earned. Trust facilitates communication and organizational cooperation. Respect for the perspectives and priorities of the other participants is essential.

**Lesson 3:** Regulatory control can be instrumental in achieving some policy objectives, but it can interfere with the development of broader cooperative relationships. It is difficult to be both a  parent  and a  peer or partner.

**Lesson 4:** Broad participation in decision making, particularly priority setting, helps develop support for ends and means and encourages compliance with decisions. Hierarchical relationships do not encourage such consensus building.

**Lesson 5:** Working through networks can create a synergy and a creativity that are lacking in hierarchical systems. Personal commitment and a sense of efficacy encourage innovation.

**Lesson 6:** The federal government  or state government, for that matter  can influence policy change even if it does not have direct authority in that policy arena. Encouragement and support can facilitate the efforts of other actors and networks involved in the effort. Attempting to impose authority is counterproductive.

**Lesson 7:** Not all networks are alike, and different skills may be necessary to cultivate relationships within each. In some cases, contractual relationships work best. In some cases, informal relationships work best. In some cases, nonparticipation may be the best choice.

**Lesson 8:** Leadership is the key to successful networks and organizations. Providing or facilitating leadership will improve the chances for success.

**Lesson 9:** A clear mission is the cornerstone for cooperation. Successful partnerships and successful networks are built upon common interests.

**Lesson 10:** Open and transparent processes facilitate understanding and encourage participation. Closed systems, limited participation, and hidden agendas confound collaboration.

What is striking about the network operations examined in this study is the personal connections among the major participants. There is considerable interaction among FEMA, IBHS, Blue Sky, FLASH, 113 Calhoun Street Center, the state emergency management agency, the local emergency management agency, and other representatives. The personal connections provide the glue that holds the network together. They facilitate communication and assure coordination of efforts. They also create a synergy that is lacking in closed systems that do not share information or other resources and do not encourage personal investments. Part of that synergy is due to the diversity of perspectives on safe construction. Conflict stimulates innovation. The synergy is also due to the mutual respect and understanding among the individuals involved in the networks and their commitment to the goal of safe construction. This does not mean that all participants are motivated or able promoters of safe construction. Effective organizational participation is still dependent upon effective leadership. Not all participants understand the need for open communication, broad community involvement, and significant personal commitments of time and energy.

What has not been addressed thus far and should be raised at least in passing is the issue of accountability. Leveraging networks may be the most effective tool for achieving national policy goals, but it is difficult to hold FEMA or any other agency responsible for the achievement of goals when it has so little direct control. In that sense, it is unfair to the agency. At the same time, it presents a problem to political leaders who desire to hold the agency accountable for its actions (see Peters, 2000: 38). This may account for some of the opposition to Project Impact by officials of the George W. Bush administration. Aside from the fact that Project Impact is the creation of a prior administration, the program is dependent upon local political support and media attention. A change in administrations always affects relationships, although FEMA's career personnel provide continuity.

FEMA's efforts to encourage safe construction through the several networks have had mixed results. Some Project Impact communities have been very successful and others have languished. However, on the whole, the efforts have advanced the cause of safe construction and undoubtedly have reduced property losses. The questions are whether other policy instruments can be as effective, particularly when the goal is as fuzzy as creating a "culture of mitigation" within the American populace, and whether public agencies can as effectively deal with the demands of network "management" to achieve public purposes as FEMA has done.

# Appendix:
## Selected Model Home Programs

### 113 Calhoun Street Center for Sustainable Living, Charleston, South Carolina

The 113 Calhoun Street Center for Sustainable Living is operated by the 113 Calhoun Street Foundation. The foundation's mission "is to create communities more resistant to losses from natural hazards—flood, wind, and earthquake—and to promote ways of living that help people conserve natural resources" (The 113 Calhoun Street Foundation homepage). The project partners are the South Carolina Sea Grant Consortium, Clemson University Extension Service, City of Charleston, Charleston County, the Federal Emergency Management Agency, and the South Carolina Emergency Preparedness Division. A Project Impact partner, the center is a 125-year old home that is being retrofitted to make it flood, earthquake, and hurricane resistant. The chief of mitigation and risk assessment of the South Carolina Emergency Preparedness Division and the director of the National Oceanic and Atmospheric Administration's Coastal Services Center serve on the foundation's board. IBHS and FEMA provide information on hazard-resistant construction (113 Calhoun Street Foundation homepage).

### Hurricane House, University of Florida/St. Lucie County Cooperative Extension Office

The University of Florida built the Regional Windstorm Damage Mitigation Training and Demonstration Center, or Hurricane House, for the Florida Department of Insurance to disseminate information on wind-resistant construction. The house is one of several located around the state to demonstrate to builders and the public how to implement hazard-reduction measures. Cut-away sections of walls permit visitors to see hurricane straps, fasteners, and other features that can be used to retrofit old homes to increase wind resistance and built into new homes (St. Lucie County Cooperative Extension Service homepage).

### Florida House Learning Center, Sarasota County Technical Institute

The Florida House Learning Center is a joint project of the Cooperative Extension Service for Sarasota County, the Sarasota County Technical Institute, the Southwest Florida Water Management District, and the Florida House Institute. The center demonstrates construction methods to encourage energy efficiency and, through the "Model Florida Yard," encourages the adoption of practices to protect water quality and reduce water usage and to encourage recycling, wildlife gardening, edible gardening, and other yard uses (Sarasota County, Cooperative Extension Service homepage).

**Protecting Home and Family Project, State University of New York (SUNY) Maritime College Campus, New York**

The mission of the Protecting Home and Family (PHF) Project is [t]o establish and promote a standard for new construction and retrofitting of residential and critical buildings in natural hazard-prone areas which will eliminate or reduce the impact of future disaster, thereby increasing the safety of individuals and families and reducing property damage and over-all disaster costs (New York State Emergency Management Office, Strategic Plan: Mitigation, Section II, p. 1). The public partners include FEMA, the New York State Insurance Department, the New York City Mayor s Office of Emergency Management, the Nassau County Emergency Management Office, and the Suffolk County Department of Fire, Rescue and Emergency Services. The private partners include IBHS, the American Institute of Archi-tects Disaster Response Corporation, and building industry and insurance firms. The program objectives are to increase the numbers of single-family residential buildings built and retrofitted to resist wind, flood, and other nat-ural disaster damage; build new and retrofit older multi-family residential structures for special populations so that they are resistant to wind, flood, and other natural disaster damage; and increase the number of hazard-resistant critical facilities and retrofit older critical facilities in those parts of the state with wind, flood, and other natural hazards. The training center project on the SUNY Maritime College campus is being built by a public/private partnership and will provide training courses to builders, architects, suppliers, engineers, building code enforcement personnel, and students. Educational programs are to be offered to government officials and the public. The project is expected to increase public and construction industry aware-ness of safe construction methods, encourage the adoption of such con-struction methods, and create a market for disaster-resistant construction (New York State Emergency Management Office, Strategic Plan).

**'LaHouse' Learning Center, Louisiana State University**

LaHouse Learning Center is being built on the Louisiana State University campus, with completion expected in 2002. Energy efficiency, durability, occupant health, marketability and cost effectiveness, and appeal are the principal criteria used in constructing the house. Durability includes resist-ance to environmental hazards, such as hurricanes and floods (*LSU AgCenter News,* June 8, 2000; LSU AgCenter, LaHouse: The Louisiana House Learning Center brochure).

# Bibliography

Agranoff, Robert, and Michael McGuire (1999). Managing in Networks, *Policy Studies Review* 16 (Spring 1999): 18-41.

Cigler, Beverly A. (1996). Coping with Floods: Lessons from the 1990s. In Richard T. Sylves and William L. Waugh, Jr., *Disaster Management in the U.S. and Canada* (Springfield, Ill.: Charles C. Thomas Publishers, 1996).

Disaster Research Center (2001). Disaster Resistant Communities Initiative: Evaluation of the Pilot Phase Year 2, Year 2 Report, Report prepared for the Federal Emergency Management Agency (Newark, Del.: Disaster Research Center, University of Delaware, March).

Evatt, Dixie Shipp (2000). Does the National Flood Insurance Program Drive Floodplain Development, *Journal of Insurance Regulation,* Vol. 18, Issue 4, Summer 2000, pp. 497-527.

Federal Emergency Management Agency (2001). Project Impact homepage (www.fema.gov/impact).

Federal Emergency Management Agency (1998). *The Project Impact Guidebook* (Emmittsburg, Md.: FEMA).

Federal Emergency Management Agency (1997a). *Strategic Plan: Partnership for a Safer Future,* September 30.

Federal Emergency Management Agency (1997b). *Report on Costs and Benefits of Natural Hazard Mitigation* (http://www.fema.gov/mit/cb_toc/htm).

Federal Emergency Management Agency/National Flood Insurance Program (2001a). *The National Flood Insurance Program* (http://www.fema.gov/nfip/summary.htm).

Federal Emergency Management Agency/National Flood Insurance Program (2001b). *Community Rating System* (http://www.fema.gov/nfip/crs.htm).

Federal Emergency Management Agency/National Flood Insurance Program (1996). *The National Flood Insurance Program's Community Rating System.*

Fischer, Frank (2000). *Citizens, Experts, and the Environment: The Politics of Local Knowledge* (Durham, N.C.: Duke University Press).

Godschalk, David R., Timothy Beatley, Philip Berke, David J. Brower, and Edward J. Kaiser (1999). *Natural Hazard Mitigation: Recasting Disaster Policy and Planning* (Washington, D.C.: Island Press).

Hy, Ronald J. (1990). Structural Failures. In *Handbook of Emergency Management,* eds., William L. Waugh, Jr., and Ronald J. Hy (Westport, Conn.: Greenwood Press).

Kunreuther, Howard (1998). A Program for Reducing Disaster Losses Through Insurance. In *Paying the Price: The Status and Role of Insurance Against Natural Disasters in the United States* (Washington, D.C.: Joseph Henry Press), pp. 207-228.

*LSU AgCenter News* (2000). "LSU AgCenter Unveils Plans for 'LaHouse' Learning Center," June 8. http://www.agctr.lsu.edu/Communications/news/NewsArchive/1ns0608.htm.

LSU AgCenter, "LaHouse: The Louisiana House Learning Center" (brochure) http://www.louisianahouse.org.

Mandell, Myrna P. (1999). "The Impact of Collaborative Efforts: Changing the Face of Public Policy Through Networks and Network Structures," *Policy Studies Review* 16 (Spring 1999): 4-17.

Mandell, Myrna P., and Toddi A. Steelman (2001). "Understanding What Can Be Accomplished Through Different Interorganizational Relationships: The Importance of Typologies, Context and Management Strategies." Paper presented at the National Conference of the American Society for Public Administration, Newark, New Jersey, March.

May, Peter J. (1997). "State Regulatory Roles: Choices in the Regulation of Building Safety," *State and Local Government Review* 29 (Spring): 70-80.

McConnaughey, Janet (1994). "Opening the Door to Hurricane-Proof Homes," *The Atlanta Journal/Constitution* (July 13), p. A4.

Milward, H. Brinton, and Keith G. Provan (2000). "How Networks Are Governed." In *Governance and Performance: New Perspectives*, eds., Carolyn J. Heinrich and Laurence E. Lynn, Jr. (Washington, D.C: Georgetown University Press), pp. 238-262.

Morrow, Betty Hearn (1997). "Disaster in the First Person." In *Hurricane Andrew: Ethnicity, Gender and the Sociology of Disasters,* eds., Walter Gillis Peacock, Betty Hearn Morrow, and Hugh Gladwin (London: Routledge), pp. 1-19.

New York State Emergency Management Office (2001). "Strategic Plan: Mitigation, Section II: Protecting Home and Family: The Program at a Glance," http://www.nysemo.state.ny.us/MITIGATION/phaf2.htm.

Nigg, Joanne, Jasmin K. Riad, Tricia Wachtendorf, Angela Tweedy, and Lisa Reshaur (1998). Disaster Resistant Communities Initiative: Evaluation of the Pilot Phase, Executive Summary. Report prepared for the Federal Emergency Management Agency (Newark, Del.: Disaster Research Center, University of Delaware, August 24.

Olson, Richard Stuart, and Robert A. Olson (1993). "'The Rubble's Standing Up' in Oroville, California: The Politics of Building Safety," *International Journal of Mass Emergencies and Disasters* 11 (August): 163-188.

Olson, Richard Stuart, Robert A. Olson, and Vincent T. Gawronski (1999). *Some Buildings Just Can't Dance: Politics, Life Safety, and Disaster* (Stamford, Conn.: JAI Press).

113 Calhoun Street Foundation homepage, "113 Calhoun Street: A Center for Sustainable Living," http://www.113calhoun.org.

O Toole, Lawrence J., Jr. (1997). Treating Networks Seriously: Practical and Research-Based Agendas in Public Administration, *Public Administration Review* 57 (January/February): 45-52.

Petak, William (1998) Mitigation and Insurance. In *Paying the Price: The Status and Role of Insurance Against Natural Disasters in the United States,* eds., Howard Kunreuther and Richard J. Roth, Sr. (Washington, D.C.: Joseph Henry Press), pp. 115-170.

Peters, B. Guy (2000). Policy Instruments and Public Policy, *Journal of Public Administration Research and Theory* 10 (January): 35-47.

Platt, Rutherford H., and Alexandra D. Dawson (1999). The Takings Issue and the Regulation of Hazardous Areas. In *Disasters and Democracy: The Politics of Extreme Natural Events* (Washington, D.C.: Island Press), pp. 131-164.

Radin, Beryl, Robert Agranoff, Ann O Sullivan, C. Gregory Buntz, J. Steven Ott, Barbara S. Romzek, and Robert H. Wilson (1996). *New Governance for Rural America: Creating Intergovernmental Partnerships* (Lawrence: University Press of Kansas).

Sarasota County Cooperative Extension Service homepage, Florida House Learning Center, http://sarasota.extension.ufl.edu/FHLC/flahouse.html.

St. Lucie County Cooperative Extension Service homepage, Hurricane House, http://stlucie.ifas.ufl.edu/wind.html.

Tierney, Kathleen (2000). Evaluation of the Project Impact Disaster Resistant Community Initiative, EIIP Virtual Classroom, moderated by Amy Sebring, http://www.emforum.org, December 13.

Twisdale, Lawrence A. (2001). What Has Happened in Florida and Other States Is There a Trend? Presentation at the Markets for Mitigation Forum, Raleigh, N.C., August 20-21.

USAA (2001). Fortify Your Home, *USAA Magazine* (May/June), pp. 12-15.

U.S. General Accounting Office (2001). *Federal Emergency Management Agency.* GAO-01-832, August 1).

U.S. General Accounting Office (1999). *Observations on the Federal Emergency Management Agency's Fiscal Year 1999 Performance Report and Fiscal Year 2001 Performance Plan,* GAO/RCED-00-210R, June 30.

Waugh, William L., Jr. (1999). Assessing Quality in Disaster Management. In *Performance and Quality Measurement in Government,* ed. Ari Halachmi (Burke, Va.: Chatelaine).

Waugh, William L., Jr. (2000). *Living with Hazards, Dealing with Disasters* (Armonk, N.Y.: M.E. Sharpe).

Waugh, William L., Jr., and Ronald J. Hy (1996). The Hyatt Skywalk Disaster and Other Lessons in the Regulation of Building. In *Disaster Management in the U.S. and Canada,* eds. Richard T. Sylves and William L. Waugh, Jr. (Springfield, Ill.: Charles C Thomas Publishers), pp. 253-269.

Waugh, William L., Jr. (1990).  Emergency Management and the Capacities of State and Local Governments.  In Richard T. Sylves and William L. Waugh, Jr., eds., *Cities and Disaster: North American Studies in Emergency Management* (Springfield, Ill.: Charles C Thomas Publishers, 1990).

## Interviews/Correspondence:

Dr. Charles A. Doswell III, National Severe Storm Laboratory, NOAA/ University of Oklahoma

Dr. Elizabeth K. Judge, Clemson University and the 113 Calhoun Street Center, Charleston, S.C.

Don Markle, Executive Director, Blue Sky Foundation of NorthCarolina

Steven Randolph, Project Impact Coordinator, FEMA Region IV

Dr. Claudette Reichel, Housing Specialist, LaHouse Project Chair, LSU AgCenter

Dr. Jasmin Riad, Dromedary Disasters International, Inc., Atlanta, Georgia

Jeffrey C. Sciaudone, PE, Associate Director of Engineering, Institute for Building & Home Safety, Tampa, Florida

Chuck Vance, Fortified Program Manager, Institute for Building & Home Safety, Tampa, Florida

**CHAPTER EIGHT**

# Extraordinary Results on National Goals: Networks and Partnerships in the Bureau of Primary Health Care's 100%/0 Campaign

John W. Scanlon
Board Member
Community Health Leadership Network

*This report was originally published in March 2003.*

## *Section I: Achieving National Goals—The Emergence of a New Kind of Leadership*

# Leadership Lessons from the Bureau of Primary Health Care

### Overview

From 1998 to 2001, a small group of managers in a federal agency went beyond their job responsibilities to create an important national movement. They produced results not only much different from what agencies usually achieve, but results that far exceeded the reach of their agency programs alone. If expected results can be called reasonable and ordinary, what this agency accomplished—by assuming a unique leadership role—was extraordinary.

This is a story about a new form of leadership in which agency managers move beyond program and agency goals to pursue a "national goal." A national goal is bigger than those of individual programs or any one agency.

Section 1 of this chapter, *Achieving National Goals—The Emergence of a New Kind of Leadership,* presents the 10 lessons learned about this new form of leadership. It addresses four questions:

- What does leadership on a national goal look like?
- What does it take for this kind of leadership to surface in an organization?
- What does it take to nurture this kind of leadership in an organization?
- What activities are undertaken to achieve national goals?

Section 2, *How to Achieve National Goals—A Case Study of Leaders Leveraging Partnerships,* is a case study of how the campaign was carried out during a four-year campaign time line. It covers the conditions in place that allowed it to start and to move from a federally led movement to a movement now led by organizations outside the federal government.

### Background: The Intent and the Setting

In 1998, a group of managers in the Bureau of Primary Health Care (the Bureau), Department of Health and Human Services, launched what they called the 100% Access/0 Health Disparities Campaign. The vision was to have every community in America provide 100 percent of its residents access to quality health care. In addition, every community would be eliminating health-status disparities, the severe and pervasive gaps in health status that show up in a community when vulnerable, uninsured populations are compared with affluent, insured populations.

The Bureau is responsible for categorical programs that contribute health service assets to needy communities, including the community health center grant program and the National Health Service Corps. The agency's mission is "assuring access to preventive and primary care for vulnerable populations." Its programs provide health care to the neediest but reach only about 10 to 20 percent of the 45 million uninsured and vulnerable. From this perspective, the 100%/0 leadership team saw the potential of a community-based solution to the uninsured problem. Their experiences told them that communities could provide access to 100 percent of their residents by restructuring the assets already in the community. The key was to create an integrated delivery system that placed the uninsured and vulnerable in "medical homes," shifting them from using wildly expensive emergency rooms to a cost-effective primary care system.

The team's vision was to have all 3,000 communities in America with integrated health systems in place  delivering 100% access and 0 health disparities. Its goal was 500 communities enrolled in the campaign within three years. The progress of these 500 communities toward the 100%/0 goal was to be tracked and assistance was to be provided to accelerate progress.

Federal staff with other full-time management responsibilities were able, in a three-year period, to launch a self-organizing, self-sustaining movement. That movement now has multiple networks of leadership at the national, state, and local levels aligned in pursuit of a common vision with measurable goals.

## The Face of Leadership on a National Goal

### What Does Leadership on a National Goal Look Like?

It looks like a self-organized group with a common vision and an impossible goal. The participants appear extroverted in their actions, always networking outside the agency, always making deals. They will strike others in their own organization as either entrepreneurial or crazy.

The core leadership group that created the 100%/0 campaign consisted of 10 people who were seasoned and relatively senior in position:

- Dr. Marilyn Gaston, director, Bureau of Primary Health Care
- Mary Lou Andersen, deputy director, Bureau of Primary Health Care
- Jim Macrae, director, Office of State and National Programs
- Chuck Van Anden, branch chief, National Health Service Corps
- Dennis Wagner, special assistant to the Office of the Director
- Donald Coleman, director, Media Center
- Rick Wilk, regional field staff, Chicago Office
- Regan Crump, director, Division of Special Populations

## Access to Health Care: A Catastrophic National Problem in Search of a Solution

The 100%/0 campaign is a bottom-up solution to a serious national problem. The nation's health care system is acknowledged to be a financial, organizational, and performance mess. It's a $1.4 trillion system that provides great care for some, some care for many, and little or no care for about 20 to 25 percent of the population. At any given point, 40 to 50 million people seem to be uninsured. National and state efforts to reform this system have foundered.

The magnitude, severity, and longevity of this situation were summarized by six former cabinet secretaries of the Department of Health and Human Services, as reported in the *Atlanta Journal-Constitution*, November 19, 2002:

> The nation's health care system is too costly, inefficient, unfair and in need of an overhaul, six former secretaries of Health and Human Services agreed Monday in Atlanta. In a rare display of unanimity among both Democrats and Republicans who headed the federal health establishment during five administrations, the former Cabinet members also agreed that, despite its flaws, the system won't be reformed any time soon.

> Donna Shalala, who served as secretary of the department during the Clinton administration, bluntly characterized the system as "a mess." "The health care system can't survive in its present state, because we can't afford the way it is organized," she said. "But there is no agreement about what the solution should be…"

> The former secretaries…warned that the real inequities in the U.S. system—which ranks first in the world in cost, and 35th in overall efficiency, according to World Health Organization surveys—aren't much closer to resolution than they were during the quarter of a century that they presided over it. The secretaries'…views on the nature of the health care problem were remarkably similar…

> "We need to shift the mix of physicians from the specialties to primary care," said Louis Sullivan, who served as HHS secretary in the first Bush administration… "The big barrier to health care is cost," said F. David Mathews, who headed the department under President Gerald Ford. The group said drug companies, doctors, hospitals, insurers and Congress share responsibility for the system's problems. But the group said the American people and their priorities also contribute to the nation's health care woes. "We have to persuade people that they have control over their own health future," said former Surgeon General David Satcher. "Sixty-five percent of Americans are obese or overweight," he said, noting that much of the problem is a result of poor dietary habits and sedentary lifestyles.

- Dr. Eric Baumgartner, director, Community Access Program
- John Scanlon, JSEA, Inc., consultant to the Office of the Director

With only two exceptions, Dennis Wagner and John Scanlon, these leaders had full-time job responsibilities in managing ongoing Bureau programs and activities and continued to carry out their full-time jobs throughout the campaign. Wagner was brought to the Bureau on detail from the Environmental Protection Agency as an expert in social marketing. He came to develop the national partnerships that would ultimately take over the campaign and was the full-time coordinator of the campaign. Scanlon served as a consultant to Marilyn Gaston on her strategic agenda and helped her translate her strategic intent into a project robust enough to achieve it. He also served as a coach to and member of the team that created the 100%/0 program.

This leadership team functioned as a group of peers, all of whom saw the world from the perspective of a grand mission they were committed to carrying out. They met weekly and interacted frequently. In the meetings, everyone at the table was proactive and ready to make commitments—there was no single person in charge.

Gaston and Andersen—the Bureau's director and deputy director—participated as team members, not acting in their roles as executives. As the Bureau's top leaders, though, they did play the special role of brokering the alignment of the campaign mission and campaign work to the agency mission and legislative charter. They kept the campaign work within the discretion allowed by law and regulation.

The team did essentially three things. First, they articulated an "impossible" national goal and crafted a plan to achieve it. Second, they continually brainstormed how events and processes that were going to happen anyway could be used to carry out the plan. The bold goals enabled them to see possibilities and opportunities already there but up to that point hidden. Third, they created partnerships to form and access networks. There were partnerships with successful communities that would serve as benchmarks for 100%/0. Partnerships with national organizations whose membership networks reached into communities. Partnerships with communities in action on 100%/0. In effect, the team built a network of networks.

Three initial lessons emerged from watching this unique group in action:

**Lesson 1: Collaborate and network.** Pursuing a national goal is an exercise in collaboration and network development. Those seeking to pursue national goals need to somehow create a "space" where hierarchy can be set aside and collaboration can happen. In this case, agency executives became part of the team rather than traditional line managers, and the "price of admission" to participate on the team was the willingness to make commitments to act. Action often means developing partnerships with networks that give the group reach.

**Table 8.1: Ten Leadership Lessons from the Bureau's Campaign for 100% Access & 0 Health Disparities**

| | |
|---|---|
| 1. Collaborate and network. | Pursuing a national goal is all collaboration and network development. |
| 2. Reveal hidden assets. | The leadership team discovers and gains access to hidden assets that they and others own by articulating a bold campaign goal. |
| 3. Operate in campaign mode. | The team takes shape around the development of a campaign goal and game plan. |
| 4. Search for national goals. | Around government programs are higher national goals, ones beyond the reach of the program, that can be achieved by leadership campaigns using the programs as "platforms." |
| 5. Find the leadership below the surface. | The leadership for national goal campaigns is already there, ready to surface and focus. |
| 6. Accept the natural resistance. | The leadership team sees organizational resistance as natural and legitimate and does not hear it as a veto. |
| 7. Distinguish the ready and the not ready. | The leadership team spends most of its time with people who are ready to play and is respectful of those who are not ready. |
| 8. Make and secure commitments. | The work of the campaign is making and securing commitments, and the tendency to create internal bureaucracy and special projects is seen as unnecessary, distracting work. |
| 9. Tell leadership stories. | Leaders generate commitments and action by conveying their leadership story and the leadership stories of others when they speak. |
| 10. Practice the discipline of leadership. | Leadership on national goals is both a calling and a teachable discipline that is available to all federal executives. |

**Lesson 2: Reveal hidden assets.** The leadership team discovers and gains access to hidden assets that they own and others own by articulating a bold campaign goal. The routine work of running federal programs creates assets for federal managers that are often not seen or acknowledged. These hidden assets involve access to people and networks, influence, credibility, knowledge. The assets are revealed by the articulation of a grand mission that one is truly committed to achieving. The campaign team referred to this phenomenon as the "abundance principle."

**Lesson 3: Operate in campaign mode.** The team takes shape around the development of a campaign goal and game plan.

Dr. Marilyn Gaston

Bringing in Wagner, an expert in social marketing campaigns, emboldened and energized the team, brought a campaign philosophy and attitude the team lacked, and rounded out the skill set of the team. His full-time role gave the team a center to turn to.

## What Does It Take for This Kind of Leadership to Surface in an Organization?

In retrospect, it seemed like the campaign was already there, ready to happen. The organization only had to relax and let it happen.

The sequence of events that created this effort began with a conversation. An assistant challenged Andersen on the strategic goals of the Bureau: "Our goal should be 100 percent access." This was way beyond the 10 to 20 percent access to primary care the programs achieved and the expected gain from incremental funding increases. A seemingly impossible goal would be rejected, and even ridiculed, in most organizations. But Andersen shared it with others and it came alive. Three factors converged to give it life:

- People were present with career-long interest in improving access to health care.
- Professionals were seeking additional meaning in their work.
- A larger mission context existed, providing legitimacy.

No one person showed up with the leadership vision for the campaign. Instead, all team members came with a clear direction to their careers. Those who joined the team had a deep, career-long commitment to the nation having an effective safety net. Gaston, for example, came to the Bureau with more than a management agenda to simply "run" her Bureau. She was an advocate for measuring and eliminating health status disparities.

---

### *Healthy People 2010:* A Public Source of National Goals for the Campaign

The vision of 100% Access and 0 Disparities flows from the goals of *Healthy People 2010*, the prevention agenda for the nation.

Developed by the Office of Disease Prevention and Health Promotion of the Department of Health and Human Services, *Healthy People 2010* states national health objectives. It identifies the most significant preventable threats to health and establishes national goals to reduce those threats. *Healthy People 2010* builds on initiatives pursued over the past two decades.

There is no funded program behind *Healthy People 2010*. The intent is for it to be used by many people, states, communities, professional organizations, and others to help them develop new ways of improving health. They all are encouraged to integrate their program's content into other programs, special events, publications, and meetings. *Healthy People 2010* offers a simple but powerful idea: Provide health objectives in a format that enables diverse groups to combine their efforts and work as a team.

This national agenda has two overarching goals: (1) increase quality and years of healthy life and (2) eliminate health disparities. It states more specific goals for 28 focus areas, one example being: Improve access to comprehensive, high-quality health care services.

The 100%/0 team was in an organizational culture that was deeply committed to the *Healthy People 2010* agenda and the goals it established.

---

She talked about the "safety net we need vs. the safety net we have." She wanted to describe that gap and put it into the policy development processes. Others on the team had similar, unrealized missions or intentions. These ambitions were held in check somewhat because they called for engaging processes, organizations, and leaders outside the Bureau and outside the federal government. But Andersen and Gaston cultivated these ambitions. A latent leadership drive among many in the Bureau was cultivated through conversations and evolved into a common leadership vision. There were many professionals in the Bureau eager to give meaning to the roles and jobs in which they found themselves. They constantly asked, "Why am I doing this?" and "What does it mean?" Already seeking, many were drawn to the campaign. The campaign helped them find a higher meaning in their jobs and gave greater purpose to what they were doing. Regan Crump described it as the opportunity to be part of a movement:

> "I never had to be convinced. 100% is such a moral imperative that we don't have to agree that 'it can be done,' it was about 'it must be done.'...

I was excited about the idea of the campaign. First it was huge. It had the big, bodacious goals that Dr. Gaston was always asking for. Second, it called for us to bring in many other organizations because we can't do it alone. Third, it required people to work across sectors—government, private sector, charity—and to go beyond health. And fourth, 100% access for everyone is so moral, so ethical, so right. It's like the civil rights movement. It's proactive, creative."

As personal interest and meaningfulness brought people together, the group needed to find a larger mission context than the categorical programs and agency mission could provide. This larger context would serve to legitimize a campaign on national goals. For the Bureau, that context has existed for decades—*Healthy People 2010,* the official prevention agenda for the nation. It is a statement of national health objectives designed to identify the most significant preventable threats to health and to establish national goals to reduce those threats. *Healthy People 2010* set forth a number of goals, including (1) improve access to comprehensive, high-quality health care services and (2) eliminate health disparities.

There is, however, no federally funded program to achieve those goals. *Healthy People 2010* is to be used by many key actors—states, communities, professional organizations, and others—to help them develop programs to improve health. 100%/0 was one way that BPHC managers and staff could articulate and pursue official national health goals. They had a kind of permission to go for it.

Two lessons emerged from watching this team form:

**Lesson 4: Search for national goals.** Associated with government programs are higher national goals that, although beyond the reach of the program, can be achieved by leadership campaigns using the programs as platforms. The mission and policy context of a categorical program and an agency can be used to legitimize and empower a leadership campaign on national goals. The program platform provides the networks, access, and events through which others can be enrolled in the campaign as partners.

**Lesson 5: Find the leadership below the surface.** The leadership of national goals is already there, ready to emerge and focus. Listen for leaders already within the organization but frequently out of sight. Create or find a "safe space" in which they can surface. As leadership spirit surfaces, put it into action—don't let it wilt under criticism, advice, gossip, wishing, or planning.

## What Does It Take to Nurture This Kind of Leadership in an Organization?

It turned out that the team was responsible for its own morale and performance. As the leadership team began this work, it found that the morale of the team depended on how it reacted to engagement with others. The

Mary Lou Andersen

team learned to draw energy from the positive engagements and to accept and not judge the negative encounters.

When the 100%/0 team brought the campaign to those outside the Bureau and outside the federal government, the members generally were greeted with enthusiasm and support. An external meeting was almost always energizing, creative, and productive. This validation and affirmation served as a market test of the campaign and as the primary source of energy and high morale for the team.

Inside the Bureau, the response was not always positive. It was a major challenge to launch a campaign like this within an organization that lacked clearly assigned responsibility for the national goal. Legitimate and natural forces resisted. Team members' reactions to negative responses had to be managed or the team would become discouraged and defensive.

Resistance showed up in two forms: criticism from peers within the Bureau and anxiety from volunteers who wanted to help. The first was overt. The team scheduled briefings with each member of Gaston's executive team to explore how the work of the entire Bureau could be used as a platform for enrolling communities and finding models that worked. The response ranged from the support of a few to harsh rejection by most. They heard statements that sounded critical:

- "As stewards of the federal dollars, we shouldn't be putting money or staff attention into anything but direct service delivery grants. Everything should be directed to serving patients."
- "This campaign is not in my job description. It looks like and feels like more work. There is no reason for me to take it on."
- "That is not our mission or role or responsibility."
- "Hogwash! I do not believe it is doable. Communities can't do it. We don't know how to show communities to do it."
- "This campaign work is a criticism of the effectiveness of our programs and it is inappropriate."
- "We are about health centers and corps placement. Period."
  Team members recalled this as an unpleasant exercise:
- "At that time many of the other managers saw us as quacks, as out-of-control entrepreneurs."(Chuck Van Anden)
- "I was frustrated at their reaction. Not that they didn't get it, but that they resisted trying to get it. It was the unwillingness to even entertain

it. They had great security in the status quo. I could see where the investment would have a big payoff, but they didn't see the possibility. It took the wind out of our sail...but we regrouped and repackaged the message." (Regan Crump)

From the experience grew important leadership values for the team and principles for the campaign. The team heard the criticism but did not take it personally or as a veto. They heard no in response to their request for help and support, but they avoided getting defensive and remained open to working with those who made critical comments.

The second form of resistance was subtler in that it first appeared to be support. Many staff stepped forward to help. They were bright, highly educated, serious people ready to lend a hand. In return, they wanted to be assigned tasks and given the necessary resources. A task agenda began to grow:

- "We need forms to fill out whenever any staff person engages a community."
- "We need someone to collect the data and produce reports."
- "We need to set up a committee to define what a community is."
- "We need to define what 100% access is so we can tell the communities."
- "We need a list of resources we can offer communities."
- "We need a technical assistance tool kit."

As the list grew, anxiety grew among the volunteer staff: "How does this relate to my performance plan? What is the budget?" The leadership team found itself under great pressure to organize all kinds of special projects that gave this work legitimacy and resources. The staff challenged them: "If you are serious, then let's build a very well-defined system and put the resources we need into it."

When the guidance and project resources failed to arrive, volunteer staff began to withdraw. One team member commented: "The staff retreated. They wanted to be helpful. They were initially interested, but these were not their primary jobs or their 'real' work. They were not committed to 100% access. And it was not their style."

At first, the requests and offers from the volunteer staff seemed reasonable and logical. But soon the team saw that creating more task and project work would sink the campaign. And it wasn't the right kind of work for a campaign. Several team members commented:

"This campaign could not be accomplished in formal structure and rules. And we know government has structure and rules. This was a proactive, fluid movement. We went way beyond what we were legally required to do. It is part of our higher mission, but it could not be done within the structure in place to run programs."

"The campaign was the most exciting and interesting kind of work. It's all about an idea, a vision, and getting people excited about it. It's not related to a program. It's not a program. It's not contingent on having dollars to spend. If it's approached as a program, it crashes. It's getting people to just do something. It's about commitments. That is the beauty of it."

Three lessons emerged from watching the team interact with individuals and groups inside and outside the Bureau:

**Lesson 6: Accept the natural resistance.** The leadership team sees organizational resistance as natural and legitimate, and does not hear it as a veto. Leadership teams manage the resistance they run into. Expressions of indifference, rejection, hostility, and cynicism will be voiced and will trigger anger and defensiveness in the team. This leadership team had to develop a mind-set that heard rejection as an expression of a different set of interests, not as an attack on the team.

**Lesson 7: Distinguish the ready and the not ready.** The leadership team spends most of its time with people who are ready to play and is respectful of those who are not ready. In this case, energy and morale came from positive conversations, mostly outside the organization, with people who were excited about something. By definition, the resources needed to achieve the goals of the campaign are outside.

**Lesson 8: Make and secure commitments.** The work of the campaign is to generate commitments. The leadership team sees the tendency to create internal bureaucracy and special projects as generating more work rather than commitments. Without legislative and budget authority, more formal structures and special projects are not appropriate or sustainable.

### What Activities Are Undertaken to Achieve National Goals?

A member of the original team described the work of the campaign as simple and easy:

"This was easy. All we did was uncover what was already going on and put a spotlight on it! We didn't create it or do it. We found people doing it, said 'great job,' showed it to others, and saw others start doing it. Shining a spotlight, encouraging those doing it, and giving courage to others to try it. People said, 'Wow, it can be done.'" (Jim Macrae)

As the team developed its confidence and approach, it came to see its work as different from traditional policy development, program management, or administrative work. Most work in organizations is planned, with a certain level of resources committed to activities designed to produce a known result. Managers know how to get the results they want from these traditional activities. They know what they don't know and can secure the expertise that will cover those areas. Traditional work requires managers to be in control of sequential work processes. It's linear, convergent, and predictable.

The work of national goal campaigns is not like that. The goals are way beyond the resources at hand, so the work has to be about developing relationships to deploy other organizations' resources. The team, generating new possibilities and opportunities, does not know what it does not know. The work is not linear. The work is about seeking multiple outcomes from activity and geometric leveraging. It's about divergent activity and paths. Finally, it is about having a bold goal, bold enough to contain all the divergent activities and paths and bring them back together. If traditional management work is "plan, allocate, do," then the work of the campaign is the work of leadership: "declare, discover, enroll."

The work of leadership on national goals turns out to be playful, improvisational, and fun. But until one gets used to it, it can be very unsettling. It calls for the leadership team to step into an empty space where possibilities exist but at first cannot be sensed or seen. As the 100%/0 team took that step, they began to develop a style and method.

The team evolved a campaign method that had five important elements:

- *Develop networks.* Build partnerships to access networks that can reach into communities and deliver assistance.
- *Generate and manage commitments.* Use requests and offers to create action and movement with every encounter.
- *Seek and deploy models that work.* Use benchmark communities and leaders as role models and blueprints for action that inspire and guide.
- *Organize call-to-action events.* Run events that cause breakthroughs in community enrollment and progress while strengthening the networks working on the campaign.
- *Adopt a signature style.* Convene and engage people in a way that generates commitments and makes things happen.

These five elements describe the nature and structure of the campaign work. They are parts of a whole. The strength and success of the campaign stem from the networks that extend the effort. The vision is conveyed by the successful communities that are showcased. The call-to-action events broadcast the campaign. The signature style is a way to be effective while doing the work of generating commitments through requests and offers. *(Section II: How to Achieve National Goals—A Case Study of Leaders Leveraging Partnerships,* the case study of the campaign, will describe these elements in action.)

The campaign's experience was that this work is easier and more fun than one might have expected. Two lessons emerged from watching the team produce extraordinary results.

**Lesson 9: Tell leadership stories.** Leaders generate commitments to action on national goals by telling their leadership story when they speak. Leadership campaigns to achieve national goals work when team members tell their personal stories and share the leadership stories of others. These stories are, first, a compelling call to action and, second, a celebration of models that work. With these stories, leaders stand for the national goal as a possibility and thus cause opportunities to appear. These opportunities are seized in the moment by making requests and offers to generate commitments.

**Lesson 10: Practice the discipline of leadership.** Leadership on national goals is both a calling and a learned discipline available to all federal executives. The discipline consists of the methods and the style that become part of a leader's everyday activity. These methods can be learned, taught, and adapted to other situations. Without them, without the discipline, the calling never comes to life. The 100%/0 team found the discipline necessary to carry out a campaign and made it their style. This leadership discipline can be seen in action in the next section, *How to Achieve National Goals—A Case Study of Leaders Leveraging Partnerships.*

## From National Goal to National Movement

From 1998 to 2001, a small group of managers in one federal agency created a national movement. They produced results on national goals generally felt to be impossible. Their goal seemed beyond reach because it required both intergovernmental and public-private collaborations. The Bureau's experience shows how federal programs can become the platforms on which to create a critical mass of collaboration necessary for realizing national goals.

Leadership on national goals is a kind of leadership that career and appointed executives throughout government can demonstrate. The potential leadership team is already just below the surface in many organizations, and existing programs have already generated the hidden assets that can be mobilized and deployed. The methods to use, while somewhat counterintuitive to an administrative or management culture, are available and teachable. National goal campaigns can deliver a high return on investment, and, for the most part, the investments have already been made.

# Section II: How to Achieve National Goals— A Case Study of Leaders Leveraging Partnerships

## Introduction

Leadership on national goals, as defined here, has the feel of creating something out of nothing. To be more exact, it takes the assets and energy that are available, but often hidden, and brings them together to produce big results that would not happen in the business-as-usual course of events. How does something like this happen?

In the 100%/0 campaign, six kinds of work were carried out as the campaign evolved from the intention of a group of leaders into a national movement.

It all began with individuals seeking leadership relationships with others. That seeking resulted in a self-directed leadership team forming itself through two *formative activities:*

- *Creating open space for leadership (1997–1998).* The career calling of several managers and staff created interest in and energy for working together. A space was created for leaders to surface and for a collaboration to form.
- *Creating a campaign (1998–1999).* A core group (called "Just Do It") formed itself and recruited others. The 100%/0 team evolved. It created the "game" to be played, a national campaign with bold, measurable goals.

The team then created the content and infrastructure of a campaign. The content is the stories of successful communities that demonstrate what a 100%/0 health care system can look like, and the leadership stories of how to bring that about. The infrastructure is the networks that enable communication among communities in action. The two *building activities* were:

- *Partnering with national networks to extend reach (1999–2000).* The team, guided by the social marketing experience of Dennis Wagner, entered into partnerships with national membership organizations. They gave the campaign team access to membership networks and thus to thousands of communities. Alliances were also created with organizations that were acting with communities on similar goals.
- *Partnering with benchmarks of the vision (1999–2001).* Communities that had successfully created 100%/0 systems were identified, and their leaders enrolled in the campaign as role models, teachers, and advocates.

The intended result of all these activities was for communities to commit to transform their health care safety net into a 100%/0 delivery system. The goal was to reach a critical mass of partnership and community enrollment that would result in a self-sustaining movement. The *outcome activities* were:

- *Enrolling communities in action (1999–2001).* Over three years, more than 500 community leadership groups were engaged in various ways to commit to 100%/0. National and local pacing events were used to enroll communities and accelerate community progress.
- *Forming a national movement (2001–2002).* By 2002, at least four organizations had formed to continue enrolling and working with communities on 100%/0. The locus of leadership had moved from the Bureau team to organizations outside the federal government. The team had successfully launched a national movement.

The time line for the six levels of work is shown in Figure 8.1. The Bureau's campaign activities extended over a four-year period. The Bureau leadership team was in action from 1998 to 2001. In 1997, the leadership forces came together to launch that work. By 2002, the campaign was effectively a national movement led by organizations outside the federal government.

How the work was invented and executed demonstrates the creative and generative nature of a leadership campaign. Jim Macrae was right when he said "the work is easy." But it's unusual work that takes getting used to. It uses a method of "declare, discover, enroll" rather than the traditional "plan, allocate, do."

# Creating Open Space for Leadership (1997–1998)

The Bureau's director and deputy director did not mandate the 100%/0 campaign—a leadership campaign cannot be ordered or regulated into existence. Instead, they created an open space where the natural leadership within the Bureau could surface and self-organize. They formed that space by declaring intent, setting up forums for leadership development, and acknowledging leadership when they heard it.

Leadership begins with intent that has passion and commitment behind it. Both Marilyn Gaston and Mary Lou Andersen brought that with them to the Bureau.

Gaston, a pediatrician, came to the Bureau as its director in 1991 from the National Institutes of Health. She found a centrally controlled set of programs being managed aggressively, like a business with a bottom line. She quickly saw that she was bringing a new approach to management (an open, participatory model) and a new strategic focus (the result we deliver is better health).

**Figure 8.1: Time Line of the 100%/0 Campaign: From Leadership Intent to National Movement**

| | | 1997 | 1998 | 1999 | 2000 | 2001 | 2002 |
|---|---|---|---|---|---|---|---|
| | | | Bureau's Leadership Team in Action | | | | |
| | 1. Create open space for leadership | Latent, hidden leadership called forth. | "Just Do It" group forms and recruits. | The 100%/0 leadership team in place. | | | |
| | 2. Create a campaign | | | Game plan developed for a campaign. | Bold goal set: Enroll 500 communities. | | |
| Six Types of Campaign Work Carried Out | 3. Partner with benchmarks of the vision | | | Leaders of Buncombe and Hillsborough join campaign as benchmarks. | New community benchmarks emerge around campaign events. | | |
| | 4. Partner with national networks to extend reach | | | Performance partnerships and alliances formed. | Performance partnership concept wins federal business award. | | |
| | 5. Enroll communities in action | | | First two pacing events: PCAs* and GHPC.** | National and local pacing events used to enroll 500 communities and accelerate progress to 100%/0. | | |
| | 6. Form a national movement | | | | | | Four new national enterprises form to assume leadership and carry 100%/0 campaign forward. |

\* PCAs = State Primary Care Associations
\** GHPC = Georgia Health Policy Center

"I found the Bureau being managed as a business, to the bottom line. The mission was to increase access to care. Performance was the number of community health centers funded, dollars spent, number of patients served. I appreciated this discipline and structure. It worked. I wanted to continue that. Yet, I felt I brought something different and wanted to see something added. I was about people's health. I brought a clinical perspective. I added 'and improve health outcomes' to the mission. I called the centers 'healing centers.' I put primary care in the name of the Bureau to have a broader view than programs and centers. I added the motto, 'The people we serve, the people we are.'"

In the mid-'90s, Gaston began talking about the "safety net we needed vs. the safety net we had." She wanted to describe the total need and the gap in order to introduce the issue into the policy-making process and the program management system.

"In speeches to the National Association of Community Health Centers, in meetings with my executive team, I began to ask about our 'penetration' into the need out there. I asked my managers to tell me not only how many we see, but also how many we need to be seeing. I asked them to give me a system for monitoring the unmet need. I wanted to be able to explain our penetration into the universe of need and show what it would take to serve everyone in need."

Her executive team did not leap into the open space she was trying to create for leadership.

"Whenever we would set program goals, the staff would avoid the gap and penetration issue. Instead I got, 'last year we served x, next year we will serve x plus a few more.' They would not say how many they wanted to serve. When I asked for bold goals, I got the number they thought they would have funding to serve in five years."

Gaston also wanted to go "beyond access to success." She called for action to eliminate health status disparities.

"In 1994, part of the Clinton administration's mission was stated as: 'reduce health status disparities.' That is not good enough. There is no urgency or call to action in 'reduce.' I had the Bureau push 'eliminate.' We want the nation to eliminate disparities. We sold it, first to Dr. Claude Earl Fox, the HRSA administrator, and then to Dr. David Satcher, the surgeon general. When people would complain that 'eliminate' is too bold, too unrealistic, I would ask 'what is the level of disparity you are willing to live with?' ...

"In 1997 and 1998, 'eliminate disparities' took on new meaning for me. Eliminating disparities was viewed by many in Washington as impossible. But I visited communities that were taking specific disparities and eliminating them! Low birth weight of African American babies vs. white babies, teen pregnancy in low-income schools vs. upper-income neighborhoods. We could show it can be done, people are doing it. That gave me inspiration and courage."

Regan Crump

In 1997, Andersen had arrived at the Bureau to be the deputy director. Then 67 years old, Andersen had been in the federal government since the mid-1970s. Early in her career, she was responsible for taking federal health programs into Appalachia and West Virginia. She found she had a knack for pulling all the pieces together on the ground: "In three years we opened 27 health clinics in West Virginia. In those days we integrated services and did it at the community level." A natural community organizer, she believed in community-based organizations and health care as the keys to social justice. She believed the way to get things done was to get things done. "Just do it" was her favorite expression.

Gaston and Andersen both were at points where they could see the time when their federal careers would end. (Andersen would retire in 1999 but continue to work as a consultant to HRSA through 2001. Gaston would retire in January 2002.) Throughout 1997, they discussed what their legacy would be. They asked who would be the future stewards of the program tradition and the future leaders of the more ambitious interpretation of the mission? They wanted to leave with the right mission and the right people in place.

Encouraged by the experiences of the Food and Drug Administration, they put in place a leadership development opportunity for the staff, a 12-month program run by the Council for Excellence in Government (CEG). A group of 20 to 30 mid-level managers spent one to three days a month in work sessions and visiting public and private organizations that are benchmarks of excellence. Experienced coaches guide participants in developing leadership behavior, and each participant takes on a leadership project.

Andersen saw the program as a strategic step. It gave her and Gaston access to staff that they couldn't easily reach by going through the line. Andersen saw Gaston's executive team as being in the old command and control school of management and resistant to her vision and requests. CEG

Rick Wilk

was an opportunity to engage another level of potential leadership. "We hand selected the participants. These were the future stars, usually deputies to the executive team. We wanted them to break free, and they did." The first class of 20 middle-level managers started late in 1997.

Much of leadership practice is sensing and encouraging the leadership of others. Andersen was very good at seeing and cultivating leadership.

She listened to staff. Early in 1997, she and Ronda Hughes, her special assistant, were planning the retreat where the Bureau executive team would set goals with performance measures and targets. Andersen asked, "What should be our target for an increase in the number of people served?" Hughes made a provocative response: "Our target goal should be 100 percent access." She then explained, "Our mission means we are responsible for all 45 million in need, not just the 9 million our programs reach. The strategic plan should also be about how we serve the 35 to 40 million our programs are not reaching!"

Andersen's immediate reaction was, "Are you crazy? Where are we going to get the extra billions of dollars to do that?" But her community organizer instincts told her that Hughes had taken Gaston's vision and quantified it as a motto she could work with: 100% access! "I knew this would not get far with the executive team. I needed to find some people to play with it and get excited about it first. I needed to know what the heck I was talking about." Andersen talked with mid-level managers in the Bureau she thought might find the idea interesting. Not only was there excitement about the idea, but many asserted that achieving 100% access was plausible, if attempted at the community level. Their experiences had given them confidence that communities could organize and create great safety nets around and beyond the federal and state programs available to them.

In addition to listening, Andersen challenged staff. Early in 1998, several CEG fellows asked her to help them collaborate on their CEG projects. "A number of the CEG fellows came to me. They were antsy to do something. I offered to convene them in my office if they were ready to have a serious conversation. They sure were ready." Andersen invited eight to 10 fellows and mid-level managers to her office for weekly meetings. Participation was voluntary. Several dropped out and others were invited. A core group quickly formed its own unique identity as the "Just Do It" group.

"Mary Lou asked us to discuss what we thought about the direction of the Bureau. We decided we stood for 100%/0. We wanted to use our programs as platforms from which to realize that vision. How do you do that? How can we work together? 'Just Do It' enabled us to refine our message and to figure out how to use our programs, our every day work, as platforms to create 100%/0." (Chuck Van Anden)

Jim Macrae

"Mary Lou convened us and urged us to go into action. Her charge was 'just do it.' Chuck Van Anden brought Nike 'Just Do It' hats to the next meeting. We became the 'Just Do It' group and agreed to take off our program hats and wear our 'Just Do It' hats when we were together. We wouldn't relate to our division, office, or branch." (Regan Crump)

"We left our program agendas at the door. We took off our program hats and became the 'Just Do It' group. We figured out how to take a big concept into action. For me the ideas were: communities can do it, communities can take control, communities can make a difference. I always believed it. Just give them courage. I came into government believing in community action, the power of people." (Jim Macrae)

It turned out that 100% access and 0 disparities were visions of the future they all felt they were called to make happen.

By expressing intent, Gaston and Andersen were finding others ready to collaborate. They were also uncovering assets they didn't know existed. An interesting example is Rick Wilk, who was in the Chicago regional office and, in a sense, out of sight, below the surface. He soon emerged as one of the campaign leaders. He brought to the team experiences and a method that the team could use.

"The CEG fellow program put me with and in front of people who were doing the mission work. This was important to me because I was out in the regional office and had no contact with headquarters.

"Early on I was one of two people selected by the class to present projects to Dr. Gaston. My CEG project was 'creating affiliations between hospitals and health centers to generate more center capacity and more access to care.' I have created these affiliations in the past, and each one generated 5,000 new people getting care with no additional federal grants! That's equivalent to putting 3 FTE physicians in the poverty community. The hospitals find it in their best interest to put in money and physicians, and to donate space, equipment, and services. Their charity care costs go down. It's a win/win deal.

"The way the Bureau usually gets more access is to hand out more grants. My message to Dr. Gaston was, 'I can get a large number of people in a community access without having to give a grant.' I know I can do it because I have done it in several communities. Right now my current workload in grant administration prevents me from putting time into forming these affiliations. Mary Lou said, 'We have to do something about this.' Soon I was reassigned to Jim Macrae and told to work on the hospital/health center affiliations as one approach to achieving 100% access.

"CEG was an incredible personal development experience for me. It was an opportunity for me, after doing the same administrative work for seven years, to grow. I learned you can do bigger work than just the tasks you are assigned. If you work bigger, it leads to greater satisfaction and more opportunity for advancement, and you see greater things happen. And the best part is that it's a lot of fun."

Wilk's advocacy and experience had a big impact on the people playing with 100% access. His personal experience with a very simple type of restructuring generated more access, more primary care access, and more resources for health centers. Here were a set of relevant experiences as well as interest buried deep in the Bureau/HRSA organization, and Gaston and Andersen created the open space for them to surface.

At the beginning of 1998, there were a few individuals with ideas and vision. During the year they became the "Just Do It" group, recruiting and attracting a core team of 10. By early 1999, they were a united force, a broader 100%/0 leadership team with a game plan ready to launch a national campaign.

# Creating a Campaign (1998–1999)

The "Just Do It" group saw itself taking on something big and important. With members meeting weekly and interacting daily, the purpose to be pursued was quickly articulated. It had three important attributes:

## Bold, Audacious Goals: The Engine of Leadership

Bold national goals startle and draw resistance in organizations. Introducing them takes courage and the willingness to deal productively with the resistance. The resistance is natural. Bold national goals always define a kind of performance that managers do not want to be accountable for, and often defy conventional wisdom.

In the Bureau, conventional wisdom was against 100%/0. The prevailing view was that 100% access called for more federal funding. Congress would have to give an additional $4 to $5 billion to the health center program to cover all the uninsured. That was not going to happen. Most felt the real solution was universal insurance coverage. The Clinton administration had failed to get health care reform in its first term and that was a dead topic. How the nation closes the gap in access to health care was considered a policy issue beyond the domain of the Bureau. The conventional wisdom said there was nothing to be done by the Bureau.

The campaign goals also went far beyond the program goals the Bureau managers and staff traditionally set, ones they could deliver with the program resources for which they were given responsibility. For example, developing so many new center grantees and National Health Service Corps (NHSC) placement sites. The 100%/0 team was making itself accountable on goals for which it did not have the required resources and was committing to find and secure those resources. That was a different kind of work than the traditional grant and program administration of the Bureau.

In May 1999, the 100%/0 team presented its goals to the Bureau executives and managers in the strategic planning process. The group was startled by these goals and resisted them. "Some felt that it was imprudent to set such ambitious goals, others felt it was not appropriate work for the Bureau. They were being honest and protective of Dr. Gaston and the Bureau." (Regan Crump)

Reasonable counter proposals were made by staff. The first was to move to a pilot approach, which involved selecting two cities and focusing on them, then doing a demonstration and evaluating it to show it can be done. Another proposal was to focus on the 10 neediest communities. The team saw these reasonable goals taking them down a different path into project management. They acknowledged the advice but stayed committed to enrolling 500 communities.

The campaign goal eventually became part of the Bureau's strategic plan. The team gained support within the executive team by promising to increase access to primary care by making relatively small investments in community development. They were promising to deliver more communities ready to apply for CHC grants and NHSC placements. The team was learning how to run the campaign to produce results that Bureau divisions and offices valued *and* perform on campaign goals at the same time.

- *It's 100% access and it's 0 health status disparities.* In the beginning it was just 100% access. Generally, team members could see how to increase access: more doctors, more clinics, more outreach, more cultural competence, all done through financial restructuring. Eliminating disparities, though, always brought people up short. That seemed harder to achieve because of issues of lifestyle, race, cultural differences, and poverty. Gaston asked that the campaign and the team work with communities to tackle disparities. The team was ready for that and agreed.
- *100%/0 can be achieved by communities today.* Gaston asserted that achieving 100%/0 was a matter of political will in communities, not one of resources or new federal programs. "I know communities can do this because I have been out there and I have seen some of them doing it. If a few can do it, the others can. This is an issue of political will." This sounded right to everyone in the "Just Do It" group—to some, because it just had to be done; to others, because they had experiences with communities similar to Gaston's.
- *It relies on evidence and data.* Gaston was constantly calling for examples backed up with data. Over time, as she became the leading public figure and spokesperson for 100%/0, she became more and more insistent on being able to present evidence. Often she would draw a line in the sand, preventing a desired event from happening or refusing to make a requested speech unless someone came up with examples she could use. The ability to track community progress and describe the results achieved by communities in action became a major priority of the campaign.

The game plan was simple: *Ask communities to do it and then inspire and guide them by showing them other communities that had done it.* The game plan had three important elements: a bold goal with a performance measure, replication of what works, and network partnerships for reach.

It took a lot of conversation to formulate a goal that was bold and audacious for the team's circumstances. The goal they came up with at first looked impossible: *Enroll 500 communities and accelerate their progress to 100%/0 by 2001.* The group constantly asked itself: How do we measure success on that goal? How do we track progress?

Chuck Van Anden of the NHSC had been assessing community experiences with Corps placements and believed he had seen communities transform health care. He accepted the challenge of translating the campaign vision and goal into a measurement system. He came up with a 10-step scale that became an important tool for articulating goals, managing the campaign, and, later, creating performance agreements with national partners.

The 10 steps defined a generic community development process. Each step was a milestone that a community was expected to achieve in building its 100%/0 delivery system.

The campaign team estimated that the country consisted of 3,000 communities. (There are about 3,000 counties in the country and 2,000 federally designated health profession shortage areas, many of them counties.) The vision of the 100%/0 campaign was now articulated as 3,000 communities across the country moving through the 10 steps. The goal was to have 500 communities being tracked on the scale in three years. Figure 8.2 identifies the 10 steps and illustrates how the scale was used to report campaign progress.

The second element of the game plan was an approach to replication of what works. Experience shows that it takes about four years for a community to move from step 1 to step 10. The campaign aimed to accelerate that rate in each community. The team believed it could help communities move through each stage fast by linking them to a network of successful communities for inspiration and guidance.

The breakthrough idea of the team is that it would first replicate the leadership behind models that work and expect the models themselves to be greatly adapted to local circumstances.

**Figure 8.2: 100%/0 Campaign Performance on 10-Step Scale**
(As reported to the administrator of the Health Resources and Services Administration, September 2001)

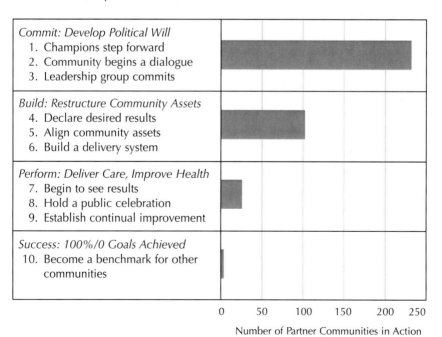

Commit: Develop Political Will
  1. Champions step forward
  2. Community begins a dialogue
  3. Leadership group commits

Build: Restructure Community Assets
  4. Declare desired results
  5. Align community assets
  6. Build a delivery system

Perform: Deliver Care, Improve Health
  7. Begin to see results
  8. Hold a public celebration
  9. Establish continual improvement

Success: 100%/0 Goals Achieved
  10. Become a benchmark for other
      communities

0     50     100     150     200     250

Number of Partner Communities in Action

Dennis Wagner

Replication was a concept that the team had experience with. The Bureau had created an annual innovation award program, called Models That Work, to identify and spread successful community health projects. The team understood that social innovations and best practices were rarely replicated on a large scale. Innovations did not transfer successfully because the passion and commitment that generated them were not present in the adopting community. The "Just Do It" group believed that while a model of success was a useful blueprint, it was the leadership that had to be replicated. They concluded they had to identify and work with leaders in each community. They would use models that work to stimulate interest, to inspire, and to guide. They would use the leaders from successful communities as role models and teachers.

The third element, network partnerships, came from outside the Bureau. The "Just Do It" group had to figure out how to reach and engage 500 communities quickly and 3,000 communities in the long run. They had no staff or budget for this work. The answer was to leverage themselves through networks. Ask organizations with networks reaching into many communities to use these channels and relationships to enroll communities in the campaign. That answer came to them from another federal agency.

In the fall of 1998, the group met Dennis Wagner. An expert in social marketing from the Environmental Protection Agency, Wagner had experience with national campaigns to achieve national goals that were not backed by legislated mandates or funded programs.

Gaston and Andersen recruited Wagner to lead a social marketing campaign for 100%/0. He joined the Bureau and the campaign team in December 1998 as the "Just Do It" group was becoming the 100%/0 team. Wagner introduced a set of methods and principles that would become an important part of the 100%/0 game plan. The four most dramatic were:

- Extraordinary results flow from public commitment to bold goals.
- Partnership networks dramatically extend reach and influence.
- Results are achieved by being tight about the what and loose about the how.
- Work is generating commitments through "requests" and "offers."

Using a simple communication model, Wagner showed how one person could reach millions by enrolling partners that controlled access to networks.

The campaign could use the communication channels of national membership organizations to reach leaders in every community. For example, a national organization such as the United Way had chapters in 50 states and every community. This approach addressed the "Just Do It" group's issue of reach. Here was a method for reaching 3,000 communities. And the partnership approach seemed more feasible than the program and project activity orientation that kept surfacing within the Bureau.

Partnering with trusted sources was a key to campaign success. Moving target audiences requires collaboration with multiple respected sources. Target audiences usually need to hear information or requests for action a number of times from a number of trusted sources before they act. Repetition and reinforcement by multiple sources increase the likelihood of action.

Going into 1999, the team was starting to make the campaign fully operational. That involved two additional stages of intensive work: creating the partnership networks of national organizations and communities, and finding the benchmark communities that show it can be done.

# Partnering with Benchmarks of the Vision (1999–2001)

A good route to success is to find out what works and do more of it. One of the most important quests of the 100%/0 team was to find examples of communities that have put in place 100% access delivery systems. The team saw that it was looking to set benchmarks for three dimensions of success:

- The service delivery system and its performance
- The process and time line the community used to build the system
- The leadership that caused it to happen

The intent was to develop a relationship with the benchmark leaders and showcase them to other communities.

The first two benchmark models came to the attention of the 100%/0 team through the Harvard Innovations in Government Award program: Hillsborough County and Buncombe County. They were as different as night and day in their origins and delivery models, yet similar and powerful in the results they produced. Both could show "better health for more people for less money" (Hillsborough's motto).

Hillsborough responded to a county financial crisis and involved a political campaign to get a sales tax passed. With elected officials and county government leading the effort, Hillsborough used a new sales tax to put in place a major delivery system reform that was organized as a health care enrollment plan and managed by county government.

The Buncombe County program emerged from a long-term concern for citizens who were underserved. Its guiding force was leadership from the physician sector. Planning and implementation grants from the Robert Wood Johnson Foundation helped launch the effort. Buncombe County saw its health care sectors self-organize into an integrated delivery system with a physician-led, "better organized charity care" program as the catalyst and the glue. Both Buncombe and Hillsborough established collaborative planning processes that involved all key players and sectors.

These two models and their differences were exciting to the 100%/0 team. They demonstrated that the work could be done, validated the process described in the 10-step scale, and proved there was more than one way for communities to do this work. The nature of these cases and the work with the leadership behind them profoundly affected the team and helped shape the method and direction of the campaign.

## Alan McKenzie and the Buncombe County Medical Society

Alan McKenzie

February 1999 was an important moment for the team. Four people from the 100%/0 team visited Buncombe County and had the team's first encounter with a full-scale, well-documented community 100%/0 delivery system. Having read a brief description of Buncombe County's Project Access in a description of the 1999 Harvard Innovations in Government Award winners, the team called to arrange a site visit because it sounded too good to be true. Project Access was a charity care program run by Buncombe County Medical Society as well as an organizing force for, and a component of, a comprehensive, integrated delivery system.

The Medical Society had created a physician-financed health care plan for specialty service for the uninsured. This initiative provided easy access to between $3 and $4 million in donated services each year. It took the charity care of individual physicians and organized it into a health care system program. The leadership of Project Access then used the charity care program to organize with other players a comprehensive set of primary care, secondary care, pharmaceutical, and hospital services. That collaboration enabled Buncombe County to serve the 18,000 residents who were uninsured and whose income was under 200 percent of the federal poverty level.

Later, the team learned that a year earlier the Innovations Award site evaluator had expressed the same excitement:

"In the Innovations application, Project Access is presented as an attempt to provide health care for uninsured patients in Buncombe County, North Carolina, through uncompensated care volunteered by the physician members of the Buncombe County Medical Society. While that presentation is entirely accurate, the site visit uncovered a much more ambitious goal— to build an integrated system of care for all the citizens of Buncombe County. Project Access has achieved much of this aim.... With a combination of positive incentives, subtle sanctions, keen political savvy, and meticulous management, the Buncombe County Program has achieved an admirable local version of health reform while avoiding the fatal pitfalls that have swamped more prominent public and private attempts to change health systems....I know of no other community where so much has been achieved." (Miles Shore, MD, Harvard University, Site Evaluator's Report to Selection Committee, July 1998)

The site visit boosted the work of the 100%/0 team. It revealed to the team how leadership was a constant force in developing an integrated delivery system and showed how these systems could be made sustainable. It gave the team a vivid picture of what the system looks like. Finally, the site visit led to a major partnership for replication.

The team went to Buncombe looking for a successful model to replicate. With that in mind, the team was excited by the widespread ownership it found on-site. Physicians, pharmacists, county executives, county health department, community health center director—all expressed compelling stories about their participation in Project Access. The team could see what a powerful experience it would be for a group from another community to visit Buncombe.

While on-site, the team explored with McKenzie his interest in having Buncombe County and Project Access play a prominent national role in the 100%/0 campaign. Given his responsibilities as executive director of the Medical Society and manager of Project Access, this was not a casual decision to make, but he agreed.

The Bureau's team was nervous about how to follow through. They had no budget with which to get McKenzie involved and no program to plug him into. One member summed up the team's conclusion: "If we are for 100%/0 and we can't figure out a way to partner with this guy and this community, we might as well quit." The team did figure out a way, though. In the fall of 1999, the Buncombe County Medical Society signed a cooperative agreement to be a performance partner with the Bureau. McKenzie agreed to enroll 45 communities over three years and to move them along the 10-step scale as they implemented their own adaptation of Project Access. McKenzie went on to play three roles in the campaign. He presented the Project Access story at state and national meetings as a 100%/0 model that works, he signed up communities to implement Project Access and coached them through the 10 steps, and he became a leader of the national 100%/0 campaign team.

The first community to replicate Buncombe County's Project Access was Wichita, Kansas. Led by Dr. Paul Uhlig, a local surgeon, this replication happened quickly. Nine months after contacting McKenzie and visiting Buncombe County, Wichita Project Access was seeing patients. In 2001, McKenzie had hired staff to handle all the requests for technical assistance. By the end of the year, the Buncombe County Medical Society was working with 50 communities and approximately 21 had begun to see patients. In 2002, the replication effort was transferred to the new, not-for-profit American Project Access Network.

## Phyllis Busansky, Cretta Johnson, Pat Bean, and Hillsborough County, Florida

Phyllis Busansky

The second model that came to the team's attention was Hillsborough County's health care plan. In addition to the Harvard Innovations in Government Award, it had received the Bureau's annual Models That Work competitive award.

An impressive plan, it replaced a fragmented, short-term, emergency-driven delivery system in financial crisis with a comprehensive, coordinated, managed care network. Hillsborough HealthCare is a comprehensive plan for indigent county residents who do not qualify for other coverage. The program is administered by the county's Department of Health and Social Services. Several networks—made up of primary care physicians, specialist, and hospitals—deliver the services. The program began in 1992, financed by property tax and a special sales tax. Of the estimated 39,000 potential enrollees, the program was seeing 34,000 by 1998.

Being a formal county government program, its performance and costs are well documented. Performance measures are tracked and audited.

# Better Health for More People for Less Money: The Hillsborough County Example

Integrated community health care systems can demonstrate better health for more people for less money. Hillsborough HealthCare of Hillsborough County, Florida, reported the following remarkable results in its 1998 annual report.

## The System
- Supported by a sustainable source of funding: a local option local sales tax of up to one-half of one cent, authorized by the state legislature and enacted by the county in 1991, along with $26.8 million per year in property taxes as mandated by the State of Florida for indigent care.
- Increased the number of health clinics (access points) from four to 12, and the number of people served from 15,000 to 28,000.
- Replaced a fragmented, short-term, emergency-driven delivery system with a comprehensive, coordinated, and managed continuum of care networks.
- Increased the number of participating hospitals from three to five, and established a panel of referral specialists where none had existed.

## The Results
- Reduced costs, per member per month, from $600 to $202 by 1997.
- Reduced the average length of hospital stay from 10.2 days before the plan to 5.1 days.
- Reduced the average number of admissions per thousand patients from 133.6 during the first year to12.4 for the year 1997.
- Saved $10 million in emergency room diversions since inception.
- Served twice as many people and spent $47 million doing so in 1997, even though in 1990 costs had been projected to rise from $35 million to $105 million by then.
- Changed the predominant reason for hospital admissions, in just four years, from "avoidable admissions" to those that are typical for the general population.
- Changed the health status of the served population, as evidenced by fewer hospital admissions for preventable conditions, for example:

|  | Percent of all Admissions | |
|  | 1992/93 | 1996/97 |
| --- | --- | --- |
| Diabetes | 26% | 3% |
| Gall Bladder | 10% | 2% |
| Asthma | 9% | 1% |

- Lowered the sales tax from one-half of one cent to one-quarter of one cent, reflecting the cost controls in place with a full access system.

Operating since 1992, the managed care network had a track record of remarkable results in both reducing costs and improving health.

In May 1999, the team invited Cretta Johnson, director of the program, to one of its first 100%/0 enrollment events. Over the next 18 months, Johnson presented the Hillsborough model at several events. In April 2000, Patricia Bean, deputy county administrator and one of the leaders in developing Hillsborough HealthCare, hosted a meeting of county commissioners from around the country to showcase the plan.

With Hillsborough, the 100%/0 team had a powerful example of a model that works. The template of system operations and performance was established. Hillsborough proved a community could do it on its own, could produce big system changes without the federal government. It had eloquent spokespersons in Johnson and Bean to describe how the process works.

But something was missing. Lacking was a good picture of the leadership force or the steps the community went through. With a "how to do it" that sounded like "first pass a sales tax, then build a health care plan," the campaign team found most audiences dismissive. One community developer put it this way: "If I had all that money, I could build a great health care system, too!" People saw the remarkable system but then dismissed any possibility that they could build one like it. They considered the sales tax initiative that made restructuring possible to be something that just happened. The idea of creating their own tax or alternative financing was beyond most people's imagination. The team felt it had to find the people who got the local sales tax in place and showcase them.

In June 2000, the 100%/0 team met the person who led the sales tax campaign, Phyllis Busansky, a former elected county commissioner. One of the champions and leaders of the two-year campaign, she was retired from politics and consulting.

Busansky described how the Hillsborough plan grew out of the financial crisis the county government faced. Florida county governments are responsible for indigent care. In the late 1980s, Hillsborough's bill was about $30 million a year and was growing at about 20 percent a year. The cost would soon exceed its property tax cap. Busansky organized a coalition to develop a solution and then launched a political campaign to put it in place. The sales tax solution required state legislature action, and they were turned down once before they finally got it. She was one of the seven county commissioners who voted for the sales tax; the one who did not vote for it was the only commissioner not to be reelected.

Busansky immediately saw Hillsborough as a model for 100%/0. She argued that, for most communities, creating 100%/0 was a matter of creating political will, and they could do that by organizing a local campaign. She believed that moving to 100%/0 required the 3 p's: "It's people, politicians, and press. You need everyone to see that this works for them. You have to realize that the politicians care and will respond. They need to hear simple things they can do and see that the voters are behind it. If you have the people, the politicians will act. You can't make this happen without local government behind it. And finally you need to involve the media. This has to be out in everyone's face. To get change you have to keep it in the public eye. Tell the press what you are trying to make happen and create events they can report on."

Busansky felt that regardless of what model a community adopted, the development of political will had to happen. Elected officials can be a leadership force and a receptive audience in a campaign to create a 100%/0 delivery system. The Bureau awarded Busansky a small contract to provide technical assistance to the political leadership in up to eight communities. She became a performance partner with the campaign and soon became a national leader in the100%/0 campaign.

### Models That Work: The Currency of the Campaign

As the campaign carried out events in 2000 and 2001, benchmark models began to proliferate. Benchmarks were continually being added to the campaign portfolio. They included financing methods such as the triple payer insurance plan of Muskegon County, Michigan, that provided coverage for employees of small businesses. They included examples of strategic elements of an integrated system such as the Jessie Tree in Galveston, Texas, a central safety net referral and assistance system.

The campaign comes alive whenever people experience successful models and the leadership behind them. Therefore, the primary campaign communication tactic is a call-to-action event where communities, success models, and coaches all come together to generate commitments and make deals. The next two sections describe how the models that work were brought to communities.

# Partnering with National Networks to Extend Reach (1999–2000)

In January 1999, the 100%/0 team began to approach national organizations that had the potential to be partners. The strategy was to create a network of special purpose networks willing, for whatever reason, to also support the 100%/0 campaign. The 100%/0 team found three sources of networks to advance the campaign: those associated with federal programs, national membership organizations, and organizations with similar access missions.

## Using Programs as Campaign Platforms

Managers on the team found that their own operations contained networks that could be engaged in this work. Grant activity and contractor initiatives that reached into many communities could be leveraged. It took a special effort to create the partnership relationship. In principle the campaign activity piggybacks on resources being spent anyway for other purposes. The managers found they had some discretion to follow this strategy.

The Bureau's Office of State and National Programs (OSNP), managed by Jim Macrae, was responsible for, among other things, support grants to state primary care associations (PCAs). Their members were primary care centers in communities throughout the state. This network of state advocates of primary care for the poor was a natural group to be enrolling communities in 100%/0. Moreover, in 1999 OSNP was about to fund approximately half the PCAs to hire community developers. The objective was to help communities meet the conditions necessary to apply for health center grants and NHSC placements. Macrae had the insight that this site development work would put them in underserved communities with community leaders who could also lead a 100%/0 transformation. It might be possible to ask the community developers to enroll the communities they work with in 100%/0 if it helped them accomplish their site development agenda.

This work could not be mandated by OSNP because it was not part of the original intent of the grant funding. But it might be possible to enroll the community developers by asking. This turned out to be the case. An enrolling meeting was held in May 1999 to secure PCA and community developer commitments to bring the communities they worked with into the campaign.

In the spring of 1999, Macrae declared to the team that the goal of 500 communities enrolled was achievable. If the 26 states with community developers each were to get 10, that would bring progress toward the goal to the halfway mark. It was becoming clear to the team that large numbers of communities could be engaged by networks natural to their agency. This same approach was used by Van Anden with the NHSC site development and later by Dr. Eric Baumgartner with the Community Access Program.

## Developing Performance Partnerships

The more networks the team could engage, the more points of influence could be turned on in any one community. With so many stakeholders in any community's health care system, hundreds of possible local champions could be engaged. The list included physicians' organizations, hospitals, pharmacists, unions, local elected officials, local government managers, and the faith community. Most local organizations and professionals belong to several national membership organizations. One of Wagner's responsibilities was to find national organizations that had members or affiliates in hundreds or thousands of communities and sign them up as partners.

The task was to find one or more people in the national membership organization who were willing to be a champion for enrolling communities. Once a champion was found, Wagner would develop a "performance contract" and enter into what he called a "performance partnership." The Bureau would provide $50,000 to $100,000 per year under a cooperative agreement to cover staff costs in working through its channels to enroll and assist communities. The organization would enter into a three-year agreement to enroll, for example, 25 communities and have them move through the 10-step scale at a specified rate. The partner would commit to performance targets and to report progress quarterly using the 10-step scale. As the communities reached step 7, the partner would report on the number of people given new access to comprehensive services and the number of dollars committed to providing access.

A community reaching step 7 was expected to generate $1 million to $100 million worth of new access depending on its size. The return on investment was extraordinary. Rather than relying on direct federal appropriation, communities were restructuring existing assets to increase access to primary care for the underserved. Very small investments in social marketing by the Bureau triggered large community reinvestments in access to care.

In 1999, Wagner put in place eight formal performance partnerships. Four of the partnerships were with national membership organizations whose members were in local communities and who had a professional interest in health care systems. They represented philanthropy, local elected officials, local government executives, and a health care specialty:
- United Way of America
- International City and County Managers Association
- National Association of Counties
- American Academy of Pediatrics

Dr. Eric Baumgartner

# The Bureau: A Platform for Reaching National Goals

The Bureau of Primary Health Care is one of four bureaus in the Health Resources and Services Administration (of the Department of Health and Human Services).

## The Health Access Safety Net Program

For the period covered by this report (1998–2001), the two cornerstone programs of the Bureau were the community health centers (CHC) program and the National Health Services Corps (NHSC). Both bring medical professionals into poor and underserved communities. They deliver comprehensive preventative and primary care services to the neediest, poorest, and sickest patients in rural and inner city areas. Both have become successful and effective programs. They are important elements of the nation's health care safety net for the poor.

## Program Scale

The Bureau manages a $1 billion grant program supporting approximately 650 community health and migrant health centers that serve 9 million people each year (40 percent are uninsured and 70 percent are below the poverty level). Grants go to community-based organizations governed by community boards. The centers provide primary and preventive health care services in designated "medically underserved" areas where income, geography, and culture limit access for vulnerable populations. About 4,500 physicians work in health centers in our neediest communities.

NHSC places medical professionals in underserved communities through scholarship and loan repayment agreements. About 2,500 professionals serve in these communities each year, and they commit to serve three years. Each year about 700 clinicians graduate and 600 to 700 are added. An estimated 21,000 alumni practice today.

## Infrastructure

A sophisticated infrastructure supports this service network. The National Association of Community Health Centers is the national trade association serving and representing the interests of America's community health centers. It is an effective developer and advocate of the federal program. Each state has a Primary Care Association (PCA), which is a membership association of all the federally funded health centers in the state. The PCAs receive federal grants to develop new sites and to improve the operations of centers. Grants are also made to state health organizations (primary care organizations) to assist in the development of need data and the designation of "medically underserved areas." The Bureau enters into cooperative agreements—with such national organizations as the National Governors Association and the National Conference of State Legislators—to transfer information and keep stakeholders informed. In addition, the Bureau manages center financing, pharmacy, technical assistance, and other support programs that assure a high-quality, sustainable primary care network.

Two of the performance partnerships were with organizations that had been funded by foundations to help communities develop their health care systems. Each had its own mission and set of relationships with many communities. The leaders of these efforts were very comfortable with the mission of 100%/0 and were excited about entering into a performance partnership:

- Coalition for Healthy Communities and Cities, Health Research & Educational Trust, American Hospital Association
- The Access Project, Brandeis University

And two other partnerships were with individuals who represented the first two benchmarks of 100%/0 community leadership:

- Alan McKenzie, president, Buncombe County Medical Society
- Phyllis Busansky, retired county commissioner, Hillsborough County

With McKenzie, the intent was to replicate the Buncombe County Medical Society's Project Access through the leadership of medical societies and physicians in partner communities. McKenzie had a template for an integrated delivery system and a process for creating it that other communities could follow. He committed to helping 45 communities. With Busansky, a prime mover in the creation of the Hillsborough model, the focus was on creating political will in local government for 100% access. She entered into a performance agreement to take eight communities through steps 1, 2, and 3 on the scale.

In September 2000, the Bureau's performance partnerships concept was one of six winners of the annual Business Solutions in the Public Interest Award given by the Council for Excellence in Government, *Government Executive* magazine, and the Office of Federal Procurement Policy (of the Office of Management and Budget). It honors agencies with innovative acquisition strategies that advance government management and performance. The Bureau was singled out because of the unique way it created partnerships to achieve its mission through social marketing. *Government Executive* described the program in its federal procurement review issue:

> "The Bureau of Primary Health Care's 100% Access and Zero Disparities campaign showcases how agencies are...taking advantage of partnerships with nonfederal entities. Upon discovering it was reaching just a quarter of the 43 million Americans who are underserved and underinsured for health care, the bureau had to find a way to reach nearly 33 million people without adding staff or budget. It is accomplishing the goal by identifying communities that have eliminated health disparities and guaranteed care to the underserved and matching them with communities in need of help. The Bureau funds efforts to replicate communities' successes, pairing civic leaders from a mentor community with those of a locality in need of assistance. The Bureau doesn't fully fund each effort. Rather, it has come to see

itself as part of a 'social marketing' effort, sharing the success of certain communities." (Anne Laurent, *Government Executive,* August 2000)

## Forming Alliances

Karen Minyard

The campaign team continually encountered organizations whose own mission and work made them natural allies for 100%/0. Some were willing to co-lead on the campaign and to use their programs and projects as campaign platforms. The alliances formed with no cost to the Bureau—a win/win relationship that extended the networks of the campaign and the alliance partners.

The most powerful alliance was formed with the Georgia Health Policy Center (GHPC) at Georgia State University. In 1997 GHPC was funded by the state at a million dollars per year to design and run Networks for Rural Health (NFRH). The program guides rural communities in Georgia through a comprehensive coalition-building effort in which they craft a health care system that works for community residents. NFRH's rural health "developers" coach community leaders through a disciplined process (seven well-defined steps) that systematically enables leadership and vision to surface, creates political will, develops knowledge, and builds infrastructure. As communities develop the social capital needed to make these changes, NFRH encourages them to "collaborate with neighboring communities" to make improvements that individual communities would be unable to accomplish. These multiple-community collaboratives are then able to acquire facilities and management information services that they could not otherwise afford. The result is integrated regional and local health care systems that provide greater access and deliver health status.

In the summer of 1999, the NFRH director, Karen Minyard, approached the 100%/0 campaign team to help her facilitate a two-day conference in which community teams from across Georgia would plan the transformation of their health care systems. This turned out to be an extraordinary event and a defining moment for the 100%/0 team. Here was someone running what was, in effect, a statewide campaign for 100%/0, and she had been doing it on the ground with dozens of rural Georgia communities since 1997. Karen Minyard became a co-leader in the national campaign. GHPC used its own resources to participate in 100%/0 events throughout the 1999–2001 period. GHPC also agreed to be the 100%/0 champion for communities in Georgia and to track their progress on the 100%/0 scale.

The Bureau's team went on to develop working relationships with other organizations deeply committed to increasing access. They included health care systems, such as Ascension Health Care and The Sisters of Mercy Hospital System, and large multi-community foundation demonstrations, such as The Community Care Network and Communities in Charge. In the end, the BPHC campaign team reached communities by using the channels of existing networks. Figure 8.3 illustrates the network of networks the team created to extend its reach.

**Figure 8.3: Partnering with National, Regional, and State Networks to Reach Community Leadership**

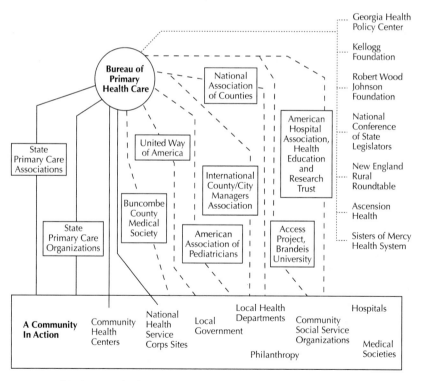

# Enrolling Communities in Action (1999 2001)

Dennis Wagner would say, "The work of the campaign is three things: making commitments ourselves, securing commitments from others, delivering on commitments. If you are not doing one of these three things, you are not doing the work." The route to success in the campaign is all about securing commitments. It is having a leadership group in the community commit to 100%/0 and then working with them as they generate the local commitments that take the community through each of the 10 developmental steps. Over three years, more than 500 community leadership groups were engaged in various ways to commit to 100%/0.

The 100%/0 leadership team used big, public events to generate commitments. Each event was designed to make deals up to and during the meeting. The team referred to them as "pacing events" and gave them names like A Call to Action. These events set the pace needed to achieve the goal of 500 communities in action by 2001. The events themselves were carefully paced to generate commitments and action.

Participants at an event were as few as 50, but typically around 200, with the most being 800 and 6,000. Events generally included four overlapping groups:

- People from communities in action or getting ready to take action
- Leaders from benchmark communities
- People from organizations that could provide assistance to the communities at each stage of development
- The national leadership team in a facilitative, coaching role

The team developed a method for making these events successful, called the campaign's "signature style." That style made these events unusual and exciting by almost everyone's experience. It was common for participants to comment: "I have never been to a meeting like this;" "I cannot believe you all are from the federal government;" "This meeting is the standard by which I want to run and judge the meetings I hold;" "This conference [June 2001, Washington, D.C.] is the gold standard for conferences;" or "This is how I want my organization to run events."

## Pacing Events Make Things Happen

The first two formative pacing events were held in 1999: the May event with the State Primary Care Association community developers and a September event with Georgia Health Policy Center's rural communities.

Over the next two years, 2000–2001, the team used more than two dozen events, an average of one a month. The more intense efforts are listed in Table 8.2. (These are distinct from the hundreds of events the partners

Donald Coleman

participated in as they spread the message and provided technical assistance.) They are organized into five types, showing the 100%/0 team s flexibility in seizing opportunity.

Three major national events gave the campaign nationwide attention and energy. Significant effort went into planning them. Each was well funded by the national partners, foundations, and the Bureau. The intent was to bring all partners together in person and in spirit. With dozens of national partners and hundreds of community partners, that means a lot of people. These three events engaged 300 people, then 800, and then 6,000, the last being a national teleconference with 190 participating sites.

Community call-to-action events were organized on both the community level and statewide. A community event was sponsored by the community itself with the intent to take all the stakeholders to a higher level of collaboration and progress on the 10-step scale. State organizations sponsored the state events and drew in large numbers of community teams. These were very effective in bringing communities into the campaign.

As the team gained experience with its approach, it realized that its partners traditionally held events each year that could be made into pacing events for the campaign. Usually they were annual learning and social networking conferences. It was easy to add the signature style of the campaign with its focus on action. The partner conferences in Table 8.2 were organized as pacing events with the campaign team facilitating the whole or major parts of the conference.

Finally, as the messaging and requests and offers became sharper, the team began to seek speaking engagements in forums that would provide access to potential community champions. Campaign presentations incorporating the signature style were made at conferences with strategic audiences.

## Creating the Signature Style of a Pacing Event

Pacing event participants secured commitments they needed for the next steps in their communities. Signature style became a way for the team to describe how to behave in meetings to get those results. They formed this style as they went from event to event.

**Table 8.2: Major 100%/0 Campaign Pacing Events**

| Type of Event | Date | Description |
|---|---|---|
| Formative Pacing Events | May 1999 | Community Development Conference with state primary care associations, 4H Center; Bethesda, Maryland |
| | September 1999 | Georgia Health Policy Center; Macon, Georgia |
| National 100%/0 Campaign Events | June 2000 | National conference of 300 people; Cambridge, Massachusetts |
| | June 2001 | Communities in Action, national conference of 800 people from several hundred partner communities; Washington, D.C. |
| | October 2001 | National videoconference on health status disparities with 6,000 participants at 190 sites across the country |
| Community Calls to Action | Fall 1999 | Community of Emanuel County, Georgia |
| | November 2000 | Community of Galveston, Texas |
| | Winter 2000–2001 | Community of Cleveland, Ohio |
| | January 2001 | Community of Northern New Mexico; Santa Fe, New Mexico |
| | March 2001 | Texas Community in Action Summit; Austin, Texas |
| | September 2001 | Community of St. Louis, Missouri |
| | October 2001 | Louisiana State Event; Baton Rouge, Louisiana |
| | December 2001 | Community of Akron, Ohio |
| Partner Events | April 2000 | National Association of Counties, annual event conducted as visit to the Hillsborough Health Plan; Tampa, Florida |
| | May 2000 | Community Access Program, Annual Grantee Conference, convening teams from grantee communities; Baltimore, Maryland |
| | April 2001 | Project Access PACE Conference; Asheville, North Carolina |
| | November 2001 | National Community Care Network Demonstration Program, annual conference; New Orleans, Louisiana |
| | November 2001 | 4th Annual New England Rural Health Roundtable Symposium; Merrimack, New Hampshire |

**Table 8.2: Major 100%/0 Campaign Pacing Events (continued)**

| Type of Event | Date | Description |
|---|---|---|
| Campaign Presentations to Strategic Audiences | September 1999 | Virginia Primary Care Association, annual meeting with keynote speaker Dennis Wagner |
| | November 1999 | Kansas Primary Care Association, with keynote speaker Dr. Donald Weaver |
| | July 2000 | Health Resources and Services Administration, Quality Conference with a session by Dennis Wagner; Vail, Colorado |
| | August 2000 | National Association of Community Health Centers, annual conference with keynote speaker Dr. Marilyn Gaston; Chicago, Illinois |
| | January 2001 | South Carolina Primary Care Association, annual meeting with keynote speaker Dr. Donald Weaver |
| | May 2001 | Society of Teachers of Family Medicine, annual conference with keynote speaker Dr. Marilyn Gaston |

The style they developed called for a highly interactive meeting designed to produce commitments. Usually the day before an event the team members on-site would meet with the organizers, the facilitators, and the benchmark leaders to review the signature style guide. A version of the guide is shown in Table 8.3.

Many of the critical elements of the style emerged from the two formative pacing events in 1999. The first was the meeting of the PCA community developers and directors on May 17 18. About 60 people met at the 4H Center in Bethesda, Maryland, at an event that began the process of developing the signature style.

A technique called effective questions was used to frame that meeting. (See Doug Krug and Ed Oakley, *"Enlightened Leadership: Getting to the Heart of Change."*) The question the meeting ran on was What can a PCA community developer do to enroll the communities they are working with into the 100%/0 campaign? All the interactions in the meeting were then viewed as conversations in which participants generated answers to that question.

The team introduced a generic model of an integrated delivery system, with primary care at the center rather than the hospital, and the 10-step

**Table 8.3: Signature Style for Community Call-to-Action Events   June 2001**

| | |
|---|---|
| **The meeting is interactive, with everyone in the room in a conversation for action.** | • Elicit the natural leader each person is by asking each person to assume that role for this event.<br>• Keep presentations short and crisp and ask speakers to speak in seven- to ten-minute blocks, followed by the audience working with what was heard.<br>• With everything needed for 100%/0 in the room, ask everyone in the room to be both faculty and student.<br>• Guide the conversations in the room with "effective questions."<br>• Create space for audience to engage in every presentation (What was said? What was heard? What was exciting? What insights did it provoke?...)<br>• Organize exercises in which participants share insights and intent, where affinity groups form to work, where people can make deals. |
| **All conversations are framed and paced to move the audience toward action on 100%/0.** | • Employ "framing," i.e., request from the audience the kind of listening that leads to action.<br>• Prepare "effective questions" and ask the audience to respond to them after each speaker. Avoid question and answer formats.<br>• Use "future newspaper headline" exercises to help groups define and express intent.<br>• Incorporate exercises to generate bold goals and commitments. Use pacing-event planning exercises to help groups move to action.<br>• Model effective expressions of commitment (action, result, date).<br>• Introduce "requests and offers" as a way to generate commitments and make deals in the room. Point to examples already happening in and around the event.<br>• Have people stand and express their commitments—and have others in positions of authority acknowledge them.<br>• Have resource organizations in the room ready to offer assistance. |
| **Participants self-organize into the conversations they are ready to have.** | • Use "open space" for participants to form around topics they define and want to work on (*Open Space Technology: A User's Guide,* Harrison Owen, 1997). Enable people to interact with each other.<br>• Plan traditional breakout sessions to give participants work time with the speakers. |

**Table 8.3: Signature Style for Community Call-to-Action Events    June 2001 (continued)**

| | |
|---|---|
| **Conversations are stimulated by examples of successful 100%/0 communities.** | Invite representatives of successful communities to be visiting coaches. Include successful leaders who can (1) inspire, (2) attest that transformation is possible, (3) show how to do it, and (4) form technical assistance relationships with communities in action. Use compelling video cases to showcase successful 100%/0 communities. (Contact Donald Coleman, Health Resources and Services Administration, Media Center.) |
| **Success is noticed and celebrated.** | Showcase leaders from other communities who have been successful. Bring in national and state leaders to hear and acknowledge community commitments, offer support, and declare success. Stimulate press coverage to bring the story of action to the community. Highlight the unique leadership nature of this work. Hold sessions for the audience on the nature of the leadership work involved using motivational speakers (such as Doug Krug, *Enlightened Leadership*). Secure commitments from visiting communities to organize future pacing events. |

development scale. With that as context, they introduced three of the early benchmark 100% leaders: McKenzie of Buncombe County, Johnson of Hillsborough County, and Uhlig of Wichita, Kansas, the first community to replicate Project Access. These 100%/0 community spokespersons proved to be powerful advocates simply by telling their leadership stories and describing the impact of the systems they created.

A national partner with resources to help communities move forward was in the room. The Access Project (different than Buncombe County's Project Access), based at Brandeis University, was funded by the Robert Wood Johnson Foundation at $10 million for four years to help communities protect and improve access to care for uninsured and underserved populations. Community champions left with a link to a helping resource.

A technique called open space was used to have meeting participants self-organize into work groups. (See *Open Space Technology; A User's Guide,* by Harrison Owen, Berrett-Koehler Publishers, 1997.) The open

---

### John Kotter on the Skill of Communicating Emotionally

People change what they do less because they are given *analysis* that shifts their *thinking* than because they are shown a *truth* that influences their *feelings*. This is especially so in large-scale organizational change  .

Change leaders make their points in ways that are emotionally engaging and compelling as possible.... They provide a means for the show to live on with physical objects that people see each day   or with vivid stories that are told and retold. But whatever the method, they supply valid ideas that go deeper than the conscious and analytic part of our brains   ideas with emotional impact.

From John P. Kotter and Dan S. Cohen, *The Heart of Change: Real-Life Stories of How People Change Their Organization* (Harvard Business School Press, 2002)

---

space technique introduced the idea that at a 100%/0 event, everyone is a speaker and a listener, a teacher and a student. The traditional professional meeting has the audience in a passive, listening role. A new dynamic was created with this technique, and the event was one large conversation.

In a session at the end of the event, participants were given an opportunity to make offers, requests, and commitments. As a voice of the campaign, Gaston joined this session and for 30 minutes received and acknowledged the commitments people made. This was an exciting, playful session with serious results. Several state groups challenged each other to a competition in enrolling communities. Community developers formed relationships with each other and with the resource people in the room.

While the 4H Center event enrolled people who would in turn enroll communities, the GHPC event later that year brought the community leadership groups themselves into the room. The program director, Minyard, brought from six to nine key stakeholders from each of over a dozen communities to Macon for two days to work on how they could transform their health care systems. Each community group included county executives, hospital administrators, providers, and citizens. She had several top state government health officials attending to hear from these communities how the state could help. A number of models-that-work speakers showed the community groups how their efforts could work.

The interactive style of the campaign was applied to this audience of 200. At one point the community groups, assisted by coaches and facilitators, spent significant blocks of time creating their own community vision and collaboration. They came back into the full session and shared their commitments with each other and state officials.

Minyard s event was able to accelerate the progress of a large number of rural communities. It created a conversation that began to align state government in support of these communities. Her convening of communities became a core part of the template for future 100% campaign pacing events.

## Understanding the Demand and Need for Pacing Events

Communities get stuck. Today, everyone agrees the health care system does not work and all the players want it to change. In every community, stakeholders are convening to fix whatever they can. But fixing calls for collaboration among parties that often have no history of collaboration. They lack the common vision that fosters it and the common language that enables it. Not surprisingly, these conversations become fragmented, settle on small projects, and eventually break down. Players have neither the time nor the patience for a process that takes time and patience. The campaign team found that many communities are willing and able to organize pacing events to get unstuck. The experience in Galveston, Texas, illustrates the situation that can create demand and the breakthrough that can result.

In 2000, Galveston s health care safety net was running out of money. They had to lower eligibility for specialty services from 100 percent of poverty to 17 percent. Leaders in the county government and the medical establishment sought advice from Phyllis Busansky. They were excited about moving forward to create a plan and a financing strategy organized around a sales tax, yet they had no plan. She suggested a community event, a call to action where they would unveil a plan. A three-day community event was scheduled for November of that year.

Just calling the event made things happen. Galveston had to come up with a plan and convene a community-wide public event. A task force was formed, scrambled to meet the deadline, and devised a financing solution of a 1 cent sales tax,  a penny for our health.  They saw that an intractable problem was not intractable. The 100%/0 team agreed to facilitate the event and ask Gaston, an assistant surgeon general, to come hear the plan. To have Gaston participate, the Galveston leaders had to agree to have a plan ready, convene the community, invite benchmark communities, and make the event a media event. The 100%/0 team arranged for other communities to attend and see a call-to-action event. The team arranged for models-that-work community leaders to attend and speak.

The day before the event, the task force had to present its sales tax plan to the city council. On the opening day of the conference, the Galveston County *Daily News* ran a lead story on the proposed sales tax, a new expense for residents. The next day, a second, more upbeat story appeared with a picture of Gaston and a front-page headline:  Official applauds county health care effort.  Gaston called Galveston a model for the nation. The next week, the paper endorsed the sales tax. The movement of the community from being stuck to being in action was captured in these three articles over a few days.

The pacing event produced a breakthrough for Galveston. On the second day, Gaston invited the leadership to come to a national event in Washington, D.C., in June 2001 to tell their story as a model for the nation. The 100%/0 team followed up. Donald Coleman of the Bureau s Media Center went to Galveston to produce a video about the initiative. The video was shown at the June 2001 event, and the Galveston team s work was celebrated. The national attention and support from November to June created energy and progress in Galveston.

## Increasing the Reach of the Campaign through Technology

The Bureau s Media Center, managed by Coleman, turned out to be one of those hidden assets that a campaign will uncover. His work had an increasingly powerful impact on the progress and effectiveness of the campaign.

Coleman stepped forward and made himself part of the 100%/0 team early in 2000:

> When I first heard 100%/0 I thought it was hogwash. I didn t hear what the team was trying to do. There were no facts or stories for me to hook onto. I was focused on supporting Dr. Gaston as she tried to inspire and rally the staff around the Bureau mission and plan. Then I was in a meeting that turned out to be a face off between the 100%/0 team and some of the Bureau staff. The team was talking about people getting health care and better health in every community. The staff was not responding. That got my attention. I envisioned women like my mother who had no guidance in making decisions about their health. My mother was not served well by the health care system. These women are without the knowledge to defend themselves.

> I began to ask  How can we do this campaign?  What are the visuals, what are the words we can give Dr. Gaston that will engage people? As I talked to the team and learned about the communities in action, it got clearer and clearer. This was about a revolution. We crafted Dr. Gaston s speeches and community story videos around the 100%/0 revolution in health care and used the song  Revolution. I went to the communities to videotape the community dynamics and the effect on the people. Visiting Sunset Park health system and clinic in Brooklyn was a big event for me. I could see the clinicians, the service, the people, and the difference it was making. We began to capture this story on video for presentations at con-

ferences and call-to-action meetings. The 100%/0 team stuck to its guns, and speaking this revolution became second nature to Dr. Gaston.

Coleman brought visual technology and videoconferencing to the campaign. He produced 3- to 12-minute video stories of the successful communities and called them  visual evaluations.  If a success story was valid, he believed, he could capture all four dimensions of success on video: the people served, the leadership, the provider system, and the quantitative results.

> We let the team tell us they have a model that works. I go there and scout it out. I get a feel for the place and do a site evaluation. Is there a story to tell? As I worked with the 100%/0 team, it became easier to capture the patients  experiences, the people s stories, the leaders  stories about transforming their community. We broke through the data challenge and began to present the heart and soul of the story in the video cases.

Coleman became producer and director of the national campaign events. He organized the June 2001 three-day event with 800 participants, using theater-in-the-round complemented by video and television projection. He created several video cases, including the one for Galveston.

A few months later, in October 2001, he produced a national videoconference with the goal of moving 0 disparities to the forefront of the national campaign. The announcement promised success stories:  Organizations, networks of organizations, and communities across the nation are mobilizing to increase and improve access to health care for all Americans  and they are succeeding. Some are even breaking through to eliminate health disparities!  Communities were asked to commit to developing and reporting on disparity campaigns, the plan being to showcase them in future videoconferences. Coleman envisioned the number of successful community initiatives growing through inspiration and celebration.

The event was a four-hour satellite teleconference broadcast by WETA in Arlington, Virginia. There were 6,000 people at four uplink communities and 187 downlink sites in 49 states, and a facilitator and a moderator at each site. A series of conference calls were used to train the site moderators and facilitators. Sites were donated videoconference facilities in participating communities. Local foundations helped fund the four uplink sites. Communities and sites registered through the Internet, and people were offered guidance in finding free videoconferencing facilities in their communities. (With a cost to the Bureau of approximately $300,000, this effort had greater reach and lower costs than did the traditional convening conference.)

The conference agenda was a series of presentations from the WETA site, followed by group interaction at the downlink sites and then reporting into Washington by video transmission or phone. Commitments made at the sites to launch health status disparity efforts were self-reported to an e-mail location. The conversation was organized around several stories of communities successful in reducing disparities:

Contra Costa County, California: A community eliminates breast cancer disparities.

King County, Washington: Network collaboration eliminates diabetes disparities.

Community health centers: Centers eliminate low-birth-weight disparities.

Leaders of these efforts spoke from the studio, and an evaluative video case was presented on each one.

The October 2001 video conference on eliminating health status disparities marked the end of the Bureau s leadership of the 100% Access/ 0 Disparities Campaign. Following this event, other organizations formed to lead the national campaign.

# Forming a National Movement
## (2001–2002)

During 2000 2001, the 100%/0 campaign was robust and moving fast. By the end of 2001, the team had seen the campaign achieve the following results:

Dozens of benchmark communities were identified that demonstrate the feasibility of 100% access. Leaders from two of the first benchmark communities  Buncombe County, North Carolina, and Hillsborough County, Florida  became national campaign leaders.

The art of replication of innovations was mastered. One 100% community model, Project Access in Buncombe County, was replicated in two dozen communities by 2001 with some 60 additional communities in the process of replicating it. A new national organization, American Project Access Network, formed to manage nationwide replication.

The discipline of reconfiguring a community health care system was captured as a teachable method by the GHPC of Georgia State University. It runs an annual institute to train developers and managers of community 100%/0 systems.

A collaboration of national partners was created to pursue the goal of 100%/0. These partners include the National Association of Counties, International City and County Managers Association, United Way of America, American Academy of Pediatrics, Health Research & Educational Trust (AMA), The Access Project (Brandeis University), American

Project Access Network, GHPC (Georgia State University), and Community Health Partners. These organizations actively enrolled communities through their networks and provided technical assistance to communities in progressing through the 10-step scale.

In 2000, the Bureau won    for its method of creating performance partnerships tied to mission achievement    an award from the Council for Excellence in Government, *Government Executive* magazine, and the Office of Federal Procurement Policy, the Business Solutions in the Public Interest Award.

The Community Health Leadership Network, a national intermediary organization, was formed in 2001 with support from the Kellogg Foundation, Ascension Health Care System, and Sisters of Mercy Health Care System. The Bureau encouraged the forming of this organization as a vehicle for expanding the leadership of the campaign.

National, regional, and community pacing events were being used to accelerate progress and bring life and energy to the campaign. At such events, hundreds of invested people came together to make commitments that created a 100%/0 future. National partners, working with state and community champions, facilitated the events.

More than 600 communities had enrolled in the campaign. The national partners could track the progress of communities on the 10-step scale and estimate overall impact in terms of the numbers of people gaining coverage through safety net health systems.

In 2001, a change occurred in the Bureau and HRSA that pulled the federal government out of its leadership role. Gaston announced her retirement, and a new administration came to HRSA. HRSA now had a challenging presidential management initiative to implement, the legislated expansion of community health centers. The new HRSA executive team stepped back from a leadership role in the 100%/0 national campaign but continued to use the message and language of 100%/0. (The 100%/0 national partners continue to use their campaign networks to help HRSA achieve its presidential goal of community health center site development.)

The locus of leadership moved from the Bureau s team to organizations outside the federal government. By early 2002, four not-for-profit organizations had formed to continue enrolling and working with communities on 100%/0. Each organization has a different area of expertise:

American Project Access Network (APAN), Asheville, North Carolina a center for replication of successful social innovations in health care. Alan McKenzie created it to manage the growing replication of Project Access. APAN promotes Project Access, and its involvement of physicians, as a core component of any integrated delivery system and a catalyst for 100%/0. Under the direction of David Werle, it is working with close to 100 communities.

The Community Health Development Institute of the Georgia Health Policy Institute, Atlanta, Georgia  a center for training community coaches, community health system developers, and the managers of integrated health care systems. Karen Minyard formed the Institute to capture and spread the learning coming out of the campaign at all levels. Over the past two years, under the leadership of Tina Smith, it has held successful training events. It sees the forming and management of collaboratives that are behind 100%/0 systems as a new, unique skill that can be taught and a vocation that can be encouraged.

Communities Joined in Action (CJA), Olympia, Washington  a center connecting the broad spectrum of leadership on the 100%/0 campaign responsible for creating the bold new goals and game plan. It was formed by Mary Lou Andersen, who currently manages it. CJAs leadership council includes national partners and community benchmark leaders.

Community Health Leadership Network (CHLN), Washington, D.C. created to be the infrastructure for the campaign. Phyllis Busansky, who led its formation and served as the first president, promotes the state and community pacing events that give life to the campaign. CHLN is developing resources to continue the community tracking system, put in place a web-based communication system, and organize and support the convening of communities.

These four organizations form a collaborative, each supporting the work of the others. (In fact, board membership and organizational membership overlap greatly.) They are leading the movement.

In 2002, leadership of the 100%/0 campaign shifted from the Bureau s team to the new intermediary organizations. Federal staff managing special purpose programs and support activities were, in a four-year period, able to launch a self-organizing, self-sustaining movement. Today that movement has multiple networks of leadership at all levels, aligned in pursuit of a common vision with measurable goals.

The Bureau s 100%/0 team has successfully launched a national movement in health care reform.

# About the Contributors

**Mark A. Abramson** is Executive Director of the IBM Center for The Business of Government, a position he has held since July 1998. Prior to the Center, he was chairman of Leadership Inc. From 1983 to 1994, Mr. Abramson served as the first president of the Council for Excellence in Government. Previously, Mr. Abramson served as a senior program evaluator in the Office of the Assistant Secretary for Planning and Evaluation, U.S. Department of Health and Human Services

He is a Fellow of the National Academy of Public Administration. In 1995, he served as president of the National Capital Area Chapter of the American Society for Public Administration. Mr. Abramson has taught at George Mason University and the Federal Executive Institute in Charlottesville, Virginia.

Mr. Abramson is the co-editor of *Transforming Organizations, E-Government 2001, Managing for Results 2002, Innovation, Human Capital 2002, Leaders, E-Government 2003, The Procurement Revolution,* and *New Ways of Doing Business.* He also edited *Memos to the President: Management Advice from the Nation's Top Public Administrators* and *Toward a 21st Century Public Service: Reports from Four Forums.* He is also the co-editor (with Joseph S. Wholey and Christopher Bellavita) of *Performance and Credibility: Developing Excellence in Public and Nonprofit Organizations,* and the author of *The Federal Funding of Social Knowledge Production and Application.*

He received his Bachelor of Arts degree from Florida State University. He received a Master of Arts degree in history from New York University and a Master of Arts degree in political science from the Maxwell School of Citizenship and Public Affairs, Syracuse University.

**Robert Agranoff** is Professor Emeritus in the School of Public and Environmental Affairs, Indiana University–Bloomington, where he remains as part of the Policy and Administration and the Urban and Regional faculty groups. Prior to his retirement from full-time status, he served as associate dean for Bloomington, director of Public Affairs/Public Policy Doctoral Programs, and chairperson, Policy and Administration Faculty (1980–2001). Since 1990, he has been affiliated with the Government and Public Administration Program of the Instituto Universitario Ortega y Gasset in Madrid, Spain.

Professor Agranoff's work focuses on public and intergovernmental management and federalism. His most recent co-authored (with Michael McGuire) book is *Collaborative Public Management: New Strategies for Local Government* (Georgetown University Press: April 2003). Previous books authored/co-authored include: *Dimensions of Human Services Integration, Intergovernmental Management: Human Services Problem Solving in Six Metropolitan Areas,* and *New Governance for Rural America: Creating Intergovernmental Partnerships.* He has contributed to many journals, including *Public Administration Review, Journal of Public Administration Research and Theory, Publius: The Journal of Federalism, International Political Science Review,* and *Federal and Regional Studies.*

Although Agranoff holds emeritus status, he remains active in research and professional service, and in his school's doctoral programs. He is currently an associate editor of the *Journal of Public Administration Research and Theory* and chairperson of the Research Committee on Comparative Federalism of the International Political Science Association.

Agranoff graduated from the University of Wisconsin–River Falls in 1962, and from the University of Pittsburgh with an M.A. in 1963 and a Ph.D. in 1967, all in political science.

**Xavier de Souza Briggs** is the Martin Luther King, Jr. Visiting Fellow in Urban Studies and Planning at the Massachusetts Institute of Technology (2002-2004) and Associate Professor of Public Policy at Harvard University's Kennedy School of Government. He has conducted nationally awarded research on young people, housing desegregation, and economic opportunity. In the world of practice, he has been a community planner in the South Bronx; a senior adviser on economic development, affordable housing, and regional change to the White House and Congress while in the federal government; and a consultant to leading national and international organizations.

A sociologist by training, Professor Briggs teaches urban policy and planning, community problem solving, negotiation, and strategy. His current research focuses on making diversity work in cities, issues of housing and urban inequality, and democratic problem solving at the local level. He is a member of the Aspen Institute's roundtable on community change and an adviser to the World Bank's Community Empowerment and Social Inclusion Project and other policy groups. Briggs holds an engineering degree from

Stanford, an M.P.A. from Harvard, and a Ph.D. from Columbia University, and has held fellowships of the National Science Foundation and American Sociological Association.

**Thomas J. Burlin** is Partner, U.S. Federal Industry and Global Government Leader, IBM Business Consulting Services. He has held this position since October 2002. In this position, he also provides global leadership to the IBM Business Consulting Services International Government Practice.

Prior to his present position, Mr. Burlin was Vice President, Federal Government Industry, IBM. His previous positions at IBM include Director, Business Development for Government and Controller, State and Local Government business unit. From 1996 to 1999, he was a program executive for operations in Australia. Mr. Burlin started his career at IBM in 1979 as a chemical engineer.

Mr. Burlin is on the board of the Reginald S. Lourie Center for Infants and Young Children. He received his B.A. degree from Ithaca College with a degree in biology.

**Samuel DeMarie** is an Associate Professor of Strategic Management in the Department of Management, College of Business, Iowa State University. Professor DeMarie earned his Ph.D. degree from Arizona State University, Tempe. He also earned an M.B.A. degree from the University of Nevada Las Vegas and a B.S. degree in accountancy from Northern Arizona University, Flagstaff.

Professor DeMarie's current research focuses on the effects of new technologies on competition and the workplace, including the emerging phenomena of virtual organizations, virtual teamwork, and e-commerce. He also works in the area of large-scale organizational change initiatives, such as restructuring and downsizing.

**Elaine Kamarck** is currently on the faculty of the John F. Kennedy School of Government at Harvard University, where she teaches courses in 21st-century government, innovation in government, and electronic democracy and electronic government. In addition, she co-directs a program on the future of public service. In January 2001, she returned to the Kennedy School from a year's leave of absence during which she served as senior policy adviser to the Gore for President campaign. She joined the Harvard faculty in 1997 as executive director of Visions of Governance for the Twenty-First Century, a new research program at the Kennedy School. She has also served as director of the Innovations in American Government Program, an award program for federal, state, and local governments.

Prior to joining the Harvard faculty, Dr. Kamarck served as senior policy adviser to the vice president of the United States, Al Gore. She joined the Clinton/Gore administration in March 1993 and, working directly with Vice President Gore, created the National Performance Review (NPR), a new White House policy council designed to reinvent government.

In addition to managing the NPR, Dr. Kamarck managed the Vice President's Commission on Airline Safety and Security that was established by the president in the wake of the TWA 800 disaster. She also served on President Clinton's welfare reform task force.

Prior to joining the administration, Dr. Kamarck was a senior fellow at the Progressive Policy Institute (PPI), the think tank of the Democratic Leadership Council. In that capacity, she and her colleague Bill Galston published many of the policy papers that were to become the New Democratic philosophy on which Bill Clinton ran for president in 1992. Before joining PPI, Dr. Kamarck worked in three Democratic presidential campaigns and worked for the Democratic National Committee.

In addition to her work at the PPI, Dr. Kamarck was a regular columnist with *Newsday* and the *Los Angeles Times* from 1988 to 1992. She has also made many television appearances for ABC News, CNN, and C-SPAN, and on *Nightline* and *The NewsHour with Jim Lehrer,* among others.

Dr. Kamarck was educated at Bryn Mawr College and received her Ph.D. in political science from the University of California at Berkeley.

**John M. Kamensky** is Associate Partner for the managing for results practice of IBM Business Consulting Services and senior fellow for the IBM Center for The Business of Government. During 24 years of public service, he played a key role in helping pioneer the federal government's performance and results orientation. He is passionate about creating a government that is results-oriented, performance-based, and customer-driven. He is the co-editor of *Managing for Results 2002* and the forthcoming *Managing for Results 2004.*

Prior to joining the private sector in February 2001, Mr. Kamensky served for eight years as deputy director of Vice President Gore's National Partnership for Reinventing Government. Before that, he worked at the General Accounting Office for 16 years, where he played a key role in the development and passage of the Government Performance and Results Act. Mr. Kamensky received a Masters in Public Affairs from the Lyndon B. Johnson School of Public Affairs, in Austin, Texas.

**Robert Klitgaard** is Dean and Ford Distinguished Professor of International Development and Security at the RAND Graduate School. He previously served as Professor of Economics at the University of Natal, Durban; Lester Crown Professor of Economics at Yale; and Associate Professor of Public Policy at Harvard. He advises many governments and international institutions on economic strategy and institutional reform, and his consulting work and research have taken him to 30 countries in Latin America, Asia, and Africa. He is the author of seven books: *Choosing Elites; Data Analysis for Development; Elitism and Meritocracy in Developing Countries; Controlling Corruption; Tropical Gangsters; Adjusting to Reality: Beyond State vs. Market in Economic Development;* and, most recently, *Corrupt Cities.* Professor Klitgaard received A.B., M.P.P., and Ph.D. degrees from Harvard University.

**John Scanlon** is a partner in JSEA Inc., a management services firm. He works with executive teams who are leading their organizations through strategic transitions. He has over 30 years' experience installing effective organizational structures and management systems that executives use to produce dramatic results.

He received a Ph.D. in applied mathematics and chemical engineering from Rensselaer Polytechnic Institute in 1967. Between 1968 and 1980, he worked in the Urban Institute's Program Evaluation Group. As director and project manager, he developed methods for assessing the management of organizations and designed information systems for evaluating large-scale public programs. He specialized in innovative evaluation strategies that were designed to improve program performance and provide timely information for policy making.

Since 1980, Dr. Scanlon has specialized in the design of leadership campaigns that enable managers to achieve extraordinary results on their missions and strategic visions. He has worked with several dozen executive teams that were facing challenges that their current management and organizational structure could not resolve. He developed the leadership stories and leadership skills of the team and put in place the campaigns that realized their vision and goals. These campaigns leverage current programs and business lines to extend reach and impact.

During the time period covered in chapter eight, Dr. Scanlon was the adviser to the Office of the Director, Bureau of Primary Health Care, on the national health care reform campaign called 100% Access/0 Disparities. This effort enabled the executive team to realize impacts on access to health care that went beyond the traditional reach of its programs. He is currently a Board Member of the Community Health Leadership Network.

**William M. Snyder** is Managing Director of Social Capital Group, a research-consulting group that helps civic leaders organize community-based approaches to social and economic development. He is a co-founder (with Etienne Wenger) of CPsquare, an association of practitioners cultivating communities of practice in private, public, and nonprofit sectors. He has consulted for 20 years on large-scale organizational change efforts in the private and public sectors, and worked at McKinsey & Company on strategic knowledge initiatives for the firm and its clients. His research focus is on community-of-practice applications in organizations and civil society—at city, cross-city, and international levels.

Dr. Snyder's publications include "Communities of Practice: The organizational frontier," *Harvard Business Review* (January-February, 2000) with Etienne Wenger, and *Cultivating Communities of Practice: A guide to managing knowledge* (Boston, Harvard Business School Press, 2002) with Etienne Wenger and Richard McDermott.

Snyder holds A.B. and Ed.M. degrees from Harvard University and a Ph.D. from the University of Southern California.

**Gregory F. Treverton** is Senior Policy Analyst at RAND and a professor and Associate Dean of the RAND Graduate School. He formerly directed RAND's International Security and Defense Policy Center, and was president of the Pacific Council on International Policy. He most recently served in government as vice chair of the National Intelligence Council. He handled Europe on the National Security Council during the Carter administration and worked on Capitol Hill for the first Senate Select Committee on Intelligence (the Church committee) from 1975 to 1976.

Professor Treverton has been a Senior Fellow at the Council on Foreign Relations in New York. He has taught public management and foreign policy at Harvard's Kennedy School of Government and has been an adjunct professor at Columbia's School of International and Public Affairs. He was director of studies at the International Institute for Strategic Studies in London. His most recent book is *Reshaping National Intelligence for an Age of Information.* His earlier books include *Making American Foreign Policy; America, Germany, and the Future of Europe; Rethinking America's Security;* and *Covert Action: The Limits of Intervention in the Postwar World.* Treverton received his B.A. from Princeton University and his Ph.D. in public policy from Harvard University.

**William L. Waugh, Jr.,** is Professor of Public Administration, Urban Studies, and Political Science in the Andrew Young School of Policy Studies at Georgia State University (GSU). He taught at Mississippi State University and Kansas State University prior to moving to GSU in 1985. Currently, he teaches graduate courses on disaster management, administrative theory/organizational behavior, human resource management, and public policy, and an undergraduate course on "global disasters." His research focuses on the design of disaster policies and programs and on the coordination of multi-organizational and intergovernmental operations.

He is the author of *Living with Hazards, Dealing with Disasters* (2000), *Terrorism and Emergency Management* (1990), and *International Terrorism* (1982); co-author of *State and Local Tax Policies* (1995); and co-editor of *Disaster Management in the U.S. and Canada* (1996), *Cities and Disaster*

(1990), and *Handbook of Emergency Management* (1990), as well as author of numerous articles and chapters published in the United States, Canada, Europe, and Asia. He currently serves as co-editor of the *Review of Policy Research* (formerly *Policy Studies Review*).

Dr. Waugh has developed college-level courses for the Federal Emergency Management Agency, conducted training programs for local emergency managers and law enforcement officers, and been a consultant to public, nonprofit, and private organizations on disaster management, strategic planning, and leadership development. He serves on the Certified Emergency Manager Commission; on the board of directors of the Family Assistance Foundation, a nonprofit organization that helps airlines deal with aviation disasters; and as academic adviser to Regional Science Institute, an international environmental analysis firm based in Japan.

He grew up on military bases in the United States and Germany and attended the University of Maryland in Munich. In 1970-71, he served in the U.S. Army. He received an A.B. from the University of North Alabama (1973), an M.A. from Auburn University (1976), and a Ph.D. in political science from the University of Mississippi (1980).

# About the IBM Center for
# The Business of Government

Through research stipends and events, the IBM Center for The Business of Government stimulates research and facilitates discussion of new approaches to improving the effectiveness of government at the federal, state, local, and international levels.

The Center is one of the ways that IBM Business Consulting Services seeks to advance knowledge on how to improve public sector effectiveness. The IBM Center focuses on the future of the operation and management of the public sector.

Research stipends of $15,000 are awarded competitively to outstanding scholars in academic and nonprofit institutions across the United States. Each award winner is expected to produce a 30- to 40-page research report in one of the areas presented on pages 382–385. Reports will be published and disseminated by the Center.

# Research Stipend Guidelines

**Who is Eligible?**
Individuals working in:
- Universities
- Nonprofit organizations
- Journalism

**Description of Research Stipends**

Individuals receiving research stipends will be responsible for producing a 30- to 40-page research report in one of the areas presented on pages 382–385. The report will be published and disseminated by the IBM Center for The Business of Government. The manuscript must be submitted no later than six months after the start of the project. Recipients will select the start and end dates of their research project. The reports should be written for government leaders and should provide practical knowledge and insights.

**Size of Research Stipends**

$15,000 for each research paper

**Who Receives the Research Stipends?**

Unless otherwise requested, individuals will receive the research stipends.

**Application Process**

Interested individuals should submit:

- A three-page description of the proposed research (please include a 100-word executive summary describing the proposed project's: (a) purpose, (b) methodology, and (c) results)
- A résumé (no more than three pages)

**Application Deadlines**

There will be two funding cycles annually, with deadlines of:

- November 1
- March 1

Applicants will be informed of a decision regarding their proposal no later than eight weeks after the deadlines. Applications must be received online or postmarked by the above dates.

**Submitting Applications**

*Online:*

businessofgovernment.org/apply

*Hard Copy:*

Mark A. Abramson

Executive Director

IBM Center for The Business of Government

1301 K Street, NW

Fourth Floor, West Tower

Washington, DC 20005

# Research Areas

## E-Government

Specific areas of interest:
- Government to Business (G2B)
- Government to Citizen (G2C)
- Government to Employees (G2E)
- Government to Government (G2G)
- Capital investment strategies
- Customer relationship management (CRM)
- Enterprise architecture
- Supply chain management
- E-Government On Demand

Examples of previous reports:
*Digitally Integrating the Government Supply Chain: E-Procurement, E-Finance, and E-Logistics* by Jacques S. Gansler, William Lucyshyn, and Kimberly M. Ross (February 2003)
*State Web Portals: Delivering and Financing E-Service* by Diana Burley Gant, Jon P. Gant and Craig L. Johnson (January 2002)
*Federal Intranet Work Sites: An Interim Assessment* by Julianne G. Mahler and Priscilla M. Regan (June 2002)
*Leveraging Technology in the Service of Diplomacy: Innovation in the Department of State* by Barry Fulton (March 2002)

## Financial Management

Specific areas of interest:
- Asset management
- Auditing
- Cost accounting
- Erroneous payment
- Financial and resource analysis
- Internal controls
- Risk management and modeling
- Systems modernization
- Financial Management On Demand

Examples of previous reports:
*Understanding Federal Asset Management: An Agenda for Reform* by Thomas H. Stanton (July 2003)
*Audited Financial Statements: Getting and Sustaining "Clean" Opinions* by Douglas A. Brook (July 2001)
*Using Activity-Based Costing to Manage More Effectively* by Michael H. Granof, David E. Platt and Igor Vaysman (January 2000)
*Credit Scoring and Loan Scoring: Tools for Improved Management of Federal Credit Programs* by Thomas H. Stanton (July 1999)

## Human Capital Management

Specific areas of interest:
- Aligning human capital with organizational objectives
- Workforce planning and deployment
- Talent: recruitment, retraining, and retention
- Pay for performance
- Leadership and knowledge management
- E-learning
- Human Capital Management On Demand

Examples of previous reports:
*Modernizing Human Resource Management in the Federal Government: The IRS Model* by James R. Thompson and Hal G. Rainey (April 2003)
*A Weapon in the War for Talent: Using Special Authorities to Recruit Crucial Personnel* by Hal G. Rainey (December 2001)
*Life after Civil Service Reform: The Texas, Georgia, and Florida Experiences* by Jonathan Walters (October 2002)
*Organizations Growing Leaders: Best Practices and Principles in the Public Service* by Ray Blunt (December 2001)

## Managing for Performance and Results

Specific areas of interest:
- Strategic planning
- Performance measurement and evaluation
- Balanced scorecards and performance reporting
- Performance budgeting
- Program delivery

Examples of previous reports:
*Using Performance Data for Accountability: The New York City Police Department's CompStat Model of Police Management* by Paul E. O'Connell (August 2001)
*Performance Management: A "Start Where You Are, Use What You Have" Guide* by Chris Wye (October 2002)
*How Federal Programs Use Outcome Information: Opportunities for Federal Managers* by Harry P. Hatry, Elaine Morley, Shelli B. Rossman, and Joseph S. Wholey (April 2003)
*The Baltimore CitiStat Program: Performance and Accountability* by Lenneal J. Henderson (May 2003)

## Market-Based Government

Specific areas of interest:
- Contracting out
- Competitive sourcing
- Outsourcing
- Privatization
- Public-private partnerships
- Government franchising
- Contract management

Examples of previous reports:
*Moving Toward Market-Based Government: The Changing Role of Government as the Provider* by Jacques S. Gansler (June 2003)
*IT Outsourcing: A Primer for Public Managers* by Yu-Che Chen and James Perry (February 2003)
*Moving to Public-Private Partnerships: Learning from Experience around the World* by Trefor P. Williams (February 2003)
*Making Performance-Based Contracting Perform: What the Federal Government Can Learn from State and Local Governments* by Lawrence L. Martin (November 2002, 2nd ed.)

## Innovation, Collaboration, and Transformation

Specific areas of interest:
- Enhancing public sector performance
- Improving service delivery
- Profiles of outstanding public sector leaders
- Collaboration between organizations
- Change management
- Providing managerial flexibility

Examples of previous reports:

*Managing "Big Science": A Case Study of the Human Genome Project* by W. Henry Lambright (March 2002)

*Understanding Innovation: What Inspires It? What Makes It Successful?* by Jonathan Walters (December 2001)

*Extraordinary Results on National Goals: Networks and Partnerships in the Bureau of Primary Health Care's 100%/0 Campaign* by John Scanlon (March 2003)

*The Power of Frontline Workers in Transforming Government: The Upstate New York Veterans Healthcare Network* by Timothy J. Hoff (April 2003)

## For more information about the Center

Visit our website at: www.businessofgovernment.org
Send an e-mail to: businessofgovernment@us.ibm.com
Call: (202) 515-4504

# Center Reports Available

## E-GOVERNMENT

**Supercharging the Employment Agency:** An Investigation of the Use of Information and Communication Technology to Improve the Service of State Employment Agencies (December 2000)

Anthony M. Townsend

**Assessing a State's Readiness for Global Electronic Commerce:** Lessons from the Ohio Experience (January 2001)

J. Pari Sabety
Steven I. Gordon

**Privacy Strategies for Electronic Government** (January 2001)

Janine S. Hiller
France Bélanger

**Commerce Comes to Government on the Desktop:** E-Commerce Applications in the Public Sector (February 2001)

Genie N. L. Stowers

**The Use of the Internet in Government Service Delivery** (February 2001)

Steven Cohen
William Eimicke

**State Web Portals:** Delivering and Financing E-Service (January 2002)

Diana Burley Gant
Jon P. Gant
Craig L. Johnson

**Internet Voting:** Bringing Elections to the Desktop (February 2002)

Robert S. Done

**Leveraging Technology in the Service of Diplomacy:** Innovation in the Department of State (March 2002)

Barry Fulton

**Federal Intranet Work Sites:** An Interim Assessment (June 2002)

Julianne G. Mahler
Priscilla M. Regan

**The State of Federal Websites:** The Pursuit of Excellence (August 2002)

Genie N. L. Stowers

**State Government E-Procurement in the Information Age:** Issues, Practices, and Trends (September 2002)

M. Jae Moon

**Preparing for Wireless and Mobile Technologies in Government** (October 2002)

Ai-Mei Chang
P. K. Kannan

**Public-Sector Information Security:** A Call to Action for Public-Sector CIOs (October 2002, 2nd ed.)

Don Heiman

**The Auction Model:** How the Public Sector Can Leverage the Power of E-Commerce Through Dynamic Pricing (November 2002, 2nd ed.)

David C. Wyld

**The Promise of E-Learning in Africa:** The Potential for Public-Private Partnerships (January 2003)

Norman LaRocque
Michael Latham

To download or order a copy of a report, visit the Center's website at: www.businessofgovernment.org

**IT Outsourcing**: A Primer for Public Managers (February 2003)

Yu-Che Chen

James Perry

**The Procurement Partnership Model:** Moving to a Team-Based Approach (February 2003)

Kathryn G. Denhardt

**Moving Toward Market-Based Government:** The Changing Role of Government as the Provider (June 2003)

Jacques S. Gansler

# HUMAN CAPITAL MANAGEMENT

**Profiles in Excellence:** Conversations with the Best of America's Career Executive Service (November 1999)

Mark W. Huddleston

**Reflections on Mobility:** Case Studies of Six Federal Executives (May 2000)

Michael D. Serlin

**Managing Telecommuting in the Federal Government:** An Interim Report (June 2000)

Gina Vega

Louis Brennan

**Using Virtual Teams to Manage Complex Projects:** A Case Study of the Radioactive Waste Management Project (August 2000)

Samuel M. DeMarie

**A Learning-Based Approach to Leading Change** (December 2000)

Barry Sugarman

**Labor-Management Partnerships:** A New Approach to Collaborative Management (July 2001)

Barry Rubin

Richard Rubin

**Winning the Best and Brightest:** Increasing the Attraction of Public Service (July 2001)

Carol Chetkovich

**A Weapon in the War for Talent:** Using Special Authorities to Recruit Crucial Personnel (December 2001)

Hal G. Rainey

**A Changing Workforce:** Understanding Diversity Programs in the Federal Government (December 2001)

Katherine C. Naff

J. Edward Kellough

**Life after Civil Service Reform:** The Texas, Georgia, and Florida Experiences (October 2002)

Jonathan Walters

**The Defense Leadership and Management Program:** Taking Career Development Seriously (December 2002)

Joseph A. Ferrara

Mark C. Rom

**The Influence of Organizational Commitment on Officer Retention:** A 12-Year Study of U.S. Army Officers (December 2002)

Stephanie C. Payne

Ann H. Huffman

Trueman R. Tremble, Jr.

**Human Capital Reform:** 21st Century Requirements for the United States Agency for International Development (March 2003)

Anthony C. E. Quainton

Amanda M. Fulmer

Modernizing Human Resource Management in the Federal Government: The IRS Model (April 2003)

James R. Thompson
Hal G. Rainey

Mediation at Work: Transforming Workplace Conflict at the United States Postal Service (October 2003)

Lisa B. Bingham

Growing Leaders for Public Service (November 2003)

Ray Blunt

# MANAGING FOR PERFORMANCE AND RESULTS

Corporate Strategic Planning in Government: Lessons from the United States Air Force (November 2000)

Colin Campbell

Using Evaluation to Support Performance Management: A Guide for Federal Executives (January 2001)

Kathryn Newcomer
Mary Ann Scheirer

Managing for Outcomes: Milestone Contracting in Oklahoma (January 2001)

Peter Frumkin

The Challenge of Developing Cross-Agency Measures: A Case Study of the Office of National Drug Control Policy (August 2001)

Patrick J. Murphy
John Carnevale

The Potential of the Government Performance and Results Act as a Tool to Manage Third-Party Government (August 2001)

David G. Frederickson

Using Performance Data for Accountability: The New York City Police Department's CompStat Model of Police Management (August 2001)

Paul E. O'Connell

Moving Toward More Capable Government: A Guide to Organizational Design (June 2002)

Thomas H. Stanton

Performance Management: A "Start Where You Are, Use What You Have" Guide (October 2002)

Chris Wye

The Baltimore CitiStat Program: Performance and Accountability (May 2003)

Lenneal J. Henderson

How Federal Programs Use Outcome Information: Opportunities for Federal Managers (May 2003)

Harry P. Hatry
Elaine Morley
Shelli B. Rossman
Joseph S. Wholey

Linking Performance and Budgeting: Opportunities in the Federal Budget Process (October 2003)

Philip G. Joyce

Strategies for Using State Information: Measuring and Improving Program Performance (December 2003)

Shelley H. Metzenbaum

# INNOVATION

**Managing Workfare:** The Case of the Work Experience Program in the New York City Parks Department (June 1999)

Steven Cohen

**New Tools for Improving Government Regulation:** An Assessment of Emissions Trading and Other Market-Based Regulatory Tools (October 1999)

Gary C. Bryner

**Religious Organizations, Anti-Poverty Relief, and Charitable Choice:** A Feasibility Study of Faith-Based Welfare Reform in Mississippi (November 1999)

John P. Bartkowski
Helen A. Regis

**Business Improvement Districts and Innovative Service Delivery** (November 1999)

Jerry Mitchell

**An Assessment of Brownfield Redevelopment Policies:** The Michigan Experience (November 1999)

Richard C. Hula

**San Diego County's Innovation Program:** Using Competition and a Whole Lot More to Improve Public Services (January 2000)

William B. Eimicke

**Innovation in the Administration of Public Airports** (March 2000)

Scott E. Tarry

**Entrepreneurial Government:** Bureaucrats as Businesspeople (May 2000)

Anne Laurent

**Rethinking U.S. Environmental Protection Policy:** Management Challenges for a New Administration (November 2000)

Dennis A. Rondinelli

**The Challenge of Innovating in Government** (February 2001)

Sandford Borins

**Understanding Innovation:** What Inspires It? What Makes It Successful? (December 2001)

Jonathan Walters

**Government Management of Information Mega-Technology:** Lessons from the Internal Revenue Service's Tax Systems Modernization (March 2002)

Barry Bozeman

**Advancing High End Computing:** Linking to National Goals (September 2003)

Juan D. Rogers
Barry Bozeman

# NETWORKS, COLLABORATION, AND PARTNERSHIPS

**Leveraging Networks to Meet National Goals:** FEMA and the Safe Construction Networks (March 2002)

William L. Waugh, Jr.

**21st-Century Government and the Challenge of Homeland Defense** (June 2002)

Elaine C. Kamarck

**Assessing Partnerships:** New Forms of Collaboration (March 2003)

Robert Klitgaard
Gregory F. Treverton

---

To download or order a copy of a report, visit the Center's website at: www.businessofgovernment.org

**Managing "Big Science":** A Case
Study of the Human Genome Project
(March 2002)

W. Henry Lambright

**The Power of Frontline Workers in
Transforming Government:** The
Upstate New York Veterans Healthcare
Network (April 2003)

Timothy J. Hoff

**Efficiency Counts:** Developing the
Capacity to Manage Costs at Air Force
Materiel Command (August 2003)

Michael Barzelay
Fred Thompson

**Managing the New Multipurpose,
Multidiscipline University Research
Centers:** Institutional Innovation
in the Academic Community
(November 2003)

Barry Bozeman
P. Craig Boardman

**Making Public Sector Mergers Work:**
Lessons Learned (January 2004, 2nd ed.)

Peter Frumkin